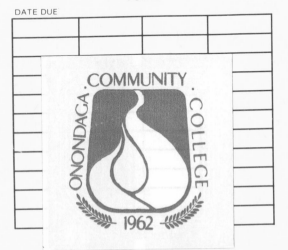

TURGENEV'S LETTERS

TURGENEV'S LETTERS

*selected, translated
and edited by*

A. V. Knowles

Charles Scribner's Sons
New York

for Sylvia

CONTENTS

PREFACE

Of all the Russian authors of the nineteenth century, if Tolstoy was the most prolific letter writer, then Turgenev was the most accomplished. His surviving correspondence of over 6550 published items (and there are more as yet unpublished) covers more than fifty years, from 1831 until almost the day of his death in 1883. It reflects the many aspects of his life, his writings, and his views on the literary, social and political events of his time. Well versed in the epistolary traditions of the past both in Russia and abroad, Turgenev was not unaware of the, albeit dubious, dictum that when writing a book one addresses oneself to friends, but when writing a letter one is speaking to the whole world. Only rarely was he annoyed when a letter of his was published without his permission – in particular one containing some scathing comment on Sarah Bernhardt's acting abilities – or when some political comment which might cause him trouble with the Russian authorities was made public. Turgenev's novels and stories have sometimes been criticized for their concentration on social problems of which he had little understanding or their doubtful characterization, but very rarely has their style been regarded as anything but exemplary.

While his letters clearly do not show the same care in composition, his facility for writing is notable. Errors in spelling or grammar (in whichever language he was using), clumsiness of expression, or failure to make clear what he meant are as rare with Turgenev as they are common with Tolstoy. Turgenev always wrote his literary works in Russian and was always cross when translations appeared before the original – usually because some French or German publisher wished to print his latest work as soon as possible (the situation complicated by Turgenev's often sending them a translation himself) – but he would write to non-Russians in French, German or English. Although he was forced to declare publicly in *Temps* in 1877 that he could not understand an author being able to express himself properly in any language other than his mother tongue, his letters would appear to contradict him. When writing in his excellent French, very passable German or adequate English (which he admitted to being able to write only hesitantly, although speaking it reasonably well) he is almost the same stylish writer as in his purely literary Russian works. Indeed, an early German publisher of his correspondence with Ludwig Pietsch wrote that Turgenev's description of the winter's cold in Weimar was better than anything comparable in the whole of German literature. Furthermore, one of his correspondents complained that so well were his letters written that the sincerity of what he was saying must be in doubt.

Very few of the letters Turgenev wrote in his youth have survived, and it is also clear that he did not write as many then as he did later on. On the evidence of his mother, as a young man he was as lazy in his correspondence as he was in other aspects of his life. When he began to live mainly abroad, which he did, in the view of his Russian contemporaries, exclusively because of his lifelong affection for the singer Pauline Viardot, he would write not so much for the information of his readers but, as he told M. A. Markovich in 1859, 'in order to receive replies'. This applied particularly to his letters from abroad to his Russian friends at home; through their replies he hoped to keep in touch with the Russia he loved. He missed speaking Russian and used letters in an attempt to overcome his loss.

Although much of his correspondence is ephemeral – arrangements and appointments (or more often than not changing them, confirming whether or not he had them right or apologizing for forgetting them), day-to-day trivia, thanks for invitations, letters of recommendation, and so on – Turgenev liked to carry on conversations by post. His letters to his great friend P. V. Annenkov constitute a fascinating literary discussion, as to a lesser extent, do those to the poet Y. P. Polonsky; many of those to A. A. Fet and V. P. Botkin are more light-hearted, yet frequently include his opinions on a multitude of subjects. He loved to argue by letter on what he considered important questions, not only about literature and the arts in general, but on social and political issues as well. While his letters to A. I. Herzen, for example, show him to be politically naive, those to M. Y. Saltykov-Shchedrin perhaps present him as more socially aware than the usual picture of him as a woolly-minded liberal might lead one to imagine, despite the reputation of *A Sportsman's Sketches* and their supposed influence on the Emancipation of the Peasants in 1861. He often fell out with people simply because of what they wrote in their letters, but nearly always tried to patch things up afterwards.

Of his 589 known correspondents 149 were women, and it was with them that Turgenev would more often discuss matters closest to his heart. This is especially apparent with Countess Y. Y. Lambert, Y. P. Vrevskaya and A. P. Filosofova, and even in the rather more flirtatious 'conversations' with the actress M. G. Savina in the later years of his life. Perhaps not surprisingly, his many letters to Pauline Viardot were less weighty, tending to be more of a detailed diary of what he had been doing, whom he had met, what operas he had seen and what music he had heard, together with comments on their mutual friends and denigrating remarks on her rivals. Many of his letters are to his Russian and Western European publishers and various translators, and all of them show him to be meticulous to a fault in regard to his writings. He was usually willing to give advice to young writers, some of whose subsequent careers he would follow with the greatest interest; he would be unstinting in his praise if he thought it deserved, but never shirked telling them if he considered them untalented or affected or if he thought there was room for improvement, although he would try to let them down as gently as he could. Through such letters some of Turgenev's criteria for a writer are revealed.

In deciding which letters to include in my selection I have tried to give due balance both to the type of correspondent (friends, relations, editors, other writers and so on) and to the content (literary, social and political views, comments on art and music, statements which reveal not only Turgenev the writer but also Turgenev the human being). I have also included some that deal with the main features of his, generally speaking, uneventful life. His biography, as he was fond of saying, lies in his books.

Turgenev has remained something of an enigma to his readers, and a study of his letters will not help those seeking an answer; it will probably only confirm their perplexities. Although a polite, charming, considerate and modest man, he was weak-willed; he found it difficult to make up his mind and then often changed it; he was a dedicated hypochondriac whose 'real' illnesses and physical complaints only fed his growing melancholia; a kind and extremely generous man who felt deeply the tight-pursed attitude of his wealthy brother; a poor father but a splendid 'uncle'; an admirer of women and happiest when in their company, yet a poor and infrequent lover; one who often fell out with others for no good reason and then regretted it, and who loved his country but was always reluctant to leave his Western European friends; generally lazy but never missing the opportunity to go anywhere when shooting was available; a man with strong views on many subjects but very few convictions; an agnostic and a lover of individual freedom. Such is the man who emerges from his correspondence. It is nevertheless the more positive sides of his character that must have impressed those who knew him well, for almost everyone liked him and children adored him. Only those of extremely strong character or determined views like Tolstoy, the editor Katkov, or Herzen, or those with more complex personalities like Dostoyevsky or Goncharov (both of whose sanity he questioned), caused him any lasting difficulty.

The English versions of those letters I have selected are based on the texts published in volumes I–XIII (2) of the Nauka edition of Turgenev's *Complete Works and Correspondence* (Moscow-Leningrad, 1961-8), A. Zviguilsky's *Ivan Tourguénev. Nouvelle Correspondence Inédite* (2 vols, Paris, 1971, 1972), or H. Granjard and A. Zviguilsky's *Ivan Tourguénev. Lettres inédites à Pauline Viardot et à sa famille* (Lausanne, 1972). Where copyright exists I have made every effort to obtain permission to translate and I am grateful to those who have granted it to me. All the versions are my own except, naturally, those Turgenev wrote in English, and the language of the original is stated before each letter; where a letter is extant in a language other than that in which it was first written this is mentioned. In an attempt to give the true flavour of Turgenev's style I have translated nearly all the letters I include in full, but on occasion I have omitted introductory or concluding passages, or lists of names, where these bear little relationship to the main drift of the letter; I have also omitted the rare play on words where there is no satisfactory English equivalent; the number of lines thereby omitted is stated. The letters are grouped into five chronological sections, each preceded by a short biographical introduction. Details of each of Turgenev's correspondents are given when a letter to them first appears; otherwise the index should be consulted.

The transliteration of Russian names is a minefield even to the wary. I have followed R. F. Christian's example in his *Tolstoy's Letters* (2 vols, London, 1978), and chosen, generally speaking, the system outlined by R. Hingley in volume 3 of his *Oxford Chekhov* (Oxford, 1964), pp. xi-xii. I have kept to the differences adopted by Christian except that I have transliterated Russian surnames of foreign origin rather than spell them in what might be assumed to be the manner of their language of origin. In cases where Russian place names and surnames have a generally accepted English spelling (e.g. Moscow, St Petersburg, Herzen, Tchaikovsky) which differs from the system adopted, I have followed the conventional usage. I have rendered the Russian combination of *kc* as *x* and preferred Alexander to Alexandr. Otherwise, with the exception of Tsar Nicholas, forenames are transliterated. When Turgenev precedes a surname with *gospodin* or *gospozha* I have used Mr, Mrs or Miss as appropriate, but I have retained his usage of M., Mme and Mlle and of Herr, Frau and Fräulein. Round brackets ( ) are employed when Turgenev used them, square brackets [ ] enclose editorial comments or additions and angle brackets ⟨ ⟩ are used for translations of words in a language other than that of the main language of the original where such words might not readily be understood by the average English reader.

Where letters were written from Russia they are dated according to the 'old style', which in nineteenth-century Russia was twelve days behind the Western European calendar, and those written from outside Russia are dated according to the normal Western system.

One of the more taxing problems of translation is how to render into English the more effusive style of Russian and European expressions of greeting and especially of valediction. For ease of reading I have generally used the more reserved English conventions and avoided a more literal translation. I have, however, retained 'I kiss your hand' (or, occasionally, 'feet'), 'I press your hand', and 'I embrace you'. Another inconvenience is that there are no widely accepted English versions for the names of Russian journals and newspapers, nor even for some of Turgenev's works. I trust my solution will not jar on English readers with a knowledge of Russian. The most frequently occurring are *Russian Herald* for *Russky vestnik*, *Messenger of Europe* for *Vestnik Yevropy*, *Annals of the Fatherland* for *Otechestvenniye zapiski* and *St Petersburg* (or *Moscow*) *Gazette* for *Sankt-Peterburgskiye* (or *Moskovskiye*) *vedomosti*. Non-Russian journals are left in the form used by Turgenev. I have also preferred *Fathers and Sons* and *A Nest of the Landed Gentry* for the best-known of Turgenev's novels, and *A Sportsman's Sketches* for *Zapiski okhotnika*. I have not translated *desyatina* (about 2.7 acres) or *versta* (about a kilometre) and have used the plural versts; rouble and copeck are spelt as such.

I would like to express my gratitude to the many friends and colleagues who have helped me on points of translation or of fact, and to the University of Liverpool for granting me a period of study leave which helped enormously in the preparation of this selection. I would also like to thank Mrs Joan Stevenson who typed the bulk of my manuscript with unfailing good spirit, charm and accuracy.

Liverpool, 1982   A.V. Knowles

I

1818–1850

Ivan Sergeyevich Turgenev was born in his parents' home in Oryol, some two hundred miles south of Moscow, on 28 October 1818, the second of three brothers. His father Sergey Nikolayevich, who was twenty-five when Ivan was born, was descended from a family of the Russian minor gentry; decorated at the battle of Borodino in 1812, he retired voluntarily from the army in 1821. In 1816 he had married Varvara Petrovna Lutovinova who was six years his senior. In contrast to her husband she was a very rich landowner and was reputed to have owned more than five thousand serfs. Her husband, handsome, cultured and a renowed womanizer, probably married her for her wealth, and his amatory activities showed little decline after the marriage. What she really thought of him is unclear, but after his early death in 1834 she kept his study as a shrine which no one was allowed to visit. Turgenev's version of their marriage can be found in the story *First Love* (1860). Intelligent and well educated, Varvara Petrovna had a reputation for capriciousness and cruelty, especially to the domestic servants on her estate at Spasskoye.

Turgenev's early education was mainly at home and received from a succession of privately hired tutors. He later spent a few months at the boarding school of the Armenian Institute in Moscow in 1829, and about a year at Weidenhammer's school in 1830 and 1831. In September 1833 at the age of fifteen he was admitted to the faculty of literature at Moscow University (which he later described in the story *Andrey Kolosov* of 1844), and he transferred to St Petersburg to read history and philology a year later. It was there that he wrote his first literary piece, a dramatic poem, 'Steno' based on Byron's *Manfred*. He never thought much of it and it was not published until thirty years after his death. In October 1834, while his mother was in Italy recovering from the birth of an illegitimate daughter, his father died. Turgenev graduated in 1837, when he returned to live on the estate at Spasskoye to indulge his lifelong passion for shooting game. He spent the years 1838–1841 mainly abroad, studying at the University of Berlin, toying in common with the rest of his generation with German Romantic Philosophy, and in travel.

After his return Turgenev spent most of his time in the country, where he got to know the peasant life he was to describe so vividly and sympathetically in *A Sportsman's Sketches*. He also became the father of an illegitimate daughter by a seamstress of his mother's. He continued writing poetry – none of which he ever valued particularly – and critical articles, and he became a regular contributor to the *Annals of the Fatherland*. In 1843 he joined government service with the Ministry of the Interior, wrote an interesting memorandum on serfdom, published the first work to establish his reputation as a writer – a short verse romance, 'Parasha' – and met the singer Pauline Viardot to whom he was to remain devoted for the rest of his life. Early in 1845 he applied to the Tsar to be released from government service on account of poor eyesight, which was almost certainly merely an excuse, and soon left for France to be near his beloved Pauline. Returning to Russia later that summer, he became involved in the resuscitation of the journal originally founded by Pushkin, the *Contemporary*, and when its first number appeared in January 1847 it contained nine of Turgenev's poems, two critical articles and the story *Khor and Kalinych*. In the spring he applied for his passport and went abroad again, where he was to stay until the summer of 1850. During this period he wrote most of *A Sportsman's Sketches*, *The Diary of a Superfluous Man*, *A Month in the Country* and four other, shorter, plays.

Turgenev's earliest surviving letters are five addressed to his uncle in 1831; there are none to either of his parents, and only about 150 for this whole period.

1. To N. N. TURGENEV

Nikolay Nikolayevich Turgenev (1795–1881) was the younger brother of Turgenev's father Sergey. By the 1830s he was a retired cavalry officer, and on the death of his brother in 1834 he ran the family estates for more than ten years. Three years after inheriting his share of the estates on the death of his mother in 1850, Turgenev appointed his uncle as his estate manager. Unfortunately he proved far from successful, as may be judged from the fact that, whereas the estates should have brought in more than 20,000 roubles a year, Nikolay managed only some 5500, out of which Turgenev nonetheless paid him 2500. When Turgenev was forced to replace him in 1867, his uncle was much taken aback and proved himself cantankerous and difficult, and their squabbles over a financial settlement received wide publicity, much to Turgenev's embarrassment. Turgenev had to sell the house he had built himself in Baden-Baden to Louis Viardot and then rent it back from him. Nevertheless, remembering the affection he had felt towards him as a boy, Turgenev was saddened by the old man's death in 1881.

When this letter was written Turgenev was twelve and still living in his parents' house in Moscow. The idea of writing in the form of a diary probably came from his father, who was keen that his sons should be competent in Russian and considered letter-writing a useful exercise.

[Original in Russian]

Moscow, 22–26 March 1831

Dear Uncle,

I'm sorry that I couldn't write you a letter on Tuesday, which is why I shall now write a very long one.

I shall write to you in the form of a diary beginning with Sunday. I begin.

Sunday, 22 March. I got up that day between six and seven o'clock; I dressed and went to church. After the service we hired a carriage and went to the Sparrow Hills; when we had passed through the city gates, we asked whether we could go on on foot; we were allowed to; I'd hardly got out of the carriage and taken a few steps, when with my usual clumsiness I slipped over and fell right in the mud: I got my fur coat all dirty and tore my trousers! What was I to do! I just got up and carried on walking. When we got to Anna Ivanovna's, I was taken into the study and my trousers were taken away; while I waited for them to be mended, I sat all alone for two hours in a dressing-gown. Alone! It would have been better if they'd put me somewhere upstairs where I would have been separated from the room where they were eating only by a partition, and not locked up! Anger and boredom! I had to eat there; because I had nothing else to do I picked up a book which was lying there. What do you think it was? A German prayer-book; I had just started to read it when they brought me my trousers; I left the study and we soon arrived back home where we didn't get any dinner, thanks to the kindness of the cook. After dinner-time Mr Lobanov[1] and I went to the Gagarins'; we danced two French quadrilles, an old and a new one, a gallopade, a mazurka and an écossaise. I didn't really want to dance, so you can imagine how annoyed I was when a cross-eyed, ugly and what's more very evil lady shouted at the top of her voice, 'Bravo, Monsieur Tourgiéneff, bravo!' I say she was evil because she kept telling everybody that her little sister was so clumsy, unintelligent, badly brought up, etc., and she said it all so nastily that when I looked at her I muttered to myself, as Pushkin says, 'A snake, a snake'.[2]

However, let's finish with all this. You probably wouldn't like her. From the Gagarins' we drove over to Mrs Yakovlev's. Mummy was already there: they asked how we were, about Daddy, and so on. At last we went home and I hurried off to bed.

Monday, 23 March. I woke up early and rushed downstairs to prepare my lessons for Mr Falantin.[3] You probably don't know, but Platon Nikolayevich[4] wants to get rid of him and replace him by some *Gregorius or other*. Please don't write to Platon Nikolayevich about this; it's a secret. Suddenly the clock strikes eight and Mr Falantin comes in, sits down and marks the translations. 'Haben sie das Buch, aus welchem sie übersetzt haben?'[5] he said. I go into the library and look – it's not there! 'I looked and looked until I was tired,' says Krylov;[6] that's how it was with me too. I tell him that it's not there, and then the teacher writes

[1] 1. Fyodor Ivanovich Lobanov, a peasant on the estate at Spasskoye; he was a valet to Turgenev's father who had paid for him to be educated. He often looked after Turgenev in his childhood.

2. From A. S. Pushkin's blank verse historical drama *Boris Godunov*, completed in 1825, published in 1831.

3. Actually Valentin, German tutor.

4. Platon Nikolayevich Pogorelsky, mathematics tutor.

5. 'Have you the book from which you translated?'

6. A misquotation from 'The Small Box' by Ivan Andreyevich Krylov (1768–1844), fabulist, dramatist and journalist.

down very clearly the fateful words, 'was not satisfied'. It turned out that Nikanor[7] had deigned to take the book that morning without asking. Platon Nikolayevich forgave me. After that it was our strictest teacher, Dmitry Nikitich;[8] we did history, grammar and poetry with him. This is what marks I received:

Grammar – very good.

Poetry – extremely good.

History – good, but the additional material not learned.

N.B. I have to thank Dmitry Nikitich for the additional material: I had quite forgotten that I should have learned it; he questioned me about it and I was forgiven.

After dinner it was Mr Gardorf;[9] he tested me and then gave me some more work. Then I went out into the courtyard, ran about and lost one of my galoshes, but it was found; thus passed Monday.

Tuesday, 24 March. Everything followed its proper course. I prepared an essay on 'L'ambition' for Mr Dublet[10] and received a 'good'. After that it was Platon Nikolayevich and geometry; I did well. After dinner it was Mr Shchyurovsky.[11] That day, though, there were no letters.

Wednesday, 25 March. That day was a holiday: the feast of the Annunciation. We went to church and then played outside: all of us got splashed with mud and then went home; we changed our clothes and after dinner went to Mrs Yakovlev's: we played blind man's buff and saw Lyovushka Yakovlev; we had a nice time and went home late. I remembered Golova in *Ruslan*[12] when she says to him, 'I want to sleep; it's already night, farewell!' etc. . . .

Thursday, 26 March. Today Mr Valentin was here and I did well. Then Platon Nikolayevich . . . Here's a problem; try to solve it:

One fountain fills a pool in twelve days, another in nine; if you turn them both on, how long will it take to fill the pool?

In the evening it was Mr Lobanov, and at eight o'clock I am already at my desk and finishing this letter; Nikolenka[13] is sitting at the teacher's desk, eating dried apricots, and reading the *Moscow Telegraph*; opposite Nikolenka sits Mr Meyer[14] reading a *Mythology*; mummy is sitting at her table learning some German words.

My diary is now finished. I'll just add a few words.

I have heard that you wrote that you're going off with the Territorials. Uncle, I won't allow it. If you do go, I'll put my arms around you so tightly that you'll

7. One of the house-servants at Spasskoye.

8. Dmitry Nikitich Dubensky (?–1863), a teacher at Moscow University, engaged by Turgenev's father to teach his sons Russian history, geography and language.

9. Greek tutor.

10. French tutor.

11. Latin and philosophy tutor.

12. *Ruslan and Lyudmila*, long poem by A. S. Pushkin (1820).

13. Turgenev's elder brother Nikolay. See headnote to letter no. 101.

14. A resident tutor in general subjects.

either have to take me with you or not go at all. But you're joking; I know you.

One piece of news. Daddy has given mummy a beautiful woollen jersey for you, and she has got a very nice little cup. Well, it's high time I realized I've been gossiping on for too long, so . . . Farewell.

I kiss you a thousand times, and remain your very affectionate nephew.

Ivan Turgenev

P.S. In your next letter tell me about Skoba. And by the way, Mr Meyer asks me to send you his respects.

Mummy will write to you tomorrow.

2. To A. V. NIKITENKO

Alexander Vasilyevich Nikitenko (1805–77) was a professor at St Petersburg University, a critic and literary historian, and one of the more sensible of the tsarist literary censors. He was one of the editors of the journals *Fatherland Son* (from 1840) and of the *Contemporary* (1846–8). Turgenev first met him at the end of 1836 and they remained on reasonably friendly terms for a number of years. Nikitenko did not like Turgenev's early works, which he found 'tendentious', but he changed his opinions after the publication of *A Nest of the Landed Gentry* in 1859. He played a leading part in settling the arguments between Turgenev and Goncharov (see headnote to letter no. 40). Nikitenko's negative opinion of Turgenev's early works did not deter him from continuing to write verse for a number of years.

[Original in Russian]

St Petersburg, 26 March 1837

Dear Alexander Vasilyevich,

In sending you my first feeble attempts in the field of Russian literature, I beg you not to think that I have the slightest desire to see them published – and if I ask your advice, it is only to discover your opinion of my writings, an opinion which I value most highly. I hesitated about including the *drama*, which I wrote when I was sixteen – my first work – because I can see so many faults in it, and in general I now dislike the whole idea behind it so much that if I did not think that at the outset of one's career it is impossible to foresee the future, and more importantly if I did not rely on your kindness, I would never have decided to send it to you. A year ago I gave it to Pletnyov[1] and he told me what I had long thought myself – that everything is exaggerated, insincere and immature . . . and if there is anything passable in it, it lies in certain details, very few in number. I feel bound to point out (and you, of course, will notice this at once) that the

[2] 1. Pyotr Alexandrovich Pletnyov (1792–1865), poet, critic and academic. From 1838 to 1846 he published the *Contemporary* and he was Rector of St Petersburg University from 1840 to 1861.

metre is very inaccurate. To rework it now is hardly worth the effort; I was about to consign it to utter oblivion when my close acquaintance with you decided me to show it to you. 'The Tale of the Old Man' – unfinished, and scarcely finishable – was written in 1835. Lastly, 'Our Century' was begun in February of this year in a fit of ill-tempered vexation at the despotism and monopoly exercised by certain people dominating our literary world. Last year was devoted to translations of Shakespeare's *Othello* (which I only completed up to halfway through the second act), *King Lear* (with large gaps) and *Manfred*. I destroyed the first two as they struck me as poor when compared to those by Vronchenko[2] and Panayev;[3] besides, this is the wrong path for me to take; I am not at all cut out to be a translator. I have not copied out *Manfred*, so I am not including it. If you would be so good as to tell me if what I have sent you strikes you as not completely worthless, then I shall send you three completed poems: 'Calm at Sea', 'Phantasmagoria on a Summer's Night', and 'Dream'. As well as these I have about a hundred shorter poems, but I have not reworked them all – they're rather incoherent. 'Our Century' is unfinished and I'm working on it at the moment. However, your advice will determine whether I shall continue writing poetry or not. There is one further request: please do not mention this letter to Pyotr Alexandrovich [Pletnyov]. Before I met you I had promised *him* my writings, but up until now I have not fulfilled my promise. His opinions, which by the way I much respect, do not coincide with mine. Furthermore, and I say this in all sincerity, from my first acquaintance with you I felt the deepest trust in you . . . I also forgot to tell you that the drama which I began at the end of last year, the first act and the general outline of which are quite finished, will be brought back, I hope, when I return from the country in September. There-fore I beg the indulgence which I have dared ask of you. In troubling you I beg you to believe in those feelings of deep respect and esteem with which I remain,

Your most obedient servant,

Ivan Turgenev

3. To T. N. GRANOVSKY

Turgenev spent the years 1838–41 as a student at Berlin University (where he studied mainly history and philosophy) and in travel. During these years the two most important of his friendships were with Granovsky and Stankevich (see headnote to following letter). Timofey Nikolayevich Granovsky was five years Turgenev's senior, and they first met in St Petersburg in 1835 when they were both students there. In 1839 Granovsky was appointed professor of history at Moscow University, where he proved himself, by all accounts, to possess one

2. Mikhail Petrovich Vronchenko (1801–55) had published translations of *Hamlet* and *Macbeth* in the early thirties.

3. Ivan Ivanovich Panayev (1812–62), writer, journalist, critic and co-editor of the *Contemporary*. His translation of *Othello* appeared in 1836.

of the more remarkable minds in Russia in the first half of the nineteenth century. Although they were never close friends – Granovsky is reported as having dismissed Turgenev as lightweight and lacking in character – Turgenev had the greatest respect for him, and on his untimely death in 1855 wrote a flattering obituary.

[Original in Russian]

Berlin, 30 May 1840

As I've been back in Berlin just over a week, dear Granovsky, and have settled down and got used to things again here, I feel I ought to write to you. I arrived here, almost without stopping, from Naples (in a fortnight), and such was my desire to return to Berlin that I left Italy without great regret. I admit that it is hard to believe now, walking along the dusty streets of Berlin in the cold wind and rain, that less than three weeks ago I was picking warm, juicy oranges from the trees in Sorrento and listening to the lap of the waves on the shores of the Mediterranean. Neither Belyayevsky nor Tritten is here – the former has left for Baden and the latter for England. Mattison, though, is here.[1] There are few Russians, and I don't know any of them yet. I got used to being in company in Italy. Every evening Stankevich, Markov[2] and I used to go to the Khovrins'[3] – you probably know them by name . . . We all liked the daughter, a pleasant, intelligent girl. I keep recalling that winter we spent together here . . . but it seems that I can never be fully happy. It's Fate! You and Stankevich are quite content with each other's company. You're united by long acquaintance, discussing ideas and sharing the same dreams. Why should you need a third? Besides, there's my illness and the many absurdities in my ⟨being⟩[4] with which I'm still dissatisfied and with which I shall probably have to struggle all my life until I lie 'in cold obstruction', as our father Shakespeare puts it. I drew a little closer to Stankevich in Rome and I would be ungrateful, Heaven knows, if I were not pleased and grateful to be on friendly terms with both you and him. ⟨'You are always what you are,'⟩[4] said Goethe. ⟨'Only know your limitations,'⟩[4] wrote Werder.[5] By the way, I'm studying with him. Things, thank the Lord, are going well. He spoke to me with tears in his eyes about the late Altenstein.[6] ⟨'He was a great spirit, in the highest sense of the word, but he had to bear leaden fetters!'⟩[4] You already know that his son Ladenberg[7] has been placed in

[3] 1. Belyayevsky, Tritten and Mattison were fellow-students of Turgenev's at Berlin University.

    2. Alexey Tarasovich Markov (1802–78), painter, academician and art teacher. He lived in Rome for most of the thirties.

    3. Nikolay Vasilyevich Khovrin, his wife Marya Dmitriyevna and their daughter Alexandra, acquaintances of Turgenev's in Moscow.

    4. Original in German.

    5. Karl Werder (1806–93), German Hegelian philosopher. From 1838 he was professor of philosophy at Berlin University.

    6. Karl Altenstein (1770–1840), Prussian Finance Minister and later an enlightened Minister of Education.

    7. Adalbert Ladenberg (1798–1853), Prussian Minister of Education. There were rumours that he was actually the son of K. Altenstein.

3. To T. N. Granovsky

charge of the Ministry *for the time being*. The king is still very weak.[8] Löwe[9] is ageing as time goes by but singing as well as ever – and with the same faults. Besser[10] returned yesterday from the Leipzig Fair – they're getting ready for a ⟨book exhibition.⟩[4] Nothing will happen in Mainz, and almost everywhere they're trying to stifle things. You are right to demand of me much of Italy, but I am unclear in my own mind as to what I brought back from there; I can say, though, that I'm sure I returned richer than when I went. It was just like a poor man receiving a large inheritance – he finds things difficult and confusing. A whole unknown world, the world of art, flooded over me, but so much of the great and beautiful merely slipped past my eyes, so poorly did I understand what I was seeing. But despite that, ⟨feelings for form and colour⟩[4] awoke within me and developed. I began to find a pleasure in art which I had not known before. I'll whisper in your ear: before I went to Italy a marble statue was just a marble statue to me, and I could never understand all the hidden delights of painting. On the other hand, however, I was disturbed by the state of the people in Rome, the artificial sanctity, the systematic enslavement, the absence of any real life... All those movements which are shaking Northern and Central Europe do not pass beyond the Apennines. No! The Russians have immeasurably more strength and promise than the Italians, especially those in the south; they have outlived their time and passed from the historical stage. Perhaps here and there in Northern Italy that proud spirit and love of freedom of the medieval Italian republics have not completely disappeared – perhaps. I don't know about Piedmont or the kingdom of Lombardy or Venice – but Rome! Naples! You just have to stroll along the *molo* in the evening and watch the priest preaching in a loud voice and pointing to the bloodstained body of Christ in every corner, and the small coins pour out of the pockets of the faithful on to the plates held out by the Capuchins – now there's a charlatan for you, an improvisator, a *pulcinello*. The people who've been lying on the sparkling sand all day now sit and listen, cross themselves and pray, while all the time someone's stealing your scarf or case, and, if they can, your watch as well. Look around, up along the coast; up there, on the top of a hill, lies a castle, by the sea another . . . a third; drums roll and there are troops everywhere. ⟨'The King of Naples is taking precautions . . .'⟩[11] Amongst the improvisators are some wonderful people, especially one, a cripple, remarkably like Mirabeau. It's a pity that I couldn't understand the Neapolitan dialect – there's a lot of the truly comical in those *pulcinelli* farces.

Werder has advised me to read the recently published works of Ludwig Achim von Arnim; he assures me that nowhere do the Middle Ages stand out so truthfully and vividly as in his novel *Die Kronenwächter*.[12] I have been reading

8. i.e. Friedrich Wilhelm III; he died in June 1840.
9. Sophia Löwe (1811–60), German opera singer.
10. A German doctor.
11. Original in French.
12. Ludwig von Arnim (1781–1831); his novel *Die Kronenwächter* was written in 1817. He was the husband of the writer Bettina von Arnim.

some contemporary German literature but so far I haven't found anything worthwhile. All you Marggrafs, Marlows, Mundts and Drechsler-Manfreds – may God be with you, my friends.[13] And what's worse is that all this isn't just rubbish; no, but you'd be surprised how ungrateful must be the soil, fertilized by new ideas, but then producing such poor and pitiful fruits. It's not that the goose is not laying golden eggs but rather that the golden goose is not laying any eggs at all. By the way, I have come across one ⟨sensible man⟩[4] – Chamisso; I don't know him (I'm speaking of his works). If you can get hold of them, read his 'Frauenliebe und Leben', 'Die Klage der Nonne', 'Das Dampfross' and 'Die Jungfrau von Stubbenkammer'.[14] As for books on history, I have started to read a very curious little one: *Maximilien I-er* by Le Glay. I've also read Feuerbach's *Philosophie und Christentum*. Oh, what a great man F. is! Tell Drashusov[15] that he would be doing me a favour if he went to my mother's house and gave my Heine and Hugo – and some others there – to my manservant Kirill Tabalenkov.

Farewell; look after yourself. Stankevich was not at all well when I left him. I haven't had any news of him since, nor from Yefremov[16] whom I've met. I'm well; don't forget me and write sometime.

Yours very truly,

I. Turgenev

4. To T. N. GRANOVSKY

Nikolay Vladimirovich Stankevich (1813–40) was the leader of one of the most influential student circles in Moscow University in the 1830s, where he was an older contemporary of Turgenev's, although they probably did not meet until introduced by Granovsky in Berlin at the end of 1838. Turgenev much admired and respected him, while Stankevich, although thinking more of Turgenev than did Granovsky, wrote of him: 'There is nothing remarkable about his talents, although he doesn't entirely lack them. He is kind and honourable.' Stankevich is depicted as Pokorsky in *Rudin* (1856).

[Original in Russian]

Berlin, 16 July 1840

A great misfortune has befallen us, Granovsky. I hardly have the strength to write. We have lost a man we loved, in whom we believed, a man who was our pride and hope . . . On 24 July, in Novi, Stankevich died. I could, I should finish

13. Hermann Marggraf (1809–64), journalist, dramatist, poet and novelist; F. Marlow, pseudonym of Hermann Ludwig Wolfram-Müller (1807–52), poet; Theodor Mundt (1808–61), novelist, critic and literary historian; Drechsler-Manfred – i.e. 'All you imitators of Byron's *Manfred*'.

14. Adalbert von Chamisso (1781–1838), poet and botanist.

15. Probably Alexander Nikolayevich Drashusov (1816–90), a fellow-student of Turgenev's at Berlin University, later professor of physics and astronomy at Moscow University.

16. Alexander Pavlovich Yefremov (1814–76); see headnote to letter no.5.

this letter here. What use are my words to you now? Not for your sake but rather for mine I shall continue the letter. I grew close to him in Rome and saw him every day. I began to value his lucid mind, his warm heart and all the charm of his soul . . . the shadow of approaching death already lay upon him . . . We often spoke of death. He saw it as the boundary of all thought, and, I think, secretly shuddered. Death has a profound significance if it strikes – as it did with him – at the heart of a fully developed life; to an old man it is a release – but to us, to him? It is the command of Fate. Why should he have died? He recognized and loved the sanctity of life so deeply and sincerely and despite his illness he enjoyed the bliss of thinking, working and loving; he had prepared himself to dedicate his life to work essential for Russia . . . The cold hand of death fell upon his head and our whole world perished. I think ⟨'The cold fist of the Devil is *not* without reason clenched in malice'⟩.[1] I received a letter from him from Florence, dated 11 June. Here is part of what he wrote: 'In Florence I sometimes get some rest, generally I've improved and things are apparently *progressing* . . . It's been finally decided that I shall spend the summer by Lake Como . . . Madame Dyakova[2] who heard in Naples of my illness . . . has arrived with her son and we'll spend the summer together.' He then confided in me his relationship with Dyakova's late sister. Do you remember Klyushnikov's 'Those beautiful eyes have closed'?[3] And *he* died, and Stankevich died! 'I found in Dyakova a real sister, as before; her concern and sympathy help the restoration of my strength more than anything.' He was very worried about his painful relationship with Berthe; he asked me to go and see her, to find out, etc . . . 'I've so many plans in my head – but when didn't I? I expect to work on a history of philosophy this winter. I've also got some ideas for some articles. Heaven knows *how* all this will come to fruition . . . Tell me about Werder; send him my regards. Tell him that his friendship has always been sacred to me and that everything in me that is decent and stable derives from it . . . Farewell, *for the moment!*'
[Five lines omitted]
A fortnight later he died, in the night, at Novi. On 12 July I received the following letter from Yefremov. 'Ivan Sergeyevich. Having recovered a little, I hasten to inform you of the misfortune which as befallen us all. In Novi, a little town about forty miles from Genoa on the road to Milan, during the night of the 24th, Stankevich died. He was going to Como. I do not know what to write. My head is in a whirl. Chaos. When I've arranged everything in Genoa, if nothing detains me I intend to come straight to Berlin. I'm doing everything necessary to organize the taking of his body back to Russia. Farewell. I hope to see you soon. Farewell.

    Yours, A. Yefremov.'

[4] 1. Original in German.

    2. Varvara Alexandrovna Dyakova (1812–?), née Bakunina, older sister of Mikhail (see next letter) and Tatyana (see letter no. 6).

    3. From 'On the Death of a Young Girl' by Ivan Petrovich Klyushnikov (1811–95), who was one of the first people from whom Turgenev sought advice on writing poetry.

I await his arrival impatiently – I'll find out everything, and write to you immediately. My God, how this blow will hit you, Neverov, the Florovs, Kenni,[4] the Bakunins and all his friends and acquaintances! I couldn't face speaking to Werder about it, so I wrote to him. How he was hit by the news! When I saw him, he said, ⟨'With him a part of us all has died.'⟩[1] He almost began to sob. He told me, ⟨'I feel it. I am halfway through my life and my best pupils, my young men are dying – I shall outlive them all!'⟩[1] He read out a marvellous poem, 'Death', which he composed just after he'd received the news. If he agrees, I'll copy it out and send it to you. I look all around and seek in vain. Who of our generation can replace this loss? Who is worthy to accept the testament of his great ideas and refuse to allow his influence to perish? Who will follow his path in his spirit and with his strength? Oh, if only something would stop me having faith in the future I could now, surviving Stankevich, bid farewell to my last hopes. Why couldn't someone else have died, thousands of others, myself for example? When will the time come when the beautiful will not suffer and perish on this earth? Up until now it has seemed that ideas were sacrilege and punishment inevitably awaited anything exceeding a blessed mediocrity. Or was it that the envy of God was aroused as it was with the Greek gods? Or are we to believe that everything beautiful and sacred, love and ideas, is but a cold irony of the Fates? What is our life, then? But no, we must not bow down our heads in dejection. We must come together, offer our hands to each other and grow closer. One of ours has fallen, perhaps the best, but others are arising and will arise in the future. The hand of God will not cease from sowing the seeds of great ambitions in the soul, and sooner or later light will conquer darkness. But to us, those who knew him, the loss is irrecoverable. Was it not Rahel who said, ⟨'Had a young man never died, we would not know suffering'⟩?[5] From the heart of the Creator flow both joy and grief, *Freude und Leid*; their sounds often tremble with the same echo and flow into each other; one is incomplete without the other. It's now the turn of grief . . .

Farewell. Make sure you stay in good health. Write me a word of reply. I think I love you more since the death of Stankevich.

Yours,
I. Turgenev

5. To A. P. YEFREMOV and M. A. BAKUNIN

Turgenev had first met Alexander Pavlovich Yefremov (1814–76) while travelling in Italy in 1840. Yefremov, like Turgenev, was a student at Berlin University at the time. They were never close friends except at this time, and after

4. Yanuary Mikhaylovich Frolov (1812–55), retired army officer and translator; Marya Vladimirovna Florova (1823–50), his second wife, and sister of N.V. Stankevich; Marya Pavlovna Kenni (dates unknown), née Galakhova, sister of N. G. Frolov's first wife.
5. Original in German. Rahel (1771–1833), wife of the German critic and memoirist K. A. Vernhagen von Ense.

5. To A. P. Yefremov and M. A. Bakunin

Yefremov was appointed lecturer in geography at Moscow University they appear to have lost touch.

Mikhail Alexandrovich Bakunin (1814–76) was the oldest of the Bakunin brothers, a revolutionary and the best-known of nineteenth-century anarchists. He and Turgenev were the greatest of friends while both were students in Berlin, where they shared a room; Turgenev soon became acquainted with the whole Bakunin family and their estate at Premukhino, and for a short time fell in love with Bakunin's favourite sister Tatyana (see next letter). Throughout his life, with one or two notable exceptions (usually connected with Bakunin's inability or reluctance to repay one of Turgenev's many financial loans), Turgenev had great affection, if scant respect, for the erstwhile friend of his youth. Bakunin is partially depicted as the eponymous hero of *Rudin*.

[Original in Russian]

Dresden, 28 October 1840

Honourable friends!

I had hoped to celebrate today, my birthday, to the clash of cymbals and the exclamations of my friends who would be crowned with roses (just imagine Yefremov dressed in sandals and a long robe with his arms bare to the shoulders and his head covered in roses), and to participate in libations dedicated to Dionysus and Aphrodite – and what am I doing? I am sitting in a room in a God-forsaken inn drinking bitter pills in a sickly mixture. But I am comforted by the Goddess of Hope; she is dancing before me, waving her garland of green, and she seems now to be no great distance away; I shall stretch out my hand and catch her. If I really am in Berlin on the first, I shall raise an altar to the Spanish fly and burn smoking candles upon it. When I get to Berlin I shall abuse Skachkov[1] roundly. Why hasn't he sent me *Vorlesung's Catalog*? Bakunin, please tell my landlady there's no need to have my room sparkling for 1 November; just warm it, clean it, put out some mignonettes and await my arrival with the trepidation of a lover. There's one nuisance, though; I've been ordered to behave respectably until the new year – no wine, *etc*. Otherwise I would have ordered a magnificent banquet. But I still fear that old bitch Fate; for no reason at all she is still giving me a slap or two. The doctor told me that ⟨it was the fourth attack⟩.[2] Why not the fifth, sixth, fifty-fifth, sixty-sixth, etc.? But there is an end to everything, even to the patience of the Germans, and it is well known that the Germans are not only patient, but courteous at the same time. For example, if the ⟨Highest Authority⟩[2] beats him with a bunch of birch twigs and in the heat of the punishment a few twigs fall out, the German will say, 'Oh, Highest Authority, four twigs have fallen out.' And so, if there is an end to such patience, so there is probably one to my illness as well. I must confess to one further thing: I have read nothing sensible except for Retscher and Hegel's *logic* because I've

[5] 1. A. Skachkov, a friend of Turgenev's at Berlin University.
    2. Original in German.

been absorbed in French romances and, heaven knows, when the blood is pounding away in your head you just can't read anything else. The most remarkable of those in the vast ocean of French books were G. Sand's *La dernière Aldini*, Souvestre's *Mémoires d'un Sans-Culotte breton*, Karr's *Une folle histoire*, and Dumas' *Le Capitaine Pamphile*.

With which, farewell.

Yours sincerely,
Iv. Turgenev

6. To T. A. BAKUNINA

Turgenev returned to Russia from Germany in June 1841 and stayed in Moscow and then with his mother at Spasskoye. Just before his return M. A. Bakunin had written to his family in terms of the highest praise of Turgenev, telling them to expect a visit.

Turgenev arrived at the Bakunin estate of Premukhino in the middle of October and stayed there a week. During this time the impressionable Tatyana (1815–71) fell madly in love with him; although not beautiful, she was by all accounts very attractive; she was also of an introspective and emotional disposition. Her letters to Turgenev are a mixture of romantic love and utter confusion, of hope and of despair – which is not surprising as Turgenev's attitude to her was at best ambivalent. Their friendship lasted but six months, when Turgenev realized that things were getting out of control, at least as far as he was concerned. The experience was, though, to have a lasting effect on him: the theme of the passionate and generous woman and the weak and indecisive man is common in his later works. The idea that it is the moral duty of a man to break off a liaison with a woman when he feels his passions cooling is the theme of his first published short story, *Andrey Kolosov* of 1844. Turgenev, however, was not such a man. His 'affair' with Tatyana, reflected in other works too, marks his parting from his flirtation with the German Romantic philosophy and a turning towards more practical, albeit more prosaic, matters.

[Original in Russian]

Moscow, *c.* 20 March 1842

I could not leave Moscow, Tatyana Alexandrovna, without saying a few sincere words. We have grown so far apart and become such strangers to one another that I do not know whether you will understand the reason why I am taking up my pen . . . You will perhaps think that I am writing to you out of propriety . . . all of that, and much worse, I deserve . . .

But I would not for one moment wish to part from you like that. Give me your hand and, if you can, forget everything painful and confusing in the past. My heart is overflowing with a profound sadness and it is quite unbearable for me to look back. I want to forget everything, everything except that look on your face which I now so clearly and vividly see . . . Perhaps I can see in that look both forgiveness and reconciliation . . . Heavens, how sad and yet how wonderful I feel – how I want to cry and press your hand to my lips and tell you everything that is now so alarmingly filling my heart . . .

I sometimes thought that I had parted from you for ever; but I had only to imagine that you were no more and had died when a deep sadness would possess me. But it was not just sadness at your death, but that you had died without knowing me, without having heard from me a sincere, heart-felt word, a word which would have enlightened me and enabled me to understand that strange union, that deep union which I sensed throughout my whole being – the union between you and me . . . Do not smile sadly in disbelief. I feel that I am speaking the truth, and I have no reason to lie.

I feel that I have not parted from you for ever . . . I shall see you again . . . my good and beautiful sister. We lived like old men, or perhaps like children – life slipped through our hands and we regarded it as children do, children who have nothing yet to feel sorry about and for whom much still lies ahead, or like old men for whom life holds no regrets. Just like the apparitions in Act II of [Meyerbeer's] *Robert le Diable* who dance and smile but know what it will cost them to move their heads – their young flesh will slip from their bones like a worn-out coat . . . In your aunt's house it is so cramped, so cold and so miserable, and you, poor girl, have been there an age.

I stand before you and firmly press your hand . . . I would like to pour hope and strength and joy into you . . . Listen, I bow down before you as a goddess; I am speaking the truth and tell you that I know I have loved no other woman as I have loved you; but I have not loved even you with a true and lasting love, and because of that I could not be as cheerful and open with you as with the others, for I loved you more than them. So I shall always be sure that you and you alone will understand me; for you alone I wanted to be a poet, for you, to whom my heart is united in some inexpressibly wonderful way so that it's almost as if I do not actually have to see you or feel the need actually to talk to you – which is why I cannot talk to you as I should – but despite all that, when I am writing, at those lonely and profoundly blissful moments of creation, you are always with me. I read to you what is pouring from my pen, you, my beautiful sister . . . Oh, if I could but once walk alone with you on a spring morning along the long, long avenue of lime trees, hold your hand in mine and feel our hearts beating as one, as everything alien and painful disappears and everything perfidious melts away – for ever. Yes, you have *all* the love in my heart, and if I could have expressed all this *myself – in your presence* – we would not have found ourselves in such a difficult position, and I would know *how* I love you.

Look how you are constantly with me in all my happiest moments. I enclose Serafina's song from my *Don Juan* (I'll tell you all about it sometime, but you will understand anyway). I know you will not imagine that Serafina is you and the man she is speaking to is me – that would be too funny, too stupid; but my feelings towards you . . .

⟨Your form, your being is always alive in me; it changes and grows and takes on new forms like a Proteus: you are my *Muse*. Thus, for example, the form of Serafina developed out of thoughts of you, as also did Inez and perhaps Doña Anna – why do I say perhaps? – everything that I think and create is in some wonderful way connected with you.

Be happy, my sister; give me your blessing on my journey and count on me – for a while – as on a speechless rock, but one in the very depths of whose stony heart true love and affection are locked away.

Be happy; I am touched and deeply moved. Be happy, my best and only friend. Until we meet again.

Turgenev⟩[1]

7. To V. G. BELINSKY

Vissarion Grigoryevich Belinsky (1811–48) was the first Russian literary critic of any great originality. He had during his short life an enormous influence on the development of Russian literature. He was the originator of the sociological or 'civic' school of criticism; he demanded that literature should be modern and true to life and, most important of all, that it should be inspired by socially significant ideas. For him content was usually more important than form, and he is generally held responsible for the fact that after him Russians tended to look for prophecy rather than entertainment in their literature. When Turgenev's 'Parasha' first appeared Belinsky hailed it as 'one of the most remarkable works of 1843', in an article which turned Turgenev, not surprisingly, into his 'disciple'. Despite Belinsky's less flattering remarks about much of Turgenev's later lyric poetry, Turgenev never wavered in his respect and veneration for him. After their first meeting in 1843 they remained firm friends until Belinsky's death five years later, despite the critic's attitude to the rising young writer being one of stern father to favourite son, and despite Turgenev's reluctance to agree with many of Belinsky's ideas.

[Original in Russian]

Moscow, 28 March 1845

Dear Belinsky,

Nekrasov[1] has asked me to send him through my brother, as I had promised, my *Landlord*,[2] and is demanding a reply. I put it all entirely at your disposal, although I cannot say that I would like to see it published on its own; in fact I

[6]1. Original in German.

[7] 1. Nikolay Alexeyevich Nekrasov (1821–77), editor of the *Contemporary*; see headnote to letter no. 24.

2. Published in 1845 and containing a caricature of the Slavophiles, especially K. S. Aksakov. Turgenev was later extremely ashamed of it and attempted to ensure it was never published again.

don't think it's at all suitable for such treatment. Perhaps it will pass off all right in polytype – but that won't make it easier for me. Do as you think fit.

I am now writing two things: 1) an article for *Annals of the Fatherland* on two of Kireyevsky's in the *Moskvityanin*,[3] and 2) a poem entitled 'A Short Love Affair' which I have spoken to Nekrasov about.[4] I shall finish it soon and would be prepared to see *this one* published separately or to give it to you (if the plan you told me about comes off).

I'm sorry not to write more, but I'm in a bad mood. Look after yourself and drop me a line if you feel like it.

Yours,

T.

8. To PAULINE VIARDOT

Pauline Viardot was born in Paris in July 1821 into a very musical family. Her father, Manuel Garcia, born in Seville in 1775, was a tenor of some repute; her mother Joaquima, née Sitchès, was a famous opera singer; her brother Manuel was also a singer, and later an influential teacher in Paris and London and the author of *Traité complet de l'art du chant* published in two volumes in 1847; and her elder sister Maria, known as La Malibran, was the most famous mezzo-soprano of her day.

Pauline's public debut was in Paris in 1838 where Alfred de Musset was overcome by her, although Berlioz did not think much of her performance. A year later she made her first stage appearance, in London, as Desdemona in Rossini's *Otello*. In 1840 she married Louis Viardot, twenty-one years her senior. Two years before he had been appointed Director of the Théâtre Italien in Paris and had engaged Pauline for the 1839 season. He was an author with an established reputation, a student of all things Spanish, and a passionate lover of shooting. Although possibly never in love with him, Pauline rewarded his devotion to her with a genuine affection, and she was more or less faithful to him. Through her friendship with George Sand, who had encouraged her marriage, she met Gounod, Liszt, Saint-Saëns and Delacrois, all of whom thought highly of her. At the end of October 1843 she made her triumphant debut at the winter season in the Imperial Opera in St Petersburg as Rosina in *Il Barbiere di Siviglia*. Turgenev was probably present, but first met her at the home of a friend a few days later. He was immediately captivated by her and loved her until he died with a quiet and, for the most part, undemanding devotion.

The earliest published letter from Turgenev to her is dated 9 May 1844; their correspondence was conducted in French, although Turgenev would often

3. Ivan Vasilyevich Kireyevsky (1806–56), a leading Slavophile philosopher, had published two articles on contemporary Russian literature in the journal *Moskvityanin* in January and February 1845. Turgenev never carried out his intention to reply to them.
4. Original title of 'Andrey' published in the *Annals of the Fatherland* in 1846.

write the more intimate and personal passages in German. When the following letter was written Pauline was fulfilling a number of singing engagements in Germany, while Turgenev remained in Paris.

[Original in French]

Paris, 25 December 1847

We were all, I swear, Madame, becoming a little worried because we had not received any news from you (it is true that you have been spoiling us lately), when your letter of the 21st, with all its charming details, filled us with joy. I performed the office of reader, as is our custom, and I can assure you that my eyes never feel better than when they are making out what you have written, the more so since, for a celebrity, you write rather well. However, your hand-writing varies a great deal. Sometimes it is quite beautiful, precise and minute – a real little mouse going at a trot across the page – while at others it marches on bravely and freely, taking long strides, but often it just presses on at an amazing speed and with extreme impatience, and then your letters become only what we can make of them.

You do well to describe your costumes. We realists hold colouring very dear. But then . . . then everything you do is done well. Your success in Hamburg gave us infinite joy. Bravo! Bravo!

Aren't we *good* to encourage you?

I thank you from the bottom of my heart for the wise and kind advice you gave me in your letter to Mme Garcia.[1] What you say about the ⟨cracks⟩[2] one always notices in a work which has been interrupted is quite true – ⟨'those are golden words'⟩.[3] Actually, since I've been in Paris I've never worked on more than one thing at a time and I've brought several of them safely to harbour – at least, I hope so. Not a week passes without my sending a large parcel off to my editors.

Since my last letter to you I've read another of Calderón's plays, *La Vida es sueño* [*Life's a Dream*]. It is one of the grandest dramatic conceptions that I know. It is full of a wild energy, a sombre and profound contempt for life and an astonishing bravado in its ideas, all combined with the most inflexible Catholic fanaticism. Calderón's Sigismond (the leading personage) is the Spanish Hamlet with all the differences there are between the Mediterranean and the North. Hamlet is more reflective, more subtle, more of the philosopher; Sigismond's character is uncomplicated, naked and penetrating like an épée; the former cannot do anything because of indecision, doubt and intellectualizing, while the latter does things because his southern blood forces him to, but in so doing he knows that life is but a dream.

I have just started the Spanish *Faust* – *El Mágico prodigioso*. I am utterly

---

[8] 1. Pauline Viardot's mother, of whom Turgenev was very fond.
   2. Original in Spanish.
   3. Original in German.

Calderonized. In reading these works, I feel they have grown naturally out of a rich and productive soil. Their taste and smell are simple and you do not sense any literary left-overs. Drama in Spain was the last and most beautiful expression of naive Catholicism and of that society it created in its own image, while in the difficult and transitional times we are now living through all artistic or literary works present in the main only the individual opinions and feelings, the confused and contradictory reflections and the eclecticism of their authors. Life is dispersed; there is no longer any one great general movement, except perhaps for industry, which considered from the point of view of the progressive subjugation of the natural elements to the genius of man will become the liberator and regenerator of the human race. So in my opinion the greatest contemporary poets are the Americans, who are about to pierce the Isthmus of Panama and speak of establishing an electric telegraph across the ocean. Once the social revolution has been achieved, long live the new literature!

Many of these reflections came to me when I was at a revue about 1847 at the Palais-Royal called 'The Oyster Bank'. It was amusing enough and made me laugh, but, good lord, how weak, timid, petty and pale when compared with what it could have been. I don't insist on Aristophanes, but at least someone from his school! A fantastic and extravagant comedy that both ridicules and moves its audience, pitiless on everything feeble or bad in society and in man himself, and which finishes by laughing at his misery, elevating him to the sublime in order to ridicule him and then descending to the depths to glorify him, to throw him in the face of our arrogance. Now, what we would give to see that! But no, we are condemned to Scribe for ever.[4] I have not lost hope of reading to you *The Birds* or *The Frogs* by Aristophanes, but I shall omit everything that is too cynical . . .

And so you're now in Berlin. Your first two campaigns are over and you now find yourself amongst a people already conquered. Your debut will be in a week. I know someone who will peruse the Berlin papers for us. In the Frankfurt *Didaskalia* there is an enthusiastic article on your performance, written from Hamburg. By the way, the *Illustration* has announced your engagement for next winter's season at the Grand Opera. They write from St Petersburg that the Italian Theatre there is in agony. I've written to your husband about *Cenerentola* and Mme Alboni.[5]

I hope you all, husband, wife and child, are as the angels, or as we are, for we are all very, very well.

Farewell, Madame. At the risk of boring you by always repeating the same

4. Augustin Eugène Scribe (1791–1861), prolific and very popular French dramatist whose comedies of manners were devoid of characterization and depended mainly on farcical plots. He also wrote a large number of opera libretti.

5. Marietta Alboni (1823–92), Italian contralto. She appeared during the winter season of 1846–7 in St Petersburg and the following season in Paris. She often sang the same roles as Pauline Viardot and considered her her main rival. Turgenev was always disparaging about her performances.

thing, I wish you all the very best of all the very best and most beautiful in the world. You know that my wishes are sincere. Be well, be happy.

Your utterly devoted,

Iv. Turgenev

P.S. ⟨May God bless you.⟩²

9.To PAULINE VIARDOT

[Original in French]

Paris, 29 April – 2 May 1848

⟨Good morning and a thousand thanks, dearest Madame.⟩¹ I shall tell you, Madame, that for the last few days the weather has been foggy, dull, unpleasant, *coldiscule* – I won't say cold – ⟨very gentleman-like⟩² – it's been atrocious! I shall wait for some more favourable sunshine before going to Fontainebleau. Up till now we've had only ⟨a real English sun, warranted to produce a gentle and comfortable heat⟩.² However, it didn't prevent my going yesterday to the Exposition. Do you know that in the whole of that awful Exposition the only thing which I really liked was a sketch by Delacroix, 'A Lion Devouring a Sheep in a Forest'? The lion is chestnut-coloured, with his mane bristling – magnificent. He is lying down and quite at ease; he is eating hungrily. Serene, yet sensual. What strength in the colouring, dark yet warm, dull and luminous at the same time. Typical of Delacroix. There were also two other paintings by him – 'The Death of Valentin' (from *Faust*) and 'The Death of Christ' – two terrible daubs, if I may put it that way. As for the rest – nothing. What a poor Exposition with which to inaugurate the Republic!

In the evening I went to see a ballet, *Les Cinq Sens*.³ It was absolutely absurd. Amongst other things it had a scene about magnetism. Grisi magnetizes Petipa⁴ to awake in him the sense of *taste* – quite colossal in its stupidity. There was a large audience and they applauded loudly. Actually Grisi danced very well but it was tedious as a ballet. Just legs, legs and more legs, very monotonous. Before the ballet they did Act II from *Lucia di Lammermoor* with Poultier!! Partheux! and a certain Rabi, or Riba, or Ribi, or Raba – in a word someone quite anonymous. This anonymous lady portrayed great fear, but she had a poor voice. It's true to say that she's also rather ugly, which didn't help her hide her age.

[9] 1. Original in German.

2. Original in English.

3. *Griseldis, ou les cinq sens*, three-act ballet to music by A. Adam.

4. Carlotta Grisi (1821–99), Italian ballerina. Marius Petipa (1822–1910), dancer and choreographer. He was subsequently to achieve fame with his striking and innovative productions of ballet in St Petersburg, most notably of Tchaikovsky's *The Sleeping Beauty* (1890), *The Nutcracker* (1892) and *Swan Lake* (1895).

9. *To Pauline Viardot*

Sunday

Good day, Madame. When one puts one's nose out of the window in the morning . . . just a minute – a verse! And as it came all alone one must be polite and provide it with a companion . . .

'Perhaps one sees nothing – something perhaps.' This is pure Hugo! But I wanted to say something else. I wanted to say (oh, this wretched pen!) that when one puts one's nose out of the window in the morning and breathes in the spring air, one cannot stop oneself desiring to be happy. Life, that reddish spark in the sombre and dumb ocean of Eternity. It is the only moment which belongs to you and you alone, etc., etc. That's very hackneyed, but it's still true. (Tomorrow I'm going to buy some new pens; the ones I'm using are terrible and spoil the pleasure I get from writing to you.) Now then, ah, thank heavens, one which is all right. What did I do yesterday, Saturday? I read a book which I have often praised without, I admit, ever having read – Pascal's *Les Provinciales*. It's quite admirable in every respect. Common sense, eloquence, humour, animation, they're all there. And what's more it's written by a slave, a slave to Catholicism. 'The Cherubims, those glorious beings composed of head and plumes' and 'those illustrious flying forms ever red and fiery' from the Jesuit Le Moine made me roar with laughter.

Then I went to the exhibition of the statues portraying the Republic, or rather the seven hundred studies representing them. I came out utterly indignant, as did everyone else. They're an unimaginable abomination. What a competition! Where is the jury?

I spent the evening at the Tuchkovs', whom I've already spoken to you about.[5] We *conducted* a conversation, which was fairly interesting but very tiring. You know those families where it is impossible to converse with a *relaxed* mind, where the conversation becomes a series of problems which you have to solve by the sweat of your mind, where the hosts have no doubt that often the most delicate of attentions is *not* to pay any attention to their guests, where every word has to be, as it were, stuck to. What torture! Such conversations are like a stage-coach journey where you are the horses.

Then I went to bed and read Count de Maistre's *Voyage autour de ma chambre* which I didn't know before. But I didn't like the voyage one bit. It's an imitation of Sterne written by a very intelligent man, and I've noticed that the most obnoxious imitations are those written by intelligent men who take themselves seriously. A fool will just copy slavishly but a clever man who lacks talent will do it pretentiously and spare no effort to be original, which is the worst of all. A captive thought in battle – a sorry sight! I have a special horror of the imitators of Sterne – egoists, full of sensibility, who luxuriate, preen themselves and are obviously proud of themselves while at the same time trying to appear simple and good-hearted. (Töpffer[6] is rather like this.)

5. A Russian family living in exile in Paris in the late forties. The father, a general, had been involved in the Decembrist movement in the 1820s.
6. Rudolph Töpffer (1799–1846), Swiss writer and painter.

My friend Herwegh's expedition was a complete fiasco. Those poor devils, the German workers, suffered a terrible massacre and the second-in-command, Bornstedt, was killed. As for Herwegh, it's said that he's returned to Strasbourg with his wife. If he comes here I'll advise him to re-read *King Lear*, especially the scene between the King, Edgar and Fool in the forest. Poor devil! He should either never have started the affair or got himself killed like the others.[7]

Is your husband returning to Paris? M. Bastide has been elected.[8] Mme Sitchès has given me all your news.[9] I hope, Madame, that you will have the kindness to write to me soon. Until tomorrow . . .

Monday, 11 p.m.

I took advantage of the fine weather today to go to Ville d'Avray, a little village beyond St Cloud. I'm thinking of renting a room there. I spent more than four hours in the forest, sad, moved, attentive; absorbed in and absorbing what I saw. The impression made by nature on a man when he is alone is a strange one. There is something in it of the *fresh* sadness which is in all the smells of the fields, a little of the *serene* melancholy in the singing of the birds. You will understand what I am saying; you will probably understand it better than I do myself. I cannot remain unmoved by the sight of a branch covered with young green leaves clearly set against the blue sky. Why? Yes, why? Is it because of the contrast between this tiny living twig, quivering at the slightest puff of wind, and which I could snap off and which must soon die but which some generous force animates and colours, and that eternal immense emptiness of the sky which is blue and radiant thanks only to the earth beneath? (For beyond our atmosphere the temperature is $-70°$ and there is very little *light*.) Ah, I cannot bear the sky; but life and reality, with all its capriciousness and dangers, with all its customs and fleeting beauty – I adore it all. Speaking personally, I am attached to the ground. I would prefer to watch the precipitous movements of the damp foot of a duck as it scratches the back of its head by the side of a lake, or the long sparkling drops of water falling slowly from the mouth of a cow as it stands motionless and up to its knees drinking water from a pond, to anything the cherubims (those illustrious flying forms) could perceive in their heavens.

Tuesday, 9.30 a.m.

I found myself last night in a philosophic-pantheistic mood, but let's think of somebody else today. I shall speak about you, which proves . . . that I'm much more sensible today.

---

7. Georg Herwegh (1817–75), German poet and revolutionary, and his wife Emma (1817–75), lived in France in the 1840s where they were befriended by Turgenev. In April 1848 Herwegh led about seven hundred young German workers living in France into Germany to raise a revolt. After their massacre by government troops he escaped to Switzerland, later returning to France. Adalbert Bornstedt (1808–51) survived; he was probably a Prussian government informer.

8. Jules Bastide (1800–79), republican politician, journalist and historian.

9. Aunt of Pauline Viardot's, the wife of her mother's brother Pablo Sitchès.

9. *To Pauline Viardot*

You will make your debut in *Les Huguenots*[10] – that's very good. But you mustn't allow people to let you do only dramatic roles. If you were to sing *Sonnambula* . . . that's Mlle Lind's[11] best part – she'll make her debut with it – but what will happen then? I imagine I can look forward to a great success. After you've heard her tomorrow, you will write and tell me what you thought of her, won't you? Whatever happens don't allow yourself to specialize only in dramatic roles. The papers say that your debut is on the sixth, on Saturday. Is that right? There'll be someone here in Paris who'll be, I'll not say uneasy, but rather out of sorts. [Seven lines of an untranslatable play on words omitted.] But I'm talking nonsense.

The day before yesterday I went to see Frédérick Lemaître[12] in *Robert Macaire*. The play is poorly written and vile but Frédérick is the most powerful actor I know. In this role he's frightening. Robert Macaire might be a Prometheus – but the most monstrous one imaginable. What insolence, what brazen-faced impertinence, what cynical self-confidence, what a challenge to everyone and what contempt for all! The public behaved perfectly – calm, cold and dignified. On my word of honour, the smallest street urchin would be able to see Frédérick's talents as an actor but would find his role repulsive. But what overpowering truth, what verve! But, you see, the feeling for the moral and that for the beautiful are two bumps which have absolutely nothing to do with each other.[13] Happy is the man who possesses both.

The weather is marvellous today. I'm going out in an hour and shan't return until late this evening. I have to find a small room outside Paris. What has stopped me deciding on Ville d'Avray is having to cross the Seine to get there on a pontoon bridge and then on foot because the boatmen have profited from the February Revolution and destroyed the railway bridge – and it now takes much longer.

I shall try to slip along to the National Assembly when it opens. If I manage it, I shall send you the most accurate description. For your part, Madame, once you have settled in will you describe your house and your salon? Please do that for me . . .

And now, Madame, please permit me to press your hand.

A thousand good wishes to Mme Garcia, your husband, Mlle Antonia[14] and Louise.[15] ⟨Look after yourself.

> Your devoted friend⟩,[1]
>
> Iv. Turgenev

---

10. Opera by Meyerbeer, extremely popular at the time in Germany.

11. Jenny Lind (1820–87), celebrated soprano, the 'Swedish nightingale', a pupil of Manuel Garcia.

12. Frédérick Lemaître (1800–76), leading Parisian actor, who specialized in melodramatic roles. *Robert Maciare* was written by him in collaboration with B. Antier and J. Saint-Amand.

13. A reference to the recently published theory of phrenology.

14. Antonia Sitchès (1827–?), cousin of Pauline Viardot, the daughter of her uncle Pablo Sitchès.

15. Louise Viardot (1841–1918), eldest daughter of Louis and Pauline Viardot.

10. To PAULINE VIARDOT

[Original in French]

Paris, *c.* [after] 15 May 1848

Exact account of what I saw on Monday 15 May.

I left the house at noon. The boulevards looked much as they always did; however, on the Place de la Madeleine there were already two or three hundred workers carrying banners.

The heat was stifling. People were talking excitedly in small groups. Then I saw an old man of about sixty get up on to a chair in the left-hand corner of the square and make a speech in defence of Poland. I approached; what he was saying was very violent, but equally trivial; however, he was wildly applauded. I heard someone near me say it was the abbé Chatel.[1]

A few moments later I saw General de Courtais[2] arrive from the Place de la Concorde on his white horse (just like La Fayette). He moved off towards the boulevards, greeting the crowds, and suddenly began to speak vehemently, making violent gestures. I couldn't hear what he was saying. Then he left by the same way as he had entered.

Soon the procession appeared. It had sixteen men in each row with flags at its head. About thirty officers of all ranks from the National Guard escorted the petition. A man with a long beard (who I later discovered was Huber)[3] rode up in a cabriolet.

I watched the procession slowly turn about in front of me (I was on the steps of the Madeleine) and head for the National Assembly. I kept on watching. The head of the column stopped for a moment at the Pont de la Concorde and then advanced up to the railings. From time to time a great cry went up: 'Long live Poland!' – a cry rather more lugubrious to the ear than 'Long live the Republic!'

Soon I could see men *en blouse* going up the steep steps of the Palais de l'Assemblée; the people around me said these were the delegates who were to be let in. But I recalled that a few days earlier the Assembly had decided not to receive the petitioners *inside the building*, as was done during the Convention, and although I was well aware of the feebleness and lack of resolution of our new legislators, I did find that a little extraordinary.

I descended from my perch and walked the length of the procession which had stopped at the railings in front of the Chamber. The whole of the Place de la Concorde was packed with people. Those around me were saying that the

[10] 1. The abbé Chatel (1795–1857) tried to establish a reformed French Catholic Church, free of the influence of Rome and based on democratic principles.

2. General G. A. de Courtais (1790–1877) was appointed Commander-in-Chief of the National Guard in February 1848, but for his 'weakness' towards the demonstrators in May he was arrested, tried, and acquitted.

3. Louis Huber (1815–65), republican and opponent of Louis Philippe; one of the leaders of the demonstrations of 15 May; he later fled to London.

Assembly was receiving the delegates at that moment and that the whole procession was going to file past inside. About a hundred *gardes mobiles* armed with rifles but without bayonets stood on the steps of the peristyle.

Succumbing to the heat, I walked for a short time along the Champs Elysées and then returned to the house with the intention of picking up Herwegh. But not finding him there, I returned to the Place de la Concorde. It would have been about three o'clock. There was still a large crowd in the square but the procession had disappeared. Only the end of it and the last banners were visible on the other side of the bridge. I had just passed the Obélisque when a bare-headed man dressed in black, anguish on his face, ran past and shouted to the people, 'My friends, my friends, the Assembly has been taken over; come to our aid; I am a representative of the people.'

I went as quickly as I could to the bridge, which I found barred by a detachment of *gardes mobiles*. Suddenly the crowd was gripped by a terrible confusion. Many left, affirming that the Assembly had been dissolved, while others denied it; all in all an unimaginable shambles.

Meanwhile, from the outside the Assembly building looked nothing out of the ordinary; the *guards* were *guarding* it as if nothing had happened. Once we heard the drums beating the fall-in, and then everything fell silent. (We learnt later that it was the President himself who had ordered the drums to cease, either out of prudence or cowardice.)

So passed two long hours. Nobody knew anything for certain, but the insurrection appeared to have succeeded. I managed to find a gap in the row of guards along the bridge and climbed on to the parapet. I saw a mass of people, but without their banners, running along the other side of the Seine . . . 'They're going to the Hôtel de Ville,' someone near me shouted; 'It's just like 24 February.'

I climbed down, intending to go to the Hôtel de Ville. But at that moment we suddenly heard a prolonged roll on the drums and a battalion of *gardes mobiles* appeared from the side of the Madeleine and moved as if to charge us. But as no one offered any resistance – with the exception of a handful of people, one of whom was armed with a pistol – they halted at the bridge and marched the insurgents off to the police station.

Even then, though, nothing appeared to have been settled. I would even say that the actions of the *gardes mobiles* were rather hesitant. For at least an hour before their arrival and for a quarter of an hour after it everyone thought the uprising had been successful, and all one heard was 'It's over', said either happily or sadly depending on the views of the person speaking.

The battalion commander, a jovial but resolute man with an eminently French face, made a short speech to his men ending with the words, 'The French will always be French. Long live the Republic!' – which hardly compromised him in any way.

I forgot to tell you that in the two hours of waiting and anxiety which I've been speaking about we saw a legion of the National Guard slowly enter the

Champs Elysées and cross the Seine by the bridge opposite the Invalides. It was this legion which took the insurgents from their rear and evicted them from the Assembly.

However, the battalion of *gardes mobiles* was greeted by the bourgeois with delight . . . Shouts of 'Long live the Assembly!' started up again with renewed force. Suddenly a rumour spread that the representatives had returned to the Chamber. This changed everything. From all sides the call to fall in rang out, the *gardes mobiles* (really mobile this time!) raised their caps on their bayonets (which, in parenthesis, produced a remarkable effect!) and shouted, 'Long live the National Assembly!' A lieutenant-colonel in the National Guard rushed up, all out of breath; about a hundred people gathered around and he told us what had happened. 'The Assembly is stronger than ever,' he shouted. 'We crushed the scoundrels . . . Ah, gentlemen, what frightful things I have seen . . . deputies insulted, assaulted . . .'

Ten minutes later all the approaches to the Assembly had been blocked off by the troops; cannon arrived, pulled with difficulty by horses at the trot; troops of the line, lancers . . . Order and the bourgeois had triumphed, and rightly, this time.

I remained on the square till six o'clock . . . I have just found out that victory also went to the government at the Hôtel de Ville. I did not manage to dine that evening till seven.

Of all the multitude of things which struck me I shall mention only three. Firstly, the *general order outside* the Chamber which reigned practically undisturbed; those cardboard toys, called soldiers, guarded the uprising as scrupulously as they could; they let it pass by and then closed in behind it. It is true to say that the Assembly for its part did everything one would have expected of it. It listened to the perorations of Blanqui[4] for half an hour without a single protest! The President never once donned his hat![5] The representatives did not leave their seats for two hours, and only then when they were forced to. If this immobility had been like that of the Roman senators when faced by the Gauls, it would have been superb! But no, their silence was the silence of fear. They sat, and the President presided . . . With the exception of a lone deputy, M. d'Adelsward,[6] no one protested. And Clément Thomas himself only interrupted Blanqui gravely to beg a word!

What also struck me was the manner in which the lemonade- and cigar-sellers circulated amongst the crowds, grasping, content, and indifferent to what was going on around them. They looked like fishermen drawing in a well filled net.

Thirdly, and this astonished me more than anything, was that I found it impossible to assess the sentiments of the people at such a moment. On my

---

4. Louis Auguste Blanqui (1805–81), left-wing revolutionary who advocated the dictatorship of the proletariat. He served a total of forty-six years in prison for his opposition to Louis Philippe.

5. Traditionally the manner in which debates were terminated in the National Assembly.

6. Member of the National Assembly, a republican; he commanded the National Guard when de Courtais was dismissed, but only lasted in the post himself till June. He emigrated during the Second Empire.

honour, I could not even guess what they wanted, or what they feared. Were they revolutionaries or reactionaries? Or simply supporters of good order? They as it were simply waited for the storm to die down. I also kept looking at the workers *en blouse*: they were waiting . . . waiting . . . waiting! What is History then? Providence, accident, irony, or Fate?

Iv. Turgenev

11. To A. A. KRAYEVSKY

Andrey Alexandrovich Krayevsky (1810–89), journalist and publisher. From 1839 to 1868 he was the editor of the *Annals of the Fatherland* and from 1862 to 1884 of the newspaper *Voice*. His relations with Turgenev were of a purely business nature, and Turgenev was always a little wary of him as he believed his talents for making money sometimes clouded his literary judgment.

[Original in Russian]

Paris, 14 April 1849

A week ago, dear Krayevsky, I received your letter with the news of the conclusive shipwreck of my ill-fated *Alien Bread*.[1] May it rest in peace! It is difficult, as the Holy Book says, to swim against the tide. But thank you for expressing your sympathy.

This is what I have to tell you. I sent off two large parcels yesterday to Shchepkin containing another three-act comedy, entitled *The Bachelor*.[2] Not only will the censor find nothing in it to remove, he should on the contrary reward me for my exemplary morality. I would of course be pleased to see it appear in the *Annals of the Fatherland*, but it is intended for Shchepkin's benefit performance and that won't be until January of next year. So you will have to wait a little longer. You can, though, write to Shchepkin and tell him that *The Bachelor* will be yours to publish. By the way, I've already written to him about it.

But you would be justified in demanding a bird in the hand rather than two in the bush. Well, I do have a couple, and one is already a fledgling and will fly off to you in a fortnight, *no later*. That *Bachelor* of mine took up a lot of time, and besides I didn't expect *Alien Bread* to be hit over the head. Here are my birds:

1. A sort of short story entitled *The Diary of a Superfluous Man*. (I think it's quite good. It's finished and only needs to be copied out again.)
2. *The Party* – a one-act comedy (also finished).

[11] 1. Two-act play satirizing the gentry, which had been banned by the censor S. A. Gedeonov (whose own plays Turgenev had dismissed as worthless a few years before) and not published until 1857.
2. A satire on St Petersburg officials. It was the first of Turgenev's plays to be staged (1849) and was dedicated to M. S. Shchepkin, Moscow's leading actor.

3. *The Student*[3] – a comedy in five acts (the first act is completed. I plan to work on this one all this year.)

You will receive the *Diary* in two weeks' time *without fail*. Thank you for sending me the *Annals* as you promised. I'll expect this year's numbers in the near future.

They're doing Meyerbeer's *Le Prophète* tomorrow. I'll send you a review for the *Annals*.

Well, look after yourself. I press your hand and remain,

Yours truly,
I. Turgenev

12. To L. and PAULINE VIARDOT

[Original in French]

Turgenevo, 18 September 1850

I have just received the collective letter you sent me from Courtavenel,[1] dear friends, and begin by asking your permission to kiss you all. It's a long time since I've been so deeply touched – truly, you are too good, all of you, and you spoil me by saying all those affectionate things. If you love me, you can be sure that I adore you and I often think with emotion of all those tender and noble hearts I have left so far away. Thank you for all you say; thank you for all your little notes; thank you for the flowers; thank you for everything! I embrace you and press you all to my heart! May the good Lord bless you a thousand times! I am happy to know that you are all reunited in the family nest and shall try to alleviate my regret at being so far away by joining in spirit in your happiness. You can be sure that I love you all very much.

So you've at last heard *Sappho*,[2] dear and good Madame Viardot. What you told me about it gave me the greatest pleasure. Our friend is a truly great composer. A thousand thanks for the details; my imagination is busy working on them. Would you please send the music for the passage, 'Come, carry the body of a faithful lover'? I promise I'll only sing it to myself. Ah, happy woman, how I envy you – no, that's not right, envy is a bad emotion – I would just like to share in your enjoyment. And dear Charles, who apologizes for not having written to me more often when it is I who am the lazybones. But tell him that I love him dearly and often think of him. He appears in my dreams almost every week and that is very significant for me. I await the first performance with great impatience. It's a role that you can work on with love. I can feel you *creating* it,

3. Original title of *A Month in the Country*.

[12] 1. Courtavenel, the Viardot home near Rozay-en-Brie, some thirty-five miles east of Paris. Turgenev often stayed there.

2. Opera by Gounod with a part especially written for Pauline Viardot. Turgenev and the Viardots were very friendly with the young composer (Pauline was mildly infatuated with him for a short time), until his marriage in 1852 when his wife was thought to have insulted Pauline.

night and day, while you're talking, or busy, or listening to something else. I've known you completely bound up in such work. May your lucky star send you great inspiration and may the holy fire burn above you! It must be much more than a triumph, it must be a revelation. This new music must appear and make itself known to the public under the auspices of a happy genius in full control of all her powers. I wish you all of this and have a premonition that my wishes will be fulfilled. You will keep me informed of all your work on it, won't you? Remember that all the happiness I get from music lies there and that at the moment I am quite indifferent to everything in music that isn't *Gounod*.

It is almost – what am I saying! – it's now over a month that you've been back in Courtavenel and you're leaving again in about a fortnight. Let's return to town together. It's eight o'clock by my watch and it'll be just after six with you. Today is Sunday. What are you doing at this very moment? I picture you at table; there are a lot of you, all happy and talking. Perhaps you're talking about me, speaking my name. The weather is fine there. As for me, I'm sitting in my little room, alone, scratching out this letter to you. It's very cold outside. My brother and his wife have gone to Mtsensk on business and my mother left today for Moscow. I went shooting this morning and bagged three snipe and a grouse. (By the way, I'm very disappointed that Viardot is unhappy with Cid, but then there's only one real dog in the world, and that's my Diane.)

My head is full of Mme Roland's memoirs. I was reading them again in bed the other night, and I dream of her and Courtavenel and you and Sappho and say, 'Thank you, Venus, my protectress!' I'm also thinking about little Paulinette and her journey[3] and then I'm always thinking about a mass of things. My heart is heavy and memories crowd in, numerous and clear, but fleeting. I can't seem to latch on to any of them. '*Guarda e passa.*'[4] I stand up from time to time and would like 'to go to Courtavenel' as you used to say in Berlin, but I haven't the courage. It's so far away and the date of my return is so uncertain. But patience, patience . . . Let's talk of something else.

If you have any spare time, please read Mme Roland's *Mémoires*.[5] Don't be put off by the Rousseau-esque phraseology (there's no question here of style; you mustn't look for any literary talent in her for she has no pretensions at all in that direction, even though you will come across some charming passages) but admire the struggles of a great soul and a strong character set in stirring times. She strides forward, dignified and noble, to the end of her road. Her last letter to Robespierre (not sent) is a masterpiece. There is an energy, a quiet disdain for death and an invincible but balanced enthusiasm which you cannot admire too much.

These memoirs apart, I've not read much of note during the two months I've

3. Turgenev's illegitimate daughter. See headnote to letter no. 43.
4. 'Look and pass by.' A quotation from Dante's *Inferno*.
5. Jeanne Manon Roland was a leading figure at the time of the French Revolution. Her salon was the intellectual centre of the Girondists. She was guillotined in 1793 and her *Mémoires* published a year later.

been in the country. I haven't had the time to work much either, even though I greatly wanted to. Once in Petersburg and ensconced for the winter in a little room, I'll get down to it. I don't plan to go out much. I don't think I'll even go to the Italian Opera very often. It will only awaken memories within me, but then, I repeat, I'm under the spell of Gounod's music.

You will see that I am numbering my letters. I'll go on doing it.

Tell Mme Garcia that it was physically impossible for me to see her in Brussels. I just didn't have a moment to myself. But also tell her that I am sincerely fond of her and hope that she has a little affection for me. I kiss her hands in filial respect. I fear that my Spanish is getting very rusty, but I understood her letter perfectly. And as for that Spanish sailor[6] – why hasn't he dropped me a line? But I love him, and his wife – and everyone!

I recall that you asked me in one of your letters if the young girl my mother is bringing up is nice or a little schemer. She's neither the one nor the other. She's not nasty or stupid but she is shallow and spoilt. And her manners are awful. She's a sort of affected grisette, lazy and vulgar. She thinks of nothing but getting herself married as quickly as possible. May God grant her this desire and may she be happy after her own fashion! My mother has become very cold towards her, although I think she's settled her future, as the saying goes. So much the better![7]

Do you want to know the name of the *old flame* I spoke to you about three weeks ago? She's called Louise Shenshina.[8] A funny name, isn't it? Just like Filosofov. I'm telling you this for there must be nothing you don't know about me. So, as we're on the subject, I'll tell you about my *affair* with my daughter's mother.[9] I was young – it was nine years ago – and bored in the country. I noticed a rather comely little seamstress whom my mother had taken on; I spoke a couple of words to her; she came to see me; I paid and left, and that's all there was to it. It's the same old story. As for afterwards she lived as best she could, and you know the rest. Everything that I do for her is aimed at improving her material condition; it's my duty and I shall do it, but it will be quite impossible for me to see her again. You are an angel in all that you say to me and in all you think about it, but I repeat I can only protect her from penury. And that is what I shall do. As for the daughter, she must forget her mother entirely. But I'll speak to you again about that. My God, how good you are, and how good I feel in confessing it to you. I beg you to give me your good and noble hands to kiss in devotion.

6. Pablo Sitchès, brother of Pauline Viardot's mother.
7. Varvara Nikolayevna Bogdanovich-Lutovinova (1833–1900), the illegitimate daughter of Turgenev's mother and A. Y. Bers (the father of Tolstoy's future wife Sofya). She took the further surname Lutovinova at the request of her mother. Turgenev's relations with her throughout his life were hardly more than formal, and it is probable that he never knew she was his half-sister; like most people he regarded her as having been adopted by his mother.
8. Yelizaveta Dmitriyevna Shenshina (dates unknown), née Karpova, a distant relative of Turgenev's; later an amateur poet.
9. A. Y. Ivanova. See headnote to letter no. 43.

I began my letter by kissing you and I shall end by doing the same. Come to me, my dear, good friends and I shall kiss you affectionately. Mme Gounod, you were too kind to write to me and I throw myself at your feet in gratitude.[10] Farewell, my dear, good friends; be happy and blessed. And you, Madame, may everything that is good in life be yours. I kiss your hands tenderly and remain your

I.T.

⟨A thousand thanks for the lovely finger-nail; I'll send you a lock of hair. I *beg* a petal that has been crushed beneath your foot. I kiss those dear, lovely feet.⟩[11] P.S. I'm sending this letter to the rue de Douai.[12] I sent one there the other day to Viardot.

13. To PAULINE VIARDOT

[Original in French]

Moscow, 24–28 November 1850

I've been here for three days, dear and good Madame Viardot, and I've only just found the time to take up my pen to send you a few brief words. This is not because my brother and I have had a lot to do – the papers won't be released for more than a week – but because we've had so many things to discuss and prepare. It is a heavy responsibility that has fallen on our shoulders.

My mother died without having seen to the things she should have. To put it frankly, she has left a mass of people who depended on her without any means of support at all. We shall have to do what she ought to have done. Her last days were terribly sad. May God preserve us from such a death. She tried only to deafen herself – on the day before she died, when the agonized death-rattle began, she ordered a band to play polkas in the adjoining room. One owes the dead only respect and pity, so I'll say no more. However, because I find it impossible not to confide in you everything I know and feel, I'll add a word or two. In her last moments my mother thought only, I'm ashamed to say, of ruining us, my brother and me. The last letter she wrote to her estate manager contained a precise and formal order for him to sell everything at a ridiculously low price and to set fire to everything if it were necessary to . . . But there it is; let's forget it. I shall take heart now as you, my confessor, know it all. I feel it would have been so easy for her to make us love her and feel sorry for her. I repeat, may God preserve us from such a death. I'll spare you any further details – what would be the use? May God grant her peace.[1]

10. Mother of the composer.
11. Original in German.
12. Where the Viardots had their Paris home at the time.

[13] 1. The complicated and distressing relations between Turgenev's mother and her two sons had their causes in her despotic and unreliable personality and in her desire to force Turgenev to return to Russia from France – where she believed he was utterly bewitched by 'that damned gypsy' Pauline Viardot – by refusing to send him any money; and in his brother's marriage, which she long refused to recognize, to Anna Yakovlevna Shvarts (?–1872), one of her housemaids.

My brother, his wife and I shall stay here till the New Year to try and arrange things as best we can. The estates left by my mother are in a decidedly unprosperous condition and unfortunately there was hardly any harvest this year. We shall have to keep a strict eye on all our expenses until next August. I have suggested to my brother that I should pay all my mother's private debts (there aren't many) and compensate all the servants. This will take all my spare money. Once these burdens have been lifted from our backs, we'll be able to proceed better and more quickly. I plan to return to Petersburg in about six weeks and then go to the country in April and stay there till November. After that, we'll see. As you know, I'm hopeless at practical matters. I intend to hand over the running of my lands to my good and excellent friend Tyutchev.[2] My brother is a very respectable person and I would be quite prepared to let him shoulder the burden, but I fear future misunderstandings. He is very careful with money and would be the same with me. He would never agree to sell any land, however necessary it might be, and I wish to avoid any possible family squabbles. I have decided to divide all our possessions into two, or rather he will do it, for he'll be a thousand times better at it than I would. I should have an income of not less than 25,000 francs and with that one is *rich*. I'll speak to you about it at some other time. But tell me what you and your husband think of my decision.

Dear and good friend, I often think of you.

Sunday

Good day, my dear and good friend, ⟨my dearest, most beloved friend⟩.[3] Yazykov's office has just sent round your kind and charming letters and I go down on my knees in thanks. Little Paulinette has arrived and you like her, you love her already! There is not a single word in your letter which doesn't breathe an inexpressible goodness, sweetness and tenderness. How can even I not end up by loving the little girl madly? You do good so simply and cheerfully that I feel as happy as a sandboy by simply knowing you. One has the feeling of doing you a great favour by giving you the chance to help somebody. I truly do not know what to say to make you realize how much your dear letter has moved and touched me. I am looking for the right words . . . I can only repeat that I prostrate myself before you in adoration. Be a thousand times blessed! Heavens, how happy the little girl must be! She must now surely be living in the bosom of Christ, as the Russian proverb says about very fortunate people. It is to be hoped that she possesses more than just intelligence; she would need to have a very unpleasant personality indeed if she failed to pick up a little goodness from living in the bosom of your family. I still trust that this big change in her life will save her. Send her a kiss from me, I beg you. Now that I am richer, I have no fear of going up to a thousand francs a year for her. Get her to learn the piano. I'll send you some money in a fortnight. I would be happy to think that you have found

2. Nikolay Nikolayevich Tyutchev (1815–78), critic, translator and journalist. A friend of Turgenev's since the 1840s, he managed his estates from 1852 to 1853.
3. Original in German.

some resemblance to me in her and that this resemblance pleases you. Send me a pencil portrait of her done by you. I repeat that I shall end up by being devoted to her as soon as I know you love her . . . Your success in *Les Huguenots* gave me infinite pleasure. I await impatiently further details.

Tuesday

⟨Good morning, dearest, most beloved and best friend. I kiss your beautiful hands in adoration.⟩[3] Good day, dear Madame Viardot. We are beginning to see a little light in our affairs. My mother has given 50,000 roubles to the young girl she adopted and we have already settled this debt. Until her marriage she will live with my sister-in-law and we'll pay her 8 per cent for maintenance. When she gets married she'll receive the 50,000. My mother left no other legacies and we have filled in the gaps. I think people will be satisfied with what we have done.

Dear friend, I have not ceased thinking of you all this time, and of little Paulinette. I feel I am growing fond of her while she is in your hands. I cannot count how many times I have read your letter. It is impossible to express all I feel when your image which never leaves me rises before me so vividly. Be a thousand times blessed! Send me news of the little girl. Are you still happy with her? And what does Mme Renard[4] say? She's been in Paris for almost a month now. What surname have you given her? I thank with all my heart the good Mme Garcia and my dear Mme Sitchès for all their kindness towards her. There is nothing to say except that you are all angels and I love you all madly.

Everyone greets me here with open arms, none more so than the good and excellent papa Shchepkin. I haven't been able to pay many visits yet, but during the week I've been here I've been to see him a couple of times and once to see a Countess Salias, a charming woman, lively and talented, who, despite what she writes, is no bluestocking. Unfortunately she does not enjoy good health.[5] The last story I wrote, *The Singers*, was very successful here.

I shall stop now in order to catch today's post. I'll begin another letter tomorrow. Tell Viardot, to whom I send my warmest greetings, that over the past few days I've been reading the volume of Montaigne he gave me in Petersburg. Send a kiss to Gounod and don't forget to tell me all about *Sappho*. All the very best to everyone. And for you, I lie at your feet. ⟨By your beloved feet will I live and die. I kiss them *for hours on end* and remain for ever your friend.⟩[3]

I. Turgenev

4. Governess engaged by the Viardots to look after Paulinette.
5. Countess Yelizaveta Vasilyevna Salias de Turnemir (1815–92), writer, especially of children's stories, and critic. She usually wrote under the name of Yevgeniya Tur, and was the sister of the playwright A. V. Sukhovo-Kobylin. Turgenev often visited her salon in the fifties, and she is the prototype of Sukhanchikova in *Smoke* and of Khavronya Pryshchova in *Virgin Soil*.

II

1851–1860

Soon after Turgenev's return to Russia from France in the summer of 1850, his mother died. As she left no formal will, her two surviving sons met a number of difficulties over their inheritance. These were, however, quickly settled between them. Turgenev and his brother Nikolay shared the various estates and properties and both became independent landowners. Although not as wealthy as he at first assumed he would be – he proved incompetent at running his estates, his writings brought him comparatively little, and he was generous to everyone – Turgenev's finances showed a marked improvement for a while. He continued to write sporadically: the plays *Conversation on the Highway*, *Evening in Sorrento* and the most successful, *A Provincial Lady*, written for the actress N. V. Samoylova, which was staged in Moscow and St Petersburg in 1851 (but this success did not change his opinion of himself as a poor dramatist, and as *Alien Bread* and *A Month in the Country* were still banned he gave up writing for the theatre altogether); the stories *Faust*, *The Inn*, *Three Meetings* and *Mumu*; and a few literary articles and reviews. With the exception of these short pieces he wrote comparatively little during the first few years after his return from abroad. The period from the summer of 1850 to July 1856 was the longest he was to spend continuously in Russia as an adult, but this was not what he would have wished.

In February 1852 the writer N. V. Gogol died, and Turgenev wrote a short obituary which he submitted to the St Petersburg censor. Gogol had been regarded as the leading satirist of the reign of Nicholas I ever since the appearance of *The Government Inspector* in 1836. His novel *Dead Souls* (1842) had led the authorities to regard him as a man determined only to slander his country. Consequently they wished his death to pass unnoticed and Turgenev's obituary was refused publication. On the advice of friends he then submitted it to the Moscow censor, who passed it, for such were the vagaries of the system that there is no reason to suppose he knew of the opinion of his colleague in the capital. It appeared in the *Moscow Gazette* in March 1852. Informed of the 'facts', the tsar, who had long regarded Turgenev with suspicion, ordered his arrest. He spent a month in prison and was then exiled to his estate at Spasskoye. Turgenev always believed it was *A Sportsman's Sketches*, which had been published individually over a number of years, that was the true cause of his arrest. There is some support for this in that when they came out as a book in August 1852 the censor who passed them, Prince V. V. Lvov, was dismissed. The edition was extremely popular and sold out in six months.

Life at Spasskoye might have seemed tedious to Turgenev, but was probably less so than he said it was. It was enlivened by visits from friends and relations, numerous shooting trips, his interest in music and chess, and by a secret visit to Moscow in March 1853 to see Pauline Viardot who was singing there. During this time he also attempted to alleviate the conditions of his peasants. After vain appeals to the highest authorities he was finally allowed to return to the capital at the end of November 1853. He entered the literary and social life of St Petersburg with obvious enjoyment.

The next few years see his attempts to find a new style of writing. He began a novel, *Two Generations*, which he discarded (a short chapter was published in the *Russian Herald* in 1859 as *The Privy Office*), and then in June 1855 he started *Rudin*, which was published the following year. It was with the novel form that he believed he had found what he was looking for – but novels where social analysis was always subordinate to human relationships and where character delineation always dominated plot. This is also apparent in some of the shorter works of the period – *A Quiet Spot, Two Friends, A Correspondence*, and in particular *Yakov Pasynkov* and *Asya*. Immediately after the completion of *Rudin* he began work on *A Nest of the Landed Gentry*, which, published in 1859, proved to be the most successful and widely acclaimed of any of his works (much in contrast to *On the Eve* of 1860).

With the death of the tsar in 1855 and the end of the Crimean War in 1856, Turgenev applied for his passport and went abroad again. For the next few years he lived in France, travelled in Italy, Germany and England, and returned twice to Russia. His relations with Pauline Viardot were not as happy as they had been before, but any coolness was all on her side and not on his. His health and finances were often at an equally low level, yet he was later to state that this was the happiest time of his whole life.

14. To PAULINE VIARDOT

[Original in French]

Moscow, 1–8 January 1851

Good day, dear and good Madame Viardot, ⟨dearest, most beloved friend⟩.[1] I do not wish to start a new year without greeting my dear, sweet patron and wishing her all the benedictions of heaven.

Alas! Is it possible that the whole of the coming year will slip away without my having the good fortune of seeing you? It is a very bitter thought but one to which I must, however, grow accustomed.

We spent yesterday evening at one of my friend's, and when midnight struck you can easily imagine to whom I raised my glass! All my being yearned to be with my friends, my dear friends over there . . . May heaven watch over them and keep them . . . I feel my heart is always with them. Until tomorrow, then. I

[14] 1. Original in German.

must go out for I have a number of visits to make. I have a mass of things to tell you. There is a reason why I've stayed so long in Moscow. I have brought a rather difficult and delicate enterprise to a happy conclusion. I'll tell you all about it tomorrow. A group of amateur actors is performing one of my unpublished plays[2] this evening at the home of Countess Sollogub.[3] I've been invited to attend but I think I'll be wise not to go; I'm frightened of appearing ridiculous. I'll tell you later what happened. Until tomorrow. But I wish to throw myself at your feet and kiss the hem of your dress, dear, dear, good and noble friend. May heaven protect you!

Wednesday

It would appear that my comedy was very successful the day before yesterday, for they're doing it again today and I have just received a pressing invitation to go. This time I will. I don't want to appear to be *giving myself airs*.

I gave a farewell dinner for my friends yesterday; there were twenty of us. I must admit that by the end of the evening we were all decidedly merry. Among the guests was a very talented comic actor, Sadovsky,[4] who nearly made us all die laughing at his improvisations of the speech and behaviour of the peasants, etc. He has such a fertile imagination and a veracity of intonation and gesture that I have almost never seen anything so perfect. There is nothing better than to see art becoming nature.

I promised you yesterday to tell you why I stayed in Moscow longer than I expected. The reason is briefly this: there were two people, two women, whom we had to get rid of as they were perpetually sowing discord. It wasn't too difficult with one of them (a widow of about forty whom my mother had taken on as a companion during the last few months of her life), and we paid her generously and begged her to find work somewhere else. The other was that young girl my mother had adopted,[5] a real Mme Lafarge,[6] deceitful, spiteful, cunning and quite heartless. It would be impossible to tell you all the harm this little viper has perpetrated. She has captivated my brother who in his innocence thinks she's an angel; she has even gone as far as slandering her real father in the worst possible way, and then, after I had quite accidentally got to the bottom of the whole affair, she admitted everything so defiantly and with such aplomb and insolence that I couldn't help recalling Tartuffe with his hat on his head telling Orgon to leave his house. It was quite impossible for her to stay any longer, but we couldn't just throw her on the street. Her real father refused to take her in (he's married and has a large family). Our position was extremely embarrassing.

---

2. *A Provincial Lady*.

3. Countess Sofya Mikhaylovna Sollogub (1820–78), wife of the writer V. A. Sollogub.

4. Prov Mikhaylovich Sadovsky, real name Yermilov (1818–72), leading actor at Moscow's Maly Theatre. Turgenev dedicated his *Conversation on the Highway* (1851) to him.

5. His mother's illegitimate daughter.

6. Defendent in a celebrated trial in France in the early 1840s, sentenced to life imprisonment for poisoning her husband.

But in the end, luckily, we found someone – a doctor friend of the girl's father – who agreed to look after her and warned her that he would keep a constant eye on her. My brother and I have given her a bill of exchange for 60,000 francs payable in three years at 6 per cent interest, all my mother's wardrobe etc., etc. She gave us a receipt and with that departed! Phew, it was an unpleasant business! I don't know what will result from her stay with my brother, but we've all started breathing again since she left. What an evil and perverse creature, and only seventeen! It promises much! It's true that she's had an abominable upbringing but . . . Well, let's speak no more of it; she's happy and so are we. I can tell you, however, that I am not cut out for such performances! I acted quite coolly and resolutely but the whole thing played terribly on my nerves. I've grown too accustomed to living with good and honest people. I'm not especially afraid of wickedness or treachery but they upset me no end. It's been impossible to work for the last fortnight. Until tomorrow. I'm leaving on Friday, or Saturday at the latest. Give me your dear, charming, gentle hands to press to my eyes and lips and may your pure, noble form drive away all these awful unpleasant memories.

Friday

Well, it appears that I had a great success the day before yesterday. The actors were abominable, especially the *jeune première* (a princess Cherkasskaya),[7] but that did not prevent the audience applauding wildly, or my going back-stage to congratulate them warmly. Despite everything I was pleased to have been present at the performance. I think the play will be a success in the theatre because people liked it in spite of the massacre by the amateurs. (It will be put on in St Petersburg on the 20th and here on the 18th.) It's rather strange, though, to see your own plays on the stage.

I'm leaving tomorrow but I'll write to you again before I go. I'm longing for a letter from you. They're not sending them on to Moscow but I expect some are awaiting me in Petersburg. Until tomorrow. (A thousand kisses for your lovely feet.)[1]

Monday

Man proposes and God disposes, dear Madame Viardot. I should have left on Saturday and here I am still in Moscow. I've got an awful cough and I shan't be able to leave my room until it's better. I hope that will be in a day or two. The delay is rather a nuisance but I must resign myself to it.

Diane gave birth to seven puppies yesterday, yellow and black like her, six male and one female. Her maternal instincts come out in an extreme ferociousness; she snarls at me when I dare to touch any of her little ones. No one else dares go anywhere near her. I am sending off this letter today, but I'll write again before leaving, probably on Thursday.

7. Princess Yekaterina Alexeyevna Cherkasskaya, née Vasilchikova (1825–88), wife of Prince V. A. Cherkassky. See headnote to letter no. 166.

Little Paulinette has been in Paris now for more than two months. How is she? Is she making any progress? I feel sure I'll read all about her in your letters which I'll get in Petersburg – I'm sure there'll be at least two there. I love you and kiss you all. I've had an idea. Shall I write to Gounod rather than you before I leave? Yes, I'll do that. Well, farewell till Petersburg.

Your
Ivan Turgenev

15. To Y. M. FEOKTISTOV

Yevgeny Mikhaylovich Feoktistov (1829–98), writer, journalist and historian. He first met Turgenev in 1850 at the home of his patron, Countess Y. V. Salias de Turnemir, when he was just starting his literary career. In the fifties he contributed to many of the leading journals. Their friendship cooled considerably in the sixties when his increasingly reactionary opinions upset Turgenev, but they continued to correspond occasionally.

[Original in Russian]

St Petersburg, 26 February 1852

You cannot imagine, my friend, how grateful I am for the details on the death of Gogol[1] which you sent me – I've already written to Botkin[2] about it. I read every line avidly, but with a sort of pain and horror. I feel that in *this* death of *this* man there is more than first meets the eye. I want to discover the sad and dreadful secret. I was deeply affected by it, so deeply that I cannot remember a similar occurrence. I was in some way prepared for it by something that happened which you'll soon hear about, if you don't know already. It's awful, Feoktistov, awful. I feel sombre and suffocated . . . as if some heavy current were flowing over my head, forcing me to the bottom, freezing and numbing me.

But more of this when we meet again, which will be quite soon if nothing else happens, for I hope to be in Moscow on 10 April.

You write about an article which I should do for the *Contemporary*, but I don't know whether I can. I cannot just sit down and write about such an event without thinking about it. One has to hit the right note, and even to think of hitting the right note when you speak of Gogol is wrong and even cruel.

I'm glad that he had the funeral service in the University Church and am pleased that you were honoured by carrying his coffin to his grave. That is something you will remember for the rest of your life.

What can I tell you about the effect his death produced here? Everyone is talking about it, but somehow coldly and in passing. But there are some people who are truly distressed. Everyone is absorbed and oppressed by other interests.

You tell me about the behaviour of Gogol's friends. I can just imagine what

[15] 1. See introduction to Section II, p. 33.
2. Vasily Petrovich Botkin (1810–69); see headnote to letter no. 29.

worthless conceit will start to pour over his grave and how they'll strut around like little cocks saying – look at us, aren't we noble, aren't we grief-stricken, aren't we wise and sensitive . . . May God be with them! When lightning strikes down an oak tree, who thinks about his mushrooms growing beneath it? We miss its strength and its shade . . .

I've sent Botkin a poem which the news of Gogol's *death* inspired in Nekrasov[3] and I've written a few words about it for the *St Petersburg Gazette* which I'm enclosing with this letter, although I don't know whether the censor will pass or change them. I don't know how they've turned out but I wept when I was writing them.

Farewell, my good Yevgeny Mikhaylovich. I'll write again soon. I expect all the news from you and Botkin as soon as you hear it. I press your hand and the Countess's and remain,

Yours truly,
Ivan Turgenev

P.S. It goes without saying that my name would not appear on my article on Gogol. That would be shameful and almost sacrilegious. You compain that I don't write to you. I wrote to you last Friday.

16.To I. S. AKSAKOV

Ivan Sergeyevich Aksakov (1823–86), poet, writer and leading proponent of Slavophile ideology. During the first half of the fifties, and especially during his exile, Turgenev was on very friendly terms with the whole Aksakov family and particulary with Ivan. It was not ideas on Slavophilism – to which Turgenev was never sympathetic – that drew them together, but rather their mutual interest in the life of the ordinary Russian peasants. Aksakov had written to Turgenev about the death of Gogol on 26 February.

[Original in Russian]

St Petersburg, 3 March 1852

I can tell you without exaggeration that I can remember nothing which made such an impression on me as the death of Gogol. What you say about it is written from the heart. It is impossible to comprehend this terrible death, this historical event; there is a secret about it, a deep and terrible secret which one must try to fathom – on that we are agreed. The tragic fate of Russia is reflected in those Russians who are closer to its roots than others; no one man can carry on the struggle of the Russian people by himself. And Gogol has perished! Indeed, it seems to me that he died because he had decided to, that he wanted to die, and

---

3. 'Blessed is the mild-tempered poet', published in the *Contemporary* in March 1852. See also headnote to letter no. 24.

that this suicide began with the destruction of *Dead Souls*.[1] As for the impression made here by his death, it is enough for you to know that the chief administrator of the university here, Mr Musin-Pushkin,[2] was not ashamed publicly to call Gogol a lackey. This happened the other day in connection with a few words I had written on Gogol's death for the *St Petersburg Gazette* (I've sent a copy to Feoktistov in Moscow). Mr Musin-Pushkin just could not be more angry at those people who have the impertinence to regret Gogol's death. It is not worth an honest man wasting his honest indignation on him. Sitting in the muck up to their necks, these people tuck into it greedily. Decent people must now keep a firmer grip than ever on themselves and on each other. May Gogol's death bring at least this advantage . . .

17. To L. and PAULINE VIARDOT

[Original in French]

St Petersburg, 1 May 1852

My dear friends,

This letter will be brought to you by a lady who is leaving here in a few days, or rather she will send it on to you in Paris after crossing the frontier, and so I can talk to you rather more openly without fearing the curiosity of the police.

I begin by telling you that I have not been outside Petersburg for over a month, and quite against my wishes. I have been under arrest by the police on the order of the Tsar for having published an article, a few lines on Gogol, in a Moscow newspaper. But this is only a pretext, for in itself the article was quite harmless. I've been regarded with suspicion for a long time and have been arrested at the earliest convenient moment. I have no complaint against the Tsar himself, for the affair has been presented to him in such a treacherous way that he couldn't have acted otherwise. They wanted to put a stop to what people were saying about Gogol's death and at the same time place an embargo on all my literary activities.

I shall be sent to the country in a fortnight to await further official instructions. None of this is very pleasant as you can see, but I must say that they're treating me reasonably well; I have a decent room and books, and I can write. I was allowed visitors from the very beginning, but that's now been stopped as there were too many of them. Misfortunes don't chase away your friends, even in Russia. To tell the truth, my *misfortune* is not all that serious. My year has just not had a spring this time, that's all. The saddest thing about it is that I shall have

---

[16] 1. In a fit of melancholy Gogol had set fire to all his manuscripts, including the projected second part of his satirical masterpiece. When Turgenev later became dissatisfied with his first novel, *Two Generations*, he flushed his manuscript down the w.c., as 'I don't want people to think I'm going the way of Gogol.'

2. Mikhail Nikolayevich Musin-Pushkin (1795–1862), extremely reactionary civil servant, head of educational services and president of the Censorship Committee in the St Petersburg district from 1845 to 1856. It was on his advice that Tsar Nicholas ordered Turgenev's arrest.

to give up all hope of being able to travel abroad. As for the rest, I've never had any illusions on that score. I well knew when I left you that it would be for a long time, if not for ever. I've only one ambition at the moment – that I'm not forbidden to move around within Russia. I hope *that* won't be refused for ever! The heir to the throne is a good man and I've written him a letter from which I hope some good will come.[1] You know that the Tsar has left the capital.

They also sealed up all my papers, or rather they sealed up the doors to my flat only to open them ten days later without examining anything, probably because they knew they wouldn't find anything illegal there.

I must admit that I'm not particularly bored in my hole. I'm profiting from my enforced leisure by learning Polish, which I started to study six weeks ago. I've a fortnight's more detention to go. I'm counting the days, I can tell you!

Well, my dear friends, that's my somewhat disagreeable news. I hope you can send me better. My health is good, but I have aged remarkably. I could send you a lock of white hair – really! However, I have not lost heart. To the country, where I can go out *shooting*! Then I shall try to arrange my affairs; I'll continue my study of the Russian people, the strangest and most astonishing people in the world. I'll work on my novel with all the more freedom because I won't have to expose it to the clutches of the censorship.[2] My arrest will probably make it impossible for me to publish it in Moscow. It's a pity, but there's nothing I can do about it.

I beg you to write to me often, my dear friends. Your letters will give me courage during this testing time. Your letters and the memory of the happy days at Courtavenel are all I have. But I mustn't dwell on things for fear of becoming maudlin. You know that my heart is with you. I can say it, especially now . . . My life is over, the charm has gone. I have eaten all my white bread and will chew on what's left of the black, while praying to heaven that it will be 'good enough', as Vivier puts it.[3]

I have no need to tell you that all this must remain utterly secret; the least mention or the least allusion to any of it in any newspaper will serve only to finish me off.

Farewell, my dear and good friends; be happy, and your happiness will make me happy too. Look after yourselves, don't forget me, write often and be sure that my thoughts are always with you. I kiss you *all* and send you a thousand good wishes. Dear Courtavenel, I send you greetings too! Write often. I kiss you again. Farewell.

Your
Iv. Turgenev

[17] 1. Turgenev wrote to Grand Duke Alexander Nikolayevich, the future Alexander II, on 27 April 1852, explaining that he had no idea that he was doing anything illegal in publishing his article in Moscow, and asking, as he had done nothing else illegal, whether he, Alexander, would do his best to have him released from custody.

2. The projected *Two Generations*.

3. Eugène Vivier (1817–1900), musician and composer, friend of the Viardots.

18. To P. V. ANNENKOV

Pavel Vasilyevich Annenkov (1813–87), writer and critic. In his last years Turgenev wrote that the people he had been most fond of during his life had been the Viardot family, Gustave Flaubert and Annenkov. Close to the Belinsky circle, he had first met Turgenev in the early 1840s and they remained close friends for nearly forty years. When possible, Turgenev always sent his manuscripts to Annenkov for his comments, which he valued highly, and he usually entrusted him with the correcting of his proofs and with looking after his literary affairs in Russia. Annenkov wrote a number of influential critical articles on Turgenev. His book *A Remarkable Decade* is a fascinating study of the intellectual movements of the 1840s in Russia, and his *Pushkin in the Reign of Alexander I* presents a notable social history of the period. Their correspondence, stretching over some thirty years and forming in part a sort of literary discussion, amounts to nearly eight hundred letters. A year before his death Turgenev appointed Annenkov executor for all his writings and correspondence.

[Original in Russian]

Spasskoye, 28 October 1852

If you were pleased to receive a letter from me, dear Annenkov, you can imagine how delighted I was to get yours. It arrived yesterday and I'm sending a word of reply on my birthday, on which I've reached not twenty-eight, as you think, but all of thirty-four. Your letter is so sensible and practical and I can see in it such a sincere attitude to me and my works, that I must thank you from the bottom of my heart. Everything you say is an undisputed truth; I feel it as deeply as you do, and I subscribe to every word. I must travel a new path – I must find one and bid farewell for ever to my old style of writing. I tried to extract from my characters drawn from the ordinary people their basic essences – *triples extraits* – and then put them into little bottles, saying, as it were, uncork them, honoured reader, and sniff – don't you sense a truly Russian type? But enough of that, enough! The question remains, am I able to do anything on a larger scale? Will I be able to draw in clear and simple lines? I don't know the answer, and I never shall until I try, but, believe me, you'll either hear something new from me – or nothing ever again. Because of that I'm almost happy at being shut away for the winter – I'll have the time to raise my spirits. The main thing is that a man living in solitude is remote from everything, especially literature and the journals, etc. Yet something will come from me only if I can destroy the literary man in me – but I'm thirty-four and it's difficult to be born again at that age. However, we shall see.

There is no argument but that solitude is a good thing, but for some use to come of it it needs, if only occasionally, to be enlivened by conversation and argument with an intelligent person whom one loves and trusts. You are such a man, and if you really care about my future as a writer then you must leave Moscow and spend a week with me. The Tyutchevs (who, I might add, have fond remembrances of you) are splendid people – although they are poor judges of literature, albeit sincere and unhypocritical, and I can draw no comfort from either their praise or their criticisms. Besides them, there is no one – or there are [?],[1] who are no good for anything. Therefore I await your arrival and beg you to come down in November.

I can understand why it must be difficult to finish writing your biography of Pushkin – but what can be done about it? A real biography of an historical person is not possible yet in Russia – besides the question of the censorhip there is that of the so-called decencies. If I were in your position I would stop *ex abrupto* and I'd put in, say, Zhukovsky's story about Pushkin's death and leave it at that. It's better for a statue to have no legs at all than to stand on tiny ones. As far as I can judge, the torso is excellent. I admit openly that I would be as happy to change my style as you would with this biography. Under the influence of Pushkin's great spirit, truly classical in its severe and youthful beauty, you have probably written something marvellous, intelligent, warm and simple. I want to hear all you've written so far. That's a further reason why you must come and see me.

Farewell, dear Pavel Vasilyevich. The guests are beginning to arrive. In another letter I'll tell you something of our life here. Did you get my second letter? I firmly press your hand and remain,

Yours,
Iv. Turgenev

19. To S. T. AKSAKOV

Sergey Timofeyevich Aksakov (1791–1859) is the author of *Family Chronicle* (1856) and *The Childhood of the Bagrov Grandson* (1858) and the father of the Slavophile writers Konstantin and Ivan (see headnote to letter no. 16). Despite the difference in their ages Turgenev and Aksakov were close and admiring friends; this is especially true of the period of Turgenev's exile in Spasskoye. Their relationship was cemented by their equally passionate interest in shooting, and Turgenev wrote two enthusiastic reviews of Aksakov's *Memoirs of a Sportsman with a Gun in the Orenburg Province* in 1852 and 1853. Thirty-nine of Turgenev's letters to Aksakov survive, and three addressed to him and his sons; thirty-eight of Aksakov's to Turgenev were published in Russia in 1898.

[Original in Russian]

Spasskoye, 22 January 1853
I received the first number of *Moskvityanin* yesterday, dear and honourable Sergey Timofeyevich, and read your biography of Zagoskin.[1] I have never read

[18] 1. Indecipherable in the original.

[19] 1. Mikhail Nikolayevich Zagoskin (1789–1852), novelist, whose *Yury Miloslavsky, or the Russians in 1612*, published in 1829, earned him the reputation of the Russian Sir Walter Scott.

a biography in Russian to match it! Taking into account the clear and profound understanding of the personality of the man to whom it is devoted, the warmth and sympathy poured into every line, the inherent cohesion and measured and masterly exposition, I would call it a model of how such things should be done. Some of what you say is remarkable for its insight. I was particularly struck by that passage where you write that on reading Zagoskin you feel 'that a sense of our national characteristics rises from the depths of the soul'. That is absolutely true. I only regret one thing: why did you include two extracts from Zagoskin's works? Besides the fact that Zagoskin is precisely the type of writer whom it is impossible to evaluate from quotations, the ones you chose (especially the couplets) are rather too trivial and could give your readers quite the wrong impression. I haven't read *Miroshev*, but I'm certainly going to now.[2] As for *Miloslavsky*, I used to know it by heart. I remember that when I was at boarding-school in Moscow in 1831 (I was twelve at the time) our tutor used to tell us all about Yury Miloslavsky in the evenings. I just cannot describe to you how absorbing it was to listen to him. I once leapt from my chair and nearly hit one of the boys, who was always talking during the readings. Kirsha, the village drunkard, Omlyash, and the boyar Shalonsky were to our generation almost members of the family, and I can remember every detail of the novel even now. Yes, such national characteristics are enviable – and given to very few! In 1832 and 1833 I often saw Zagoskin at my father's house; he and my father were very good friends. The impression he made upon me was vastly different from the respect I had for his novel; actually it wasn't respect but rather a warm, friendly feeling, as one has for an elder brother (I mean in relation to *Yury*). The reason why I was not reverential towards Zagoskin himself is twofold. On the one hand he was too nice and straightforward: he would sometimes even argue with me, and a young boy, which I was then, cannot revere something on his own level; and on the other hand there was a sort of good-natured boasting in connection with women, which I disliked even more because he usually spoke on these occasions in very inaccurate French. Yet when I remember all those writers whom I later met – hardly any of whom could match Zagoskin – and recall their petty irritability, their arrogant self-importance and affectations (I dare not recall my own faults of like kind), I cannot marvel enough at the modesty of an author who really had no equal for a certain time in the hearts of the people, and kept it to the end. Zagoskin, with whom I, a thirteen-year-old boy, could behave without ceremony, was a splendid man!

I hope you will like my small article on your book, if only half as much as I liked your biography.

Did Ketcher[3] get my *The Coaching Inn* for you? Have you read it yet? As it is impossible to say when we shall see each other again – and I like to submit my

2. *Kuzma Petrovich Miroshev*, Zagoskin's novel of Russian life in the reign of Catherine the Great in the second half of the eighteenth century, published in 1842.

3. Nikolay Khristoforovich Ketcher (1809–66), Moscow doctor and translator of Shakespeare into Russian. He is portrayed in *Rudin* as 'the young forty-year-old'.

works to your judgment – I shall try to arrange that you get my novel [*Two Generations*] in manuscript. But this is between ourselves. It will have twelve chapters and I've already written seven.

I am sure you will have noticed the story about *Frol Skobeyev*[4] in the first number of the *Moskvityanin*. It is really remarkable. All the characters are excellent and the simplicity of the way it's told is very touching. But the poems by Shcherbina are even less to my taste than those by Mrs Pavlova or Mrs Rostopchina.[5] It's a sort of impassioned chirping which they are trying to pass off as antiquity. And if only the poems were any good! No, this sort of poetry will just not do.

Farewell, dear Sergey Timofeyevich; be in good health and good cheer. Since 12 January the weather here has been cold and sunny; it's probably the same with you. We've had the right conditions for cholera fairly frequently, but so far nothing untoward has occurred. My men have slaughtered a mass of rabbits, but as I feel the cold rather a lot I'm giving it a miss. I'm feeding up twelve partridges and shall breed them in March. I've sent one of my men to a village in the steppes with orders to catch some more and bring them back.

I firmly press your hand and those of all your family, and remain,

Yours very sincerely,

Iv. Turgenev

P.S. Is it true that Katkov is getting married and moving to Petersburg?[6]

20. To K. N. LEONTYEV

Konstantin Nikolayevich Leontyev (1831–91), thinker and publicist of extremely anti-democratic views. Starting his professional life in the 1850s as a writer, he later developed into one of the most brilliant and original of Russia's literary critics. Turgenev first met Leontyev when the latter was still a young medical student and attempting to get his plays and stories published. Turgenev overestimated his talents at first, giving him much advice and even lending him money, but the two never became friends. Of the twenty-four surviving letters which Turgenev wrote to Leontyev the bulk belong to the 1850s, before Leontyev's increasingly anti-European and nationalistic views drove the two apart.

4. Eponymous hero of a notable picaresque novel from the late seventeenth century.

5. Nikolay Fyodorovich Shcherbina (1812–69), poet and translator; Karolina Pavlovna Pavlova (1807–93), née Yanish, poet, novelist and translator; Countess Yevdokiya Petrovna Rostopchina (1811–58), née Sushkova, writer and poet.

6. Mikhail Nikiforovich Katkov (1818–87), editor of the *Russian Herald*; see headnote to letter no. 56.

[Original in Russian]

Spasskoye, 9 June 1853

I hasten to reply to your letter, dear Konstantin Nikolayevich. I'm glad that you've made the acquaintance of Krayevsky, but allow me as a man more experienced in literary matters to point out the following: in the first place, both for your sake and for the future of your talents, please do not imagine that you can play with the public – that you can write, as you put it, 'something full of falsehood and flattery' for money, and then appear later in your true colours. You should remember that you won't fool the public for a moment; it's far more intelligent than any of us; and you should also remember that in giving it all of yourself, your blood and sweat, you should still be grateful if it understands and appreciates your sacrifice or pays any attention to you. That should be taken as read; even more, it's just. The public doesn't need you, you need it. If you want to conquer it, then you'll have to strain every muscle. I don't mean by this that you should just set out to please the public and pamper to its tastes; on the contrary, be as God created you, give of everything that is in you, and if you have any originality or your personality is interesting the public will recognize you, take you up and make use of you as, for example, in a different field of activity, it accepted gutta-percha because it found it useful and convenient. Do not distort any of your sincerely held ideas because of the censorship, but try to select inoffensive subjects. Your *Summer on the Farm* would, I think, offend no one. I'm sorry that *The Germans* was not passed for publication, because it's quite good; we must hope that it's not wasted and will be published in due course. My second request is that you do not accept any *feuilleton* work. Besides its being for dilettantes, I cannot see in you not so much the qualities but rather the faults of the feuilletonist. You're too young for such things, too fresh and, in the best sense of the word, too inexperienced. Krayevsky would be pleased to derive some profit from you. He's a very clever entrepreneur but there's no need for you to play into his hands. Finish off *Summer*, do it with love, in your own good time, and offer it to the *Annals of the Fatherland*. It will be good and useful and, as a start, very advantageous for you.

I hope your health remains good – that's the main thing; everything else will sort itself out. I think I've already written to you that there's nothing to be regretted in starting to be published late. How much I would give for some of my latest works (I'm not thinking about my first poor verses) to have remained unpublished! And to write just for money is difficult and awkward. Even Menshikov didn't succeed in taking anything, to start with, from Constantinople.[1] Time is needed for everything. Just sow healthy seeds and a good harvest will come along in time.

As for myself, my stomach is giving me a lot of pain. We all have our cross to bear.

---

[20] 1. In February 1853 General Prince A. S. Menshikov was sent on a delicate diplomatic mission to Constantinople, but as things turned out he only succeeded in making relations between Russia and Turkey worse, and war between them became inevitable.

Well, farewell. I wish you once again good health and beg you not to take offence at my advice – that's an old man's privilege.

I remain,

Yours very sincerely,

Iv. Turgenev

21. To S. T. AKSAKOV

[Original in Russian]

Peterhof, 31 May 1854

I am writing to you, dear and honourable Sergey Timofeyevich, as both the St Michael's Days in May have passed (do you remember?) and nothing out of the ordinary has happened to me![1] I am living here in a little house two versts from Peterhof and half a verst from the sea, which I can see from my windows across the top of a pine forest. I have brought a horse and carriage with me and plan to stay here until the autumn. Unfortunately the weather is quite unspeakable; there are just no words to describe it. Cold, rain, the wind howling around everywhere – depression! Oh where are those golden days that we enjoyed in Abramtsevo?[2] I must arm myself with patience. I can literally sit here by the sea and await fairer weather. I haven't yet been to Kronstadt, which is only some five versts away. It appears that the English are in the vicinity, but they haven't yet shown their faces.[3]

Let us talk a little about literary matters. Firstly, I shall tell you that I have met Baratynsky's widow[4] (between ourselves she's quite mad), and she gave me an album in which she has collected everything which belonged to her husband, letters, and so on. One could write an interesting enough article. Tolstoy, the author of *The History of my Childhood*, has sent me the sequel, *Boyhood*; people are saying it's splendid.[5] A translation of my story has appeared in Paris with a long introduction – a lot of nonsense, I'll be bound.[6]

Baratynsky is not a real poet in the Pushkin sense, but one cannot help respecting his noble, artistic honesty, his continual and disinterested striving for the highest ideals of poetry and life. Your son Konstantin would like him, despite his Westernism. He has much intelligence, taste and perception, perhaps too much; every word of his bears the traces of the chisel, the file. His poetry

[21] 1. Turgenev always imagined that the name Mikhail (Michael) had unlucky associations for him.

2. S. T. Aksakov's estate near Moscow.

3. A squadron of the British navy under Sir Charles Napier was patrolling the Baltic and the Gulf of Finland.

4. Yevgeny Abramovich Baratynsky (1800–44), poet, contemporary of Pushkin's. His widow was Anastasiya Lvovna, née Engelgardt (1804–60).

5. Lev Nikolayevich Tolstoy (1828–1910); see headnote to letter no. 26. His *Childhood* had been published, much to his annoyance, as *The History of My Childhood*, in 1852.

6. *Mémoires d'un seigneur russe*, translated by E. Charrière: a French version of *A Sportsman's Sketches*. Turgenev was most dissatisfied with the translation.

never strains or hurries. Here is one of his unpublished poems (which you must not allow to be copied), in which you can see all the main elements of his Muse. [Poem omitted.] One can catch the echo of our great classical epoch in the style of his poetry.

Nekrasov, whom you so dislike, has written several good poems, especially one about an old peasant woman lamenting her dead son.

My address is simply Peterhof. I have already arranged things with the post office and any letters will reach me. Please drop me a line with news of yourself and about how things are going in Abramtsevo, which I really love.

Please send my greetings to your wife and all your family. I cordially press your hand and Konstantin Sergeyevich's and remain,

Yours sincerely,

Iv. Turgenev

22. To Y. Y. KOLBASIN

Yelisey Yakovlevich Kolbasin (1831–85), writer, journalist, literary historian, and friend of Turgenev's from the fifties. He accompanied Turgenev on his visit to England in 1858. Thirty-eight of Turgenev's letters to him have survived.

[Original in Russian]

Spasskoye, 29 October 1854

Dear Kolbasin,

My heartiest congratulations on passing your examinations and on your victory over Musin-Pushkin. It is clear that you are not unsuccessful in everything. And in connection with another matter I am beginning to think that, on the contrary, you are the luckiest of men. Long may it continue!

I shall be in Petersburg by 20 November, and I have written to your brother[1] and asked him about a flat. Would you be so kind as to help him? We shall find you some sort of a post for the winter; don't worry about it.

I am very pleased at the success of *Boyhood*. May God grant Tolstoy a long life! I firmly believe that he will surprise us all. He is a first-class talent. I've made the acquaintance here of his sister (she has also married a Tolstoy). A most charming and attractive woman.[2]

I am in excellent health and my stomach rarely troubles me. I am not playing much chess at the moment, but when I do I am winning. The local gentlemen here are not making any progress at all. Do you remember those heavenly games at Peterhof?

[22] 1. Dmitry Yakovlevich Kolbasin (1827–90); he would often carry out commissions for Turgenev when the latter was away from Russia.

2. Countess Marya Nikolayevna Tolstaya (1830–1912) and Count Valerian Petrovich Tolstoy (1813–65); see headnote to letter no. 30.

Farewell; look after your health, and be happy. Please remember me to all my friends. I shall write to Minitsky[3] by the next post. He's the nicest of men.

Yours,

Iv. Turgenev

23. To O. A. TURGENEVA

Olga Alexandrovna Turgeneva (1836–72) was a distant relation of Turgenev's. In 1854 he grew very fond of her and at one time considered asking her to marry him, but veiled opposition from Pauline Viardot and a haunting belief that an artist should not marry (in case it made him happy) led him to change his mind. They did, however, remain friends. This relationship with Olga was probably a real-life reflection of those situations in his works where the hero fails to find happiness either through his own lack of decision or through an infatuation for a woman whose character is stronger than his own. This is the theme of *A Correspondence* (1854) and of *Torrents of Spring* and *Smoke*, in which Olga was in all probability the model for Tatyana. Although Olga later married and had four children, Turgenev wrote to his friend Annenkov when she died: 'One beautiful, pure person fewer in the world. I remembered a lot and the memories were bitter. Shadows keep falling on my life . . .'

[Original in Russian]

St Petersburg, 6 January 1855

Olga Alexandrovna, may I first of all thank you for deciding to write to me. I have myself long wished to speak sincerely to you, and without your letter our relations would have ceased in silence and mutual confusion.

I thank you for your trust in me, and I am especially grateful that you have given me the opportunity to express those feelings of sincere respect and heartfelt friendship which you have aroused in me and which I hope to retain for ever.

You ask for *my* forgiveness, but of the two of us, Olga Alexandrovna, it is I alone who am to blame. I am older than you and it was *my* duty to think for us both. I should not have allowed myself to give way to an unaccountable passion, especially when it was not clear to me just what sort of passion it was. I should not have forgotten that you were risking much and I nothing. But I did. At my age it is ridiculous justifying thoughtlessness over first impressions, but I can offer no other justification, for it is the truth. And when I later became convinced that the feelings within me were beginning to change and weaken I also behaved badly. Instead of giving myself up to those senseless, peevish tricks which you bore with such simplicity and gentleness, I should have left immediately. You

---

3. Ivan Fyodorovich Minitsky (dates unknown), schoolteacher; he lived for many years in Odessa and consequently saw Turgenev very rarely.

can see that it is all my fault. Only the generosity of a woman's, a maiden's, pure heart can still refuse to blame a man behaving in that way, and then almost blame herself!

You beg me not to *hate* you, but I would consider myself the most unworthy of men if I did not respect you deeply. Believe me, I knew how much I valued you, and despite all that has passed between us I consider my friendship with you to be one of the happiest events of my whole life. I now consider it my first duty to avoid frequent meetings and close relations with you. We must stop all the rumours and gossip which my behaviour towards you is causing. Yet I would be deeply hurt if you ascribed my present parting from you to any other cause. On the contrary, I dare to hope that when everything has returned to normal we can become friends again, should you so wish it. Believe me, whatever the future holds in store for you and whatever fate awaits me, that feeling of affection I have for you will never fade. Forgive me, Olga Alexandrovna. I shall only forgive myself when I see you surrounded by that happiness which you so deserve. Give me your hand and allow me to press it firmly, and please accept along with my deep gratitude the expression of my sincere devotion.

Yours,
Iv. Turgenev

24. To N. A. NEKRASOV

Nikolay Alexeyevich Nekrasov (1821–77), poet and literary editor and publisher. The main themes of his poetry were the miseries of the poor classes, upon which he did much to focus the attention of educated Russians. He edited the *Contemporary* from 1847 to 1866 and later the *Annals of the Fatherland*. Turgenev first met him in the mid-forties and they remained close friends for a number of years. Nekrasov published many of Turgenev's works, including *A Sportsman's Sketches*, *A Month in the Country*, *Asya*, *Rudin* and *A Nest of the Landed Gentry*. From the mid-fifties relations between them became increasingly strained, largely because of the influence on the *Contemporary*'s opinions of the radical critics Chernyshevsky and Dobrolyubov. The final break came in 1860, after which they met only once, in May 1877, just before Nekrasov's death; this is reflected in *The Last Meeting*, one of Turgenev's *Poems in Prose*, published in 1878.

[Original in Russian]

Spasskoye, 10 July 1855

Your letter found me here, dear Nekrasov, thanks to an outbreak of cholera which is raging in the very place I was going to shoot grouse – Zhizdrensk. My friends have returned with tales of the wonders of the area, but what can I do? I'm passionately fond of shooting, but I'm more afraid of cholera. So I'm sitting here and working on a long story[1] (I've already written 120 pages), although I don't know how it'll turn out. I was delighted to get your letter, but it also grieved me, because of what you say about your health. I console myself with the thought that although it's not exactly marvellous, it's not too bad, as you yourself admit. You just see, you'll keep going longer than all those in the pink! Only lead a proper life and don't expose your somewhat dimmed flame to the blast of the passions. Take note of what you've been told.

Your poem *To K**** is pure Pushkin; I'm now learning it by heart. Would you please send me your story in verse.[2] I'm sure there are wonderful things in it. I fully approve of your intention to write your autobiography. Your story is one of those which, putting aside all self-esteem, should be told because they present much of what no Russian can fail to respond to deeply. My gratitude in advance for the dedication, but I hope the public doesn't find out about it too soon. (By the way, I was very flattered by Tolstoy's dedication.[3] What a marvellous thing his *Sevastopol* is.)[4]

To my great annoyance, I've left my copy of Burns in Petersburg. Would you ask Vasenka[5] to pop into a bookshop and buy another copy (there are plenty of them) and send it to me? I'm sure that you'll be delighted with Burns and will have immense pleasure translating him. I promise I'll select the best of him and mark the metre for you. Burns is a source of pure poetry. Try for the moment to write something on the following, which is in his favourite metre. [Six lines of I. I. Kozlov's Russian translation of 'To a Mountain Daisy' omitted.]

Do you understand it? This metre is suitable for elegiac and pensive subjects. Burns used it in his famous poem about the daisy that he had cut down while ploughing. Don't forget to send me the original.

From the fact that I've asked you to send me the Burns you will conclude that I won't be able to come and see you. Unfortunately, it's quite impossible for many reasons which I've no need to go into. Perhaps it'll be possible next year.

Thank you for your encouraging words. I really was, and up to a point still am, as you say, if not exactly demoralized about things, then at least full of doubts about myself. I can see only too clearly my faults, and my self-confidence vanished along with my faith in myself. But I shall do my very best at least to justify the good opinion of me held by my friends. I shall be very interested to know what you think about my story; I've thought about it for a long time and have for the first time written out a detailed outline before getting down to the actual writing.

We are all really happy and lively and there is not a mention of cholera. Do you know that Druzhinin[6] is an excellent fellow? His article in the *Reader's*

[24] 1. The novel *Rudin*.

2. *Sasha*, published in 1856 and dedicated to Turgenev.

3. Tolstoy's *The Woodcutting Expedition*, dedicated to Turgenev, was published by Nekrasov in the *Contemporary* in 1855.

4. *Sevastopol in December*, the first of Tolstoy's three *Sevastopol Stories*.

5. V. P. Botkin, who was sharing a flat with Nekrasov at the time.

6. See headnote to next letter.

Library on Annenkov's edition of Pushkin is very good. I must admit I was a little cross at the *Contemporary* for not toning down as it should have the carrion produced by Chernyshevsky.[7] It's scarcely disguised hostility to art. Everywhere's awful, and all the more so with us. If only we could rid ourselves of *that* enthusiasm.

Please write to me; I promise to reply. Don't forget the Burns and your poem. Are you planning to go abroad? Vidert[8] is expecting you in Berlin just like Toggenburg awaiting his bride.[9]

Farewell, old chap. Be happy and in good health. I press your hand affectionately. Remember me to Botkin – I wrote to him recently.

Yours,

Iv. Turgenev

25. To A. V. DRUZHININ

Alexander Vasilyevich Druzhinin (1824–64), writer, translator and critic. As a young man he served in the army and later as an official in the Ministry of War. His first novel *Polinka Saks* (1847) was very popular. He translated several of Shakespeare's plays and his articles on various English authors received wide recognition. His reputation as a critic began in 1849 when he became a regular contributor to the *Contemporary*; but his faith in the aesthetic rather than the utilitarian values of literature led to conflicts with the editors, and he broke with them in 1856 to become editor of the *Reader's Library*. In 1859 he was the founder of the Literary Fund, a society formed to help needy writers and scholars.

[Original In Russian]

Yushkovó, 20 August 1855

I am replying to your letter, dear Alexander Vasilyevich, from the country, where I arrived a couple of days ago in the hope of shooting snipe, but the marshes have all dried up thanks to the prolonged drought of the summer and early autumn, so there's no game. I'm preparing to go to Karachev which is about twenty-five versts away – perhaps I'll have better luck there.

I was pleased to get your letter. If I may speak plainly, you are one of those people whom one doesn't take to at first but the more one gets to know you, the more attracted to you one becomes – and I can say that about very few people. If I can manage it, I'll get myself to Petersburg in mid-November, and I can already foresee frequent meetings, conversations and arguments throughout the winter. I think that we look on many things from a different point of view. Our

7. A reference to N. G. Chernyshevsky's master's dissertation 'The Aesthetic Relationship of Art to Reality', just published in the *Contemporary*; it is a very utilitarian view of art.

8. Avgust Fyodorovich Vidert (1823–88), writer and translator.

9. See Schiller's *Ritter Toggenburg* where the hero awaits patiently but hopelessly the appearance of the woman who has rejected him.

personalities are different, but as we are both as far as possible honest and sincere in what we are trying to do, that very honesty will draw us together probably more than any similarity of views.

I've recently been reading Gogol's *Confessions of a Writer*[1] and I thought of you. All that disturbed nonsense and that conceited concern with himself is so pitiful when compared with the clear, healthy, impersonal artistry of Pushkin. But I think our literature needs the two of them. Pushkin's influence might have slipped into the background at the moment but I hope it will come to the fore again – and not simply to replace Gogol's. We really need Gogol's influence – both in literature and in life.[2] We'll be able to discuss all this – and more than once.

I'm very happy about your forthcoming article on Crabbe.[3] I'm sure it'll be a delight. You're a master at such things, probably the only one in Russia.

I carried out your commission with regard to the Tolstoys.[4] These unceremonious and good people completely excuse you and send you greetings. Everyone here asks to be remembered. Anna Semyonovna[5] had a terrible fever but is now a little better although she is still in bed.

Poor Karatayev stayed with us just before leaving to join the militia.[6] We drank his health with champagne and wished him every good fortune. He was very nice and amusing, though sad at the same time, and we were all sad for him. I didn't manage to see Lavrov, but I hear he's flourishing.[7]

I've heard a rumour that someone of Granovsky's circle has been allowed to publish a journal in Moscow. Is it true?

At the moment I've put my novel [*Two Generations*] in the drawer. There's a lot in it which I don't like, so I'll have to rework it. I've written a long story – the first story, if the truth be told, at which I've worked conscientiously.[8] We'll see how it turns out. I read it to Countess Tolstaya and she liked it, but that's no guarantee, of course. I have a kind of feeling that my literary career is over. This story will settle it one way or the other.

I have started writing to Olga Alexandrovna's family again, and received a

[25] 1. In 1855 an edition of the posthumously discovered works of Gogol was published, including his explanation of what he was planning to do in the second part of the novel *Dead Souls*. The editors entitled it *Confessions of a Writer*.

2. A reference to the arguments of 1855–6 between the 'art for art's sake' critics, notably Druzhinin and Annenkov, and the utilitarians Dobrolyubov and Chernyshevsky, who used Pushkin and Gogol respectively to support their views. As was to be expected, Turgenev refused to join either camp.

3. Druzhinin published six articles in the *Contemporary*, entitled 'George Crabbe and his Works'. This was the first time the English poet had been properly introduced to the Russian reading public.

4. Druzhinin had apologized for not calling on the family of Countess M. N. Tolstaya and her husband.

5. Anna Semyonovna Belokopytova, sister-in-law of N. N. Turgenev, Turgenev's uncle.

6. Vasily Vladimirovich Karatayev (1830–59), neighbour of Turgenev's. His unpublished story *A Moscow Family* provided the basic idea behind Turgenev's *On the Eve*.

7. A neighbour of Turgenev's.

8. *Rudin*.

very charming letter from her the other day. They're all well and hope to return to Petersburg in the middle of September.

I said my 'literary' career; I meant to say my career as a 'bellettrist', because I hope to die a writer and don't want to be anything else.

Well then, farewell. I affectionately press your hand and wish you health and happiness. Please send my sincere good wishes to your mother.

Yours sincerely,

Iv. Turgenev

26. To L. N. TOLSTOY

Lev Nikolayevich Tolstoy (1828–1910) first met Turgenev in November 1855 when he had just returned from the front during the Crimean War, where he had been present during the siege of Sevastopol; he stayed with Turgenev in his flat in St Petersburg. They met frequently from 1856 to 1861 both in Russia and abroad. Although almost always respectful of each other's qualities as writers, Turgenev's opinion of Tolstoy was higher than Tolstoy's of him, and the differences in their personalities and outlooks led to many arguments and quarrels. In June 1861, while both were visiting the poet A. A. Fet, they had a huge row, ostensibly over the education of Turgenev's illegitimate daughter, and both stormed out of the house. Further misunderstandings all but led to their fighting a duel. Relations between the two ceased until April 1878 when Tolstoy wrote suggesting a reconciliation. Their differences, however, did not prevent Turgenev doing his utmost to make the writings of his fellow-countryman better known in Western Europe. Forty-two of Turgenev's letters to Tolstoy are known and seven from Tolstoy to Turgenev.

[Original in Russian]

Pokrovskoye,[1] 3 October 1855

I have wanted to make your acquaintance for a long time, dear Lev Nikolayevich, if only by letter, but up until now it has proved impossible. But I have just been to see your sister in Petersburg and I wish now to carry out my desire. Firstly, my sincere thanks for dedicating to me your *A Woodcutting Expedition*; nothing in my literary career has so flattered my self-esteem. Your sister has probably written to you about my high opinion of your talent as a writer and how much I expect of you, and I have been thinking of you a lot recently. It's terrible to think of where you are at present. Although, on the other hand, I am glad that you're experiencing all these new sensations and ordeals. But there's a limit to everything, and there's no need to tempt fate. She's only too willing to harm us at every opportunity. It would be a very good thing if you

[26] 1. The estate of Marya Tolstaya, Tolstoy's sister, some fifteen miles from Turgenev's at Spasskoye.

managed to get away from the Crimea. You've given enough proof that you're not a coward, and a military career is not for you. Your calling is to be a writer, an artist in words and ideas. I have dared to say this because in your last letter which I received today you suggest that there's a possibility of some leave, and moreover I love Russian literature too much not to want to know that you're beyond the reach of stupid stray bullets. If you really can manage to get to Tula even for a short time, I will definitely leave Petersburg in order to make your acquaintance personally. I know that's not much of an enticement, but for your own sake and for literature's please come. I repeat: your weapon is the pen and not the sword. The Muses cannot stand vanity – and they're jealous too. I think we could become friends. We have much to talk about, and possibly our acquaintance would be useful to us both.

I would have liked to tell you much about yourself, about your writings, but that's quite impossible by letter, especially in one such as this. I shall postpone it until a personal meeting, of which I don't despair.

I've seen a lot of your relations this summer and have grown very fond of them. How much we regretted the departure of Nikolay Nikolayevich.[2] It is annoying to think that being such close neighbours we got to know each other so late.

You would greatly honour me by a reply. My address is Stepanov's House, by the Anichkov Bridge, Fontanka, St Petersburg.

I press your hand, dear Lev Nikolayevich, and wish you all the best, especially your health.

I remain, yours respectfully,

Ivan Turgenev

27. To COUNTESS Y. Y. LAMBERT

Yelizaveta Yegorovna Lambert (1821–83) was the daughter of Nicholas I's Finance Minister, Y. F. Krankin, and wife of General Count I. K. Lambert, aide-de-camp to Alexander II. Turgenev first met her in 1856 when he was applying for permission to travel abroad, and she provided him with much assistance. She was a well educated, intelligent and sensitive woman and Turgenev valued her friendship and their correspondence, where he would frequently discuss with her his ideas and literary plans, his joys and his despairs. They were closest during the winter of 1858–9, which Turgenev spent in St Petersburg. The strong religious overtones to *A Nest of the Landed Gentry*, completed soon after this period, derive in part from his friendship with the serious-minded and rather ascetic Countess, even though she thought it the 'work of a pagan who has not renounced his worship of Venus'.

2. Tolstoy's older brother.

[Original in Russian]

Spasskoye, 10 June 1856

I was very happy to receive your letter from Revel,[1] dear Countess, and feel a little ashamed. I do not deserve all the charming words with which you have filled it, and I know (although I have only read thirty pages of the book you recommended) that the human heart is made in such a way that even undeserved praise affords a certain sweetness or at least the pleasure of humility . . . these are all dangerous feelings and it's perhaps better not to speak of them. I am grateful that you haven't forgotten me and sincerely hope that you remain satisfied with your stay in Revel.

I will say a few words about myself. Firstly, I have heard from St Petersburg that my passport will be granted and I shall leave Russia sometime after the twentieth of next month, so we shall still be able to write to each other. I hope that even when I am abroad our correspondence will continue. The permission to go abroad has cheered me up, although at the same time I must admit that it would probably be better for me to stay. Going abroad at my age means condemning myself finally to the life of a gypsy and giving up all thoughts of a family life. But what can be done about it? Such is obviously my fate. This means to say, of course, that people not possessing strong characters like to invent for themselves a 'fate' which relieves them of the necessity of having a will of their own and also of being responsible for their own actions. In any case ⟨'the wine is drawn, it must be drunk'⟩.[2]

I haven't got a proper house here. I used to, but it burnt down and I'm living in an old annexe. But there is a large and beautiful garden and a pond. I have no female neighbours, especially none like Tatyana; and I'm not much like Onegin anyway.[3]

The shooting season hasn't started yet. I should tell you that the story I told you about the young lady who charmed me in spite of myself is not the same one you write to me about.[4]

Did you know that you write most charmingly in Russian, not a single mistake, even in spelling! But write to me in French. I can detect some effort to find the exact words, for you seem to think in French and then translate. It will be easier for you to write in French and then you'll write more willingly.

It's a pleasant thought that we shall, albeit rarely, exchange our ideas and feelings; it's even more pleasant that, God willing, we shall see each other again and, I dare hope, be friends. In a man's life, just as in a woman's, there comes a time when one enjoys more than anything relationships that are peaceful and lasting. Those clear days in autumn are the best of the whole year. I trust that I

---

[27] 1. Now Tallinn, capital of Estonia.

2. Original in French.

3. Countess Lambert had written that she imagined Turgenev was living in the country flirting with the girls, just as Evgeny Onegin did with Tatyana in Pushkin's novel in verse.

4. Pauline Viardot.

shall then be able to convince you that you need have no apprehension about reading Pushkin – or will you still feel 'alarm'?[5]

I no longer count on any happiness for myself, i.e. happiness in that same *alarming* sense with which it occurs in young people. One mustn't think of flowers when blossom time is over. May God grant at least some fruit – this vain nostalgia will only hinder its development. One must learn from nature her proper, peaceful course, her humility . . . In your words, we're all foolish men: as your first stupidity passes by, you chase after it.

When I look back over my life it seems I have done nothing else except chase after stupidities. At least Don Quixote believed in the beauty of his Dulcinea, whereas our Don Quixotes can see that their Dulcineas are ugly, yet still chase after them.

We have no ideal – that is where all this comes from – and an ideal springs only from a strong social life, from art (or science) or from religion. But not everyone is born an Athenian, an Englishman, an artist or a scientist, and religion is not given to everyone. We must wait and believe and realize that for the moment we are making fools of ourselves. This realization at least can be useful.

Well, that's enough philosophizing. So meanwhile, with your permission (you remember you told me I could) I respectfully and cordially press your hand and wish you all the best. I remain,

Yours very sincerely,

Iv. Turgenev

P.S. My respects to your husband.

28.To A. V. DRUZHININ

[Original in Russian]

Paris, 11 November 1856

I received your letter yesterday, dear Alexander Vasilyevich, and am replying today. First of all, thank you for remembering me: everything Russian is now doubly dear to me and greetings from good friends such as yourself are a real treat. Kolbasin gave me your news and I asked him to remember me to you. I am very pleased to hear from you personally that you are well and have moved to Petersburg. As for me, I've been in Paris for just over a week but couldn't find a decent flat anywhere and so, as they say here, was *en l'air*. But I've at last rented a small room at no. 206 rue de Rivoli, and am about to get down to some serious work because I led a decidedly lazy life in the country. To my great distress my wretched bladder is playing up – after six years of silence it has suddenly started up again. They tell me that neuralgia has the tendency to return when a man is in the place where he first developed it. The doctors have reassured me by saying it can't last long, but nevertheless I'm upset. Whatever will be, will be!

5. The Countess thought that reading Pushkin's poetry, especially his love lyrics, raised dangerous thoughts in his readers, especially young ladies.

I'm happy with the keen interest you're taking in the *Reader's Library* and I'm sure that the journal will flourish with you as editor. I can foresee, though, that I shan't be in agreement with you over everything, but there's no harm in that. There's more than one side to Truth, thank heavens! It's large enough for that, too. And then I know that you'll express much of what is important and dear to me so that all I'll have to do is to thank you, as I did with your article on Pushkin. It's a very good thing that you've a lot of material. I would dearly like my piece to come your way. You'll receive my article this year, on my honour, so long as I'm still alive. You can print it whenever you can fit it in, but have a word with the *Contemporary* first. I'm very glad that you liked my *Faust*[1] – that's my guarantee, as I have faith in your taste. You say that I couldn't go on writing like George Sand; of course I couldn't, just as I couldn't write, say, like Schiller. But this is the difference between us: for you all this present trend is a delusion which has to be rooted out, while for me it is part of the Truth, which will always find (and must find) followers at those periods in human life when the full Truth is inaccessible. You think it's time to start building the walls, while I'm suggesting we should still be digging the foundations. I could say the same about Chernyshevsky's articles. I'm cross with him for his dryness and stale taste, and also for his unceremonious treatment of living people (for example, in last September's *Contemporary*), but I no longer find any 'carrion' in him. On the contrary I find in him a living spirit, although it's not one which you would like to see in a critic. He doesn't understand poetry very well but, you know, that's no bad thing. Critics don't create poets, nor do they kill them. But he understands – how shall I put it? – the demands of our real contemporary life, and in him this is not the result of a disorder in the liver, as dear Grigorovich[2] once put it, but the very core of his being. But enough of that; I find Chernyshevsky useful. Time will tell whether I am right. And anyway as a 'counterweight' to him there'll be you and your journal, which is why I'm delighted about it. Do you remember that I, a supporter and devoted follower of Gogol, once suggested to you that we needed a return of the Pushkin element as a counterweight to that of Gogol? Impartiality and a desire to seek only the Truth are two of the good qualities for which I am grateful to nature for having given me.

Thank you for the news of our writer-friends, especially of Grigorovich. Is he really going to spend another winter in the country? When you write to him send him a friendly word from me.

I can get the *Contemporary* here from Brandus's music shop. I can't wait to see *King Lear*, and it was a wonderful idea of yours to translate *Coriolanus* – he's somewhat to your taste, you most charming of conservatives! Could you arrange for me to get the *Reader's Library* here in the same way as the *Contemporary*, starting in October, or even September? I'll willingly pay you in advance and would be very grateful. Please do it, if you can.

[28] 1. Story in letter form, published in the *Contemporary* in 1856. It contains a detailed description of Turgenev's estate at Spasskoye.
2. Dmitry Vasilyevich Grigorovich (1822–99), writer. See headnote to letter no. 228.

However, it's time to finish. Look after yourself. I press your hand. Send my sincerest respects to your mother and the Maykovs[3] and all my other friends. Until my next letter.

Yours,

Iv. Turgenev

29. To V. P. BOTKIN

Vasily Petrovich Botkin (1810–69), writer, historian, literary critic and traveller. In the 1840s, when he and Turgenev first met, he was a liberal, almost a radical, in his opinions, but as the years passed he grew increasingly conservative, which nonetheless did not prevent Turgenev from remaining fond of him. The eldest son of a wealthy tea merchant in Moscow, he was closely involved with his family's commercial activities and became comparatively rich. This is usually given as the explanation for the fact that he published very little, but his *Letters on Spain* (1847) were enthusiastically received.

[Original in Russian]

Paris, 7 December 1856

My dear Botkin,

Your letter has been received and read with great emotion. Your words are golden and I listen to them as a man on a desert island listens to the song of a bird of paradise. Everything you say about my writing is sensible and to the point; everything has been taken into consideration and the appropriate action taken. In the present anarchic times only you, and perhaps Annenkov, have any critical sense – although in you it is sometimes a little capricious and is somewhat clouded by an incorrigibly confusing way of expressing things, added to a sort of native cunning. But I have received the most salutary warning from the two of you and am prepared to admit that I haven't taken it enough to heart. But what can I do? All men are to some extent good-for-nothings and I, sinner that I am, the more so. Consequently, please do not stop putting me on the right path and I shall try to ensure that your efforts are not in vain. It seems to me that the main fault in our writers – and this applies to me especially – is that we come all too rarely into contact with real life, that is with real live people; we read too much and think in the abstract. We are not specialists and so produce nothing special. Merck[1] puts his finger on it when he says, 'With the ancients ⟨everything was local and topical and so became eternal'⟩.[2] We write in some hazy, distant spot for everyone and for posterity and hence for no one.

If one of us does pay some attention to the 'local', he immediately tries to

---

3. Apollon Nikolayevich Maykov (1821–97), poet, and his younger brother Vladimir.
[29] 1. Johann Heinrich Merck (1741–91), German writer and literary critic, a friend of the young Goethe.
2. Original in German.

make it universal – that is, he gives it a universality of his own invention and so produces nonsense.

I mentioned Merck. I have been reading a lot of him lately and plan to introduce him to the Russian public. He was a truly great critic whom one could compare only with Lessing. Those who know him (and there are very few of them) think that Goethe based his Mephistopheles on him and no one else. This is partly true, and to be the prototype of such a character is an honour in itself. But there is more to Merck than just ironic negation. I finally managed to find his *Selected Works*. It's not a long book, only 350 pages (including a biography), but I came across some splendid passages. For example, can there by anything better than the following? He once said to Goethe, ⟨'All your endeavours, the path which you follow unwaveringly, are directed to giving poetic form to reality. All the others try to turn the so-called poetic, the imaginative, into reality, and from that comes only nonsense.'⟩[2]

If you can get hold of his book, *Ein Denkmal*, read it, and I promise you the greatest pleasure.

I have also been reading lately *The Confessions of an English Opium Eater*.[3] It's amazing! I've never come across anything like it.

All in all I've been reading a tremendous lot lately. My bladder has been preventing me writing; it's ruining my peace of mind and stopping me seeing things clearly. I just don't feel free; it's like having a candle held under your foot until just before the skin melts. But I have been a little better lately – I've started to take quinine – and perhaps fate will take pity on me and deliver me from my misfortune. If not, then so much the worse for my literary activities! I've read Suetonius, Sallust (whom I have come to hate for his over-refined style) and Tacitus and have just started on Livy. I find these writers, especially the first, very modern.

Delaveau[4] has rushed off my *Faust* and squeezed it into the December number of the *Revue des Deux Mondes*. The editor (de Mars)[5] came round to thank me and assures me it is being very well received. But I don't really care what the French think of me, especially as Mme Viardot didn't like *Faust*.

The most worthy Polonsky[6] has told me, amongst other things, that Tolstoy is in Petersburg. I sent him a letter at your Moscow address. Give it to him; and as you have probably read his *Youth*, tell me what you think of it – I'm very keen to know. I enjoyed what you said about Tolstoy; and Nekrasov's success is remarkable. The public *needs him* and that's why they've snatched him up.[7]

3. Turgenev read Thomas de Quincey's book in English, although there had been a Russian version published in 1834.

4. Hippolyte Delaveau (?–1862), French writer, critic and translator of many Russian authors. He lived in Russia for a number of years and was instrumental in introducing the writings of Herzen, Nekrasov, Ostrovsky, Pisemsky, Tolstoy and Turgenev to the French reading public.

5. Victor de Mars (?–1866), main editor of the *Revue des Deux Mondes* at the time.

6. Yakov Petrovich Polonsky (1819–98), poet; a neighbour and lifelong friend of Turgenev's. See headnote to letter no. 93.

7. An edition of his poems with a print run of 1400 copies had sold out in a fortnight.

Please stay in Petersburg a little longer and turn your whole attention to the *Contemporary*. Write and tell me in all honesty what the public thinks of my *Stories*. I've not received a copy yet, even though it was sent off a long time ago.[8]

I hardly ever see any French people here, but I do see one or two Russians, including Melgunov.[9] What an odd fellow! But he's nice. It's bad, though, that you've caught something. Under the influence of the news I took some *capotis en caougutta perfectionnée*, although I didn't need it at all.

And so, farewell. I cordially press your hand, and remain,

Yours sincerely,

Iv. Turgenev

30. To COUNTESS M. N. TOLSTAYA

Countess Marya Nikolayevna Tolstaya (1830–1912), younger sister of L. N. Tolstoy. When she was seventeen she had married a distant cousin, Count Valerian Petrovich Tolstoy (1813–65), by whom she had four children between 1849 and 1852. Although the early years of her marriage were not unhappy, her husband's dissolute and cynical behaviour led her to leave him in 1857. She went abroad, travelled extensively, had an affair with a Swedish viscount and bore him a daughter; she returned to Russia in 1864. She could never settle, however, and grew more and more capricious, irritable and unhappy. Always deeply religious, she finally became a nun and settled in the Sharmordino convent in 1891.

She first met Turgenev in the autumn of 1854 when people were first becoming interested in her brother's literary activities, and a close friendship developed between them which lasted until 1859. Turgenev was probably in love with her for a short time. Tolstoy, who was always very close to her, strongly disapproved of their relationship and thought Turgenev's treatment of her when his affections were cooling was quite despicable. Vera Yeltsova, the heroine of Turgenev's *Faust* (1856), is based on her and the story is dedicated to her. She is also depicted as Lyuba in her brother's *Childhood, Boyhood and Youth*. Seventeen of Turgenev's letters to her survive, together with a further eight addressed jointly to her and her husband.

[Original in Russian]

Paris, 6 January 1857

Well, how delighted I was to receive your letter, dear Countess. I heard a rumour that you are very ill, and although from what your husband writes and from your handwriting I can see that you are not really well, at least it seems that things are not as bad as I had thought. Get fully fit and then the summer will pass

---

8. The three-volume *Tales and Stories*. Y. Y. Kolbasin wrote to Turgenev that it was not selling very well.

9. Nikolay Alexandrovich Melgunov (1804–67), writer and music critic.

pleasantly. I shall definitely return to Spasskoye at the end of May. I'll write to your two brothers, Lev and Nikolay, and we'll see what we can arrange. I was very pleased you liked my *Faust* and also at what you said about there being two men in me. That's very true, but perhaps you don't know the reason for it. I'll be open with you too. You see, I felt very sad to think I was growing old without achieving complete happiness or building a quiet nest for myself. My heart was still young; it had its hopes and its yearnings. But my mind, tempered by hard experience, was occasionally overcome by the passions of the heart and retaliated against its weakness with bitterness and irony. But when my heart in turn asked of my mind what *it* had done to create a good and sensible life, it was forced into silence and to hang its head. And then both heart and mind grew depressed. But all of that has now changed. When you first knew me I still dreamed of happiness and did not wish to give up all hope, but now I have waved all that goodbye. Everything has quietened down, the ups and downs have evened out. I no longer reproach myself and there's no point in raking over the ashes. Why all this happened is a long story – time has taken its toll. When you see me again, you'll be surprised at my ⟨equanimity⟩.[1] There's no point in wondering what bitterness might lie behind it. One mustn't delve that deeply into anyone. *Faust* was written at a turning point in my life. My heart was afire with the last flames of memories, hopes and youth. That will never occur again. But you talk in vain of my happiness; the grass always appears greener on the other side, and other people more fortunate than yourself. But enough of all this. I repeat that I'll try and come to see you this summer, and we'll pass the time like happy and contented old friends.

I correspond with your brother Lev fairly often. I think he's made a change for the better. May God grant him peace and quiet. I'm not exaggerating when I say that he'll become a great writer and a splendid person. At the moment he's very close to Druzhinin. I could have wished for a better companion for him, but it's difficult to be on good terms with him. Until he makes himself sick (if you'll excuse the crude expression) from some dish or other he won't stop eating it and praising it – and he goes on praising it even though he's got a pain in his stomach. Druzhinin is a good chap but not for your brother. But I suppose all this will shake the wheat from the chaff. Let's hope so!

And what of your other brother, the good and estimable Nikolay Nikolayevich? Is he still in the Caucasus? Does he want to stay there for ever? How pleased I'd be to see him.

I'm very sorry that there seems to be no hope for your illness. If you can, I would advise you to jot down on paper all the thoughts which pass through your head. There's nothing to be done about it, just be patient, happy days will return, and you'll get better. You mustn't worry about a pulse of 130 – it's happened to me. If it's not caused by pneumonia, it's not dangerous.

Please remember me to your husband. Does he subscribe to the *Reader's*

[30] 1. Original in French.

Library? They've announced the appearance of *School Lane* by Y. Y. Kolbasin, the author of *Hi, ha, ho*.[2] By the way, did you get your copy of my *Tales and Stories*?

Farewell, dear Countess, and please get better. I press your husband's hand and, if I may, kiss yours.

Yours very sincerely,
Iv. Turgenev

31. To S. T. AKSAKOV

[Original in Russian]

Paris, 8 January 1857

Dear and honourable Sergey Timofeyevich,

I received your letter a long time ago, and have been intending to reply for some time but have not been in the right mood to chat with old friends. And I cannot blame the 'whirl' of Parisian life, either. I'm living almost like a hermit here, and anyway Paris with all its bustle and glitter can turn the heads only of the young – or, perhaps, the old. I'm not old yet, but goodness knows how long it is since I was young.

Since I last wrote I've met a lot of writers here. Not the great old ones, the former literary generals – for, as they say, old goats that they are, you get no milk or fur from them – but some of the leading younger ones. I must admit however, that they're all very petty, prosaic, empty and untalented. Wherever you look what you see is a sort of lifeless vanity, a precociousness and vacuous impotence, or a complete lack of understanding of anything that's not French; the absence of any faith, any convictions, even artistic ones. The best of them sense this themselves but only grunt and bemoan it. There aren't any critics, just rubbishy indulgence of all and sundry. Everyone mounts his own hobby-horse and flatters everyone else in his own way so as to be flattered in turn – that's all there is. One poet states that we must 'advance' realism and with great effort and strained simplicity sings of 'Steam' and 'Machines', while another shouts that we must return to Zeus, Eros and Pallas and writes hymns in their praise, happily putting their names into his poor French verses. And there's not one iota of poetry in either of them. Through this petty noise and babble you can just hear, like the voices of ancient poets, the jingling sounds of Hugo, the puny whining of Lamartine, and the babbling gossip of Sand. Balzac is revered as an idol, and the new school of realists grovels in the dust before him in reverence to Chance which they dignify by the names of Reality and Truth, while the general level of morality declines with every day and everyone is tired out with chasing after gold – that's France for you! If I live here it's not for France nor for Paris but because of circumstances beyond my control. But spring is coming, and I'll fly

2. Kolbasin's story *In the Country and Petersburg* (1855) was given this name by Turgenev because of the distinctive laugh of its hero.

to the motherland where life is still young and overflowing with hope. With what joy I'll greet the steppes! I'll definitely be with you in Abramtsevo in May.

I was very upset by the news of the illness of your daughter and your personal troubles. May God grant an improvement and let everything return to normal!

The article on your *Chronicle* was written by a certain Delaveau who lives here and knows Russian well; I helped him by explaining things a little. The article should soon appear in the *Revue des Deux Mondes*. Your idea of writing a story of a young boy for children[1] is an excellent one, and I'm sure you'll do it better than anyone else with that epic clarity and simplicity that marks you off from all our current writers. The *Russian Herald* which contains an extract from your *Chronicle* has been promised to me by Prince Trubetskoy (the friend of your son Konstantin).[2] I see quite a lot of him and he's a decent enough man – and is very fond of you all. He always gets *Russian Conversation*, but no. 4 hasn't arrived here yet![3]

Please send my best wishes to your wife and to all your family, Konstantin and Ivan in particular. Ask Konstantin to write to me; I'll reply at once. And come the spring what arguments we shall have! I love arguing with him because, despite all the heated words we might exchange, our friendship for each other never deserts us and is there in every word, while with others you can agree on everything and have nothing to argue about and yet there is still a huge gap between you.

I see Vasilchikov here, the brother of the general whom Ivan worked with.[4]

Well, farewell, good and honourable Sergey Timofeyevich. Look after yourself and may God grant you the time and inclination to write to me. For some reason I don't seem able to do anything; it's as if my hands have seized up. Perhaps things will improve. Until the spring.

Yours ever,
Iv. Turgenev

P.S. I can't tell you how upset I am with the news of both the Kireyevskys.[5]

---

[31] 1. *The Childhood of the Bagrov Grandson.*

2. Prince Nikolay Ivanovich Trubetskoy (1807–74) who, opposing the policies of the Russian government, had emigrated to France with his family in the early 1850s and adopted Roman Catholicism. He was satirized by Konstantin Aksakov in his play *Prince Lupovitsky* and mentioned by Turgenev in *Smoke* as 'Prince Koko'.

3. It contained Aksakov's *Literary and Theatrical Memoirs.*

4. Prince Alexander Illarionovich Vasilchikov (1818–81), liberal economist and agriculturalist. His brother Viktor (1820–78) headed a commission after the Crimean War to investigate maladministration in the Russian armies in the area. Ivan Aksakov was a member of the commission.

5. The brothers Kireyevsky, Ivan and Pyotr, both of whom Turgenev knew well, died in 1856 within four months of each other.

32. To L. N. TOLSTOY

[Original in Russian]

Paris, 15 January 1857

Dear Tolstoy,

I do not know whether you are pleased to receive my letters, but yours certainly console me. There is evidently some change going on within you – which is a very good thing. (I apologize for, as it were, patting you on the back, but I am all of ten years older than you and feel I've become a sort of tutor and confidant for you.) You are calming down and things are becoming clearer to you. And most importantly of all you are freeing yourself of all your former opinions and prejudices. Looking to the left is just as pleasant as looking to the right – the world is large enough for both. There are 'perspectives' everywhere. (Botkin stole that word from me.) You only have to open your eyes. May God grant that your field of vision continues to expand! Systems are only valued by those who do not possess the whole truth and want to grab it by the tail. Any system is like truth's tail but truth is just like a lizard – it leaves its tail in your hand, knowing full well that another will grow in its place. This comparison is not particularly apt, but the fact is that your letters console me. There's no doubt about it.

I have received a very nice and rather long letter from your sister. I was delighted to get it. I am sincerely fond of her and the news of her illness distressed me a lot. She also liked my *Faust*, but it's had a rather strange fate. Some people didn't like it at all, amongst whom, to my very great regret, was Mme Viardot. And what unpleasant rumours you are hearing! Her husband is as fit as ever, and I am as far from getting married as, for example, you are. But I love her more than ever and more than I've ever loved anyone. That's the truth.

Your *Childhood and Boyhood* is causing a furore amongst the Russian ladies here. The copy I was sent is being read by everyone and I've already had to promise many people that I'll introduce them to you. I'm always being asked for your autograph and, in short, you're more in fashion than the crinoline.

From the letters I get from Petersburg I gather that the literary life has got a hold of you – and not only the literary life! Sometimes I feel a little annoyed that I can't be there with you all, and I even think (how conceited) that I could be useful to you. But I cannot consider leaving here before April, and so I shall postpone all such thoughts until next winter. But you probably won't be there then. You write that you won't even be spending this winter in Petersburg. What are you thinking of in going to the Caucasus? You'd do better to get your brother back from there.

Don't forget to send me everything you write that doesn't appear in the *Contemporary*.

I'm delighted that you've made the acquaintance of Shakespeare, or rather that you've returned to him. He is like Nature. She sometimes wears a repulsive face (just recall one of those days on the steppes in October, damp and drizzling), but even then there is certainty and truth and (be prepared: your hair will stand on end) expediency. You must also read *Hamlet, Julius Caesar, Coriolanus, Henry IV, Macbeth* and *Othello*. Don't allow any external incongruities to put you off. Get to the heart, the core of their creation, and you will see the harmony and profound truth in their great human spirit. I can see you from here laughing at these lines, but consider that perhaps T. is right. We'll just have to wait and see.

I haven't said anything about the people I've met here. I've only come across one nice girl[1] – and she's Russian, and one intelligent man[2] – and he's a Yid. I'm afraid that I can't take to the French. They might make excellent administrators and soldiers but their prejudiced thoughts all rush along the same narrow track. Anything that isn't French appears to them quite alien and stupid. ⟨'Ah, but a French reader would never admit it,'⟩[3] and when he pronounces these words a Frenchman cannot imagine that you might have something to say in reply. The devil take them!

Well, farewell, dear Tolstoy. If you grow as broad as you have already grown deep, we shall all one day sit in your shadow and admire both its beauty and its coolness.

Yours,
Iv. Turgenev

33. To P. V. ANNENKOV

[Original in Russian]

Paris, 15 April 1857

I am still here, dear P. V., but all by myself. Tolstoy suddenly left for Geneva, and has already written an amazing letter in which he calls Paris Sodom and Gomorrah and compares himself to a rock on a river-bed which is slowly getting silted over and suddenly feels it has to tear itself away and seek another where there might be less silt. Paris certainly doesn't suit his personality. He's a strange man and I can't quite understand him. A mixture of poet, Calvinist, fanatic and landowner's son; somewhat reminiscent of Rousseau, but more honest; highly moral but at the same time not someone you can warm to. He intends to stay for a long time on the shores of Lake Geneva, but I expect to see him in London in a month's time. I'm going there on 1 May.

I have nothing to tell you about myself. I am living through – or rather living out – a spiritual and physical crisis from which I'll emerge either smashed to smithereens – or rejuvenated! Well, no, hardly rejuvenated, but propped up like they prop up a dilapidated barn with logs. And there are occasions when such

[32] 1. Princess Y. N. Meshcherskaya (1838–74), who later married P. P. Ubri, Russian ambassador to Berlin from 1871 to 1879.

2. H. B. Oppenheim (1819–80), radical German politician, but later a strong supporter of Bismarck.

3. Original in French.

barns stay up a long time and are put to a variety of uses. But enough of that.

Permit me now first to reprove and then to praise you (but even here I can't avoid some reproof). The reproof comes from the fact that you lavished praise upon that totally flabby, bad and obscure play by Ostrovsky where, except for Yusov (and then only in Act III), everything is unbearably coarse and lifeless.[1] It's just like a frozen pig's carcass. I had relied on you and decided to read it aloud to a certain (very nice and intelligent) Russian family . . . We moaned, groaned and howled from boredom. I am ready to sign what I say in my blood. Henceforward I've no faith in Ostrovsky. But enough, again.

The praise is due for the first two articles on Stankevich in the *Russian Herald*. (I haven't seen the third one yet.) You have reminded me of that open expression on his face; you have taken me back to the time of my youth; you have captured the whole essence of his life and reproduced it extremely accurately and faithfully. But why do you sometimes write so strangely? On occasion you somehow grow very florid and complicated. You cease to be Annenkov and seem like some meritorious German diplomat from the Ethico-Philosophical Department. And then the word 'utmost' will drop from your pen only to be followed by your qualifying it in some way, etc. But clearly one must accept every man as he is, as a whole, and I would be the first to accept you, with the greatest of pleasure, because I realize that everything you do could not be done better by anyone else. Once again, my sincere, heartfelt thanks. For heaven's sake publish his letters as soon as possible; I've already promised them to Tolstoy. He'll revel in them. I'll stake my life on it.

I received a letter today from Nekrasov in Rome, written in Italian. Sultry and full of atmosphere, but miserable and weary. He's coming here soon with A. Y. Panayeva.[2]

On none of my previous visits to Paris have I met so many people as on this one. Just before I left I met the Dumas family,[3] but I can't say I derived any pleasure from it. I dined with Mérimée[4] who is a real Druzhinin writ large. He's just as cold and loves all sorts of obscenities.[5] I haven't met a single remarkable or interesting person. Everything is dry, constrained, flat and limited.

---

[33] 1. Alexander Nikolayevich Ostrovsky (1823–86). See headnote to letter no. 139. His play, *A Profitable Position*, was published in *Russian Conversation* in January 1857.

2. Avdotya Yakovlevna Panayeva (1819–93) was the wife of I. I. Panayev, Nekrasov's co-editor of the *Contemporary*. For nearly twenty years she and Nekrasov lived together. She left some amusing anecdotal memoirs which belong largely to the realms of fiction. She detested Turgenev, who in turn considered her a 'coarse and nasty woman'.

3. Alexandre Dumas *fils* (1824–95).

4. Prosper Mérimée (1803–70) first met Turgenev in 1857 when the latter awoke in him an interest in Russian literature, which he began to write about and translate. He wrote the foreword to the French edition of *Fathers and Sons* (1863), translated a number of Turgenev's short stories (*The Jew*, *Petushkov*, *The Dog*, and *Ghosts*) which were published in a collection *Nouvelles Moscovites* in 1869, and edited the French version of *Smoke* (1868). Mérimée's letters to Turgenev were published in France in 1952, but all of Turgenev's to him were destroyed in a fire in 1871.

5. Druzhinin wrote a number of erotic poems and stories which were known to his friends as *Black Magic*.

I also dined, old chap, with Kiselev,[6] which is why I'm now rather subdued. I see Prince Orlov[7] every day; he seems an excellent fellow. The other day he took me to church where, to my great surprise, I heard an intelligent and elegant sermon for the first time in my life. It was given by our local priest, Vasilyev.

There is nothing to report on the theatre. *Fiaminna*, which everyone is talking about, is rubbish.[8] *Question d'argent* is a piece of witty chat, but tedious.[9] The French have lost all capacity for truth in art, and art itself is dying out here. With which, *addio*. Write to me in London.

Iv. Turgenev

P.S. Did you give my letter to Countess Lambert? Have you met her yet?

34. To P. V. ANNENKOV

[Original in Russian]

Sinzig, 9 July 1857

Without the attached sketch, dear Annenkov, you would probably never find the little town where I've been for a week drinking the waters and taking the baths to cure all my ailments. You probably won't find Remagen on the map either, so look for Andernach which isn't far away. Dr Godenus, whom I consulted in Dresden, advised me to go either to Ems (which is a three-hour journey from here) or to Sinzig. I chose the latter. There's almost no one else here and so I can get complete rest and quiet and work as hard as I am able – something which I haven't done for more than a year. Russians seem to turn up everywhere, even here, and I've met a very decent fellow, a certain Nikitin. He's an army officer who has given up his career to become a painter (I think he's got some talent). He's very ill and probably incurable. Two other very pleasant Russians, one Saburov and his sister – they come from Moscow, have their own house, etc. – left here today after visiting him. We all took a long excursion yesterday along the valley of the Ara, which is very picturesque.

Since I last wrote I've been to England, and thanks to two or three successful letters of introduction I made many pleasant acquaintances of whom I shall mention only Carlyle, Thackeray, Disraeli and Macaulay. Had I stayed longer I would have been introduced to Palmerston and Prince Albert. (I would also have met the duc d'Aumale.) But I decided to postpone it all to a more convenient time and come here for my health. You will probably laugh, but I am talking in all seriousness when I say that the return of my illness has killed me off. I feel a dead man, a living corpse. While this serpent continues to gnaw away at me I can take no interest in anything and am quite good for nothing. I don't

6. Count Pavel Dmitriyevich Kiselev (1788–1872), leading civil servant, Russian ambassador to Paris from 1856 to 1862.

7. Probably Prince Nikolay Alexeyevich Orlov (1827–85), general and diplomat.

8. Play by Mario Uchard (1827–93).

9. Play by Alexandre Dumas *fils*.

know whether the waters here will help me, but I think I'm getting worse. I am assured that this is the effect of the waters at first, but I've ceased to believe in the doctors. But enough of this.

While I was in England I went to Manchester and saw a multitude of wonderful things[1] – but I'll tell you all about it and about my stay in England in general when I see you. What I will say, though, is that the English made a much better impression on me than I had expected, and I'm not saying this simply because I met some princes. They're a really great nation.

I returned to Paris from England with Nekrasov and accompanied him and Mrs Panayeva to Berlin. He was going back to Russia and is probably already in Petersburg. He's a very unhappy man. He is still in love with that coarse and nasty woman and she's driving him crazy. His health, however, is a little better, although he's in no way cured. When I return to Petersburg in October, I'm going to try to get him away to a warmer climate for the winter.

Write to me and tell me what you're doing in Simbirsk and what life's like there. Although I'm very down and feel nothing for anything, I know that I'm fond of you and would love to see that ragged Astrakhan coat again. If you write as soon as you receive this letter, you'll still find me here. I'll be here for another six weeks.

Tolstoy is in Switzerland at Clarens, which he likes a lot. He's walking in the mountains, writing, keeping very fit, and he feels, as he puts it, beauty flowing through his eyes and into his soul – an almost physical sensation. I've written to him, but don't know whether he'll bother to reply. Botkin and Druzhinin are in Italy, but where exactly is unknown. Kovalevsky[2] is in Plombières. All our London friends are fit and well. I often saw them.

Well, farewell until October. You will find me a different man from when you last saw me. I wish you good health, firmly press your hand and remain,

Yours sincerely,

Iv. Turgenev

35. To L. N. TOLSTOY

[Original in Russian]

Rome, 7 December 1857

Dear Tolstoy,

Botkin brought me your letter three days ago. I thank you and reply. (By the way, I didn't get your long letter in Fécamp because I never went there, but I've written asking for it to be sent on, if it can be found.) The reason why I've come

[34] 1. A fine art exhibition, opened by the Prince Consort, was held in Manchester in a specially constructed building. It contained a magnificent collection of paintings, mostly Italian and Dutch, as well as much else of interest.

2. Yegor Petrovich Kovalevsky, writer and traveller (1811–68), one of the founders of the Literary Fund and its first President.

to Rome instead of returning to Russia is very simple, although there are really three or four reasons. 1) I fear returning to Russia for the winter. 2) I didn't want to go back empty-handed and hoped to do some writing in Rome, which I have. 3) I was attracted by the idea of seeing Rome with Botkin. 4) If I return to Russia in the spring, I'll be able to see all my old friends again. Everything here would have been very, very good if only my damned illness had not started to nag away at me again. I'm afraid it might force me to leave.

While Botkin and I have been travelling around the area, seeing the sights under 'favourable' skies, we have thought of you constantly. We would have liked you to be with us. I think you'd like Rome and it would do you good. You would probably be able to work hard here. Even I have managed to throw off my lethargy and have written a story[1] which will be sent off to Petersburg in a day or two. I read it to Botkin and he gave me some useful advice which I have taken.

How are things in Moscow? Living with your sister will be easy – but you don't seem to be able to live easily. You seek completeness and clarity in everything. You are continually feeling the pulse of your relations with other people and of your own emotions. All of this prevents your days passing calmly and smoothly. I expect that you'll get bored with Moscow and be buffeted about. You need to work quietly and peacefully. I wouldn't like to think that the present literary preoccupations with legal matters will put you off. I have just read Shchedrin's *The Fiancé*[2] and cannot imagine how such a coarse story can have any importance; it might be useful, but to allow it to have the slightest influence on your own work would be unforgiveable. Follow your own path and write – but, please, no more politico-moralistic homilies like *Lucerne*. Botkin has told me how much he liked the beginning of your story about the Caucasus.[3] You say you're pleased that you didn't take my advice to be just a writer. I shan't dispute that you might be right but, sinner that I am, and however low I might hang my head, I just cannot imagine what you are if not a writer. An army officer? A landowner? A philosopher? The founder of a new religion? A civil servant? A businessman? Please help me out of my difficulty and tell me which of these is correct.

I'm joking, of course, but I would really like to see you finally sailing full steam ahead. With what pleasure I could then sit between you and your sister and discuss things until we dropped. Your brother Nikolay would also be there and he would interrupt our speeches from time to time with a telling word! Send him my greetings, please. Is he writing anything? There were some marvellous pages in his last story.[4]

Do you see anything of the Aksakovs? How are things between you? I'll write

[35] 1. *Asya.*

2. Mikhail Yevgrafovich Saltykov (1826–89), social and political satirist; he wrote under the name of N. Shchedrin. See headnote to letter no. 120.

3. *The Cossacks*, published in 1863.

4. *A Shooting Trip in the Caucasus.*

to Sergey Timofeyevich soon; I would like to renew our correspondence.

I have already heard once again that my uncle is not running my estates as he should. But what can I do about it? I can't cope with them myself. And I did all I could, i.e. I arranged for the small sum of 3600 roubles for me to live on. And then I've decided to devote the whole of next year to a final settlement with my peasants – I might even give them everything and cease being a *barin*. I'm absolutely determined to sort it all out and shan't leave the country until I have and it's all settled.

Botkin is a changed man here. His leg doesn't hurt any more and he's very hale and hearty. Of the other Russians there's a certain painter, Ivanov.[5] He's a remarkable and intelligent man, whereas all our other painters are fools and imitators of Bryullov[6] and quite untalented. Well, perhaps not that; they've all got some ability but they haven't a clue what to do with it. They live with whores, pour abuse upon Raphael, and nothing more. At the moment there is no Russian painting.

The weather is marvellous. The roses are in bloom, but that brings me little joy. I'm convinced the climate here is no good for me, but it would still be a pity to leave.

Write to me in Rome, poste restante. Remember me to all my friends in Moscow (that won't be difficult – there are very few of them) and press your sister's hand for me. I haven't paid the postage on the letter, so you'll more likely receive it sooner. Do the same.

Keep well, and do some work.

Yours sincerely,
Iv. Turgenev

P.S. Send me your address.

36. To PAULINE VIARDOT

[Original in French]

Spasskoye, 25 June 1858

Dear friend,

I have just returned to Spasskoye after an absence of four days and found your letter awaiting me with its sad news.[1] I did not dare tell you of my forebodings. I had endeavoured to convince myself that everything would turn out well. But he is no longer with us. I am extremely sorry for him and for all that he has taken

5. Alexander Andreyevich Ivanov (1806–58). His best-known painting is *The Appearance of Christ before the People* on which he worked for more than twenty years and completed just before his death.
6. Karl Pavlovich Bryullov (1799–1852). His romantic painting *The Last Days of Pompeii* is said to have inspired E. Bulwer-Lytton's historical novel of the same name (1834).
[36] 1. The death of the painter Ary Scheffer in Paris on 15 June. Scheffer was a devoted admirer of Pauline Viardot and it is not improbable that she returned his affections to a certain extent.

with him. I deeply sense the cruel grief that his loss has caused you and the void which you will be able to fill only with great difficulty. He was very fond of you. Viardot and Louise must be very upset. When death strikes at our ranks, the friends who remain must cling all the more closely together. I cannot offer you consolation but I can offer the hand of a friend and a devoted heart on which you can rely as much as you did on the one which has just ceased to beat.

I cannot help thinking of the last time I saw Scheffer. He was so well that the thought that it would be the last time I would see him never entered my head. He was painting a Christ with the Samaritan. I sat behind and we had a long conversation. I told him all about my trip to Italy in early May. Never had I seen him so affable or in such good humour. What a terrible blow for his daughter.

I am too affected by this sad news to be able to tell you much about myself. I spent two very enjoyable days with my friends [the Tolstoys], two brothers and a sister. The latter is an excellent woman but very unhappy. She has been forced to leave her husband, a sort of rural Henry VIII and a most disgusting man. She has three children who are growing up well, especially since the absence of their father. He brought them up in a very strict manner and took great pleasure in treating them like Spartans while leading his own life in quite opposite fashion. Such things often happen; people can give themselves thereby the pleasures of both vice and virtue, but the virtue comes at the expense of others.

Of the two brothers, one is rather insipid while the other is a most charming man, rather lazy, phlegmatic, not a good talker but at the same time very kind, very gentle, with delicate tastes and feelings – a real original. The third brother (Count L. Tolstoy, the one I told you about, is *one of our best writers*; this will make you smile and think of Fet,[2] who is a neighbour of mine and whom I'm going to see tomorrow – but to Tolstoy, he is really and truly extremely talented and one day I hope to convince you of it by translating for you his *Childhood*. I shall now end this interminable parenthesis) – the third brother, I was about to say, is expected here but hasn't arrived yet. The sister is quite a good musician and *we* have played some Mozart, Beethoven. etc . . .

Iv. Turgenev

37. To PAULINE VIARDOT

[Original in French]

Spasskoye, 30 July 1858

. . . Here is what I've been doing over the past nine days. I've done a lot of work on a novel which I've started to write and which I hope to finish before the onset of winter.[1] Then I've been shooting some 150 versts from here and passed five wasted days. The marshes were still empty, because the snipe haven't started to

2. Afanasy Afanasyevich Fet (1820–92), lyric poet, friend and neighbour of Turgenev's. See headnote to letter no. 46.

[37] 1. *A Nest of the Landed Gentry*.

migrate yet. At the same time I've been busy with my uncle trying to arrange things with my peasants. From the autumn I'm putting them all on *obrok*, that is to say that I'm letting them have their own land for an annual rent and hiring others to cultivate mine. This is only a temporary measure until we have some decision from the official commissions; but nothing definitive can be expected from them just yet.

I mentioned a novel I was writing. How happy I would have been to show you the outline and to explain the characters and the purpose I have in writing it, etc. How precisely I would have followed the advice you would have given me. This time, though, I have thought about the subject for a long time and I hope to avoid those sudden and impatient conclusions which so rightly have jarred upon you in the past. I feel in the right mood for writing, and the ardour of youth has long since deserted me. I am writing with a calm which astonishes me. I only hope it's not reflected in the novel! Whoever said 'cold' meant 'mediocre'. . .

Iv. Turgenev

38. To V. P. BOTKIN

[Original in Russian]

St Petersburg, 10 February 1859

Please excuse me, dear Vasily Petrovich, for not having replied before now; various affairs, new friendships, etc. prevented it. And even now I am not sending a letter but a brief note, or rather a call to come here for the holidays. Stay for a fortnight or so, and bring Tolstoy with you. A number of new faces have turned up; Mrs Markovich (who writes stories in Ukrainian under the name of Marko Vovchok), a charming lady who looks as if (as they say in Petersburg) she doesn't know which hand to hold a pen in.[1] Besides her I have met a whole colony of Ukrainian men and women and all of them, with the exception of the obtuse and guttural Kulish,[2] are nice people. The violinist Laub has arrived from Berlin – a very remarkable player.[3] My *Sportsman's Sketches* have been passed for publication, and we are giving a dinner in their honour which would be particularly graced by the presence of you and your bald patch. Martynov has created a new role, dramatic and without a trace of humour, in a big new play written by the actor Chernyshev – he's really good in it.[4] These are just some of the reasons, not to mention the many others, which should make you get on a train and come here.

I have already written to you about the dispatch of the money, and you should get it soon.

[38] 1. Marya Alexandrovna Markovich (1834–1907). See headnote to letter no. 47.
   2. Panteleymon Alexandrovich Kulish (1819–97), writer and Ukrainian nationalist.
   3. Ferdinand Laub (1832–75), Czech composer, violinist and teacher.
   4. Alexander Yevstafyevich Martynov (1816–60), a leading actor at the Alexandrinsky Theatre in St Petersburg. He usually specialized in comic parts. *Money Doesn't Bring Happiness* by Ivan Yegorovich Chernyshev (1833–63) had its premier on 30 January 1859.

Until we meet again, dear Vasily Petrovich, and please come.

Yours,

Iv. Turgenev

P.S. That friendship I made at the masked ball of course came to nothing, but it did have some amusing elements, which I'll tell you about when I see you.
P.P.S. Alexandra Petrovna[5] has absolutely worn me out. No, brother, once every three months is quite enough at our age.

39. To V. Y. KARTASHEVSKAYA

Varvara Yakovlevna Kartashevskaya (1832–1902), née Makarova, minor writer. Turgenev first met her at the beginning of 1859, and she introduced him to 'the little world' of Ukrainian writers and artists who used to meet frequently at her house or that of her brother N. Y. Makarov. Turgenev was fond of her, although he later wrote that she 'was only a piece of female flesh whom I once found beautiful', one of the few unflattering remarks about women he ever allowed himself. Although the group was strongly nationalist and politically active, Turgenev's interest in it was only literary and social, and as far as is known he never visited the Ukraine (or Little Russia as it was known in tsarist times). Fifty-four of Turgenev's letters to Kartashevskaya have survived.

[Original in Russian]

Spasskoye, 31 March 1859

Dear Varvara Yakovlevna,

Well, madam, how are things with you, your family, and your little Russian world?

I shall tell you what I am doing. I am at home, sitting by the window in my little house, looking at the melted snow, the drab countryside, the dead grass and the bare trees; a continuous drizzle is falling from a grey sky and I am listening to the softly whining, moaning wind. I am thinking that I would much rather be in that splendid city of Petersburg with my dear friends than admiring this far from beautiful scene! But there's nothing to be done about it. There's no hope of returning yet, especially as all the ice on the rivers has melted and there's nowhere to cross. But all in all I did well to return here, because of various matters which I need to deal with. The woodcocks, though, are making me wait; not a single one has flown in yet. Perhaps you don't know what a woodcock is? It is a bird with a long nose and it eats anything, even the innards of things, even . . . etc. But it's a wonderful bird not only for its tastes but also for the way it soars through the trees making the sportsman tremble and admire, and forcing him to regret what a poor shot he is! You fire, miss, and stand there like a 'wet cat' . . .

5. It is not known to whom Turgenev is referring.

73

Have you met Mrs Markovich yet? I haven't yet received the translation of *The Boarding-Schoolgirl*[1] and I shall definitely need the original. I hope Kulish will send it to me. I went to see Sergey Timofeyevich [Aksakov] in Moscow. He is not at all well, and nor are his sons, especially Konstantin whom one just cannot admire too much; his self-sacrifice knows no bounds. Sergey Timofeyevich will go on suffering, for there is scarcely any possibility of an improvement in his health. Perhaps he can be taken to a warmer climate in the spring . . .

I found everyone here fit and well. But to my great sorrow a certain Karatayev, a splendid young man – almost our only decent neighbour – died about a fortnight ago, and, as far as I can judge, from a lack of care by his family and his doctor. I am now busy with the plan for a story, the idea for which comes from one of Karatayev's and, if I complete it, I shall dedicate it to his memory. I shall try to depict him in one of the characters.[2]

Drop me a line; my address is Mtsensk, Oryol Province. Do you still like Annenkov? And what is Shevchenko doing, and your brother, your husband, Belozersky, Nadya?[3] And Nadya will turn a few heads in her time, I swear it. I find you all fascinating.

Just imagine what it is like to have left an area where cholera is raging: I am eating radishes! lettuce! ! cucumber! ! ! and drinking cream! ! ! ! and all in huge quantities, and I've given up mint! ! ! ! ! I am definitely beginning to feel the presence within me of some heroic spirit.

Until we meet again in three weeks. Look after your health, all of you, and I firmly press everyone's hand, and yours even more so.

Yours sincerely,
Iv. Turgenev

40. To I. A. GONCHAROV

Ivan Alexandrovich Goncharov (1812–91), writer, civil servant, censor and author of three major novels – *An Ordinary Story* (1847), *Oblomov* (1859) and *The Precipice* (1869) – the second of which has become a classic and has been translated into many languages. The two writers first met in the mid-forties and became friends in 1856, after Goncharov's return from a round-the-world voyage which he described in his *The Frigate 'Pallada'*. Their habit of discussing with each other the subject matter of their current writings led to a very curious

[39] 1. Turgenev's translation of Markovich's novel appeared in 1860.

2. V. V. Karatayev is partially portrayed in *On the Eve* as Pavel Shubin.

3. Taras Grigoryevich Shevchenko (1814–61), the greatest Ukrainian poet; Kartashevskaya's brother was Nikolay Yakovlevich Makarov (1828–92) a journalist and civil servant; her husband Vladimir Grigoryevich Kartashevsky (?–1876), a high-ranking St Petersburg civil servant, whose mother Nadezhda was S. T. Aksakov's sister; Vasily Mikhaylovich Belozersky (1823–89), Ukrainian writer, journalist and publicist; Nadya was Kartashevskaya's young daughter.

incident. Goncharov began to write *The Precipice* at the same time as he was finishing *Oblomov*. In the winter of 1857/8 he became convinced that Turgenev was stealing all his ideas and using them for his own novels and stories. He was sure that his should have been the credit for Turgenev's success. His belief was strengthened with the subsequent appearance of *A Nest of the Landed Gentry*, *On the Eve* and *Fathers and Sons*. Furthermore Goncharov was adamant that Turgenev had passed on all his plans to his friends, and believed that all of Auerbach's novels and even Flaubert's *Education Sentimentale* had been plagiarized from *The Precipice*, via Turgenev. He ascribed his novel's lack of success to the fact that everything in it had been published beforehand. Goncharov's public avowals of his beliefs led Turgenev to call for a 'trial', which was organized by A. V. Nikitenko; the 'judges' were S. S. Dudyshkin, A. V. Druzhinin and P. V. Annenkov. While admitting that there were certain similarities between the output of the two writers and many other contemporary authors, they completely absolved Turgenev from the 'charges'. Although they patched up their differences in 1864, Goncharov never forgave Turgenev. Goncharov wrote his version of the affair as *An Unusual Story*, which was unknown until 1924.

Five of Turgenev's letters to Goncharov have survived, all only in extracts copied out by Goncharov himself. The following letter dates from an early stage in their quarrel, before Goncharov's increasingly somewhat pathological behaviour made relations between them impossible.

[Original in Russian]

Spasskoye, 7 April 1859

I cannot hide from you, dear Ivan Alexandrovich, that I take up my pen to reply to your letter with less than my usual pleasure; for what pleasure is there in writing to a man who considers one a thief of other people's ideas (*plagiaire*), a liar (you suspect that in my latest story there are hooks with which I wanted to pull the wool over your eyes) and a gossip (you suggest that I told Annenkov of our conversation)? You will agree that, whatever 'diplomacy' I might possess, it is difficult to laugh and be polite when one receives such onslaughts. You will also agree that you would yourself be angry at receiving a half – what am I saying? – a tenth of such accusations. But I thought – put it down to weakness on my part, or pretence, or what you will – he's still got a good opinion of me; and I was amazed that you could still find something to like in me. For that, much thanks! I can say without any false modesty that I looked upon my *A Nest of the Landed Gentry* as 'instructive'. What would you have me do? I cannot go on repeating *A Sportsman's Sketches* ad infinitum. And I don't want to give up writing, either. I am left with writing stories where, without pretending that my characters are either complete or strong or that I have penetrated life to any depth or described its many facets, I could write what came into my head. There will be deficiencies and patently obvious gaps, etc. But what can I do about it? He who wants a novel in the epic sense of the word must not look to me. Whatever I might want to write, what turns out is but a series of sketches. E *sempre bene*! But you probably see in this only 'diplomacy'. Even Tolstoy thinks I sneeze and sleep and drink, just for words. Take me as I am, or don't take me at all. But don't ask me to change, and most importantly of all don't think of me as just another Talleyrand! But enough of all this. It doesn't help anybody. We're all going to die and we'll all smell when we're dead.

Spring has arrived here and nearly all the snow has melted, but it's still unpleasant and lifeless. The days are damp, cold and grey. The fields are still a deathly yellow. However, in the woods the grass is beginning to come up. There isn't much game yet. I hope to finish everything here by the twentieth and get to Petersburg by the twenty-fourth. (As you know, I'm going abroad on the twenty-ninth.) We'll see each other in Petersburg and perhaps abroad as well, although I'll probably be advised to take different waters from you. I trust your visit to Marienbad will be as beneficial to you as it was in 1857.[1] Send my best wishes to all my friends and also to Maykova.[2] I learnt today of the death of Bosio and was very sad about it.[3] I saw her on the day of her last performance in *Traviata*. She had no idea then that when she was portraying a dying woman she would soon be doing it in real life. Decay and death and falsehood – such is life in this world. Farewell, unjust man! I press your hand.

I've forgotten the most important thing: my letter to Kushelyov about Solyanikov's translation. I'll write to him tomorrow, although I must admit that I don't expect anything from that mean old moneybags.[4]

41. To COUNTESS Y. Y. LAMBERT

[Original in Russian]

Vichy, 24 June 1859

Dear Countess,

I have received two letters from you to which I should have replied immediately, but I have been a little tardy, for which I beg your forgiveness. I have been in Vichy for five days now. I'm taking the waters and bathing to cure all my ailments. We'll see if anything comes of it. First of all may I thank you for all you did for Belenkov[1] and Mrs Zmeyeva.[2] I know that giving you the opportunity to do some good is to be in your debt, but to thank someone you love is pleasant and you will not wish to deprive me of that pleasure. I'm very glad that Belenkov's affairs have been settled. As for Mrs Zmeyeva – between

[40] 1. While Goncharov was in Marienbad he wrote a large part of his masterpiece *Oblomov*.

2. Yekaterina Pavlovna Maykova (1836–1920), writer and friend of Goncharov's.

3. Angelica Bosio (1824–59), Italian prima donna at the St Petersburg opera.

4. Count Grigory Alexandrovich Kushelyov-Bezborodko (1832–70), publisher of the journal *Russian Word* from 1859 until his death. P. A. Solyanikov's translation of *Hegel and his Times* was published as a book in 1861.

[41] 1. Ivan Belenkov, a young Oryol landowner and army officer who had requested help in obtaining a transfer from his post in the Caucasus.

2. Nothing is known of this woman.

ourselves – I find her decidedly uninteresting. Her unbearable, intimate, vulgar, empty-headed, insensitive and delighted gossiping is quite repulsive, and her daughter will probably lose very little by being separated from such a mother – although one must, of course, do one's best to bring them together again. In any case, I kiss your dear hands in pleasure and gratitude.

May God grant that the salt-water baths will help you. I often think of you and feel I am deeply and sincerely attached to you. I am in that half-elated, half-depressed mood which always takes possession of me before working;[3] but if I were younger I would stop working altogether, go off to Italy and breathe that now doubly beneficial air. Is there any enthusiasm for anything left in the world? Do people still know how to sacrifice themselves? Can they enjoy life, behave foolishly, and have hopes for the future? If I could see it all, I might know.[4] But I have grown too fat and lazy to jump from the path which I have laid for myself, even though 'life's chariot' still creaks and bumps along it. All the passion I have left is spent on writing. Everything else is cold and still.

I often saw my daughter in Paris and sometimes wondered how I would introduce her to you. It's not that there is much to boast about, for she is nothing out of the ordinary. She has some rather serious faults, but she's a very pure and honest creature and will make someone a good wife. But how that will come about I just don't know. She received her education in a French *pension* – i.e. the very worst it is possible to get. I can already see something of me in her. I don't mean by this that she takes after me – quite the contrary, for I don't have these characteristics either – but simply that that's the way she is. This explanation reminds me of Molière's ⟨'That's why your daughter is dumb'⟩[5] – but almost all explanations are like that. In short, I'm satisifed with my daughter and pleased to be so. She'll leave the *pension* in the autumn. I'm placing her for the winter in a good home with an estimable family. Before I return to Russia, perhaps we'll be able to take a little trip down the Rhine together. I shall definitely be back in Russia by September.

I met Count Karl Lambert in Paris.[6] He was the first to tell me you were in Gapsal. He can hardly walk now.

Please send my greetings to your charming husband and all my good Petersburg friends.

I haven't said antyhing about Vichy. It's a rather dirty little French town; there's no shade or any decent places to go for a stroll; there's only one pleasant spot, an avenue with a few lime trees which are now in full bloom. Their sweet smell reminds me of Russia, but there are none of those huge fields with wormwood around their edge or ponds surrounded by willow trees, etc. Whatever you may say, a man is far more like a plant, a plant with *roots*, than he imagines.

3. Turgenev was working on *On the Eve*.
4. A reference to Italy's struggle for unification led by Garibaldi.
5. Original in French.
6. Countess Lambert's brother-in-law, Karl Karlovich (1815–65).

42. *To I. S. Aksakov*

Once again I kiss your hand and beg it, that hand, to write to me in Paris, poste restante. I'm staying here for only three weeks. Look after your health, that's the main thing.

Yours,
Iv. Turgenev

42. To I. S. AKSAKOV

[Original in Russian]

Spasskoye, 22 October 1859

I passed through Moscow so quickly, dear Ivan Sergeyevich, that I didn't manage to see anyone. I was in a hurry to get back here to work and go shooting, but I now wish to send you a word and, more importantly, to hear how you and yours are getting along.

My story is soon told. After I stayed with you in the spring (a few days before the death of your father; the news reached me when I was already abroad. I was very upset, even though I had expected it) – after my visit I went to France and England and took the waters in Vichy. And that's all. I came back here and went shooting – most unsuccessfully, as there was very little game about. And then I caught a most stupid and unpleasant cold with pains in my chest and a sore throat. I cannot speak; I can't even whisper and I have a hacking cough. And it's all been going on for three weeks. Naturally I haven't seen a soul – there's no one to see anyway. I worked hard, though, and wrote a long story for the *Russian Herald*.[1] I very much hope you like it. I didn't read anything while I was abroad and am reading nothing here. I've, as it were, retired from the literary world, although I've heard a lot of praise for your journal.[2] I've managed to settle things with my peasants almost entirely successfully (leaving them, of course, with the same amount of land as before); I've moved them (with their agreement), and from next winter they're all going over to the quit-rent system at three roubles per desyatina. I said that I've done all this, but rather it was my uncle, for whom *the new arrangements* go very much against the grain, but he understands that we cannot return to *the old order*. Before parting from their 'lords' the peasants become, as we say, 'Cossacks', and they try to get all they can from their masters – corn, wood, animals, etc. I can quite understand it, but for the first time in this area the forests are disappearing; everyone is selling them off in a frenzy. Never mind, though, they'll be planted again, but this time not any-old-how but according to scientific methods. There is no *sobriety* round here; it's a very drunken part of the world. So the peasants will be on quit-rent with *their own land* until the new arrangements are decided from above. In this region no one wants to hear a thing about the *mir*, the peasant commune, or about any civic responsibilities. I'm almost convinced that it will have to be *imposed* upon the

[42] 1. *On the Eve.*
2. *Russian Conversation*, a Slavophile journal.

peasants in the form of administrative or financial regulations. They just won't agree to anything themselves. They value the *mir* only from a legal point of view, a sort of mob law, if I can put it that way. They can see nothing else in it for them.

That is all the news I have. Have you any for me? (My address is Mtsensk, Oryol Province.) On account of my illness I cannot say when I'll be able to leave here. I would have liked to go to Moscow for a day or two before 15 November and then return here for three weeks or so (for Christmas) so that I could supervise the printing of my story. But I can't guarantee anything at the moment, although I still hope to fulfil my plans. Please send my best wishes to your mother and all your family; also Khomyakov, the Yelagins[3] and my other good friends. Look after your health, that's the main thing. Goodbye. I press your hand.

Yours sincerely,
Iv. Turgenev

43. To PAULINETTE TURGENEVA

Turgenev's passing fancy for a seamstress of his mother's, Avdotya Yermolayevna Ivanova, resulted in the birth of an illegitimate daughter in 1842. The baby was christened Pelageya Ivanovna. Turgenev never denied his paternity and looked after the mother financially until her death in 1875. The daughter was brought up by a laundress on the estate at Spasskoye until 1850, when Turgenev realized his responsibilities towards her. He wrote to Pauline Viardot about her, and she generously offered to bring her up with her own children. At first the Viardots paid for her upkeep, but after the death of his mother Turgenev paid his daughter an annual allowance of 1200 francs, which, by the standards of the time, was not at all ungenerous. In 1857 she was legally recognized as his daughter, but only in France, consequently she was not allowed to inherit anything of Turgenev's in Russia. From 1860 to 1863 she lived in Turgenev's home in Paris together with an English governess, Mrs Innes. In 1865 she married Gaston Bruère, the manager of a glass factory; they had two children. In 1882 her husband's firm went bankrupt. His behaviour towards her, which for some time had not been the most admirable, grew worse and she was forced to flee the country, accompanied by her children. Turgenev had to sell his collection of paintings, of which he was very fond, to support her. Because of the complicated legal position, on the death of her father she was left without any inheritance.

3. Alexey Stepanovich Khomyakov (1804–60), theologian and philosopher, the most outstanding of the older Slavophiles; Alexey Andreyevich Yelagin (?–1846) and his wife Avdotya Petrovna (1789–1877), who had been married previously and was the mother of the Slavophile thinkers Ivan and Pyotr Kireyevsky.

43. *To Paulinette Turgeneva*

Turgenev was never an affectionate father, but he carried out what he considered to be his legal duties to his daughter as best he could. Three hundred and forty-nine of his letters to her survive.

[Original in French]

Spasskoye, 10 November 1859

My dear daughter,

I must now write this *long* letter, which I have been promising for so long and for which you are waiting with, probably, no great impatience. Alas, my child, if I have hesitated for so long it is because I do not have many pleasant things to say to you. But pleasant things are not always the most useful and I beg you to read this letter in the same spirit as it is written in, that is, that the truth must be our first consideration.

Frankly, I must tell you that I was little pleased with you during my last visit to France. I found that you possessed some rather serious faults which were less developed a year ago. You are touchy, vain, obstinate and secretive. You do not like being told the truth and you too readily turn away from those you should love the most as soon as they stop pampering you. You are also jealous. Do you think that I failed to understand why you affected to avoid my presence during the last few days of my visit to Courtavenel? From the moment that you felt that I was not occupied with you exclusively I saw nothing of you – you disappeared. You are mistrustful. How many times have you failed to continue a friendship which you yourself have started? You only like dealing with people you consider inferior to yourself. Your self-esteem makes you take on the airs of a savage and, if this continues, your mind, by not coming into contact with people who are more intelligent than you, will cease to develop. You are even mistrustful of me, a man who has done nothing to hurt you. Do you think that a good daughter would not have written a single line to her father from whom she has been parted for more than two months? You will say that I haven't written to you either and that you were awaiting my letters. You would be right if you were a barrister pleading his case to a stranger, but such considerations are out of place in the relations between a father and daughter. You have many good qualities, and if I do not speak of them it is because I would consider it as improper as talking of the good qualities which I might possess myself. You are too close to me and I love you too much not to consider you a part of myself. I prefer to point out your faults with a possibly exaggerated sincerity. I am sure you will not attribute my words to anything but a desire to see you turn out as perfect as possible. And if my words are too harsh you must not feel hurt but see in them further proof of my affection for you.

My dear girl, I would like to love you even more than I do already. This depends only on your removing those obstacles which prevent it. Think about what I have told you and you will see that it is not too difficult. At your age I also was sulky and mistrustful and wanted nothing better than to keep myself to myself; I also believed that I could do without the affection of others. But, my child, affection is something so rare that it is foolish to reject it, from whichever quarter it may come, and even more so when it's from a father who desires only to cherish his daughter.

Well, I've finished. This letter will be hard for you to read, and it hurt me to have to write it. I hasten to kiss you, very hard, as Didie[1] would say, in recompense.

I'm leaving Spasskoye, God permitting, in a week's time. Write to me in St Petersburg.

I kiss you again.

Your loving father,
I. Turgenev

44. To N. I. TURGENEV

Nikolay Ivanovich Turgenev (1789–1871), writer, historian and economist. Possibly a distant relation of Turgenev's, he was a member of the Decembrist organization, the first Russian revolutionary movement of the nineteenth century, formed after the Napoleonic wars. On the accession of Nicholas I in 1825, the Decembrists staged a poorly organized and badly conducted uprising which was rapidly put down by government troops; it resulted in five of their number being hanged and many others being exiled to Siberia. N. I. Turgenev did not take part himself since he had emigrated in 1824 – as he later admitted, 'perhaps wisely'. However, he was not allowed to return to Russia for more than thirty years. Turgenev had first met him in 1845 when the older man might well have influenced the young writers's views on serfdom, for after this time he began to believe not in the reform of the system but in its abolition. In the fifties and sixties they saw a lot of each other in Paris, where N. I. Turgenev and his wife Klara lived with their family; they took a lively interest in the upbringing of Turgenev's daughter Paulinette. On his death in 1871 Turgenev wrote a sympathetic obituary for the *Messenger of Europe*.

[Original in Russian]

St Petersburg, 10 February 1860

Dear and honourable Nikolay Ivanovich,

I returned from Moscow yesterday, where I had gone for a fortnight but was forced to remain for more than a month thanks to an illness which attacked my throat. As I had not requested any correspondence to be forwarded to me, I only received your letter yesterday. I hasten to thank you very sincerely for all the

---

[43] 1. Claudie, or Didie, born in 1852, the second daughter of Pauline and Louis Viardot. Turgenev always lavished on her the affection he could not feel for his own daughter, a fact which has led some to suggest that he was her real father. While this is not utterly impossible, the available evidence would suggest that it is improbable.

interest you are taking in my daughter and for your help with Father Vasilyev.[1]
My daughter may consider herself fortunate in having found such good and
caring patrons as you and your family.

You will probably have read in the papers of the death of Rostovtsev.[2] He was
buried yesterday. His death in the present circumstances is a calamity. There is
no reason to suppose that it will change the government's views on the emancipation, but you yourself know how much can depend on individuals. I haven't
yet managed to see anyone here, but I've heard, and it's probably true, that he
won't be replaced and that the Commission will finish its work without a
chairman, particularly as things are so far advanced. It is difficult to see the
outcome of the whole business, but it appears that a modest allotment is the
favoured recommendation, although many people are against even this. I have
already finalized things on my own estates. I have given my peasants an amount
of land equivalent to that which they worked previously and placed them all on
quit-rent at three roubles a desyatina. I haven't forced any of them to move, but
those who have chosen to have been given timber and everything necessary for
the building of a house without charge; I have also left them in control of their
old fields for a period of three years. This measure was perhaps too successful. I
thought that they would have chosen to move over a period of two or three
years, but almost all of them decided to go more or less at once, which cost me
no small amount of money. But I didn't want to go back on my word. Of the
rest of my lands I shall work two estates with hired labour and rent out the rest.
During the first year I shall lose a little more than a quarter of my whole income,
but it must be hoped that in the fulness of time the results of employing hired
labour and the proper use of my capital will make up the deficiency. Farm
labourers do not cost a lot and are easy to find. I don't yet know how the
quit-rent will be paid, and the peasants are unwilling to give a collective
guarantee. But in any case, whatever arrangements the government decide upon
they will not be far removed from what I have done, and I am sure that I have
already made this change in my life much easier. And I'm not alone in doing
what I've done. In our province alone many landowners have already gone over
to the quit-rent system. If the government in calculating the quit-rent at 5 per
cent were to give us bonds at sixty roubles an acre, we would all (in Oryol
Province) be very satisfied.

I would very much like to read your two articles but I can't see any way of
laying my hands on them here. I shall have to postpone that pleasure until the
spring, i.e. the end of April when I hope to be in Paris. My story *On the Eve* has
recently appeared in the *Russian Herald*. I would like you to read it and let me
have your opinion.

[44] 1. Turgenev was keen that his daughter should continue to have religious instruction from the
priest at the Russian embassy, Father I. V. Vasilyev.

2. Yakov Ivanovich Rostovtsev was chairman of the committee set up to draft proposals for the
Emancipation of the Peasants. He died on 8 February 1860. Contrary to Turgenev's view, he was
replaced by Count Viktor Nikitich Panin (1801–74), later Minister of Justice.

I don't know your address in the rue de Lille so I'm sending this letter via my daughter. I trust that you and all your family are in good health. Please send my sincerest greetings to your wife. I press your hand.

Yours sincerely,
Iv. Turgenev

45. To P. V. ANNENKOV

[Original in Russian]

Soden, 8 July 1860

Dear Pavel Vasilyevich,

I have received your letter and now reply. The story you relate is very interesting. What would we have done if you'd been shot?[1] And you probably wouldn't have defended yourself! Bullets don't choose their victims! We'll have a lot to talk about when we meet up on the Isle of Wight; I don't think we'll see each other before then. My plans have suffered a slight alteration which I should tell you about. I'm staying here until the sixteenth, when I shall travel directly to Courtavenel to see Mme Viardot. I shall stay there till the first of August when it's possible to bathe in the sea on the Isle of Wight. This is what Mme Viardot wishes, and her word is my command. Her son very nearly died and she went through a lot during his illness. She wants to take a quiet holiday in the company of friends. And talking of death, just imagine what sad news I received from Pisemsky.[2] Polonsky's dear, gentle wife has died. I cannot tell you how sorry I am about it, and you will no doubt share my grief. Why couldn't she have lived and given poor Polonsky a little relief from his continuing sorrows?[3] Where is the justice?

Our life here in Soden is very quiet. My health is excellent. Unfortunately the weather is very cold and miserable: non-stop rain. You write about a heat-wave and I've just proved myself not overly sensitive to the cold by driving in an open coach from Ems, where I'd been to visit Countess Lambert, to Schwalbach to see M. A. Markovich. She's a very nice, pleasant and intelligent woman with a poetic soul. She'll be on the Isle of Wight with us so you'll be able to get to know her. Mind you don't fall in love with her! You're quite likely to, despite her not being exactly beautiful. I think we're a couple of pickled herrings whom no one would choose. Kartashevskaya has rushed over here with her brother and they're now living in Bonn at the Hotel Belle-Vue under Dr Kilian. She'll stay there a month and I've sent her your address. You can go and see her and bathe together in the green waters of the Rhine.

[45] 1. Annenkov, who was staying near Milan, had told Turgenev that he had almost taken a coach that had been waylaid by bandits and two of its occupants had been shot.

2. Alexey Feofilaktovich Pisemsky (1821–81), novelist and playwright. See headnote to letter no. 115.

3. Polonsky's son had also died, six months earlier.

I see more often than anyone else here Lev Tolstoy's brother Nikolay. He's a splendid fellow but is in a very poor way. He's got incurable consumption. He's expecting his brother and sister, but heaven knows if they'll come. Rostovtsev writes to me.[4] He's at Ventnor on the Isle of Wight. There aren't the words in any language to express just how little I'm doing here. My fingers ache whenever I take up my pen. Am I really a writer?

Well, farewell. Surely after all our postponed meetings we shall see each other in Ventnor? I somehow feel that we shall have an enjoyable time there. Look after yourself, and try and keep your round and charming chin above water.

Yours,

I.T.

46. To A. A. FET

Afanasy Afanasyevich Fet (1820–92), poet and translator, neighbour and friend of Turgenev's and Tolstoy's. Fet's parents were German, but his mother left his father when she was pregnant and went to live with Afanasy Shenshin in whose home Fet was born. He was christened as Shenshin's son before his mother was divorced from his father. When Fet was fourteen the Orthodox Church authorities declared the christening illegal, and he was forced to assume the name of Fet and forfeit has status and all future inheritance. After a successful university career Fet joined a cavalry regiment in the hope of gaining the gentry status he felt was rightly his, as it was automatically conferred on serving officers on reaching a certain rank. After some eleven years in the army he retired, bought a large estate at Stepanovka, not far from Tolstoy's home at Yasnaya Polyana, and became a prosperous landowner. As a poet Fet is best remembered for his short lyrics, which are dominated by the themes of love and nature; many of them were inspired by his love for Marya Lazich whom he once thought of marrying; even after her early death and his subsequent marriage to the sister of V. P. Botkin, much of his poetry is dedicated to her memory. Fet was also a prolific translator from English, German and Latin.

Fet and Turgenev first met in 1853 during Turgenev's exile in Spasskoye, and they remained close friends for more then ten years until Fet's increasing conservatism and support for the ideals of a serf-owning society drove them apart; the final break occurred in 1874. Four years later Fet tried to start up his correspondence with Turgenev again, but their former friendship was not to be repeated. A hundred and twenty-one of Turgenev's letters to Fet have survived, but only six from Fet to Turgenev. Fet's *My Reminiscences* published in 1890 contain much useful biographical information on Turgenev.

---

4. Nikolay Yakovlevich Rostovtsev (1831–87); his father was one of the leading proponents of agricultural reform in the fifties. See also p. 82.

46. *To A. A. Fet*

[Original in Russian]

Courtavenel, 28 July 1860

My dear Afanasy Afanasyevich,

I have already written to you from here, but yesterday I received your letter which you sent to me from Mtsensk on 2 July (the post here is like a capricious woman: it's always surprising us by its unreliability) and I hasten to reply. Up to a point I have a duty to reply, as you state that you are feeling depressed because of the introspection which you say *I caused in you*. Well, really! In the first place, as far as I can recall you have suffered from this epidemic, as you call it, ever since I've known you; and in the second place, in our arguments I have always protested against your rectilinear and mathematical abstract thinking and I've even wondered how it could coexist with your poetic nature. But that's not the point. I wish to dispel at least one of your delusions. You call yourself a retired officer, a retired poet and a retired person (and who isn't a retired person, I might ask?), and ascribe the fact that *you're feeling clogged up* and depressed to the lack of any proper work. My dear fellow, it's not that at all. Your youth might have passed but you're not an old man yet, and that's why your arse is all knotted. I'm also going through that dismal and difficult period, that time of sudden impulses all the more powerful because they're not at all warranted, a time of peace without rest, where hope is similar to regret and regret to hope. Let's be patient, my dear Afanasy Afanasyevich, quietly patient, until we finally reach that peaceful harbour of old age and the possibility arises of doing things suitable to old age, even perhaps experiencing its joys, so splendidly described by Cicero in his *De senectute*. A few more grey hairs in our beards, a few more teeth removed, a little rheumatism in our backs or legs – and then all will go smoothly! And in the meanwhile, so that time will not drag too much, we'll go shooting game.

And talking of grouse, I had hoped to receive from you a description of your trip to Polesye – and you're still getting ready for it! That's bad. I was sure that by this time you would have already made up for your errors and would have been heartily sick of shooting. And goodness knows when the season will start here in France. It's just like winter: freezing cold and rain every day; utterly miserable! No one is even predicting when they'll start the harvest. And what shooting, anyway! Just the same old partridges and rabbits! As for when I'll return to the motherland, I'm afraid I cannot say anything definite at the moment. I'll decide in a day or two whether to spend the winter in Paris or return to the snipe at Spasskoye.

As regards your plans to buy some land and put your capital to some use, etc., I can only give you this advice: don't let it become an obsession with you, don't allow it to take on the form of an *idée fixe*. 'Don't strain after things,' as our wise Tyutchev[1] puts it, 'for that way lies madness.' The time will come, the opportunity will arise, and all will be well. But it's madness to chase after either the time or the opportunity. ⟨Everything comes to him who waits.⟩[2] You mustn't

[46] 1. Fyodor Ivanovich Tyutchev (1803–73), poet.
2. Original in French.

buy an estate simply because it happens to be up for sale.

As far as I know the Tolstoys are still in Soden; probably someone will write to me poste restante in Paris. I'm leaving here in a few days for England where I'm going sea-bathing on the Isle of Wight, so long as the sea hasn't frozen over.

Ten thousand greetings to your wife and Borisov.[3] I firmly press your hand and remain,

> Your absolutely innocent of causing
> you any introspection,
> Iv. Turgenev

47. To M. A. MARKOVICH

Marya Alexandrovna Markovich (1834–1907), née Vilinskaya, Ukrainian writer and translator, better known under her *nom de plume* of Marko Vovchok. She first met Turgenev in 1859, and the two were close friends for a few years; Turgenev liked her stories and translated some of them into Russian. Her increasing radicalism in the early sixties and the influence of Herzen, Ogaryov and Chernyshevsky, with whom Turgenev was having notable disagreements, spelt the end of their friendship. Forty-one of Turgenev's letters to her survive.

[Original in Russian]

> Ventnor, 13 August 1860

Dear Marya Alexandrovna,

I have been here since yesterday and today moved into a delightful little house overlooking the sea. The weather, as if intentionally, is marvellous, and I just can't tell you how delightful this island is. Woods, flowers, cliffs, the smell of new-mown hay – in a word, luxury! Of our Russians friends Rostovtsev is here, and Kruze.[1] Annenkov hasn't come; he's stayed in London. Herzen has rented a house although not here on the Isle of Wight, but in Bournemouth. He's got a mass of empty rooms and has invited me there; but I fear *the noise* and prefer my own company. I am sure he'll invite you too, and I might add in parenthesis that I too have a spare room for which I'm paying and which I do not need. At least drop me a line to tell me how you are and what plans you have. Shall I really not see you? My address here is Rock Cottage, Ventnor, Isle of Wight. I shall impatiently await your letter. The weather is still marvellous.

I firmly press your hand and ask you to come here. You only need the money for the crossing; don't worry about anything else.

> Yours,
> Iv. Turgenev

---

3. Ivan Petrovich Borisov (1832–71), neighbour and friend of Turgenev's. See headnote to letter no. 76.

[47] 1. Nikolay Fyodorovich Kruze (1823–1901), Moscow censor, dismissed in 1859 for 'being too indulgent'.

48. To COUNTESS Y. Y. LAMBERT

[Original in Russian]

Courtavenel, 3 October 1860

Here I am again writing to you in Petersburg, dear Countess, and you will read this letter in your nice little room which, alas, I shan't see for the whole of the coming winter. Instead of Petersburg, I shall be living in Paris, which I can't say is a very happy prospect. I cannot stand the Parisians; my daughter and I (and I must admit it, although she's a charming girl) have very little in common, and some rather dark clouds have been hanging over that other friendship which you know about. However, there's nothing to complain about and I shouldn't moan. Any hope of finding *personal* happiness in life has long since faded for me, and I must now school myself to some *real* self-sacrifice and not to the sort of which we talk so much when we are young and which presents itself in the form of love, which is still nonetheless something pleasurable, but rather to one that gives nothing to the individual except perhaps a feeling of having done one's duty; and you will note this feeling is cold and alien, without any trace of enthusiasm or passion. You know all this already for we are tarred with the same brush, but I am saying it to you to support both you and me in thinking about it.

I got little pleasure from our last meeting in Paris. You were constantly taken up with some heavy burden, some *préoccupation*, and I felt cold and listless. Indeed we saw very little of each other. Sometimes letters alleviate things for you; write and tell me what you are thinking at present. I have no need to tell you with what warm and friendly feelings I accept everything from you. Incidentally, I have rented a flat, 210 rue de Rivoli – write there. It's quite pleasant, even perhaps a little large, but it means I shall have a separate place to work in. I shall probably spend most of my time at home as I have started a long book[1] and would be very happy if I could complete it this winter.

I would like to explain to you why exactly my daughter and I have little in common. She doesn't like music, poetry, nature – or dogs – and that is all I care about. From this point of view it is hard for me to live in France, where poetry is petty and miserable, the scenery is positively ugly, music descends to the level of vaudeville or joke, and the shooting is disgraceful. For my daughter all that is quite all right and she replaces what she lacks with other more positive and useful qualities. But for me, between ourselves, she is just another Insarov.[2] I respect her but that is not enough.

Please do not forget to do your best and put in a word where possible for our project.[3] Annenkov will obtain for you an accurately transcribed copy.

I have received another letter from my acquaintance N. R. Tsebrikov, whom I

[48] 1. *Fathers and Sons.*

2. The hero of *On the Eve.*

3. While on holiday in Ventnor in August 1860, Turgenev, Annenkov and a group of Russian friends discussed the almost non-existent possibilities for Russian peasants of receiving an education. Turgenev drew up a draft proposal for founding a 'Society for the Spread of Literacy and Primary Education'. Nothing came of the 'project'.

asked you about and recommended as an excellent, honest and hard-working man.[4] He still hasn't found a post of estate manager and wants one which will pay 1200 roubles. If the opportunity arises please don't forget him; I can answer for him.

Look after your health, dear Countess, and don't lose heart – that's the most important thing. Please remember me to all your family and friends, and I firmly, firmly press your hand.

Yours sincerely,
Iv. Turgenev

49. To P. V. ANNENKOV

[Original in Russian]

Paris, 12 October 1860

Just a little news. I've rented a flat and moved in with my daughter and the most wonderful English governess, whom God helped me find. I intend to work like a slave. The general outline of my latest story [*Fathers and Sons*] is finished to the last detail, and I'm eager to write it. What will come of it I do not know, but Botkin, who is here, is enthusiastic about the ideas which lie behind it. I would like to finish it by the spring, by April, and bring it back to Russia myself.

The Century may consider me as one of its most devoted and serious contributors. Please send me its programme, and when I take time off from my novel I shall write some short articles which I shall try to make as interesting as possible.

Thank you, old man, for the books you sent. And for the forty roubles you gave to that dissolute cousin of mine. 'For all and everything I thank you.' That crazy good-for-nothing who was nicknamed Shamil in the province had at one time a very decent estate, and then became a monk, a gypsy and an army officer and would now appear to have dedicated himself to the profession of drunkard and cadger. I have written to my uncle and told him to support this dissolute buffoon at Spasskoye.[1] As for the hundred roubles, you can ask the editor of *The Century* to give them to you and I'll repay them by the end of the month.

Please give the attached note to I. I. Panayev. If he wishes to know the real reason why I no longer wish to contribute to the *Contemporary*, ask him to read the June number of the *Contemporary Review*, p. 240, three lines from the top, the passage where Mr Dobrolyubov[2] accuses me of deliberately making my Rudin a

4. Nikolay Romanovich Tsebrikov (1800–62); he had been a participant in the Decembrist movement in the early twenties.

[49] 1. Mikhail Alexeyevich Turgenev (1829–?), whose story Turgenev told in *The Desperado* (1882).

2. Nikolay Alexandrovich Dobrolyubov (1836–61), literary critic, friend and protégé of Chernyshevsky's. Turgenev never much liked his literary criticism published in the *Contemporary*, and his negative review of *On the Eve*, entitled 'When will the real day come?', caused the final rift between them.

caricature in order to please my wealthy literary friends in whose eyes anyone who is poor is a scoundrel. This is too much, and to participate in a journal like that is just not something a decent person can contemplate.

Will you fix something up, or rather try to fix something up through Yegor Kovalevsky (to whom I send friendly greetings), for Markovich.[3] His wife is here and suffering from poor health. But things will pass and she'll improve. The most important thing, however, is that she is penniless. Although her husband won't send for her, if he had a regular income then at least he wouldn't have to rob her. Makarov is still here but returning soon.

Poor, noble Nikolay Tolstoy has died in Hyères. His sister will spend the winter there and Lev Nikolayevich [Tolstoy] is still there.

Well, farewell. I send a tender kiss for your lips and await a reply. Greetings to all my friends. What is poor Polonsky doing?

Yours sincerely,
I.T.

3. Afanasy Vasilyevich Markovich (1822–67), Ukrainian folklorist and nationalist, husband of M. A. Markovich.

III

1861–1870

In October 1860 Turgenev rented some rooms in the rue de Rivoli in Paris, where he settled with his daughter Paulinette and her governess, Mrs Mary Innes. Turgenev did not like Paris, for he believed his health was always worse there, and his affection for the French was at this time not remarkable. Pauline Viardot's voice had begun to deteriorate although she was only forty, and she decided that she would no longer sing for the Paris Opera; her husband Louis was finding the political atmosphere in France increasingly distasteful, and so in 1862 the Viardots set up home in Baden-Baden in the Black Forest area of Germany. The villa which they bought on the outskirts of the town became an important musical and social centre. Turgenev followed them there in 1863 with Paulinette and Mrs Innes, but relations between his daughter and Pauline Viardot, never noticeably amicable, created problems, and he and Paulinette returned to Paris within a few months. Turgenev made continuing efforts to find a suitable husband for his daughter, and in 1865 she married the manager of a glass-factory, Gaston Bruère – a union which was to prove disastrous.

The period of Turgenev's stay in Baden-Baden, interspersed with visits to Russia, France and England, was on the whole extremely happy. This was despite arguments with Goncharov, Tolstoy, Dostoyevsky and Herzen; an inquiry by the Russian Senate into his supposed political activities; and, although his literary earnings were not inconsiderable, financial worries caused in the main by his uncle Nikolay's mismanagement of his Russian estates. He was forced to replace him in 1866 with N. A. Kishinsky, a man found for him by Annenkov. Unfortunately this apppointment was ultimately to prove equally unsuccessful.

The pleasant and congenial life in Baden-Baden came to an end. In order to provide a better education for their children, the Viardots moved in 1868 first to Karlsruhe and then to Weimar. Although they returned to Baden in the summer of 1870, the outbreak of the Franco-Prussian War had an adverse effect on their finances and they decided to set up home in London, where Pauline hoped to supplement their income from concerts and by giving singing lessons. They moved to England in October. Not wishing to be apart from Pauline, Turgenev followed them a month later.

During this period Turgenev continued his literary activities, although without the intensity of the previous five years. He published the novels *Fathers and Sons* and *Smoke*, the stories *Ghosts, Enough,* and *The Dog,* six of the eleven sketches which since 1874 have been known as *Literary and Social Memoirs* (a twelfth, *A Fire at Sea,* was added in 1884), and a small number of other stories and literary reviews and articles. Turgenev was also becoming known as a writer in Western Europe. Translations of his books, especially into French, German and English, were appearing with increasing frequency, although, much to his disappointment, he considered most of the translations (except those into German) to be of a rather poor quality, and they brought him little financial reward.

50. To L. N. TOLSTOY

[Original in Russian]

Paris, 22 March 1861

If I might speak plainly, dear Tolstoy, I was delighted to receive your letter. It marks the end of those, if not exactly hostile, then at least cold, relations which have existed between us. Our last meeting in Paris had already pointed to it, and I even wrote about it yesterday in a letter to your sister. What we had both admitted to ourselves is now expressed openly, and there's an end to our past misunderstandings. I am sure that we shall meet again in Russia as good friends and shall remain so, God permitting. To ruin one's life is only permissible to a young man, and neither of us is that. I thank you again for thinking of writing your letter, which has straightened out the former kink in our relationship once and for all.

The long-expected but nonetheless sudden news from Russia has aroused in me even more strongly the desire to return home.[1]

There is no possibility of arranging a marriage for my daughter in the near future, and so I shall leave here in five weeks with the idea of returning in the autumn, and I shall spend all the intervening time, i.e. spring and summer, in the country with the object of finally settling everything with my peasants. I am very pleased that I persuaded my uncle last year to set up a farm at Spasskoye and to transfer the peasants on all my other estates to quit-rent. That means that there will now be fewer difficulties. Thoughts about my journey to Russia and my stay there now preoccupy me almost constantly. In my mind's eye I can already see myself with Fet and Borisov (and, from today, with you too) in our fields and woods and in our little wooden houses; I can picture going shooting, etc., etc. There is one sad thing, though; your good and unforgettable brother Nikolay will not be with us.

Write and tell me when you plan to arrive at Yasnaya Polyana; I seem to remember your wanting to stop off somewhere on your journey; however, your phrase 'I'm waiting for some money in Brussels' is not at all clear. I hope to be in Spasskoye by the beginning of May.

So you didn't like the English. I had half expected it. It would appear that you had neither the time nor the opportunity to appreciate that spirit of sincerity

[50] 1. A reference to the Edict of Emancipation of the Peasants, issued on 19 February 1861.

which beats in the hearts of many of the characters in the novels of Dickens and which flows strongly in the veins of the people in general and in each individual Englishman. You must not forget that they are so modest and so reserved that they cannot express themselves openly.

And Herzen is, as you say, very old, poor chap! Ogaryov[2] has something of Moscow about him which I don't find much to my taste, although I know he is an excellent and kind-hearted man.

I shall say just a few words about the Russians who are here in Paris. Borkin's health is improving only slowly; he has fallen into a kind of gentle sluggishness and softness of manner, but his mind is as ever lively, subtle – and capricious. Chicherin[3] continues to survey the whole of the Parisian scene. Dolgorukov[4] – but it's better to say nothing about him.

It is a pity that you didn't see either *Orphée* (which they are doing again) or *Alceste* at the Conservatoire.

I firmly press your hand and bid you farewell,

Yours sincerely,
Iv. Turgenev

51. To V. Y. KARTASHEVSKAYA

[Original in Russian]

Paris, 26 March 1861

Each of my letters to you, dear Varvara Yakovlevna, should begin with an apology; my laziness and irregularity make me blush to the roots of my hair; and you, as if preparing for mass, decide to beg *my* forgiveness! After that, any beautiful lime tree, under the shade of which a traveller takes shelter from the burning heat of the sun, should beg that traveller's forgiveness! Do not put me to shame but rather accept the expression of my gratitude for remembering me and for your kind letters. I hope to have the opportunity of thanking you in person in the very near future, and to spend a few hours together as we used to, either at your home or in the flat of that charming young couple.[1]

I was saddened by the news of the death of Shevchenko; the poor man knew freedom for so short a time. I can imagine the impression it made on all your Little Russian world.

2. Nikolay Platonovich Ogaryov (1813–77), poet, publicist and revolutionary theorist, a life-long friend of A. I. Herzen (see headnote to letter no. 57); many of his ideas were later adopted by Lenin. Turgenev was friendly with him in the 1840s but later insisted to Herzen that Ogaryov's influence could only be detrimental to Russia's cause.

3. Boris Nikolayevich Chicherin (1828–1904), jurist, philosopher, historian, politician with Western views and professor at Moscow University. From 1882 to 1883 he was mayor of Moscow. His *Reminiscences* are an interesting historical document.

4. Probably Prince Pyotr Vladimirovich Dolgorukov (or Dolgoruky) (1816–68), émigré and writer of exposés of the tsarist government and the Russian aristocracy.

[51] 1. P. V. Annenkov had just married a relation of Kartashevskaya's, Glafira Alexandrovna Rakovich (1831–99); he was forty-nine and she twenty years younger.

We all attended a service here in honour of the Emancipation. The priest gave a short sermon which moved us all to tears. We all prayed for the Tsar.

My health has remained good throughout the winter, but I now have a slight cough again. I haven't done much work.

Thank your brother for sending me *The Spark* and the first two volumes of my new edition. My greetings to everyone, and I cordially press your hand.

Yours sincerely,

Iv. Turgenev

52. To COUNTESS Y. Y. LAMBERT

[Original in Russian]

Spasskoye, 21 May 1861

Dear Countess,

I received your two letters almost immediately ⟨one after the other⟩. [1] Might I congratulate you, Tsebrikov and myself on his appointment as your estate manager. I am sure you will find him satisfactory and the peasants will see him as both firm and considerate. May God grant that my words come true!

You paint a rather sombre picture of comtemporary life in Russia and of the Russian character in general. Unfortunately an honest man will have to subscribe to almost all you say. Has history made us as we are? Are there elements in our very natures of all that we see around us? We, of course, in the sight of heaven and aspiring to it, continue to sit up to our ears in the mud. Some astronomers state that comets become planets when they change from a gaseous to a solid state. The general *gaseous* nature of Russia upsets me and forces me to think that we are far from the *planet* stage. Nowhere is there anything firm or solid; nowhere is there any core. I am not talking about our institutions but about the people themselves.

You have probably already heard the rumours that the people *have no desire* to transfer from corvée to quit-rent. This remarkable and, I must admit, quite unforeseen fact only goes to show that the people are ready to forgo an obvious advantage (the cost of the corvée has been estimated at eighty roubles and yet quit-rent is nowhere more than thirty) in the hope that, as they say, there'll be a new edict and the land will be given to them as a gift, or the Tsar will give it to them in two years. And yet the quit-rent system is *already in operation*, i.e. the peasants are already working under certain determined conditions. Some of my quit-rent peasants have complained to me that those still on corvée have an obvious advantage – three days' work instead of six for their masters, while they themselves have received nothing. This also goes to show how well the various laws, enacted since the time of Peter the Great, have been observed – that landowners should demand no more than three days' corvée. The government has acted on the assumption that laws have their force, that they will be observed

[52]1. Original in French.

– it would be silly for it to behave otherwise -- and it turns out that the government has in some way been unjust: it has rewarded some people while leaving others just as they were before. As for the peasants agreeing to redemption payments, there's no question of it, not even in thirty-six or forty years. But if you say to our peasants that if they pay the odd rouble for only five years they will acquire land for their very own sons, they will not agree. In the first place they think only of today and in the second they do not trust their masters. We'll pay for five years, they think, and then a new rule will be announced – pay for another five. And in this they're not absolutely mistaken. We are now reaping the bitter harvest of the past thirty or forty years. Recently a friend of mine hired a free labourer and concluded with him an extremely favourable (to the labourer) contract, and after a few days the labourer's father arrived and, quite grief-stricken, said, 'Oh master, master, why have you led my poor son by the nose? He's stupid and cannot think for himself – while you . . .' 'And are the conditions unfavourable?' my friend interrupted. 'No, I can't say that they are unfavourable,' replied the old peasant, scratching himself on the back of the head, and then, rather quietly, 'But still, why did you lead him *by the nose?*'

And we still go on about legalities, responsibilities, division of power, etc., etc.

Fortunately, last year I managed to transfer at least some of my peasants to quit-rent.

You do not write anything about when you plan to leave Petersburg for the Ukraine. You'll probably stay a few days in Tula where your husband now is. If I knew when this will be, I could come and meet you. A visit by you to my modest Spasskoye home would be a delight. But that is probably daring to hope for too much. One of the gardens here is particularly worth seeing, especially now when all is green, bright and luxuriant.

In any case, until we meet again. I am grateful that you haven't forgotten me. I send my best wishes to you all and firmly press your hand.

Yours sincerely,

Iv. Turgenev

53. To M. A. MARKOVICH

[Original in Russian]

Spasskoye, 22 May 1861

Heavens above, dear Marya Alexandrovna, you are the most incorrigible of women! Is it possible to send a letter five lines long all the way from Italy to Russia and not say anything at all? Judge for yourself: your letter took eighteen days to get here, which means that this one will take just as long and not get to you before the middle of June, and at that time no foreigner is staying in Rome for fear of catching malaria; and *you* won't be there either, yet you tell me to write to Rome, poste restante, which I shall do, although I know that my letter will be lost almost certainly. Not a word about where you plan to go from

53. To M. A. Markovich

Rome, or where you're going to spend the summer, or whether you're returning to Paris for your things, or what your companions are doing, or whether you still have any companions, etc. I really ought to write to you in the same way and then you would know how nice such letters are.

However, your letter does manage to say something pleasant. You say that you will be attached to me *for ever*. This means a lot to me, but I know that you are not without a certain cunning – which you are aware of yourself. There is no doubt that I am attached to you, but besides this there is another rather strange feeling, which makes me want to have you near me – as in my little room in Paris; do you remember? When I recall our conversations then I cannot help admitting that you are a very strange person whom it is very difficult to make out; at least, it is not at all clear what to make of everything that happened. What rubric should I place it all beneath? When we see each other again – when and where that will be I just don't know – I shall tell you what decision I have come to – or the most probable one – although it's not very pleasant from my point of view.

Now I shall tell you briefly what my plans are. I shall stay in the country until 3 August or perhaps the fifteenth, and finish my novel, sort everything out with my peasants and set up a school, etc. Then I shall go to Baden-Baden where my daughter and Mrs Innes should be waiting for me, and perhaps we shall all go to Northern Italy together; by the middle of September I shall be back in Paris. I should be very grateful if you would tell me your plans. But doubtless they don't depend on you alone . . . and on whom they depend is a secret from me.[1]

I saw Belozersky and a few others in Petersburg. (Annenkov is married – there's a delight!) I was given four numbers of *The Fundamentals* from which I may conclude that there are no people on earth superior to the Ukrainians and that, in particular, we, the Great Russians, are rubbishy nonentities. We, the Great Russians, stroke our beards, quietly chuckle and think: let the children amuse themselves while they are still young. They will learn some sense as they get older. For the moment they are intoxicated with their own words. And their journal is so wonderful . . . and Shevchenko is such a great poet . . . Play on, dear children, play on!

Spring was very late here, and then suddenly burst out, as if everything was showered in green. You do not see such things abroad. But it is hard for an old man with an embittered heart.

Farewell; try to write rather more sensibly – including your address. I press your hand, and something else, to which you have never responded. Give a kiss to Bogdan[2] – about whom you wrote not a single word – and send my best wishes, assuming there is someone to send them to.

Yours,
Iv. Turgenev

[53] 1. Turgenev disapproved of the fact that Markovich was in Italy not with her husband but with another man. Like many of his contemporaries he had a very puritanical view of the way women should behave, at least in public.

2. Markovich's young son.

54. To L. N. TOLSTOY

[Original in Russian]

Spasskoye, 27 May 1861

Dear Lev Nikolayevich,

In reply to your letter I can only repeat what I considered it my duty to declare to you at Fet's: that, overcome by a feeling of involuntary hostility, the cause of which this is not the place to discuss, I insulted you without there being any positive cause on your part – and I apologized. I am prepared to repeat it now by letter and apologize again. What happened clearly shows that any attempt at friendship between two people of such incompatible personalities as yours and mine can lead to no good; consequently I shall the more readily carry out my duty towards you, as this letter is probably the last manifestation of any relationship between us. I hope in all sincerity that this will satisfy you and declare my agreement to whatever use you might see fit to make of it.

I respectfully have the honour, Sir, to remain your most obedient servant,

Iv. Turgenev

Ivan Petrovich [Borisov] has just brought my letter over to me. My manservant had stupidly taken it to Novosyolki rather than Bogoslov. I most humbly beg you to forgive this unwitting and foolish mistake.[1]

55. To L. N. TOLSTOY

[Original in Russian]

Spasskoye, 28 May 1861

Your manservant informs me that you desire an answer to your letter, but I cannot see that I can add anything to what I have already written.[1]

I fully recognize your right to demand satisfaction from me in a duel, but the fact that you chose to be content with an apology, which I repeated, was your privilege. I can say in all honesty that I would willingly have faced your fire in order thereby to make amends for my really insane words. The fact that I did utter them, which is so far removed from my habit of a lifetime, I can only ascribe to vexation provoked by that extreme and constant antagonism which

[54]1. Tolstoy visited Turgenev at Spasskoye on 25 May where he was given the manuscript of *Fathers and Sons*. Turgenev was infuriated with him when, after reading a few pages, he fell asleep. On the following day they both visited Fet's estate at Stepanovka, where their famous quarrel took place. The cause was ostensibly some of Tolstoy's forthright comments on the education of Turgenev's daughter Paulinette, and Turgenev threatened to punch Tolstoy on the nose. Both then promptly left Fet's house. Tolstoy went to I. P. Borisov's estate at Novosyolki and wrote to Turgenev demanding an apology. This letter is Turgenev's reply, but by the time it arrived Tolstoy had left and was at the posting-station of Bogoslov not far from Spasskoye.

[55] 1. Because of the mix-up over the delivery of the previous letter, Tolstoy wrote again, challenging Turgenev to a duel. Before Tolstoy had received this reply from Turgenev he had already written to Fet explaining that he had challenged Turgenev but now regretted it. Despite Fet's strenuous efforts the two were not reconciled for some seventeen years.

exists between us. This is not an excuse, nor do I think of it as a justification, but an explanation. And so, in parting from you for ever – such events are indelible and irrevocable – I consider it my duty to repeat once again that in this whole affair it was you who were in the right and that it was I who was in the wrong. I might add that there is no question here of *courage* – which I may or may not want to prove – but the recognition that you had the right either to call me out, of course in the accepted way (with seconds), or to excuse my behaviour. You chose as you thought fit and it only remains for me to submit to your decision.

I once again beg you to be assured of my complete respect.

Iv. Turgenev

56. To M. N. KATKOV

Mikhail Nikiforovich Katkov (1818–87) studied philosophy at the University of Moscow, where he was associated with liberal student circles and especially Stankevich and Belinsky. He first met Turgenev in the early 1840s when both were in Berlin, before returning to Moscow to become professor of philosophy in 1845. When the study of philosophy was banned for 'provoking dangerous thoughts', he turned to journalism. His generally liberal views soon earned him a wide reputation, but after the Polish rebellion in 1863 he grew increasingly reactionary. He published the *Russian Herald* from 1856 and later the *Moscow Gazette*. Although Turgenev never liked him, after he broke with the *Contemporary* he published in the *Russian Herald* (*On the Eve*, 1860, *Fathers and Sons*, 1862, *Smoke*, 1867, etc.). Katkov had what Turgenev found the extremely annoying habit of cutting and changing passages in those works he published, and Turgenev finally broke with him in the early 1870s when he transferred his allegiance mainly to the *Messenger of Europe*. When he subsequently suffered from frequent attacks of gout Turgenev would refer to them as 'Katkovitis'. Thirty-nine of Turgenev's letters to Katkov survive.

[Original in Russian]

Paris, 11 November 1861

Dear Mikhail Nikiforovich,

I wrote to you recently but, having received your letter yesterday, I feel I ought to send you a few words in reply. I agree with your comments [on *Fathers and Sons*] – well, with almost all of them – especially those about *Pavel Petrovich* and Bazarov himself. As for Odíntsova, the unclear impression which this character has made on you convinces me that I must do some more work on her. (By the way, the *argument* between P. P. and Bazarov has been completely re-written and shortened.) It is clear that we shall have to postpone things, *for the time being*, because of both the present circumstances[1] and the story's internal

[56] 1. In the autumn of 1861 there were serious student demonstrations in the capital leading to many arrests and the temporary closure of the university.

unfinished nature. You too will agree to this. I am very sorry that it has turned out this way but, particularly with subject matter such as this, one must appear before the reader fully armed. I want to look over everything again at my leisure, as it were to replough it. I suppose that all the *present* difficulties, both external and internal, will have disappeared by the time I return to Russia, i.e. in the spring, in April, and that we shall be able to let my little creation appear.

I cannot agree, though, to one thing: Odintsova must never speak ironically, nor must the peasant appear superior to Bazarov, even though the latter is empty and impotent. Perhaps my opinion of Russia is more misanthropic than you suppose. In my opinion he is the real hero of our times. The hero is good and the times are good, you will say . . . But that's the way it is.

I repeat my request to hold the story back. I firmly press your hand and remain,

Yours sincerely,
Iv. Turgenev

57. To A. I. HERZEN

Alexander Ivanovich Herzen (1812–70) was the illegitimate son of a Russian nobleman and his German mistress with whom he lived but never married. Given the surname Herzen at birth, he was brought up as a normal son and heir. He entered Moscow University in 1829 to study the natural sciences, philosophy and literature, and there developed his radical ideas based, as was current at the time, firstly on German romantic idealism and then on Utopian socialism. After graduating he joined the civil service, but his ideas soon began to upset the authorities and he was twice exiled, where he wrote stories, articles and novels wherein he denounced many of the social and political practices of his day.

On the death of his father in 1846 he inherited his father's wealth and, convinced that the conditions prevailing in Russia would offer him little opportunity to satisfy his ambitions, he decided to emigrate. In 1847 he left with his wife and family for Western Europe. They were caught up in the revolutions of 1848, where he was generally sympathetic to the aims of the republicans. After the unsuccessful outcome of the revolutionary movements and a number of personal tragedies, he moved to England in 1852. He established two journals *The Polar Star* in 1855 and *The Bell* two years later, which were both smuggled illegally into Russia, where they had considerable influence. After the Emancipation of the Peasants in 1861 he grew increasingly disenchanted with many of the activities of the various Russian radical movements, and his influence subsequently declined. In 1865 he set up home in Geneva. His best-known works include the novel *Who is to Blame?*, the political essays *From the Other Shore* and *The Russian People and Socialism* and the long autobiographical memoirs *My Past Life and Thoughts*.

Herzen and Turgenev first met in the early 1840s. Herzen was at first unim-

57. To A. I. Herzen

pressed with his younger contemporary, whom he found 'educated and clever' but 'superficial and fatuous' but he changed his opinion of him after the publication of *A Sportsman's Sketches*. Till the end of his life, despite the divergence of their views and numerous misunderstandings, Herzen thought Turgenev a first-rate writer who had helped the radical movement by his writings, but his feelings for him as a man were always slightly contemptuous. Their correspondence over twenty years contains a mass of material on social and political matters.

In May 1862 Turgenev paid a short visit to London and argued with Herzen over the future of Russia. One of the results of their debate was a series of eight articles which Herzen wrote for *The Bell*, entitled 'Ends and Beginnings' and cast in the form of open letters to a friend. Turgenev had originally planned to publish his replies in *The Bell*, but after warnings from the Russian authorities he decided it would be wiser to respond to Herzen in private letters.

[Original in Russian]

Paris, 11 February 1862

Dear Alexander Ivanovich,

I reply at lightning speed.

1. *The Bell* has not been banned here, and was still on sale yesterday evening *everywhere*.

2. Have nothing to do with *The Future* and advise Trübner not to either.[1] It hasn't even covered its costs and has had no success whatsoever. *Believe you this*, as our former landowners wrote beneath their former instructions.

3. I know nothing of Sadovsky[2] and you would be wise not to become involved in the matter. Dolgorukov is quite immoral and is scarcely up to it. You did all you could in *The Bell*: you had to suppport him as a matter of principle, but now leave him to his fate. He'll get stuck in your throat and you'll have to cough him out. It goes without saying that you won't get any support from the Vorontsovs. Be like Jupiter and stand aloof from all these petty squabbles.[3]

4. There is certainly a lot going on in Russia, but leave Golovnin alone.[4] Except for one or two things he just had to do, and they aren't very important, everything he's doing is for the good. (Remember his decision to allow Kavelin[5] and others to give public lectures, etc., etc.) I am getting very good reports on him. Don't worry; if he goes off the rails we'll 'hand him over' to you, as the

[57] 1. Russian-language journal published in Leipzig. Nikolay Trübner (1817–84) was Herzen's London publisher.

2. It is not known to whom Turgenev is referring.

3. A reference to various political trials in Russia and the acrimony that they had caused on all sides.

4. Alexander Vasilyevich Golovnin (1821–86) was Minister of Education from 1861 to 1866. He was also in charge of censorship.

5. Konstantin Dmitriyevich Kavelin (1818–85), jurist and historian. See headnote to letter no. 169.

peasants say when they bring criminals to the local courts for punishment.

5. *Et tu, Brute!* You attack me for publishing in the *Russian Herald*. But why did I quarrel with the *Contemporary* under Nekrasov? In their programme they announced they weren't going to accept anything I wrote and that I was somewhat backward, but ⟨you will not be taken in⟩[6] by this manoeuvre. I know that I gave up Nekrasov because he's not an honourable man. Where else could I have placed my stories? In the *Reader's Library*? No, when all's said and done the *Russian Herald* is not all rubbish, although much of what appears there makes me sick.

6. I shall have to call you out for a duel if you continue suspecting me of being friends with Chicherin.[7] And you're not even right about the people in Moscow, many of whom abhor him. He would have been impossible in Petersburg – and you still curse the place!

7. That dromedary Bakunin was here, procrastinated, bumbled, and left, leaving me the address of some brothers Lafare who must be paid the 1000 francs Michel had borrowed from them. I have opened up a subscription for him, but I've only added 200 to the 500 francs I've already given. I hope, all the same, to get the whole amount. I am prepared to give it to him *before* I leave here, but then it would have to come out of the three-year pension I gave him (well, not exactly – I promised him 1500 francs a year, and 1000 roubles plus 500 francs is a little less than that). But please talk him out of sending for his wife at the moment. It would be stupid; let him work things out first.[8] He will have to see what resources he has at his disposal, and they can't be great. Botkin won't keep on giving him money, etc.

Well, farewell my friend, or rather till we meet again.

Yours,
Iv. Turgenev

58. To F. M. DOSTOYEVSKY

Fyodor Mikhaylovich Dostoyevsky (1821–81) and Turgenev first met in November 1845. Dostoyevsky wrote to his brother: 'A poet, a talent, an aristocrat, superbly handsome, rich, clever, educated – I can't think what nature has denied him. Above all, straight as a die, schooled in kindness.' But their friendship rapidly cooled when Turgenev and Nekrasov wrote a satirical poem about him early the following year. They were on reasonably friendly terms in

6. Original in French.
7. B. N. Chicherin was reported to be publicly supporting the retention of corporal punishment in the army.
8. Bakunin's wife Antoniya Ksaryevna, née Kvyatkovskaya (1840–?), was still living in Irkutsk in Siberia where she had followed him into exile. With Turgenev's help she was soon permitted to return to European Russia; she later emigrated to London. Turgenev's involvement in this affair led to some difficulties for him with the Russian police. See letter no. 72.

the first half of the sixties; Dostoyevsky liked *Fathers and Sons* and Turgenev published his *Ghosts* in Dostoyevsky's journal *Epoch* in 1864. After this time, though, their widely different ideologies drew them apart, and the publication of *Smoke* led to a quarrel between them in Baden-Baden in July 1867, when Turgenev was accused of being an atheist, a Germanophile, and one who 'needed a telescope to see what was really going on in Russia'. They never forgave each other. Turgenev was convinced that Dostoyevsky was insane, an opinion that was confirmed when Turgenev found himself mercilessly satirized as Karmazinov in *The Devils* of 1871–2.

[Original in Russian]

Paris, 30 March 1862

Dear Fyodor Mikhaylovich,

I have no need to tell you how delighted I was with your review of *Fathers and Sons*. It is not a question of flattering my vanity, but of the conviction that I am probably not mistaken and have not completely missed the mark – and that my labours have not been in vain. It was even more important to me that people whom I trust (I'm not speaking of Kolbasin) had seriously advised me to throw the manuscript in the fire. What's more, Pisemsky recently wrote to me (but this is between ourselves) that the character of Bazarov is quite unsuccessful. With such comments how am I supposed not to have doubts and feel confused? It is difficult for an author to know *immediately* to what extent he has managed to get over his ideas, whether they are correct, whether he has expressed them properly, etc., etc. When he thinks of his own writing, it's as if he's walking in a forest.

You have probably often experienced this feeling yourself. And so I thank you again. You have grasped so well what I wished to express through Bazarov that I can only raise my arms in amazement – and satisfaction. You have got to the heart of things and have even sensed what I thought unnecessary to express. May God grant that this is not just the acute sensibilities of a master but that it can be understood by the ordinary reader as well – that is, may God grant that everyone can see albeit only a part of what you have seen. I am now not worried about the fate of my story. It has done its job and I have nothing to repent.

There is one further proof of how well you understand the character: during the meeting of Arkady and Bazarov, where you feel that something is missing when Bazarov talks of the duel and makes fun of the *upper classes* and Arkady listens to him, inwardly shuddering, etc. I cut a lot of it out, and now regret it. Generally speaking, I made a lot of changes and cuts under the influence of adverse criticisms, and perhaps from this results that slow development that you noticed.

I received a nice letter from Maykov and I shall reply. I shall be attacked fiercely, but shall have to put up with it like rain in summer.

I would be upset if I didn't find you still in Petersburg. I'm leaving here at the end of April, i.e. in a month's time. I can now tell you *for certain* that I shall bring my story with me, completed; it's not only going ahead extremely well but is approaching its conclusion. It will be about fifty pages long. It's turning out strangely. It's precisely those *Ghosts* over which we had the argument with Katkov a few years ago. I don't know if you remember it. I was about to start something else but was suddenly seized with the desire to finish this one and worked on it enthusiastically for several days. I only need to finish off a few pages.

I am delighted with the success of *Time*, but it's annoying that you couldn't arrange for it to be sent here regularly. I say this not only from personal interest – for I'm returning to Russia soon anyway – but it would have been to your own personal advantage. The *Russian Herald* arrives here regularly, although I haven't received the February number yet.

I very firmly press your hand and thank you yet again. Please send my affectionate greetings to your wife, and look after your health.

Yours sincerely,

Iv. Turgenev

59. To A. A. FET

[Original in Russian]

Paris, 18 April 1862

First of all, dear A. A., thank you for your letter. You would have had an even bigger thank you if you hadn't considered it necessary to wear kid gloves while you were massacring me. Believe me, I have learned how to take even the most unpleasant truths from my old friends. And so, despite all your euphemisms, you don't like *Fathers and Sons*. I bow my head, for what else can I do? But I would like to say a few words in my defence even though I know how improper it is – and futile. You ascribe the whole trouble to *tendentiousness, introspection*, or in a word, to intellect. But you really ought to have said simply that I lacked the necessary skill. It would appear that I am more naive than you suggest. Tendentiousness! Where is the tendentiousness in *Fathers and Sons*, might I ask? Did I want to tear Bazarov to pieces or to extol him? *I don't know that myself*, for I don't know whether I love him or hate him. There's the tendentiousness for you! Katkov blew me up for turning Bazarov into the apotheosis of the *Contemporary*. You also mention *parallelism*; but where, might I ask? Where are these pairs of characters, the believers and the non-believers? Pavel Petrovich – is he a believer or isn't he? I don't know. I just wanted to depict through him the Stolypins, Rossets and other Russian ex-lions.[1] It's strange that you should accuse me of parallelism when others write and ask me: Why hasn't Anna Sergeyevna got a superior character so that she would be more of a contrast to Bazarov? Why aren't Bazarov's parents more patriarchal? Why is Arkady rather commonplace?

[59] 1. Guards officers from the 1820s and 1830s who later became leading members of the gentry class.

And wouldn't it have been better to portray him as an honest young man who got suddenly carried away? What's the point of Fenichka? And what conclusions can be drawn from her? I can say one thing. I drew these characters as if I were drawing mushrooms, leaves, or trees; they caught my eye, so I began to draw them. But to rid myself of any personal impressions simply because they are similar to tendentiousness would have been rather silly and laughable. I do not wish you to draw from all this the conclusion that I am saying that I'm a splendid chap. On the contrary; but what you do conclude is even more insulting to me – that I have overreached myself and failed. But the truth is paramount. *Omnia veritas.*

I definitely plan to leave here in three weeks. As if on purpose, some suitors will turn up before then, but I know nothing will come of it – and it mustn't. One has to fulfil one's duty to the very end.

We'll certainly see each other again in Russia – and our great Vasily Petrovich [Botkin] – I'm already looking forward to Stepanovka, to our conversations, to going shooting, etc., etc. The trees are in full blossom here, but spring hasn't yet arrived. It's cold, cold!

Please send my most affectionate greetings to your wife and to my other friends. I press your hand in friendship and remain as ever,

Yours sincerely,

Iv. Turgenev

60. To K. K. SLUCHEVSKY

Konstantin Konstantinovich Sluchevsky (1837–1904), poet, journalist and government official. After receiving negative reviews of his early poetry, he emigrated to Western Europe and studied in France and Germany from 1861 to 1864. He returned to Russia after gaining a doctorate, and published a series of reactionary articles on Russian life; Turgenev thought them nonsense, and never had a high opinion of him, either as a man or as a writer. Sluchevsky is portrayed as the careerist Voroshilov in *Smoke*.

[Original in Russian]

Paris, 26 April 1862

I hasten to reply to your letter, for which I am very grateful, dear S. One cannot but value the opinions of young men, but I would nonetheless like to avoid any misunderstandings about my intentions. I shall reply to the points you make.

1. Your first criticism is reminiscent of that made of Gogol and others – why aren't there any *good* people amongst all the others? But Bazarov *does* stand above all the other characters in the book. The character I gave him is not accidental. I wanted to make him a tragic figure, and this was not out of any feelings of tenderness. He is honest and upright, and a democrat to his fingertips,

and yet you cannot find a *good* side to him? He recommends *Stoff und Kraft*[1] precisely because it's a *popular*, i.e. a simple, book. The duel with P[avel] P[etrovich] is specifically introduced as clear proof of the emptiness of the smart landowning classes, which are portrayed as almost exaggeratedly comic. And supposing he had not refused it, surely Pavel Petrovich would have killed him? In my opinion Bazarov gradually destroys Pavel Petrovich, and not the other way round. And if he calls himself a Nihilist, one should read: Revolutionary.

2. What you say about Arkady, the rehabilitation of the fathers, etc., only shows – my fault! – that I have not been understood. *All my story is directed against the gentry as the most important class.* Just look at the characters Nikolay Petrovich, Pavel Petrovich and Arkady. Weakness, inertia, limited outlook. The aesthetic sense forced me to take precisely those *good* representatives from the gentry class in order the more accurately to prove my argument: if the cream is off what about the milk? To take high officials, generals, thieves, etc., would have been crude, ⟨hackneyed⟩[2] and inaccurate. All the real *denunciators* of our system whom I have known (Belinsky, Bakunin, Herzen, Dobrolyubov, Speshnev[3] and so on) have all come without exception from reasonably good and honest parents. And herein lies a crucial point: it removes from *the activists*, the denunciators, any shadow of *personal* indignation or irritation. They take the road they do take only because they are more sensitive to the demands of our national life. Countess Salias is wrong when she says that characters like Nikolay Petrovich and Pavel Petrovich are our grandfathers. Nikolay Petrovich is me, Ogaryov and thousands of others; Pavel Petrovich is Stolypin, Yesakov, Rosset and many of our contemporaries. They are the best of the gentry class and that is precisely why I chose them, to show their bankruptcy. The portrayal on the one hand of bribe-takers and on the other of an ideal young man I shall leave to others. I wanted something better. At one point Bazarov said (I removed it because of the censorship) to Arkady, that same Arkady in whom your Heidelberg friends see *a more successful type*, 'Your father is an honest sort of fellow, but even if he took bribes all the place you would go no further than a noble humility or perhaps just get cross, because you're from the gentry class yourself.'

3. Heavens above! Kukshina, that caricature, is in your opinion the most successful of all! There is just no reply to that. Odintsova is as little *in love with* Arkady as with Bazarov; how did you not see this? She is a representative of those lazy, dreamy, curious, cold and epicurean ladies of our gentry class, our female landowners. Countess Salias understood *this* character completely. At first she wishes to stroke the fur of the wolf (Bazarov), provided he didn't bite her, and then the curls of the young man – and then, cleansed, to go on living as she did before.

[60] 1. By Friedrich Karl Büchner (1824–99), German materialist philosopher.

2. Original in French.

3. Nikolay Alexandrovich Speshnev (1821–82), a member of the circle which met under the leadership of M. V. Petrashevsky to discuss Russia's social and political problems. In 1849 thirty-five of its members (including Dostoyevsky) were arrested and exiled to Siberia. Speshnev returned to European Russia in 1860.

4. The death of Bazarov (which Countess Salias sees as *heroic* and consequently criticizes) should; in my opinion, put the final touch to his tragic character. And your young friends find it merely accidental! I shall conclude with the following: if the reader does not love Bazarov, despite the fact that he is crude, heartless, pitilessly cold and abrupt, if the reader does not love him, I repeat, then the fault is mine and I have not succeeded in doing what I set out to. But I did not wish, as he would say, to 'romanticize', although had I done so I would have had the younger generation immediately on my side. I did not want to gain popularity by such a compromise. It is better to lose a battle (and it would appear that I have lost it) than to win it by subterfuge. I wanted to create a character who was shadowy, strange, lifesize, only half developed yet strong, fearless and honest but nonetheless doomed to failure because he still stands on the threshold of the future. I wanted to create a strange sort of counterpart to Pugachov,[4] and so on. But my younger contemporaries say to me, shaking their heads, 'You've made a fool of yourself, old man, and have even insulted us. Your Arkady has turned out the purer; you should have worked harder on him.' All that's left to me, as they say in the gypsy song, is 'to remove my hat and bow down yet lower'. Up till now Bazarov has been fully understood, i.e. my intentions have been understood, only by two people – Botkin and Dostoyevsky. I shall try to send you a copy of my story. But enough of this for now.

Your poems have unfortunately been rejected by the *Russian Herald*. This is unjust, for they are ten times better than those by Shcherbina and many others which have appeared in that journal. With your permission I'll take them and get them published in *Time*. Drop me a line about it. Do not worry about your name; it won't appear.

I haven't yet received a letter from Natalya Nikolayevna,[5] but I've heard news of her from Annenkov whom she knows. I shan't be coming to Heidelberg, even though I could have met the young Russians there. Send them my greetings despite their considering me backward. Tell them that I would like them to wait a little longer before pronouncing their final sentence on me.

You can show this letter to whomsoever you wish. I firmly press your hand and wish you all the best. Carry on working and do not rush to finish things.

Yours sincerely,
Iv. Turgenev

61. To P. V. ANNENKOV

[Original in Russian]

Spasskoye, 8 June 1862

Well, here I am at last in my old nest, dear Pavel Vasilyevich, and I take up my pen at once to thank you 'for everything, for everything', and to remind you of my existence. I was very disappointed to have missed you in Petersburg; I

4. Leader of a popular uprising in 1773–5, during the reign of Catherine the Great.
5. N. N. Rashet (*c.*1830–94), writer and translator.

understand why you couldn't linger any longer, and I was detained for three weeks, as if on purpose, by an illness. But I intend to correspond with you frequently and hope that you will stay with me again at Spasskoye on your way back, because you can hardly go back to Petersburg via Vienna, as some wagging tongues are suggesting. All my friends are coming to see me here (at this very minute Botkin and Fet are chatting in the next room) while you, the best of them, have not favoured us with a visit. We shall welcome you and your wife with all possible honours, a triumphal arch, solemn music, fusillades from the arquebus, etc., etc.

I arrived in Petersburg on Whit Sunday, the day before the dreadful fire at the Apraxin Dvor, the Ministry of Internal Affairs etc., and spent four days there, saw both the fire and the people, heard all the rumours . . . and you can imagine what I felt and thought. All these stupidities, all these crimes, all this chaos – what can you say about them in a letter! It is to be hoped that the Tsar, our only strength at this time, will remain firm and calm in the face of all the attacks coming from right and left. It is frightening to think how strong the reaction will be, and one cannot but admit that to a certain extent it will be justified. The security of the State must come first.

I am also being flooded again with the old questions and discussions about *Fathers and Sons*. This is also a sort of chaos. On hearing some of the compliments I wished the ground would swallow me up, while some of the attacks were even quite pleasing. Pisarev's[1] article in the *Russian Word* seemed to me rather remarkable. My story fell into our lives when it did like oil thrown on to a fire purposely to liven it up, as the saying goes, at just the right moment.

But at least I'm not going to repent, even though most of the younger generation are cross with me. I even dare to think that I've been of some use, although Samarin (Yury)[2] in a letter to I. S. Aksakov accuses me – of what do you think? – of civic cowardice. He would have preferred me to cover Bazarov with mud, while others are attacking me for having slandered him. In a word, chaos. All will sort itself out in due course, and even if my reputation is destroyed, the affair itself will triumph and surely that's the main thing. All the rest is rubbish.

Can you imagine it? I made the journey from Petersburg to Moscow with Nekrasov. We chatted very politely, but briefly and without enthusiasm. He was even conscience-stricken, but he's long ceased to exist for me. Maslov[3] and Alexander Stankevich[4] were also travelling with us. I arrived here with Botkin, who has grown very decrepit and is turning into a real old woman. But he's still as clever and sharp as ever. We found Fet already here and argued till we all got hoarse. By the way, I was very pleased to see that he likes you . . .

[61]1. Dmitry Ivanovich Pisarev (1840–68), literary critic and thinker. See headnote to letter no. 90.

2. Yury Fyodorovich Samarin (1819–76), Slavophile publicist and politician. He took an active part in the preparations for the Emancipation of the Peasants.

3. Ivan Ilyich Maslov (1817–91), friend of Turgenev's. See headnote to letter no. 77.

4. Alexander Vladimirovich (1821–1912), younger brother of Nikolay Stankevich.

62. To F. BODENSTEDT

Friedrich Bodenstedt (1819–93), German poet. He lived in Moscow from 1841 as a tutor to the children of Prince M. Golitsyn, studied Russian language and literature and travelled widely in the Crimea and the Caucasus. In 1854 he was appointed Professor of Slavonic Literature at the University of Munich, and he became Director of the Meiningen theatre company in 1866. He wrote extensively on literature, history and music and translated Shakespeare's sonnets into German, as well as many poems by Pushkin, Lermontov, Koltsov, Tyutchev and Fet, some of which were set to music by Pauline Viardot and published in two albums in St Petersburg in 1864 and 1865. Bodenstedt first met Turgenev in the summer of 1861 in Munich, and between 1862 and 1865 he translated *Mumu*, *Yakov Pasynkov*, *Faust*, *A Trip to the Forest Belt* and *First Love*, and published a two-volume edition, *Erzählungen von Iwan Turgenew* (1864–5). Thirty-five of Turgenev's letters to him have survived.

[Original in French]

Paris, 31 October 1862

My dear Monsieur Bodenstedt,

I arrived back in Paris two days ago where the letter you wrote to me in May had been forwarded, and which has therefore remained unanswered until now as I was not in Paris. I went to Russia without being able, to my great regret, to pass through Munich. I have returned here for the winter and hasten to renew our correspondence.

First of all I must begin by saying a word about your translation of my story *Faust*, however egotistical that might be. I have just read it and was literally *delighted* with it; it is quite simply perfect. (Naturally I am speaking of the translation, not the story.) It is not enough just to have an excellent knowledge of Russian, but one has to be a great stylist oneself to create something so completely successful. My great good fortune has given me a taste for more. This is what I would like to propose. I would be very happy if I were introduced to the German reading public through someone as excellent and popular as you, and if you wish to select a number of my stories for publication I would be delighted to place at your disposal whatever you consider suitable as an honorarium, for I well know that present-day editors are not at all well disposed towards anything Russian and will take on no more than the printing costs. If this suggestion is acceptable to you, please drop me a line. For my part, I would willingly go up to a thousand thalers. That is by no means too much for having the opportunity to be exposed to a *reading public* as large as yours. In any case would you be so kind as to tell me what you think?

As for that unfortunate article which you sent to Petersburg, that is another matter. It must be admitted that we have been rather unlucky. In the space of a year the review (the *Contemporary*) has lost its two most influential editors through death, while two of the others have been sent to prison (and Chernyshevsky will be tried by the Senate).[1] And then it was forced to suspend publication for eight months, which means for ever.[2] Its *paper-work* was always rather disorganized but now it's just chaotic, so I fear that I shan't be able to recover your article. However, one of my friends is actively engaged in trying to find it and I do not yet despair. I shall write to you immediately I have any positive news.

I trust that you are in good health and that your eyes are causing no trouble. Please send my compliments to your family and remember me to M. Paul Heyse.[3] If you should see Mme Nelidova,[4] tell her that I am waiting for a reply to the letter I wrote her from Baden-Baden. I sent her at the same time a copy of my last novel, *Fathers and Sons*. If you would like to read it, please ask her for it, or I could send you a copy from here. I expect a reply in the near future. I cordially press your hand.

Yours sincerely,
Iv. Turgenev

P.S. In your translation, p. 69, line 15, there is probably a misprint. In the original: zu starr (intent, *fixe*) for children's eyes and not feurig (fiery), which would contradict what has gone before.

63. To A. I. HERZEN

[Original in Russian]

Paris, 8 November 1862

What a correspondence we have had, dear Alexander Ivanovich![1] Perhaps it has not been to your taste – I've heard a rumour to that effect. This letter is in response to your last one to me, which you published in *The Bell*. It is quite remarkable, although written if not a little fancifully then rather abstrusely for many readers, who will not immediately understand the origins of Pan or *pre-Punic* – but these are trifles. You put foward your diagnosis of contemporary man with unusual subtlety and sensitivity – but why specifically *Western* man and not *bipeds* in general? You're just like a doctor who, having studied all the symptoms of a chronic illness, announces that the whole trouble stems from the fact that the patient is French. Enemy of mysticism and absolutism, you mystically bow down before the Russian sheepskin coat and see in it the great abundance, innovation and originality of future social forms – *das Absolute*, in a

[62]1. Dobrolyubov had died in November 1861 and Panayev in February 1862. M. L. Mikhaylov was arrested in September 1861 and Chernyshevsky in July 1862.

2. The *Contemporary* was closed on the orders of the Minister of Education A. V. Golovnin in July 1862.

3. Paul Heyse (1830–1914), German novelist. See headnote to letter no. 137.

4. Princess Olga Dmitriyevna Nelidova (1839–1918), née Khilkova.

[63]1. See headnote to letter no. 57.

word, that same *absolute* which you so scorn in philosophy. All your idols are destroyed, but one cannot live without them. And you raise your altar to this new unknown god, the blessings of whom are practically unknown, and you can again pray, believe and expect. But this god does nothing that you expect of him – in your opinion this is temporary, accidental and violently forced upon him by an external power. Your god loves madly what you hate and hates what you love. Your god accepts precisely what you reject on his behalf. You turn your eyes and cover up your ears and in an ecstasy – that ecstasy of all sceptics whose scepticism has grown tedious – in a special, ultra-fanatical ecstasy you affirm 'spring's freshness, beneficial storms' etc. History, philology, statistics all mean nothing to you. Facts mean nothing to you, even the undoubted fact that we Russians belong by language and birth to the European family, *genus Europaeum*, and consequently by the same immutable laws of physiology must travel the same road. I have never heard of a duck who, belonging to the duck species, breathes through gills like a fish. And because of your spiritual pain, your weariness, your thirst to place a fresh snowflake on the parched tongue, you attack everything that should be dear to every European and consequently to us too – civilization, legality and finally the revolution itself – and, having filled the heads of the young with your half-fermented socio-Slavophile views, you send them out intoxicated and befuddled into a world where they will stumble at their first step. That you do this conscientiously, honestly, and with complete and sincere selflessness I have no doubt at all, and you are sure that I have no doubts either – but that does not make it any easier. You can do one of two things: either serve the revolution, the European ideals, as before, or, if you are convinced that it cannot be achieved, then have the spirit and courage to look it in *both* eyes and say ⟨guilty⟩[2] – before *all Europe* – and not draw either obvious or implied conclusions about Russia's mission, in which, in essence, you personally believe as little as you do in Europe's. You will say that this is terrible and that you will lose both your popularity and the possibility of continuing your activities. Agreed, but on the one hand to continue as you have been doing will be fruitless, and on the other I can see in you, to your misfortune, enough strength of character not to fear any repercussions from the expression of what you consider the truth. We await further comments, but that's enough for the moment.

Yours sincerely,
Iv. Turgenev

[P.S. omitted.]

---

2. Original in English.

64. To TSAR ALEXANDER II

[Original in Russian]

Paris, 3 February 1863

Your Imperial Majesty, Most Gracious Sovereign,

I have twice had the good fortune to address myself to Your Majesty by letter, and on both occasions my requests were graciously received. Grant me on this occasion also, Sire, your consideration.

I have today received instructions from our Ambassador here to return to Russia immediately. I must state in all sincerity that I cannot understand why I warrant such a show of mistrust. I have never hidden what I think, my actions are known to everyone, and I know of no reprehensible behaviour on my part. Your Majesty, I am a writer and nothing else. Everything in my life is expressed in my works – and I should be judged by them. I dare think that anyone who cares to look at them will be convinced of the temperance of my albeit independent but none the less sincere convictions. It is difficult to understand, Sire, that you, who have made your name immortal by a great act of justice and humanity[1], could at the same time suspect a writer who, in his field, has propounded, as far as he is able, the same high ideal. The state of my health and some extremely urgent personal affairs do not permit me to return to Russia at present and therefore I beg you, Most Gracious Sovereign, to condescend to send me the questions to which answers are required; I give you my solemn promise that I shall reply to each of them immediately and with complete honesty. Please believe, Sire, in the sincerity of my words. To the feelings of loyalty which it is my duty to express to your Majesty is enjoined my personal gratitude.

65. To P. V. ANNENKOV

[Original in Russian]

Paris, 6 February 1863

Dear friend, Pavel Vasilyevich,

The rumours about which you told me and which, because of their implausibility, I did not believe, have proved to be true. I really have been required to return to Russia. I cannot go immediately, for family affairs keep me here, so with the approval of our ambassador I have written to the Tsar asking him to do me the honour of sending to me here the questions to which answers are required and telling him that I shall reply in all openness. This task will not be difficult, for I have nothing to hide. I just cannot imagine of what I am being accused. I also cannot believe that the authorities are annoyed with me on account of the friends I had in my youth, who are now abroad and with whom I have long parted, and for ever, from a political point of view. And what sort of

[64] 1. i.e. the Emancipation of the Peasants.

political being am I? I am a writer, as I told the Tsar himself, albeit an independent one, but a writer with a conscience and of moderate opinions – and that's all. It remains for the government to judge to what extent I am useful to it or harmful, but it must be recognized that it is acting harshly with its 'secret supporter', as I remember you once called me. However, I am not at all worried and shall calmly await a reply. I cannot but tell you that Baron Bugberg (our ambassador) showed his best side throughout this whole affair.

What you write to me about the turn for the better that can be seen in our society is extremely gratifying. May God grant that you are right! By the way, I read with real pleasure your article on Uspensky[1] in the *St Petersburg Gazette*. The news from Poland has been received with sorrow here too. Blood and horrors once again . . . When will it all stop? When will we be able to have normal and proper relations with her? One can only desire the quickest possible end to this insane uprising, just as much for Russia's sake as for Poland's.

My health is, as usual, nothing to write home about and I am working without much enthusiasm, whilst you on the other hand seem to be in full working order and pressing ahead. Have the subscriptions to the *St Petersburg Gazette* been good? . . .

66. To N. V. KHANYKOV

Nikolay Vladimirovich Khanykov (1822–78), geographer and orientalist; he lived in Paris for many years, where he met Turgenev. After his death Turgenev raised a subscription to pay for a monument on his grave, which was carved by the sculptor M. Antokolsky. Fifty-nine of Turgenev's letters to Khanykov are known.

[Original in Russian]

Brussels, 15 February 1863

Dear Nikolay Vladimirovich,

I had a long conversation with your historian, the same Prince N. A. Orlov, after which I am still of the same opinion about the conscription in Poland, and here is why:

1. The fact that conscripts are being selected not by the police but by recruiting officers is neither here nor there because the clear, unconcealed objective of Wielopolski,[1] and *consequently* of the government, is to call up all the so-called revolutionaries, and this objective will certainly be carried out to the full according to the *instructions of the police*.

[65] 1. Nikolay Vasilyevich Uspensky (1837–89), writer. Annenkov had favourably compared a recently published collection of his short stories with Turgenev's *A Sportsman's Sketches*.
[66] 1. The Marquess Alexander Wielopolski (1803–77), Polish politician, generally in favour of cooperation between the Poles and their Russian masters. During the Polish insurrection of 1863 he was vice-president of the State Council and headed the civilian government under the Russian governor-general.

2. They are certainly calling up people between the ages of nineteen and twenty-three – i.e. the most dangerous age-group in the eyes of the government.

3. The method of conscription about which you write definitely obtained in Poland for thirty years, but *it was formally and finally replaced by a new law in 1859*, so it is now being employed again illegally. The illegality is compounded by the fact that the present call-up, as far as its size is concerned, should have been made *from all classes*, but it has been concentrated on one only – i.e. they did *not* say we'll take three thousand legally from the townspeople and consider another three thousand as arrears from the peasantry, or excuse them altogher, but announced that all *six thousand* would be taken from the townspeople. It is this and the absence of any prescribed system which is so blatantly and disgracefully unjust, and it is no less unjust because something similar is happening in Italy.

I shall give all these facts to Lanfrey,[2] and he can judge what best use to make of them.

Yours sincerely,
Iv. Turgenev

67. To COUNTESS Y. Y. LAMBERT

[Original in Russian]

Baden-Baden, 9 May 1863

Dear Countess,

I arrived here a week ago and have only just managed to settle in, find myself a flat, etc. I was just about to write to you – although not fourteen pages but my normal four – when your long letter suddenly appeared, and naturally, despite your pitiless severity on me, I hastened to carry out my intention. I will say a few words, not in justification, but by way of explanation.

You censure me both as a man (in the sense of a political animal, a citizen) and as a writer. I think that with the first you are quite correct, but not with the second. You are right in saying that I am not a political animal and in affirming that the government has nothing to fear from me; my convictions haven't changed since my youth. But I have never engaged in political activity, nor shall I ever do so. Such matters are alien to me and uninteresting and I concern myself with them only insofar as I need to as a writer who deals with contemporary life. But you are wrong to demand of me literature which I cannot produce, fruits which, as it were, do not grow on my tree. I have never *written for the ordinary people*. I write for that class to which I belong, from *A Sportsman's Sketches* to *Fathers and Sons*. I do not know whether I've been of any use, but I do know that I have been unwavering in my aims and in this respect do not deserve your reproach. You suggest that it is merely out of laziness that I do not write, as you

2. Pierre Lanfrey (1828–77), French historian, publicist and politician. His *Etudes et Portraits Politiques* (1864) contains a chapter on the Polish question but makes no mention of the information provided by Turgenev.

say, simple and moral stories for the people, but how do you know that I haven't tried twenty times to do something along these lines and have not done so because I am convinced that it is not in my province, that I *do not know how to*? This is precisely where you can see the weak side of the most intelligent people who are *not* artists: having grown accustomed to arrange their lives according to their own free will, they just cannot understand that a writer often has no control over his own offspring and are ready to accuse him of laziness, epicureanism, etc. Believe me when I say that every person does only what is given him to do, and to coerce him is both useless and fruitless. That is why I shall never write stories for the ordinary people. For that one needs a quite different cast of mind and character.

I can place my hand on my heart and say that I don't think I live abroad simply to enjoy staying in hotels and so on. Circumstances have up until now determined that I spend only five months a year in Russia, and it's now even less. I trust you will believe me when I say that I would particularly like to be in Russia now and to see at first hand what is happening there, for it is something I really feel for.

I still haven't found a husband for my daughter; she'll be writing to you herself. I am sorry that I didn't thank you for the marvellous album which you sent for her, which arrived safe and sound and now graces her table. I would be very pleased if you were advised to go abroad; I would then have *une chance* to see you.

Look after your health and write me albeit indignant letters. You know that I love you sincerely and value your friendship. I firmly press your husband's hand.

Yours,
Iv. Turgenev

68. To F. BODENSTEDT

[Original in Russian]

Baden-Baden, 6 July 1863

Dear Sir,

I was extremely sorry to hear of the accident which befell you and nearly crippled you, and trust that you are now fully recovered. You have had a troublesome winter and would do well to come here for a fortnight to recuperate. I have no need to add what a pleasure it would be for all your friends here. Mlle Steinbach,[1] whom I have just met, tells me that it was your intention to come – so please do.

Would you also permit me to make a request which I hope you will not find too disagreeable? A great friend of mine, Mme Viardot (the celebrated singer),

---

[68] 1. Actually Augusta Eichtal, a friend of Bodenstedt's.

has profited from her stay in Baden-Baden by putting her immense talents to excellent use. She has set to music several Russian poems which I selected for her. (She is also studying our language.) The musical quality of these romances is so high that we have decided to publish them in an album in Karlsruhe – with both the Russian and the German texts. When we began to consider the translations, I naturally thought of you, the most perfect and delicate of translators. And so my request is that you associate yourself with this publication. As you will see, it won't involve a lot of work. The album will consist of six poems by Pushkin and five by Fet, which I enclose. It is possible that you have already translated some of the Pushkin, which will make your task easier. It goes without saying that the measure and the rhythm of the originals must be retained exactly, but that will present you with no difficulty. If you accept this small task you will be giving us a real present and we would be very happy to acknowledge it.

Would you please have the kindness to let me have a few words in reply.

Yours very respectfully,

Iv. Turgenev

69. To A. I. HERZEN

In *The Bell* of 10 July 1863 Herzen reprinted a story taken from I. S. Aksakov's paper *Day*, which related a story which its Paris correspondent attributed to Turgenev: a Cossack colonel in charge of a regiment of Russian soldiers in Poland berated his batman for giving him English mustard rather than French to accompany his meal of roast Polish children. Herzen added that although Turgenev understood nothing about politics, he was surely still a human being who must be revolted by the atrocious treatment being meted out to the Poles by the Russians. Herzen added, though, that he did not believe Turgenev was the author of the story.

[Original in Russian]

Heidelberg, 22 July 1863

Dear Alexander Ivanovich,

I have just read *The Bell* and have noticed the passage about 'French and English mustard'. I thank you for not believing that frightful story, but I think you would have expressed yourself more clearly if you had said you believed none of it. Never has a single insulting or sarcastic word directed at the Poles ever passed my lips, especially as I have not lost all conception of the meaning of 'tragic'. And now is no time for laughter.

I ceased writing to you for reasons which you well know, and who would wish to exchange letters like our last ones? Our views are too far apart, and what is the point of our fruitlessly abusing one another? I am not suggesting that we should renew our correspondence, but I should be obliged if you would print the following in the next number of *The Bell*: 'We have received positive information that the words attributed to Mr I. Turgenev are a complete fabrication.'[1]

I am also writing to I. S. Aksakov. I am deeply insulted by the filth which is being splattered over my secluded, almost subterranean, existence.

I wish you a quiet life, as far as that is possible, and beg you in the name of our former relationship not to consider me capable of any worthless word or deed.

Iv. Turgenev

P.S. I am living at 277 Schillerstrasse, Baden-Baden, and have only come here for the day to consult a doctor.

70. To PAULINE VIARDOT

[Original in French, translated from the Russian]

St Petersburg, 10 January 1864

Dear and good Mme Viardot,

I hasten first of all to thank you for your letter, which I received yesterday (and the one from the children). It was very kind of you . . . You will notice that for my part I am not being tardy.

I must give you an account of the past two days. In the morning, or rather on both mornings, I made and received a number of visits. The evenings were dedicated to music. Two days ago I saw *Faust*. The auditorium was packed but it was only an average success, more of a *succès d'estime*. Here is my report; Tamberlick (Faust) was awful – his voice has completely gone; Mme Barbot, a subtle and intelligent actress, gave an almost poetic performance, but her voice is poor; Everardi (Méphisto) is a wonderful singer but a weak and limp actor. Meo (Valentin) is poor, heavy-footed and has no power at all; the orchestra was good but the chorus was *absolutely terrible*: after the Soldiers' Chorus there was not a single clap. The decor was pretentious and in bad taste, *à la* Roller. All those Italians were not at home with the music; it's as if they were wearing second-hand clothes which were too tight and prevented free movement.[1]

Yesterday evening I went to a concert at the Philharmonic Society under Rubinstein.[2] They played large extracts from *Oberon* (with a certain Mlle Prokhorova[3] who has a beautiful voice, but cannot sing at all; however, she's

[69] 1. Herzen printed the statement.

[70] 1. Enrico Tamberlick (1820–89), eminent Italian tenor; Caroline Barbot (1830–?), French soprano; Camillo Everardi, real name Camillo François Evrard (1825–99), Italian baritone; Meo, Italian baritone; A. A. Roller, real name Andreas Leongard, born in Germany (1805–81), leading scene-painter and designer for the Imperial theatres in St Petersburg.

2. Anton Grigoryevich Rubinstein (1829–94), the pianist and prolific composer; in 1862 he founded the St Petersburg Conservatory. Turgenev never much liked his music but he admired his playing.

3. Kseniya Alexeyevna Prokhorova-Mavrelli (1836–1902), soprano. By all accounts Turgenev's opinion of her was harsh.

still very young). A motet by M. Hadyn and Mozart's *Ave verum* were performed impeccably. Then I went to a reception given by the Italian ambassador,
Marchese Pepoli.[4] There was music here too: an extensive patriotic cantata
performed by all the leading singers. I liked Mme Fioretti's voice a lot.[5]

I saw many people I knew, including Mme Adlerberg[6] who inquired after
you. Prince Dolgorukov (just you listen!),[7] the head and director of all the police
in the Empire and one of the most influential of all government officers, came up
to me and we chatted for several minutes, and Prince Suvorov[8] was extremely
pleasant with me. All this goes to show that I am not looked upon as a
conspirator. And one of my inquisitors, the corpulent Venevitinov,[9] whom you
know, told me that my case was trivial. All of this reassures me. I'm telling you
this so that you can banish any worrying thoughts you may have on my
account.

Let us now discuss something more important – your Song Album.[10] It is
being published by Iogansen and the manuscripts have already been passed by
the censor – this was unavoidable. They are just about to engrave the plates for
'The Little Flower'. Rubinstein has suggested the following order: 'The Little
Flower', 'In the Mountains of Georgia', 'A Still Night', 'Images at Midnight',
'Whisper', 'Incantation', 'The Tomtit', 'Two Roses', 'At Night', 'Prisoner',
'Bird of Paradise' and 'Stars'. As you see, we are publishing only twelve. The
publisher thought this was enough. The other three we can hold over for next
year's volume, for there will be one. Rubinstein made the selection. He left out
'To the River-Banks', 'Cradle Song' and 'During a Sleepless Night'. The
print-run will be 1000 copies, exclusively for sale in Russia. You will get 2500
francs, which I shall bring you. If you nonetheless would like the other three
included in the album, drop me a line. Nothing would be easier than to add them
on to the rest. The album will appear in six weeks. Reply immediately.

Embrace the children for me and tell them that I will write something to them
in my next letter, which I'll post on *Monday*. I was happy to hear that you have
started up your little salon again. A thousand greetings to Viardot and all my

4. Joaquim Napoléon (1825–81). He married the soprano Marietta Alboni.

5. Elena Fioretti (1837–89), brilliant Italian soprano.

6. Cóuntess Yekaterina Nikolayevna Adlerberg, née Poltavtseva (1822–1910), wife of Count A.
V. Adlerberg, important court official and personal friend of Tsar Alexander II.

7. Prince Vasily Andreyevich Dolgorukov (1803–68), Minister of War from 1853 to 1856 and
later Chief of Gendarmes and Head of the Third Section, the tsarist political police.

8. Prince Alexander Arkadyevich Suvorov (1804–82), general, member of the State Council and
from 1861 to 1866 Military Governor of St Petersburg.

9. Alexey Vladimirovich Venevitinov (1806–72), important civil servant, brother of the poet. He
was later a member of the Literary Fund.

10. Poems by Pushkin, Fet and Turgenev, set to music by Pauline Viardot and published in St
Petersburg in 1864; a second volume appeared the following year. The albums were also published
in German versions in Leipzig. See also letter no. 68.

good Badeners. As for me, you know more than I could tell you. A tender kiss to both your hands.

⟨Your⟩[11]

I. Turgenev

P.S. My leg has been hurting *a little* for two days. I wouldn't have mentioned it if I hadn't promised to share with you all my ailments.

71. To PAULINE VIARDOT

[Original in French]   St Petersburg, 11, 13 January 1864

Yet another letter from you, ⟨dearest friend⟩.[1] You really are spoiling me, but I shall not object, and I ask you to continue in the same spirit. If you often think of me, I can tell you that my thoughts are never far from Baden. You well know that I shall feel happy only when I return to that charming little valley.

I am very pleased to hear that all the changes the house needed have been completed. Everyone should feel happy there. As for me, my foot has been a little troublesome and I await the return of Botkin's brother, a leading doctor, for a consultation.[2]

Rubinstein has told me that he has had to postpone the 'Cradle Song' to the next collection because there is one to the same words by Glinka which he says is very fine and popular, although I've never heard it.[3] 'The Sleepless Night' seems rather too bizarre in his opinion, and as thirteen is an unlucky number he has removed 'To the River-Banks' as well.

I've heard parts of *Rogneda*[4] for the second time – Botkin heard it too – and my opinion of it hasn't altered. My fastidious friend also finds things of great beauty in this new music.

Monday

I hasten to inform you of the result of my second visit to the Senate. It was entirely satisfactory. There wasn't even a formal meeting. They contented themselves with giving me the whole dossier (which, in parenthesis, shows their trust in me), pointing out those pages where my name appears. I wrote several comments, or rather some additional explanations, which seemed to satisfy my six judges. Evidently the whole affair was quite innocuous. My judges didn't even interrogate me. They preferred simply to talk to me about this and that, and it only took a couple of minutes. I have to go back to the Senate tomorrow, probably for the last time. As you can see, everything is turning out fine and nothing can now prevent my return. In five or six weeks at the latest ⟨God

11. Original in German.

[71] 1. Original in German.

2. Sergey Petrovich Botkin (1832–89) was a professor at the Medico-Surgical Academy in St Petersburg. There is still a clinic in Moscow named after him.

3. Rubinstein was mistaken. Glinka's 'Cradle Song' was to words by Pushkin. Pauline Viardot had set Lermontov's poem of the same name to music.

4. Opera by A. N. Serov (1865).

willing⟩⁵ I shall have the pleasure of seeing you again. My absence will be no longer than two months, in any case. I am very happy about it all, especially as my presence here had become unavoidable and any further delay would have had unfortunate consequences for me. My return to Russia has silenced a mass of rumours which were as unpleasant as they were stupid. I shall tell you about them sometime, very soon now, sitting by your side in your little salon. And so there is now nothing at all to worry about. We must just have a little more patience. That is a word that I find myself repeating frequently these days.

My foot is a little better today and I have kept my boots on all day.

I fear that this letter will not find you still in Baden. I shall write to you tomorrow in Leipzig. I haven't seen many people these last two days. I spent yesterday evening at my good Countess Lambert's; her health is apparently improving. I am completely avoiding the literary world here. Those gentlemen are just like cowbells – small, empty and making too much noise. I've been amusing myself by leafing through the reviews and journals that have appeared during my absence – not very edifying reading. There's an almost complete absence of talent. The young men state that talent is no longer necessary, that it's rococo and that they're just honest labourers, like M. Josse.⁶

Until tomorrow, dear and good friend. I just cannot say how often I think of you. If the truth be told, my thoughts are always with you. Please give the enclosed little note to the children. Kiss them for me. A thousand greetings to Viardot and all the others. I tenderly kiss your hands.

⟨Your⟩¹

I. Turgenev

P.S. By the way, I haven't yet received Bodenstedt's translation of 'The Prisoner' or 'The Bird of Paradise'. Write and ask him to send them to me immediately.

72. To A. I. HERZEN

When Turgenev was requested by the Senate, who were inquiring into the activities of certain radicals and their connections with the émigrés grouped around Herzen's paper *The Bell* in London, to state his relations with them (his name cropped up in a number of letters the police had confiscated), he had first replied by letter. He answered reasonably truthfully, although not in full. Rumours reached Herzen to the effect that Turgenev was denying he had any current contacts or former friendship with Herzen's circle. In January 1864, while Turgenev was actually back in Russia answering the charges in person, Herzen published in *The Bell* a short note stating: 'Our correspondent tells us of a certain grey-haired Magdalene (of the male sex) who wrote to the Emperor

5. Original in Spanish.
6. Character from the *Amour Médecin* by Molière. The name has come to be applied to people who are, as it were, 'in the trade' and so do not give unbiased advice.

that she had lost sleep and appetite, her rest, her white hairs and her teeth, tortured by the thought that the Emperor does not yet know of the repentance which has overtaken her, on the strength of which "she has broken all contact with the friends of her youth".' Turgenev hesitated three months before replying.

[Original in Russian]

Paris, 2 April 1864

Since my return from Russia, I have hesitated for a long time over whether to write to you in connection with your comments in *The Bell* about 'the grey-haired male Magdalene, whose teeth and hair have fallen out in repentance', etc. I must confess that this statement, clearly referring to me, made me very angry. That Bakunin, who borrowed money from me and subsequently placed me in a very uncomfortable position (he has completely ruined some others) by his stupid gossip and flippant behaviour, that Bakunin, I say, went about spreading the most coarse and filthy slanders about me, is quite in the order of things, and, knowing him of old, I could hardly expect anything else. But I did not expect that you would throw mud in exactly the same way at a man you have known for almost twenty years, simply because he no longer subscribed to your ideas. You are no different from the late Tsar Nicholas, who also sentenced me without even telling me of what exactly I was guilty. If I could show you the replies which I gave to the questions I was sent, you would probably be convinced that I hid nothing and not only that I did not betray any of my former friends but also that I did not even wish to disavow them. I would have considered that quite unworthy of me. I admit that I recall my replies with a certain pride – replies which, despite the tone in which they were written, earned the respect and trust of my judges. As for my letter to the Tsar, which you presented in such an unfavourable light, here is what I wrote . . .[1]

Yes, the Tsar, who did not know me at all, nonetheless understood that he was dealing with an honest man, and because of this my gratitude to him increased. And my old friends, who should have known me better, should have had serious doubts about accusing me of repudiating them and about publishing their opinions in the press. If I were dealing with the old Herzen, there would be no need to ask you not to abuse my trust in you and to destroy this letter immediately. But I do not know now what to think of you, and I beg you not to cause me any more trouble – there has been enough in the past. However, this letter should prove to you that my former feelings towards you have not vanished altogether. I am not going to waste any words on Bakunin. Look after yourself.

Iv. Turgenev

[72]1. See letter no. 64.

73. To COUNTESS Y. Y. LAMBERT

[Original in Russian]

Baden-Baden, 3 September 1864

Dear Countess,

First of all I must say that for some inexplicable reason your letter written on 18 August arrived only yesterday. This was doubly unpleasant for me; firstly because you might think I was being slow in replying, and secondly that my reply will not find you still in Wiesbaden. But so be it; I do not want to waste a minute now. I am very grateful for your letter, even though you reprove me and seem to be bidding me farewell. But I can see that you haven't forgotten me and even feel some friendship for me. Fortunately for me you never possessed any of that virtuous but arrogant inability to understand – and sometimes even to forgive – the faults of others which I have noticed in many Christians, both men and women, of the upper classes. You reproach me, it is true, but in the first place there is kindness in your reproaches and in the second they give me the chance to justify myself. From your point of view I have two important faults; one, the absence of . . . Orthodox faith, and two, residing outside my native land, which stems from the desire to live the life of an epicurean – in a word, from egoism. I shall not expand on the first point: I am not a Christian in your understanding of the term and probably not in any sense, and so I'll leave the question to one side – it can only lead to serious misunderstandings. As for the second, please allow me to protest at your application to me of the word contempt. Only young and passionate people can feel contempt, and I have never sinned in this way, even in my youth. You say that one must serve one's country. Agreed, but you will grant that I could not serve Russia as a soldier or a civil servant, or an agronomist or industrialist. I can be of use only as a writer, as an artist. I might also note here that for every artist there comes a time, and even the right, to fall silent. I wish only to point out to you the fact that there is no need for a writer to live continuously in his native country in order to see all the changes going on there. I have worked rather hard in that field, anyway, and how do you know that I might not now intend to write something that is not specifically about Russia and to set myself a wider task?

You will reply that I am only thinking up some favourable prologue for my future laziness . . . but you would not be quite right.

In brief, I can see no reason why I should not settle in Baden. I am doing it not from the desire for pleasure (that's also a mark of youth) but simply to build myself a little nest where I can await my inevitable end.

Well, I've had my say and no doubt failed to convince you. In your letter you say nothing about your health or your plans. Despite the *twenty-four-hour* period which you falsely apply to such things, I would of course come and see you if I knew for certain where you would be and for how long. Please drop me a line, and let us, in general, continue our correspondence. In spite of all our disagreements we are close to one another. In the expectation of a letter, I firmly press your hand and remain,

Yours very sincerely,
I.T.

74. To COUNTESS Y. Y. LAMBERT

[Original in Russian]

Baden-Baden, 25 December 1864

I was very pleased to receive your letter, dear Countess; I was beginning to lose hope of any renewal of relations between us. I must assume that you did not receive the letter I sent to you in Vienna last summer. I regret its loss only because it might have convinced you that your opinion that I am forgetful is unjust. However that may be, our relationship has been renewed and we must try to avoid its being interrupted again. These interruptions are all the more annoying as we must give each other something like a report on how we are feeling every time we write, to keep each other *au courant*. And this isn't always convenient, especially in just a few lines. Any confession should be full, but we are forced to restrain ourselves and find some brief but expressive words. However, I am not about to confess on this occasion; I shan't talk about myself.

I shall tell you first of all a piece of news which is very important for me. My daughter is to be married at the end of February. Her fiancé is M. Gaston Bruère; he is a young man (twenty-nine), from a good family and lives almost continuously in the country, where he has a large glass factory. He was introduced to my daughter by Mme Delessert,[1] a great friend of mine, who has known him since his childhood. My daughter liked him and everything was settled. I'm going to Paris soon to make all the necessary arrangements. If you care to write I shall be staying at 10 rue Basse, Passy. I am very pleased about it all; it will remove my daughter from the false position in which she finds herself, and will release me from a great responsibility.

May God grant that you find the rest and peace of mind you need in the country. But I hope to see you before your departure from Petersburg; I am going to Russia immediately after my daughter's wedding and shall stay in Petersburg until 15 April. It is absolutely essential for me to be in Russia in order to arrange all my affairs, which my dear uncle has let get quite out of hand.

Count [K. K.] Lambert's marriage (which, by the way, I only learnt of through you) was no surprise to me, and I think he's taken a wise and sensible step. It would appear that his [army] career is over, and to spend the remaining years of his life alone would be difficult for a man as energetic as he. Write and tell me where he is; if he's in Paris I shall seek him out.

Please send my best wishes to your husband. I affectionately press your hand. I shall write to you in more detail from Paris. Thank you for remembering me.

Yours sincerely,

Iv. Turgenev

[74] 1. Countess Valentine Delessert (1806–94); see headnote to letter no. 78. Turgenev was exaggerating in saying that Gaston Bruère owned a factory. At the time he only managed the one owned by Mme Delessert's son-in-law, Roger de Nadaillac.

75. To PAULINETTE TURGENEVA

[Original in French]

Baden-Baden, 19 January 1865

My dear Paulinette,

I am writing to you today just to let you know that I have received your last letter and am expecting another in which you will tell me about the soirée you spent with your 'intended'. I hope everything is proceding well. All the necessary documents were sent off some time ago, and I sent some money to Mme Innes yesterday. Would you tell her, please, in this connection, that I do not wish to spend more than 3000 francs on your trousseau; and also, would it not be more sensible to arrange the wedding breakfast in Passy at a good restaurant rather than at the Grand-Hôtel? These two requests are necessitated by my having to make as many economies as possible. I know that I spoke of the Grand-Hôtel when I wrote to her yesterday, but I have had second thoughts. However, I give her *carte blanche* and trust in her judgment.

Annenkov and his wife have sent me a letter full of congratulations for you – I'll send it on.

I shall see you soon. Look after yourself, and do not worry. I do not think it would be a good idea to return to Paris during the first few days of your marriage. It would be better to stay in Rougemont,[1] even though it will be February and the house still not finished. You must face up to your new life from the very start – and also it will be the best way of preventing your mother-in-law from putting ⟨her finger in the pie⟩.[2] I forgot to mention this yesterday to Mme Innes, but I know she will agree with me, as will Mme Delessert. You will do well to think about such things yourself from now on.

I kiss you and cordially press Mme Innes's hand.

I. Turgenev

76. To I. P. BORISOV

Ivan Petrovich Borisov (1832–71), landowner in Oryol Province, a friend and neighbour of Turgenev's, Fet's and the Tolstoys'. A gentle, kind man, he had an unhappy life. His father was hanged by his own peasants and he was brought up by a neighbour who cared little for him. As a young man he fell in love with Fet's sister, Nadezhda, proposed, but was rejected. He spent eight years in the army, returned, proposed again and received the same answer; he tried to commit suicide but the pistol misfired. Finally in 1857 Nadezhda consented to marry him, he resigned from the army and the couple settled down to being minor landowners. A year later a son, Pyotr, was born. Ten years later in 1869

[75] 1. Rougemont (Eure-et-Loire), some eighty miles to the south-west of Paris, was the site of the factory managed by Paulinette's future husband, and the home of his parents.
2. Original in English.

76. To I. P. Borisov

Nadezhda, who had suffered since childhood from periodic serious mental disorders, died under the most pitiable conditions in an asylum. Sadly, their son developed the same illness as his mother and died in hospital aged only thirty. Borisov bore his misfortunes better than most could have done, and it was his friendly and mild personality, and his love of shooting, which drew Turgenev to him. Sixty-five of Turgenev's letters to Borisov survive.

[Original in Russian]

Baden-Baden, 28 March 1865

Dear Ivan Petrovich,

You will not believe how much I enjoy receiving letters from you. While they of course remind me of a man of whom I am sincerely fond, they are also almost my only contact with a certain 'essence' of Russian life which grows weaker with every day and with which I am losing touch. I must admit that it is entirely my own choice – and it probably could not have been otherwise – but there are times when something akin to regret stirs in my soul. It would have been even deeper if I did not consider my work completed and so can live out my days anywhere. But I wish neither to upset myself nor to speak of myself; better to express the pleasure with which I recall our last meeting 'in the spring, to the song of the nightingale'.

Since your letter arrived I have managed to read Ostrovsky's play *The Voivode* and have begun Tolstoy's novel[1]. To my great regret I find the novel positively bad, tedious and unsuccessful. Tolstoy has lost his way – and all his faults appear clearly. All those little details, subtly observed and fancifully expressed, those trivial psychological observations which, under the pretext of 'truth', he draws from the armpits and other dark places of his heroes – how wretched all this is on the vast canvas of an historical novel! And he thinks this sad product is better than *The Cossacks*! All the worse for him if he is speaking sincerely. How cold and dry it all is, and how one senses a lack of imagination and the naivety of the author as the same trivial, incidental and unnecessary detail is paraded before the reader. And what sort of young ladies are these! All of them scrofulous poseuses. No, we just cannot have this; it's a waste, even with his talents. I find it very painful, and would hope that I am wrong.

On the other hand I found Ostrovsky's *The Voivode* very moving. Never before has such wonderful, tasteful and pure Russian been written. The last act (especially where the voivode chases after his fiancée to *tickle her to death*) is poor, but Acts II and III are perfection! How one can sense the smell of our Russian woods in summer. Even in that splendid scene 'The House Spirit'. Ah, our bearded one is a master, a master! And he knows exactly what he is doing. None of that 'striving to be over-particular', *chercher la petite bête*, as the French say. He has stirred my literary blood no end.

---

[76] 1. *1805*, the original title of the early parts of *War and Peace*. The first few chapters had been published in the *Russian Herald* in January and February 1865.

I am not 'avoiding' Katkov, as you suggest, although personally I'm not over-fond of him. But my larder is bare and I've swept out the last crumbs. What can I do now? I don't know what will turn up in the future, but at the moment I can only look at what others are doing.

I don't know what the weather is doing with you, but here and indeed over the whole of Europe it's simply terrible. It's been snowing heavily since yesterday evening and there's not a single bud on any of the trees. I've had enough of January! I must be thankful, though, that there's no typhus or anthrax. Come the first fine days and I shall leave for Novosyolki and Stepanovka.[2] Please send my best wishes to the owner of the latter and tell him that I can't wait to see his red nose again and listen to his charmingly bellowing voice. Send a greeting from me to your poet, Petya.[3] I shake your hand.

Yours sincerely,

Iv. Turgenev

P.S. My daughter was married a month ago and I am getting very happy letters from her. Her husband is a really pleasant and nice man. And very good-looking. His name is Bruère.

P.P.S. If someone is in pain, then he ought to mention it. If you should see my uncle, tell him that the 'bonds' (he'll know what I mean) are giving me no peace day or night.

77. To I. I. MASLOV

Ivan Ilyich Maslov (1817–91), civil servant, music critic, and close friend of Turgenev's throughout his life. They had first met in 1843 when Maslov was secretary to the Commandant of the Peter and Paul Fortress in St Petersburg. In 1860 he was appointed Director of the Office of Crown Lands in Moscow. When Turgenev was in Moscow he usually stayed at Maslov's flat. Forty-three of his letters survive.

[Original in Russian]

Spasskoye, 18 June 1865

Dear Ivan Ilyich,

Today I need to speak to you not about selling land nor about money, but about something completely different. Listen.

In 1851, 1852 and 1853 a young girl, by name Feoktista, lived with me here and in Petersburg. I formed a liaison with her. I later helped her get married to a minor official at the Navy Ministry and she is now prospering in Petersburg. When she left me in 1853 she was pregnant, and she later gave birth to a son, Ivan, in Moscow, whom she handed over to a foundling hospital. I have

2. The home of A. A. Fet.
3. Borisov's son.

sufficient reason for supposing that the son is not mine, but I cannot swear to it. He might be my offspring. This son, called Ivan, ended up with a peasant family in a small village in the country. Feoktista, who visited him last year without telling her husband, could not tell me where the village is or in which area exactly it lies; she could only say that it's about fifty versts away and is called Prudishche. She also thinks that a certain lady took the child in – conditions in the village were bad – but then was admitted to hospital. From this you may conclude that Feoktista is not the brightest of people. Now she's going to Moscow again (she dropped in here to see me – her husband's been sent to the Bogoroditsky district for a month) and I directed her to you to see if you could help her in her search. If this Ivan is alive and can be found, I would be prepared to send him to a trade school, and pay for him.[1]

78. To VALENTINE DELESSERT

Valentine Delessert (1806–94), née Countess de Laborde, was a friend of Turgenev's from the time he lived in Paris in the 1860s. She took a fond interest in the upbringing of his daughter and in fact first introduced her to Gaston Bruère, who worked at the time for her son-in-law. Thirty-nine of Turgenev's letters to her are known.

[Original in French]

Baden-Baden, 22 October 1865

Dear Madame Delessert,

Your short letter awoke in me feelings of both tenderness and gratitude which it would be difficult to define but which you will understand. I have just received (after a delay of three months) the last letter which you wrote to me in Spasskoye – the one where you speak about the branch of a lime tree, an allusion which I missed when I saw you in Paris – and I was about to break my long and unforgivable silence when news arrived about Paulinette's unfortunate accident[1] – and then your letter. I beg you to allow me to thank you sincerely. My son-in-law writes that Paulinette is making rapid progress and that there are no consequences to fear. I am told that such things often happen to young women recently married, and then they're both still young and so I still have the time to be a grandfather many times over. I must resign myself to having been deceived this time – and wait.

I have been thinking a lot of you recently. I have no doubt that the dangers of the illness[2] now sweeping Paris have been exaggerated, but it was painful (and still is) for me to think that you are still there. The air in Passy, and especially

[77   1. No information has survived on the existence or fate of this child.

[78] 1. Paulinette had just had a miscarriage.
    2. Cholera.

where you live, is extremely good, but you would do well to make many trips like the one you are making now, judging by the date of your letter. I shall stop worrying when winter has set in, for it is said that the cold is the best defence against infectious diseases.

The shooting season is in full swing here. Great *battues*, much slaughter of the rabbits, etc. I've enjoyed myself immensely, and a slight sensation of fatigue, not at all disagreeable, grips me continuously. The weather has been splendid so far, but I fear rain is on the way and I shall take advantage of it by getting down to some work, if I still can. My house is completely finished on the outside and I am at present laying out the garden. It will soon be November – the time for planting. It has taken up a lot of my time. Unfortunately the news from Russia is not good – cattle fever and the early frosts have caused me considerable losses – and money is hardly arriving in abundance. Also the exchange rate has fallen by at least a quarter. In a word – here too – one must be patient and wait.

I have received a pleasant letter from M. Mérimée – I have replied; today even! I am very fond of him and feel that he likes me a little too. I would like to continue writing if only to give him some work and to have the pleasure of seeing myself translated by him.

A thousand greetings to you and yours, starting with Mme de Nadaillac.[3] I plan to come to Paris sometime this winter, and it goes without saying that my first visit will be to you. Meanwhile, look after yourself, and please accept my most heartfelt gratitude.

Yours very sincerely,
I. Turgenev

79. To A. A. FET

[Original in Russian]

Baden-Baden, 6 April 1866

On the day when, according to the popular proverb, 'even the ravens stop building their nests',[1] I write to you, dear Afanasy Afanasyevich. I received your letter ten days ago, from which you may conclude that my laziness has not deserted me – but neither has my affection for you. I am sincerely glad to see that your health is satisfactory and that your affairs are going well. I am no less pleased (on behalf of the whole district) about your appointment as local councillor. And I suppose you are losing no sleep over the failure of Vasily Petrovich [Botkin] to arrive at Stepanovka. May God grant you all the best in your little nest on the steppes! And all of us over here will be able to read your letters 'From the Country' in the *Russian Herald*, which I await with great impatience.

Of the two poems that you sent me, the one (published) addressed to

---

3. Mme Delessert's daughter, Cécile.
[79] 1. i.e. 25 March, old style, the Feast of the Annunciation.

Tyutchev is excellent – it breathes of the old (or rather the young) Fet. The other is not satisfactory. 'Why?' you will ask. 'Critic, explain yourself!' With your permission, I shall. In the first place it reminds me – in tone and also in certain details – of two poems by Pushkin and Tyutchev, both of which are much better: 'I remember the wonderful moment' and 'As the stars in heaven at night'. Secondly, what is 'To send a greeting *from memory*'? That's very ugly. How is it possible to 'delight someone's sadness'? 'All the simplicity of your heart' and 'The star and the rose' are pale prose. And finally, 'In the dark sky and the water' – you might just as well have written 'in the washbasin'. There is one other thing that I have noticed: all your personal, lyrical love poems, especially the passionate ones, are weaker than the others. You have simply composed them, when no subject for a poem existed.

I have received a letter from Mrs Engelgardt[2] and have already replied.

It would appear that I shan't be coming to Russia this year and so I shan't see you unless you would like to come and stay with us. Viardot and I have hired another shoot to add to the one we have already, and so now we can invite our friends. We'll be able to bag up to three hundred rabbits alone.

I am getting the journals this year and am again following Russian literature – without much pleasure. The best thing is the revival of *The Messenger of Europe* by Kostomarov.[3] The first part of Dostoyevsky's *Crime and Punishment* is remarkable but the second smells of fusty introspection. The second part of *1805* is also weak; it's all so petty and complicated, and surely Tolstoy gets bored with all those *interminable discussions* about, say, Am I a coward, or am I not? All this pathology of battle. Where are the main features of the period, the historical colour? The figure of Denisov is well drawn, but he would have been better as part of the background – but there is no background.

However, *basta!* I've done nothing but carp today. I shall conclude by embracing you and sending greetings to your wife.

Iv. Turgenev

80. To P. V. ANNENKOV

[Original in Russian]

Baden-Baden, 18 April 1866

You may easily imagine, dear Pavel Vasilyevich, the feelings which were aroused in me by the news of that disgraceful event in Petersburg.[1] Furthermore, there was a rumour here that the Tsar had been seriously wounded.

---

2. Sofya Vladimirovna Engelgardt (1828–94), minor writer who used the pseudonym of Olga N.
3. Nikolay Ivanovich Kostomarov (1817–85), Russo-Ukrainian writer and poet.

[80] 1. On 4 April 1866 a conspiratorial group calling itself 'The Organization' arranged the first attempt on the life of Alexander II. As the Tsar was taking his usual stroll in a park in St Petersburg, one of the group's most fanatical members, Dmitry Karakozov, a twenty-five-year-old law student, shot at him. Fortunately one of the bystanders knocked the pistol upwards and the bullet missed. Karakozov was arrested and hanged.

Fortunately I soon heard of the true contents of the telegram. All the Russians living here attended a thanksgiving service and I can say that just this once there was no difference of opinion. Everyone's feelings were the same. One cannot help shuddering at the thought of what would have become of Russia if this act of villainy had succeeded. But now I have an urgent request to make of you: you must tell me all you can find out about this Petrov.[2] It's not simply idle curiosity; it's extremely important for me to know all about his past and what could have brought him to commit such a crime. I imagine it will be some time before the journals report any positive information. You will greatly oblige me if you can fulfil my request.

I cannot write about anything else. I have been too shaken by this one event to think properly. I have read my story[3] in no. 85 of the *St Petersburg Gazette* and expect some offprints. And so farewell, look after your health . . .

81. To P. J. HETZEL

Pierre Jules Hetzel (1814–86), French publisher, novelist and writer of children's stories under the name of P. J. Stahl. He first met Turgenev at the beginning of the sixties and they were friends for the rest of Turgenev's life. Hetzel published in French almost all of Turgenev's works written after 1862. A hundred of Turgenev's letters to him have survived.

[Original in French]

Baden-Baden, 7 June 1866

Dear Sir,

I have just received a letter from the kind and excellent Mérimée who with his customary kindness has offered to put his name to the volume you plan to publish. I have also heard from M. de Mars that the story about which I wrote to you (*Ghosts*) will appear on 15 June in the *Revue des Deux Mondes*. This will delay (at least I believe so, not knowing the practice here) the appearance of a separate edition. But in any case you know I have the following ready for the printer: 1) *The Jew*, 2) *Petushkov*, 3) *Annushka* (which Mérimée has read with M. Pagon-kin[1] and which he quite likes), and 4) a story which I forgot to mention called *The Dog* which Mérimée is at present translating. These will make quite a large volume if we also include *Ghosts*. You have only to say the word and I'll send you copies of the originals. But perhaps we would do better to postpone it until the winter. But please do as you think best.[2]

2. First reports stated that the would-be assassin was Alexey Petrov.
3. *The Dog*.

[81] 1. The only thing known about him is that he collaborated with Mérimée on the translation of *Annushka* and probably did one of *Asya* as well.
2. The collection appeared as *Nouvelles moscovites* in 1869.

The Viardot children thank you effusively – no, children cannot thank *effusively* – rather they thank you very much for the charming books which I gave them in your name.

We are anxiously awaiting the first cannon shot here. But when will that be? I cordially press your hand.

Ever yours,
Iv. Turgenev

82. To W. R. S. RALSTON

William Ralston Shedden Ralston (1821–89) was one of the pioneers in introducing Russian history and literature to the English reading public. He was a librarian at the British Museum in London for over twenty years and played a crucial part in building up its Russian collections. His publications include a translation of Turgenev's *A Nest of the Landed Gentry* entitled *Liza*, an edition of Krylov's fables, a series of Russian folk songs and a collection of folk tales; he also wrote a series of introductory lectures on early Russian history and a number of articles and reviews on Russian literature. He visited Russia a number of times and his knowledge of the language was ultimately excellent. He first met Turgenev in the mid-sixties and the two became friends. They subsequently met frequently in London, Paris and Baden-Baden. In the summer of 1870 Ralston stayed with Turgenev at Spasskoye. His reputation in Russia was high, and he was elected a corresponding member of the Imperial Academy of Sciences. It was Ralston who first suggested the idea of awarding Turgenev an honorary degree at Oxford. Forty-four of Turgenev's letters to Ralston have survived.

[Original in French]

Baden-Baden, 19 October 1866

Monsieur,

I have received the letter which you had the kindness to send me, together with a copy of the *Fortnightly Review*. (Might I ask your permission to write in French? I know your country's literature well and I speak English reasonably fluently but it would be difficult for me to write in it.)

I read your excellent article on Koltsov[1] with the greatest of interest. I hardly knew him personally and only met him once or twice in Petersburg, but I was closely involved with a number of his friends, especially Belinsky, who also wished him to be better known and wanted his influence and the social role he played to be more widely appreciated. Koltsov was a true poet of the people – as

---

[82] 1. Alexey Vasilyevich Koltsov (1809–42), poet; the son of a peasant, he received no formal education; his poetry, dealing mainly with nature and peasant life, remains popular in Russia to this day. Ralston's article 'A Russian Poet' appeared in the *Fortnightly Review*, no. 6, 1866.

far as that is possible in this day and age – and if you do him too much honour in comparing him with Burns, whose nature and gifts are far wider and richer, there are nonetheless certain points of comparison between the two, and there are a score of his poems which will survive as long as the Russian language itself.

I cannot be other than happy to see that you intend to expand the knowledge of our literature amongst your compatriots. Apart from Gogol, I think that the works of Count Lev Tolstoy, Ostrovsky, Pisemsky and Goncharov would be of interest in that they show a new method of understanding and writing literature. It cannot be denied that since Gogol our literature has taken on an original character, but it remains to be seen whether this character is pronounced enough to be able to interest other nations. The approbation and sympathy of your country in particular would be most welcome – you must know how strong the influence of England is with us and how much your writers are appreciated. I repeat, I can only applaud your intention and congratulate my country on its good fortune.

It would be very agreeable to me to make your personal acquaintance and I willingly place myself at your disposal to supply any information you may need. I beg you to count on me for anything.

I plan to spend February, March and April in Russia, but I fear that I shall have left again by the time you arrive. I have no doubt that you will receive a warm welcome here, and I should be happy to contribute to it.

I learn with pleasure that the Mr Lewes[2] with whom I studied in Berlin in 1838 is the same man as the eminent biographer of Goethe. Please send him my regards and accept my sincerest good wishes.

I. Turgenev

P.S. If you wish to reply, please feel free to do so in English.

83. To M. N. KATKOV

[Original in Russian]

Baden-Baden, 25 December 1866

Dear Mikhail Nikiforovich,

I have just received your letter with the enclosed bills of exchange for 1200 roubles, for which I thank you. With regard to your wish to publish my novel [*Smoke*] in next year's first number of the *Russian Herald*, may I state the following? I could actually send you now the rewritten first half, but the fact is that I have never published any of my works without having heard the opinions of my literary friends and in consequence of which made numerous changes and corrections. This is now even more necessary than ever. I have been silent for rather a long time and the public, as always happens on such occasions, looks upon me with a certain mistrust – the more so now as this novel touches on

2. George Henry Lewes (1817–78), philosopher, writer, editor and critic. His *Life of Goethe* was published in 1855. See also headnote to letter no. 183.

many questions and has, for me at least, great significance. Consequently I would be very grateful if you would allow me not to alter my original plan, which was to bring the novel with me to Petersburg at the end of January, to have it read, and then to deliver it to you in Moscow at the very beginning of February so that it could appear in the February number. (*Fathers and Sons* also appeared in February.) Various matters prevent my returning to Petersburg before the end of January. You could announce in the January number of the *Russian Herald* or the *Moscow Gazette* the forthcoming publication of the novel, and you can do this with complete confidence, for I give you my word of honour that you will have the manuscript, fully corrected, in your hands by the beginning of February.

I would be very happy if my arguments have convinced you. Please accept, together with the expression of my gratitude, my sincere respects.

Iv. Turgenev

84. To T. STORM

Theodor Storm (1817–88), German poet and novella-writer. He was a master of the so-called frame technique of narrative writing, and his novellas have a strong feeling of his native North Germany. Perhaps his best-known works are *Immensee* and *Der Schimmelreiter*. He and Turgenev first met in Baden-Baden in 1865, when he stayed with Turgenev. Seven of Turgenev's letters to Storm are known.

[Original in German]

Baden-Baden, 20 January 1867

My dear friend,

You have probably already decided that I am a lazy correspondent and not very grateful for your extremely kind present. The fact is I did not want to write to you before I had read your charming little book, but I couldn't seem to find the opportunity, and when I at last read it – with great pleasure – on a journey to Strasbourg, I was then laid low by an enemy I had not encountered before – namely, gout. I had a rather serious attack and still haven't fully recovered, and I am writing to you in a semi-recumbent posititon. The pain, though, has almost disappeared. Old age has somewhat rudely knocked upon my door . . . but one has to put up with things if one can do nothing about them.

Your story [*Von jenseits des Meeres*] could not be better written nor more touching, and there is a quite unique poetic air around the figure of Jenny. The night with 'the marble statue' is a minor masterpiece. Such things give me great happiness amidst all the triviality and affectation of current literature.

I am very pleased that you like my stories. As for *First Love*, it is perhaps based too closely on my own personal experience, too realistic, and many think it rather overdone. Perhaps they are right. I can tell you nothing definite about a sequel to the two small volumes. I think my publisher feels they've not been very successful and is waiting to see how things finally turn out.[1]

I have been busy with a long novel [*Smoke*] which I am just completing. I am going to Russia in February and will have the thing printed in Moscow. I shall be back in Baden at the end of April and hope then to move into 'my little castle', as you call it.[2] I was overjoyed at what you told me of your life. You have built yourself a nest and are now sitting there cosily.[3] A large and beautiful part of your 'I' might have died, but that happens to everyone over forty. Young life is throbbing around you, the foundations of which you have laid yourself. If a man should desire more, the gods will punish him if they think they have granted him everything he deserves earlier. But such favourites are rare, and like all favourites they do not deserve the kindness afforded them. But one cannot change it.

I would also have preferred your story to have had a tragic ending, particularly from an aesthetic and misanthropic point of view, but younger people will like it better as it is. And one must bear them in mind too.

Mme Viardot thanks you for your greetings. She has composed a lot this winter, but all instrumental pieces for violin and piano. Her son Paul is making great progress as a violinist. She is soon going to Berlin for a couple of months. That will please the good Pietsch.[4]

Well, I cordially press your hand and wish you all the best in your 'grey town by the sea'.[5]

Yours,
Iv. Turgenev

P.S. I have passed on your greetings to Frau Anstett.[6] She was very touched and thanks you warmly.

85. To PAULINE VIARDOT

[Original in French]

St Petersburg, 26 February 1867

No. 1 (from Russia)

Dear and good Madame Viardot, ⟨dearest friend, my only adored being⟩,[1]

---

[84] 1. Two volumes of Turgenev's stories, translated by F. Bodenstedt, had been published in Munich. As they sold poorly, a planned third volume never appeared.

2. Turgenev actually moved into his new house on the Thiergartenstrasse in Baden-Baden in April 1868.

3. Storm had just married for the second time.

4. Ludwig Pietsch (1824–1911), German painter, writer and critic, a close friend of Turgenev's and the Viardots'. See headnote to letter no. 109.

5. A quotation from Storm's poem 'Die Stadt' (1852).

6. Minna Anstett (1818–1900); she and her husband owned a large house in Baden-Baden in which Turgenev rented rooms from 1863 to 1867.

[85] 1. Original in German.

85. To Pauline Viardot

Well, here I am in Petersburg and settled into a fine and well furnished room at old papa Botkin's – whom I found slightly aged and greying. My foot, which was looking decidedly poorly the day before yesterday when I dropped you a line from between Königsberg and Elbing, is a little better; the inflammation has almost disappeared, and I hope that two or three days of complete rest will restore it to the condition it was in Berlin. I was made to suffer a little at the frontier and at the customs, for I had to get out of the train and walk, etc. But it wasn't too terrible and you must not be at all apprehensive about me. I promise to write to you *every day*.

Annenkov has come to see me, of course. His wife has been seriously ill: she had peritonitis, like Jeanne,[2] but she's started to improve. My estate manager is here and I hope to see him today. It would appear that my uncle is being as stupid as ever and my presence at Spasskoye is unavoidable. I am writing to Katkov in Moscow to see if I have to go there immediately or whether I can stop off there on my way to the country, or vice versa. The first reading [of *Smoke*] is fixed for this evening. I shall stay here in any case for five or six days and you can send your reply to this letter here. I've sent a telegram with a pre-paid reply and sincerely hope it arrives today.

Here, and since I crossed the frontier, winter has set in, all white and cold, snow everywhere, sleighs, etc., etc.

I have begun to come to my senses a little, or rather, to keep my head above water. ⟨I cannot tell you how unbearably sad I was. Those days in Berlin; those unexpected and wonderful meetings; everything; and then the cruel parting. It was all really too much for me. I felt myself overcome by the weight of those unforgettable events, the like of which I had never experienced before. Ah, my feelings for you are too strong and powerful. I can no longer live apart from you. I must feel and delight in the nearness of you. A day which is not lit up by your eyes is lost. But enough, enough, or I shall lose control of myself . . .⟩[1]

I thought of you a lot yesterday evening while chatting to my two old friends. You were with Pietsch and I imagined you singing 'Räthsel', etc., etc. By the way, I think I've learned to sing it myself. You must have conquered everyone. I hope you'll send me the details, and about the Queen's soirée – your letter is on the way, is it not?

I must end here in order to catch today's post. I kiss Didie and send a thousand kind words to Désirée,[3] her mother, the kind M. Halpert,[4] who saw me off at the station – and I prostrate myself with inexpressible tenderness at your beloved feet. Be a thousand times blessed. (*Lock yourself in every night.*) Be well and happy!

⟨Your⟩[1]

I.T.

2. Jeanne Pomey, née Fawtier, wife of the French poet, translator and painter Louis Pomey.
3. Désirée Padilla, nee Artôt (1835–1907), Belgian soprano, a pupil of Pauline Viardot's.
4. A friend and neighbour of Turgenev's in Baden-Baden.

86. To N. A. KISHINSKY

The ravages to his estates and to his income which Turgenev believed were caused entirely by his uncle Nikolay's mismanagement of his affairs finally convinced him that he needed to replace him with a new manager. With the help of Annenkov, Turgenev appointed at the beginning of 1867 Nikita Alexeyevich Kishinsky (?–1888). Unfortunately for Turgenev, Kishinsky was to prove over the nine years he was in charge of the estates that if he was not incompetent at least he was dishonest. Despite Turgenev's innocence in business and financial matters, his own estimate that more than half of the income he had expected during Kishinsky's stewardship had somehow failed to materialize is probably not too far off the mark. Two hundred and forty letters to Kishinsky have survived, dealing mainly with the problems of Turgenev's estates.

[Original in Russian]

Moscow, 14 March 1867

Dear Nikita Alexeyevich.

I am still in my bed but the fever has passed and I shall be fully recovered within a week. I have written at length to my uncle telling him to hand over everything to you without waiting for me to get there and to provide you with all the papers, books, accounts and so on; in brief, everything. I do not think it necessary to repeat that you need not demand a full report but simply take over what you are given and make an inventory of it all. I have written to my uncle that he can stay in Spasskoye for as long as he wishes and that the servants looking after him and his family remain a charge on me. As for all the other people, that will depend on what arrangements you make. Besides the inventory, would you please send me a list of the old house servants whom I must still maintain. I also wish you and my uncle to decide at once which horses, cows, etc. will stay on the estate and which can be got rid of. Would you also check the current stocks of corn in the stores and see to it that no one thinks of taking advantage of the change in stewardship and removes them. I have also asked my uncle to do this and so help you. I've also written to him telling him to send me any money he has for me in the office, as I'm in need of it. Write to me immediately and tell me how my uncle greeted your arrival and how things are at Spasskoye generally. I suggest you move into the annexe.

Did you find the papers I mentioned and have you sent them on?

Yours sincerely,

Iv. Turgenev

87. To I. P. BORISOV

[Original in Russian]

Moscow, 16 March 1867

Dear Ivan Petrovich,

No doubt you know of the misfortune that befell me, namely the illness that struck me in Serpukhovo and forced me to return to Moscow and so postponed our meeting. However, my health soon improved and I am hoping to go out today for the first time. But a further obstacle has arisen. The first proofs of my story [*Smoke*] have been brought round to me from the *Russian Herald* and so I just can't move until I have corrected them, i.e. at least for the next ten days. And in ten days' time who knows what state our roads will be in? It might even be that terrible period when you cannot get through either by carriage or even on a sleigh. But needs must, even if I cannot for the life of me see how I can get there. My uncle won't agree to hand over the estate if I'm not there, and you can't do these things by letter. (I've already sent off my new estate manager – with luck he'll have already reached Serpukhovo.) The necessity of changing my manager will become clear to you from the following figures:

According to my uncle's reckoning, over the last eleven and a half years I have received 127,371 roubles and the odd copeck. Of this the capital (redemption dues, sales of forests, etc.) amounts to 63,564 roubles. Consequently I should have received 63,807 roubles, i.e. about 5500 a year. The quit-rent estates bring in 5756 roubles a year and my payments to the local authority are 3409, consequently I should receive 2347 roubles. If you add to this sum the money from rented property, the mill etc. I should have got an annual income here of about 5500 roubles. Furthermore it turns out that my vast estates, Spasskoye, Tapki, etc., have brought me literally not a copeck. Show all these figures to Fet, who wrote to Botkin that in getting rid of my uncle I've behaved like Satan. Would he be satisfied with an annual income of 5500 roubles from nearly 15,000 acres? [Ten lines omitted]

What is my dear Petya up to? Send him my best wishes and tell him that if the main road is still open and the rivers haven't inundated the whole of Tula Province I shall soon see him. Meanwhile I cordially and firmly press your hand and bid you farewell. I shall send you a copy of my latest story as well as my novel. But all of that lies in the future. Look after yourself.

Yours very sincerely,

Iv. Turgenev

88. To PAULINE VIARDOT

[Original in French]

Moscow, 28 March 1867

A climacteric year, a climacteric year, dear Madame Viardot! I cannot seem to get out of it. My foot is a little better and the reading planned for Saturday should now take place tomorrow, Wednesday. A further misery: Mr Katkov is creating so many difficulties over my unfortunate novel that I'm beginning to think it won't be possible to publish it in his journal. Mr Katkov is insisting that I turn my Irena into a virtuous matron and make all the generals and other gentlemen who appear in the novel exemplary citizens. As you can see, we are far from seeing eye to eye. I have made a few concessions but today I ended up by saying, 'That's enough!' We shall see if he gives way. As for me, I am determined not to budge an inch. An artist must also have a conscience and I do not want to give mine occasion to reproach me. So, in brief, you can see what a mess it all is, but come what may I'm leaving on Friday. I swear that as soon as I am back in Baden-Baden I shall heave such a sigh of relief that the mountains of the Black Forest will tremble!

Naturally things are going wrong with my uncle too. On top of all this the weather is awful; the snow for ever before one's eyes. It's making me quite ill!

But let us talk of other things. I am absolutely smitten by the Queen of Prussia, and if she should ever offer me her hand to kiss, I shall do it with the greatest of pleasure. It is impossible to be more gracious and one feels that she has the greatest affection for you, something which makes her charming in my eyes. Despite all that, it is not impossible that your military march will sound over the battlefield – near the Rhine. People are very worried here. The terrible fall on the Paris stock exchange which was announced here today by telegraph has given the most carefree of people pause for thought, and it is being said that despite the Exposition the French and the Prussians are going to take up arms against each other this summer. One must not deceive oneself; if it happens, Russia will clearly be on the side of Prussia, just like in 1815. Public opinion is very anti-French in our country and yet it's strange, isn't it, that in this affair it is Prussia that stands for progress, civilization and the future, and France, the son of the France of 1830, for routine and the past! . . . .

I know that it is unbearably long and tedious to copy out music, but do it, both for Gérard[1] and for your publisher in Berlin. I am sure that it will be very successful and encourage you to continue.

If God grants me life, in a week's time at this hour I shall have crossed the frontier, but one can know nothing for sure. In the meanwhile a thousand, thousand greetings to everyone. I affectionately kiss your hands.

Iv. Turgenev

89. To M. HARTMANN

Moritz Hartmann (1821–72), Austrian poet, publicist and journalist. An active liberal, he participated in the revolutions of 1848 and subsequently emigrated

[88] 1. Emile Gérard, a music publisher in Paris, was bringing out an edition of six pieces for violin and piano written by Pauline Viardot.

until 1862. He knew many of the Russian exiles, including Herzen, Bakunin and the various Turgenevs. During the Crimean War he was the correspondent for the *Kölnische Zeitung*. From 1859, three years after first meeting Turgenev, his poetry appeared in Russian periodicals. He translated many of Turgenev's works into German, including *Smoke*, *Mumu* and *Three Meetings*. Twenty-three of Turgenev's letters to him survive.

[Original in German]

Baden-Baden, 15 May 1867

My dear friend,

Mme Rashet has been here and has probably told you what is going on in Baden. The weather is marvellous, peace has been ensured, and my foot is getting better. I dare not hope that I shall see you here in the near future, but should you come with your dear wife, whom I thank for her kind wishes (I send her mine in return), you must stay with me. I am a confirmed bachelor, but whole ménages have already stayed with me.[1] Now, just reflect on that!

I was greatly honoured by your article on me in the *Ergänzungsblätter*. Unfortunately I do not know of any book specializing on my literary, etc., activities; there have been, though, many comments on me in the Russian press, but I'm afraid I do not have any to hand. The gossipy chatter which emanated from Lamartine (he honoured me with the whole of one of his *entretiens*)[2] will be of little use to you. As for biographical facts, luckily there haven't been any for the past three years – ⟨no news is good news⟩.[3] I have written a few new things – and that's all. You have the French translation of *Fathers and Sons*. Of all my works this little book has had the most influence on the formation of present-day Russian society, or at least on a part of it – and it would appear that I am the godfather of 'nihilism', about which so much has been said recently.

I am delighted at Catherine's good fortune; it is a real blessing for the whole family.[4] The shameful slanders that Catherine was the mistress of the King of the Belgians (!!) and that her child was *his* because Orlov was *impotent* (!!!) have now thankfully been disproved. Such things are disgraceful enough to have been hatched up by Prince Dolgorukov.

And so, until we meet again, the warmest of handshakes to you and your dear wife.

Yours,
I. Turgenev

[89] 1. Louise Héritte, the eldest daughter of Pauline Viardot, and her son had been the latest visitors.

2. Alphonse de Lamartine, the French poet, writer and statesman, published his 'Iwan Turguéneff' in volume XXII of his *Cours familier de littérature* in 1866. Although Lamartine included many wrong facts and some none-too-flattering literary judgments, Turgenev was later to say that Lamartine, and Mérimée, had done the most to further his reputation in Western Europe.

3. Original in French.

4. Princess Yekaterina Nikolayevna, née Trubetskaya (1840–75), the wife of the general and diplomat N. A. Orlov, had just given birth.

90. To D. I. PISAREV

Dmitry Ivanovich Pisarev (1840–68), literary critic and thinker, the chief representative of Russian Nihilism. He had a strong influence on the younger generation in the 1860s, and turned their attention away from the traditional social and literary values and towards the natural sciences. Almost alone of the radicals, he found praise for *Fathers and Sons*; certainly no revolutionary, Pisarev believed that Russia would be changed only by an intellectual élite which would emerge from the ordinary Russian people, and he saw Turgenev's Bazarov as the prototype of such an élite. While dismissing most art for its lack of any practical value, he insisted that his interest in Turgenev was utilitarian in that he showed what was wrong in society and pointed to a better way. While Pushkin was worth less than a pair of boots, Turgenev was useful. When the two met in 1867, Turgenev found his own views had much in common with those of the younger man, a rare occurrence for Turgenev.

[Original in Russian]

Baden-Baden, 4 June 1867

Dear Dmitry Ivanovich,

If you knew me better, you would probably not have felt it necessary to resort to reservations; there is nothing 'insulting' in your letter. I am not insulted very easily and am innocent, I think, of such a sin. On the contrary, I was very pleased with your review and am prepared to correspond with you – as a meeting between us does not look possible in the near future.

In common with most of my Russian readers, you do not like *Smoke*. In the face of such a unanimous response, I cannot but doubt the qualities of my creation; but your opinions seem to me somewhat unjustified. You remind me of 'Bazarov' and inquire 'Cain, where is your brother Abel?' But you have not considered that if Bazarov is still alive – of which I have no doubt – then one cannot refer to him in a work of literature: to deal with him from a critical point of view is not necessary, and from any other is not proper. And finally, he can now only *announce*, himself, that he is Bazarov; and while he has not yet done so it would be quite wrong, even hypocritical, to talk about him. Such a 'watch-tower' is probably unsuitable, and yet the little hill I chose for myself is not so low as you suggest. From the heights of European civilization one can still survey the whole of Russia. You think that *Potugin* (you must mean him and not Litvinov) is Arkady all over again. I cannot but say that your critical sense has deceived you here – between these two characters there is absolutely nothing in common. Arkady has no convictions whatsoever, while Potugin will die an inveterate and passionate Westernizer, and my writings have all been in vain if this fierce and inextinguishable fire does not come over. Perhaps this character is dear only to me, but I am glad that he has appeared, and is being attacked from all sides, at the very same time as a Pan-slavic intoxication has overtaken everyone in Russia. I am glad that at precisely this moment I have emblazoned the word 'civilization' on my banner, and may it be sprayed with mud from all directions. *Si etiam omnes, ego non.* There is nothing to say about Litvinov. He is not Arkady either; he is an ordinary, honest fellow and that says it all. It would have been very easy for me to include a sentence along the lines of 'there are now, however, sensible and powerful people working in silence', but out of respect for these people and their silence I preferred to proceed without it. There is no need to raise false expectations in the younger generation – at least, that is what I think.

And as for the 'roulade' at the end, you are aware that in opera there are occasionally 'inserted' grace-notes while other numbers are excluded; when the text is published separately everything is restored.[1]

You write to me that you are alone, that you do not have a circle of friends; this is both good and bad. A writer, especially a critic, should not be alone. You will tell me that loneliness is often something out of our control, and you would be right. I would not want to think that ⟨I am offering you biased advice⟩,[2] but there is scarcely a better motto for a sensible and practical journalist than 'European Civilization', even in the Potugin sense.

And so I wish you all the best – tranquility and activity – and with the greatest of respect, I remain

Your most obedient servant,
Iv. Turgenev

91. To V. P. BOTKIN

[Original in Russian]

Baden-Baden, 6 October 1867

Dear Vasily Petrovich,

Mr Schuyler, my American translator, passed through here and gave me four copies of *Fathers and Sons*, and so there is no need to worry about them.[1] It is clear from the translation that it was made from the French and that Mr Schuyler's knowledge of Russian is rather limited. He has been appointed American Consul in Moscow and has already arrived there.

What you say about the operettas is true, but the second, *Le dernier Sorcier*,[2] belongs to precisely the type that you recommend, and I know of no music more poetic than that composed for it by Mme Viardot. Everybody who has seen it (and amongst them are some excellent musicians – as, for example, Mme

---

[90] 1. A reference to the omission of certain words from *Smoke* due to worries about the censorship; when the novel appeared as a book Turgenev planned to reinstate them.
2. Original in French.
[91] 1. Eugene Schuyler (1840–90), diplomat, poet and translator. He published translations of *Fathers and Sons* (1867) and of Tolstoy's *The Cossacks* (1873).
2. One of four operettas, music by Pauline Viardot, libretti by Turgenev, which they concocted between 1867 and 1869.

Schumann,[3] Rubinstein, Rosenhaim,[4] and Lewy, the director of music in Karls-ruhe) has recommended her to orchestrate the score; they also say that there is no reason why *The Last Sorcerer* should not be staged anywhere. I am certain that it would be a great success. The music critic of the *Athenaeum*, Chorley, is of the same opinion.[5] It has, amongst other things, a love duet the like of which I know in very few other operas. You will be able to hear it all if you come to Baden next year. The performances are staged in my house. I am not living there for the time being and can scarcely see myself there before the spring, as my uncle has quite ruined me, even fleecing me – over all of ten years – of the interest on his worthless bills of exchange. I shall definitely get hold of the articles by Ambros which you recommended, and read them.[6]

Everything proceeds here calmly and peacefully; the weather, though, is enough to make you ill. It's as cold as winter already. No one can remember such an October.

The conviction that war will break out next spring is very widespread here and there is general horror at the financial chaos in France. Matters have clearly taken a turn for the worse there.

Milyutin[7] is a little better and was well enough to attend one of Mme Viardot's little soirées. We're expecting Cherkassky,[8] Samarin and even Arapetov.[9] Where do you plan to spend the winter?

I affectionately press your hand.

Yours sincerely,

Iv. Turgenev

92. To P. I. BARTENEV

Pyotr Ivanovich Bartenev (1829–1901), eminent historian. From 1859 to 1873 he was director of the Chertkov Library in Moscow; in 1863 he founded the journal *Russian Archive*, which he edited until his death and which contained a mass of documentary material on eighteenth- and nineteenth-century Russian history and literature. Seven of Turgenev's letters to him are known.

3. Clara Schumann (1819–96), the widow of the composer, settled for some time in Baden-Baden and was a frequent visitor to the home of Pauline Viardot.

4. Jakob Rosenhaim (1813–94), German pianist and composer.

5. Henry Chorley (1808–72), writer and critic, editor of the London *Athenaeum* for a number of years and a friend and correspondent of Turgenev's.

6. August Wilhelm Ambros (1816–76), German music critic and historian, teacher and composer.

7. Nikolay Alexeyevich Milyutin (1818–72), deputy Minister of the Interior, important civil servant, influential in the preparations for the Emancipation of the Peasants, and close friend of Turgenev's.

8. Prince Vladimir Alexandrovich Cherkassky (1824–78), writer, political and social figure; a Slavophile, he also played an important part in the preparations for the Emancipation of the Peasants.

9. Ivan Pavlovich Arapetov (1811–87), important liberal civil servant. Turgenev portrayed him as Pomponsky in *A Quiet Spot*.

93. *To Y. P. Polonsky*

[Original in Russian]

Baden-Baden, 3 January 1868

Dear Pyotr Ivanovich,

It has come to my attention that a letter (which must not be published before 1890) written by Mr Dostoyevsky has been sent to you at the Chertkov Library, in which he sets out various outrageous and preposterous opinions on Russia and the Russians which he attributes to me. These opinions, which contain my supposedly deepest convictions, were expressed by me in his presence, according to Mr Dostoyevsky, during the only meeting with which he honoured me in Baden-Baden this summer. Leaving aside to what extent such a misuse of trust might ever be justifiable, I feel obliged to state on my part that I would consider any expression of my deepest convictions before Mr Dostoyevsky quite inappropriate, inasmuch as I consider him a man who, because of his epileptic fits and other things, is not in full control of his mental faculties; furthermore this opinion of mine is shared by many other people. I have met Mr Dostoyevsky, as I said before, only the once. He was with me for no more than an hour and, having relieved himself of the most savage abuse of the Germans, of myself and my last novel, he left. I had scarcely the time nor the slightest desire to argue with him. I repeat that I treated him as I would a sick man. It is probable that his disturbed mind led him to draw those conclusions which he would like to have heard from me and has attributed to me – his own . . . report to posterity.

There is no doubt that by 1890 neither Mr Dostoyevsky nor myself will attract the attention of our fellow-countrymen; however, should we be not utterly forgotten, we will be judged not by unilateral declarations but by our whole lives and works. I nonetheless felt it my duty to protest here and now at such a distortion of what I think.

It remains for me to crave your forgiveness for having approached you without knowing you personally, and also to accept the expression of my complete respect and sincerity.

I remain your most obedient servant.

Iv. Turgenev

93. To Y. P. POLONSKY

Yakov Petrovich Polonsky (1819–98), poet and writer. He first met Turgenev in Moscow in 1841 and they remained close friends for forty years. Turgenev would often advise Polonsky on his poetry and frequently supported him financially. He was a deputy editor of the *Russian Word* for a number of years.

[Original in Russian]

Baden-Baden, 14 January 1868

Dear Yakov Petrovich,

My conscience was already troubling me terribly because I had not replied to your long letter containing your two poems when your latest missive arrived, and I can only hang my head in shame and reply immediately – and in orderly fashion.

In your marvellous poem *The Bacchante and the Satyr* 'she sought the hill' is wrong – not because I dislike it for its cynicism – I'm not afraid of that – but because it's funny, i.e. it has amusing connotations. She has such a large, excuse me for saying it, arse, that she would probably need at least a hill to sit down. And I just cannot allow the epithet 'windy' – it's completely the wrong tone . . . but the poem is nonetheless excellent.

Unfortunately I cannot say the same about the other two. The idea behind 'The Eagle and the Snake' is original, but how could you suddenly lose the thread of the allegory to such an extent that you make the snake speak of his *fateful* ambitions and of having been born to be a genius!
[Twelve lines omitted]

Everything that you write about your life and what you are doing, and about the state of literature today, is extremely interesting. As far as I can judge from this distance, it appears that there is something of a renaissance; we shall see what comes of it. The lack of any talented people, especially talented authors, is our misfortune. Since the appearance of Lev Tolstoy there has been nothing – and his first story was published in 1852! One cannot deny that all these Sleptsovs, Reshetnikovs, Uspenskys[1] etc. are competent writers, but where is the imagination, the strength, the flight of fantasy, or the *inventiveness*? They cannot *invent* a thing and, if you will, are pleased about it. They say we think we are closer to the truth. But truth is like air: without it you cannot breathe; yet art is like a plant, sometimes admittedly a little strange, but which ripens and develops in that air. And these gentlemen are *sterile*; they cannot *bring life* to anything.

Fet will be well advised to keep his word and cease writing poetry. What's the use of going on repeating himself in such a weak and paltry way? I am very fond of him, though, and we correspond with each other and argue in every letter.
[Five lines omitted]

I shall see you in April and shall be able to embrace you. Until then, look after your health and be happy. Please send my cordial greetings to your wife (and when I get to Petersburg I shall teach her to play chess better); I press your hand.

Yours,
Iv. Turgenev

---

[93] 1. Vasily Alexeyevich Sleptsov (1836–78), realistic writer and radical, mercilessly lampooned in Leskov's *No Way Out*. Fyodor Mikhaylovich Reshetnikov (1841–71), whose vivid novel of peasant life *The People of Podlipnoye* (1864) was to play an important part in the creation of the 'repentant noblemen' of the later sixties and seventies. The writers Nikolay Vasilyevich Uspensky (1837–89) and his cousin Gleb Ivanovich (1843–1902). See also headnote to letter no. 208.

94. To P. J. HETZEL

[Original in French]

Baden-Baden, 25 February 1868

My dear friend,

I am very happy to learn that you have arrived safely in Paris and have taken a good supply of fresh air with you.

I shall send you immediately the two sheets.[1] There is an old custom of writing two fs at the end of Russian names, but like many an old custom it doesn't make a lot of sense. The Russian f is far *weaker* than the French – but down with habit! As for the I. before my name (I am Ivan or Jean as you prefer), I think you'd better include it because there is another Turgenev who writes in French[2] and we do not want him to have to defend a book which is causing so much indignation.

Prince Golitsyn[3] has written to me specifically to request that we do not mention his name, and as we have had to make so many changes we shall name no one.

Our poor friend Viardot is not at all well. He has had bronchitis and it has now gone on to his lungs. He has been confined to his bed for a few days, and that is what has kept me here. But I hope to come to Paris towards the end of this week. The train leaves at six in the morning; I shall inform you at nine, and we can eat together at eleven.

Yours sincerely,

Iv. Turgenev

95. To P. V. ANNENKOV

[Original in Russian]

Baden-Baden, 26 February 1868

Your letter found me still here, dear Pavel Vasilyevich. I was detained in Baden by a very serious illness which struck Viardot and which only ceased to give concern two days ago. If everything turns out well, I shall be leaving on Sunday to spend a week or so in Paris. But I wish to have a word with you first. Firstly, would you give the enclosed letter to Korsh[1] and ask him to print it in the *St Petersburg Gazette*? I have always been sorry for that unfortunate young man; he is still being kicked around even after his death.[2] Secondly, I can tell you that I've

[94] 1. Proof copies of the French translation of *Smoke*.

2. i.e. Nikolay Ivanovich Turgenev.

3. Prince Avgustin Petrovich Golitsyn (1824–75), the original translator of *Smoke* into French.

[95] 1. Valentin Fyodorovich Korsh (1828–89), journalist and literary historian, editor of the *Moscow Gazette* from 1856 to 1862 and the *St Petersburg Gazette* from 1863 to 1874.

2. Artur Ivanovich Benni (1840–67), radical journalist, with British citizenship; arrested for distributing Herzen's works in Russia, he was tried in 1865 and deported. Turgenev's letter, defending Benni's reputation, was published in the *St Petersburg Gazette* on 6 March.

read Tolstoy's novel and your article on it.[3] I don't wish to flatter you, but it is the best thing that you've done for a long time; the whole article is evidence of the subtle and accurate critical acumen of its author and only in one or two places is there an obscure or slightly confusing phrase. The novel itself aroused in me the most lively interest: there are whole dozens of pages which are marvellous, first-rate – all the domestic and descriptive passages (the hunt, the sleigh-ride at night etc.); but the historical addition, with which his readers are particularly delighted, is a puppet comedy and charlatanism. Just as Voroshilov in *Smoke* casts dust in people's eyes by quoting the last pronouncements of science (without knowing the first or the second, which is something, for example, that conscientious Germans cannot conceive of), so Tolstoy amazes the reader with the toe of Alexander's boot and Speransky's laugh, forcing one to think that he knows *everything* because he has gone into even these details – but it is only these details that he knows. A trick and no more – but the public has fallen for it. And there is much that could be said about Tolstoy's so-called 'psychology'; there is no real development in any of the characters (which, by the way, you pointed out very well yourself), and there is the same old way of transmitting the vacillations and vibrations of one and the same feeling or situation or what he so mercilessly puts into the mouths and consciousness of each and every one of his heroes. I love, someone says, but actually I hate, etc., etc. How sick and tired one is of these quasi-subtle reflections, these thought processes, and the observation of their own feelings. Tolstoy is either unaware of any other psychology or he intentionally ignores it. And how wearisome are those deliberate and insistent repetitions of the same old trait – the down on Princess Bolkonskaya's upper lip, and so on. But despite all this there are things in the novel which no one in the whole of Europe but Tolstoy could have written and which have aroused in me the chill and fever of ecstasy.

I have already written to you that I have received all the journals safely, but no copies of the translation of Ducamp's novel have yet arrived!![4]

Mérimée's two articles on Pushkin appeared in two issues of the *Moniteur* sometime between the tenth and the twentieth of January; the fifteenth, I think.[5]

I cordially press your hand, and remain,

Yours sincerely,
Iv. Turgenev

---

3. Annenkov's review 'Historical and Aesthetic Problems in Tolstoy's *War and Peace*' appeared in the *Messenger of Europe*, February 1868.

4. Maxim Ducamp's novel *Forces perdues*, which had an introduction by Turgenev, appeared in Russian at the end of 1867. See also headnote to letter no. 105.

5. Mérimée's articles, 'Alexandre Pouchkine', appeared in the *Moniteur Universel* on 20 and 27 January 1868.

96. To Y. P. POLONSKY

[Original in Russian]

Baden-Baden, 18 March 1868

Dear Yakov Petrovich,

Your last letter was filled with such despondency that I would have willingly paid good money to find the right words to cheer you up and reassure you.

I shall say only this: just as in the final analysis no one can pass himself off for more than he really is, so it is true that something that is really there will be recognized – in the long run. Your talent is not something which you have imagined – it is really there and will probably not fade and die. That things should at times go badly for you in this anti-poetic age is not something you can do anything about. But you mustn't grow despondent. If a man doesn't help himself, no one else will bother to.

For instance, you ought to try to get rather more out of Volf,[1] and then, sitting by the sea, await fair weather – but not just sitting with your arms folded, but working. Whatever they may say, you are a poet, if only for 'The Grasshopper'; and your 'Grasshopper' will be read when many of our clever modern people and inventions have long since sunk into obscurity.

I am very glad that in connection with my *Story* you prefer to trust your own impressions rather than the sentence pronounced by Mr P. Kovalevsky.[2] This gentleman (and I say this not because he criticizes me but from comments made about him), after the death of a certain Russian émigré, V. I. Kasatkin, showed himself to be in my eyes the stupidest of all our contemporaries.[3] That Privy Fool with a portrait of the goddess of idiocy in his buttonhole! With a very fitting flair for such things, he sits in the mire and affirms that my little bagatelle was rushed off as if it were a *feuilleton*. I have never worked harder on anything – I rewrote the wretched thing three times! But enough of this.

There is no article by Annenkov on *War and Peace* in the *Russian Herald*, but there is one in the *Messenger of Europe* – and everything he says in it is very wise and sensible, although some of it is a little obtuse. Tolstoy's novel is a wonderful thing but its weakest side is precisely what everyone is delighted with: the history and the psychology. His history is a trick, the throwing of subtle little details in one's eyes, and the psychology is just a capricious and monotonous concern with the same sensations. But all the domestic, descriptive and military passages are first-rate. And we haven't any great writers other than Tolstoy.

The lines you wrote about me can also be an instructive example for you: you see, a certain gentleman quite unashamedly asserts that I have sacrificed my honour for the sake of my hurt pride, just like Chernyshevsky announced in print that I had been *bribed with money* to change Rudin's character for the worse.

[96] 1. Mavriky Osipovich Volf (1825–83), St Petersburg publisher and bookseller.

2. Pavel Mikhaylovich Kovalevsky (1823–1907), poet, writer and art critic, had been, according to Polonsky, very scathing about Turgenev's *The Story of Lieutenant Yergunov* (1868).

3. Viktor Ivanovich Kasatkin (1834–67), writer. He was closely connected with the activities of Herzen in London. He is probably the prototype of Pishchalkin in *Smoke*.

Well, my brother? These things are like the torrents of spring – they rush along but leave no trace of their passing. But you've no need to grieve over it.

I cordially press your hand and wish you all the best, especially to be of good heart.

Yours sincerely,
Iv. Turgenev

97. To M. HARTMANN

[Original in German]

Baden-Baden, 21 March 1868

Dear friend,

What you say about my novel has delighted me.[1] You are correct in thinking that it has made me a lot of enemies, but one true friend as yourself outweighs a thousand such enemies. In the final analysis every honest man must express the truth as he sees it, even if he should be hit by the ricochet. Things started to go badly for me with my *Fathers and Sons*. I am now possibly the most unpopular man in the whole of Russia. I have insulted our national pride and *that* is more unforgivable than anything. Never mind! Things will sort themselves out. I haven't lost any sleep over it.

I do not think that *Smoke* will translate very well into German; it is too Russian. You can of course judge better than I, but I am very dubious.

I am very pleased that you have translated my *Diary [of a Superfluous Man]*. It contains a slice of real life. If you have the time, read *The Upas-tree* from my *Sportsman's Sketches* and tell me what you think of it.

I would like to repeat that your suggestion of translating my works gives me no little pride.

I am going to Paris for a week and then I shall return here before going to Russia at the end of May. Will we see you here before then? That would be splendid! All the Viardot family send you their best wishes. I press your hand and ask to be remembered to your dear wife.

Yours,
Iv. Turgenev

98. To PAULINE VIARDOT

[Original in French]

Paris, 25 March 1868

Dear Madame Viardot,

I have just come back after a performance of *Hamlet* at the Opéra.[1] Do you

[97] 1. Turgenev had sent Hartmann the French translation of *Smoke*.
[98] 1. A. Thomas's *Hamlet* was first performed on 9 March 1868.

recall Saint-Victor's[2] review of it? What he wrote is absolutely right. The music is quite empty. It's cold, impotent, vulgar, insignificant, colourless, lifeless – in a word, nothing! Except perhaps for two arias. But I hasten to add that Nilsson[3] was quite charming and one could not wish for anything more graceful than her big scene in Act IV. As for her bearing and manner, imagine Mlle Holmsen,[4] but *extremely* idealized. She also has those quick little movements of the head and arms and that same sort of harsh and jerky pronunciation. It's probably because she's Swedish, but her performance as a whole was charming, pure, virginal, almost severely virginal – *herb*, as the Germans would say. She has a pretty voice but I fear that she will not long be able to resist the *urlo francese*. Faure[5] was, as ever, 'magisterial' with an irreproachable bearing and diction. But ultimately he is tedious. It's the professor who is singing. The libretto is quite simply absurd! In the last act the father's ghost appears in full view of everyone, even the villainous king, and orders Hamlet to slay the tyrant with his sword, which the latter does to general satisfaction, and the tyrant permits himself to die with resignation, just like a rabbit in a *battue*, the ghost being the beater and Hamlet the sportsman. The decor was *admirabilissime*, as were the costumes, and the production was splendid. I have never seen anything more beautiful than the scene in front of the court in the fourth act . . . But you must see Nilsson. The auditorium was full and in the Royal Box – the Emperor and Empress, and they stayed till the end!

I observed closely Viardot's friend,[6] and I could not have found him less attractive. I managed – in the end – to see his thick-lipped mouth behind all those moustaches; it is the same repulsive colour as the skin on his face; and that slightly sneering smile which goes from his right eye, or rather from the corner of his right eye, along his pale, wrinkled cheek, all making him look, as Viardot well knows, like a man untouched by intelligence. Now I've seen him, I would swear to it. He is a man who is clearly tired and satiated with life, but he is not ill in any way. There were a dozen or so cries of 'Vive l'Empereur' from the supers at his entrance. But that was all. The Empress has somewhat baggy cheeks and in general looks like a cocotte who has seen better days.

But enough for today. It is time for bed. A thousand greetings to everyone. I kiss your hands.

Yours,

Iv. Turgenev

2. Comte Paul de Saint-Victor (1825–81), French drama and art critic.

3. Christina Nilsson (1843–1921), Swedish soprano who sang at the Théâtre Lyrique in Paris from 1864 to 1866 and later at the Grand Opéra.

4. A pupil of Pauline Viardot's.

5. Jean-Baptiste Faure (1830–1914), French baritone and composer, popular at the Opéra Comique in the fifties and the Grand Opéra in the sixties.

6. i.e. Emperor Napoleon III. Louis Viardot, a staunch republican, had vowed never to visit Paris while the Emperor lived there.

99. To M. V. AVDEYEV

Mikhail Vasilyevich Avdeyev (1821–76), writer, particularly of novels – *Tamarin* (1852), *The Reef* (1860, dedicated to Turgenev), *Between Two Fires* (1868) etc. In 1862 Avdeyev was arrested in connection with the trial of M. L. Mikhaylov, co-author of a revolutionary pamphlet 'To the Younger Generation', and sentenced to internal exile. He escaped and emigrated to Western Europe in 1863. Although he and Turgenev had first met in the mid-fifties, it was not until both were living abroad that they became friends. Eighteen of Turgenev's letters to him have survived.

[Original in Russian]

Baden-Baden, 30 April 1868

I have just received your letter, dear Avdeyev, and hasten to reply as things are evidently rather urgent. First of all, about your translations. It is very difficult to get translations from foreign languages published in Paris because they do not sell well. We are no match for Dickens – and none of his novels has ever reached a second edition, while a certain *Monsieur, Madame et Bébé* by G. Droz is already in its twentieth. My books are indeed translated, but I have personally never received a single copeck for any of them. Occasionally, out of great kindness, the translator might receive three or four hundred francs. So as you can see, the prospects are not dazzling. I have no need to add that none of my books has ever sold all of even their first editions, i.e. 2400 copies. I was asked to talk my publisher, Hetzel, into printing *at no cost to him* an excellent translation of [A. K. Tolstoy's] *Prince Serebryany*, but I doubt if he'll agree. On top of this there is another difficulty. Your translation has been done by a Russian and is probably (I know Mme Chekuanova) in that Moscow French which the French find quite awful. It will be necessary to rewrite the whole thing, for we Russians do not even begin to suspect what purists they are. Two of my books were done in this way and the translators were informed that such a thing would not be accepted again. But despite all this, if you still want to try, send me the manuscript and I shall do everything I can. But I warn you, the publisher will be showing you extreme generosity if he even agrees to print it *at no cost to him*. (N.B. I received nothing at all for *Smoke*, which, *from the point of view of its sales in Paris*, is by far my most successful novel.) If they should pay even 300 francs, they will think it's the end of the world . . . Russian ladies who wish to earn their living should think of something else. But I repeat, send the manuscript; I'll do all I can.

My *Story* [*of Lieutenant Yergunov*] has pleased no one in Russia – without exception. Usually I am willing to agree with the critics, but I think this little story was undeserving of such dissatisfaction. If only I had expressed some *ideas* in it! I thought I had, but evidently I was mistaken.

I am setting off for Russia in a month's time, but I shall be in Petersburg only for a day or two. I shall have to spend six weeks in Moscow and in the country. It would be nice if we could see each other. I shall then return here to spend the winter.

I liked your novel less than your previous writings. It is written well and intelligently but seems rather long drawn out and intense. And there are rather too many love scenes.

I fully concur with your opinion of *War and Peace*, but parts of it are first-rate.

So, do not delay in sending me your manuscript. I cordially press your hand.

Yours sincerely,
Iv. Turgenev

100. To PAULINE VIARDOT

[Original in French]

Spasskoye, 13, 14 June 1868

I am here at last, dear and good Madame Viardot, at the end of my 'courageous journey'. I arrived at about 9 p.m. and Fet and G.[1] detained me almost by force. My estate manager is sporting a splendid beard.

My old chasseur, Afanasy, is falling into decrepitude, and my mother's ex-doctor, one Porphiry, with whom I made my first visit to Germany, has arrived to rent a little land I have in Oryol Province.

The whole house has been re-limed and painted, eveything is in order and not too unworthy of your visit with Didie which will be . . . in two years?

I haven't yet been to the gardens but I shall take a long walk tomorrow and have much to discuss with my estate manager. He will bombard me with requests all of which I am firmly resolved to fend off. I shall not lose a minute and trust I shall no longer be here in a fortnight.

At the moment Russia is making a disastrous impression on me. I don't know whether it's on account of the recent famine but it seems to me that I have never seen the houses so neglected or so many of them in ruins. All the faces are so emaciated, and so sad. Taverns everywhere and perpetual misery. Spasskoye is the only village I have seen up till now where the thatched roofs aren't full of holes, and the Lord knows how far Spasskoye is from the smallest little village in the Black Forest!

As I write this and think of the enormous, the infinite distance which separates us, my blood turns to ice. I beg you all to look after yourselves, all of you, the whole household!

I shall go to bed with a strange feeling. I feel that I shan't fall asleep at once. The ancient walls seem to look on me as a stranger, which I suppose I am. Sleep well, over there in my dear Thiergarten, and think of me. Until tomorrow.

Well, well, I was wrong. I slept very well and woke up rather late. I have just taken a long walk around the gardens, which looked immense. I think they

---

[100] 1. It is not known to whom Turgenev is referring.

would hold the whole of the Thiergarten valley. Memories of childhood assailed me, as they always do. I saw myself as a little boy again, much younger than Paul,[2] running along the avenues, lying in the strawberry-beds and stealing the fruit. There is the tree where I killed my first crow; there is the spot where I found an enormous mushroom; the place where I witnessed the battle of a snake and a toad, a battle which caused my first doubts about the goodness of Providence. And then there were memories of the young student and the grown man. I went to the grave of my poor Diane where the headstone I had erected had disappeared. All the trees have grown tremendously during my three-year absence; I could hardly believe my eyes! The lime trees are magnificent, the grass is alive with flowers although it is not as tall as usual; spring was cold and it is no warmer now. If it goes on like this and we have no rain, we shall have another poor harvest. There are still, here and there, a few lilacs in bloom.

I am sending Didie a sketch of a mendicant priestess who wanders from village to village. You will admit that it could not have been better drawn.

I hope there will be something for me in today's post. A thousand good wishes to Viardot and a thousand tender words to everyone. I kiss both your hands.

Yours,
Iv. Turgenev

101. To N. S. TURGENEV

Nikolay Sergeyevich Turgenev (1816–79) was Turgenev's elder brother. He was a pupil at the Artillery School and later served for three years in the Guards; from 1840 to 1849 he worked in the Ministry of Crown Lands. After a quarrel with his mother over his marriage to one of her maids, Anna Yakovlevna Shvarts, he settled on his father's estate at Turgenevo, which he inherited on her death. The two brothers had very little in common. While Ivan was kind, generous and practically and financially incompetent, Nikolay was cold, avaricious and an astute businessman. While not sharing any of his brother's tastes in painting or music (or even shooting), Nikolay did from time to time take an interest in Ivan's writings. Never at all close to one another, they nonetheless managed to be reasonably amicable when they met, although after Ivan's decision to spend as little time in Russia as he could, these occasions were rare. Their correspondence is concerned, in the main, with financial matters and inquiries about each other's health. On Nikolay's death Turgenev seemed, however, genuinely upset. 'We seldom met,' he wrote to Annenkov, 'we had no interests in common . . . but still, a brother! There is an unconscious bond of blood which is stronger than many others.' A hundred and forty-nine of Turgenev's letters to his brother survive.

2. Paul Viardot (1857–1941), later a well-known violinist.

101. *To N. S. Turgenev*

[Original in Russian]

Baden-Baden, 28 July 1868

Dear brother,

Your letter from Karlsbad found me consigned to bed at Maslov's in the grip of a painful attack of gout which, according to the doctors, I had no right to expect so soon after last year's visitation. On this occasion, however, it was reasonably bearable and just about allowed me to drag myself here three days ago, and although it was worse by the time I arrived, it's now troubling me less – because I am home. I shall certainly have to drink the waters somewhere next year. I spent a fortnight at Spasskoye and can say along with Marius that I sat in the ruins of Carthage. In the current year 'that ill-starred old man'[1] has robbed me of money, cattle, carriages, furniture and other effects to the tune of 36,500 roubles (and I had to pay a debt of his of 5000 roubles), to say nothing of the fact that he has left the estate in the most sickening disorder, swindled everyone and paid no one. I didn't find him at Katushishchi and was very glad. Throughout the time I spent at Spasskoye I felt like a hare on the run. I could hardly put my nose outside without being surrounded and assailed by house-servants, peasants, merchants, retired soliders, young girls, old women, the blind and the lame, neighbouring landowners and their wives, priests and sacristans, my own and other people's, all popping out from behind the trees, from under the bushes and even from out of the very ground – and all of them ragged and starving, with their mouths gaping like jackdaws, shaky on their feet and crying hoarsely, 'O master, Ivan Sergeyevich, save us, save us; we're dying'. In the end I had to save myself; I fled in order that I myself should have something left. On top of all this it appears the present year will be terrible – the spring wheat has failed, the amount of straw from the rye will be enormous but there is not a grain to be seen on it. What a sight Russia is at the moment, that Russia which everyone is convinced is such a rich land! The roofs are *all* full of holes, the fences are falling down, nowhere is there a new building to be seen – with the exception of taverns. The horses and cattle are dying and the people hollow-cheeked. Even three coachmen could hardly carry my trunk! Clouds of dust are everywhere, everything is on fire all around Petersburg – the forests, the houses, *the very land* itself. And the people – sleeping, stretched out flat on their stomachs. Debility, inertia, poverty, everything in an awful state. The picture is not a happy one – but it's *accurate*.

I trust both you and your wife will soon be fully recovered. Can you not come to Baden? The packet sent by Mr Zhikharyov (whom, by the way, I don't know) contained a photograph of Chaadayev's study; I've already been given *eight* such photographs. I'm beginning to think that my leg is being pulled.[2]

[101] 1. i.e. Turgenev's uncle Nikolay.

2. Pyotr Yakovlevich Chaadayev (1794–1856), thinker, who suggested in his famous 'Philosophic Letter' of 1836 that Russian history had no meaning – 'we are a blank on the universal landscape' – and that Russia would only have a future if she accepted the traditions of Western European civilization and joined the Roman Catholic Church. He was declared insane by the Russian authorities and placed under house arrest. Mikhail Ivanovich Zhikharyov (1820–?) was his nephew.

Write to me here, for I shall be here for a long time. I embrace you and send my best wishes to your wife.

Your affectionate brother,

Iv. Turgenev

102. To M. D. KHMYROV

Mikhail Dmitriyevich Khmyrov (1830–72), writer on history and geography, a biographer and genealogist. He wrote to Turgenev in connection with the preparation of the second volume of his *A Portrait Gallery of Famous Russians*, which was published in 1869.

[Original in Russian]

Baden-Baden, 20 October 1868

Dear Mikhail Dmitriyevich,

I have received your letter and willingly comply with your request. You will excuse me for not being able to reply to certain of your questions in detail; I am living abroad and do not have some of my works to hand and so cannot check them, and there are other things which I cannot remember.

1. I was born in Oryol on 28 October 1818.

2. My father was Sergey Nikolayevich Turgenev; he was from the Tula gentry and reached the rank of colonel in the army. My mother, Varvara Petrovna Lutovinova, was the daughter of Pyotr Ivanovich Lutovinov, a land-owner in Oryol Province.

3. My early childhood was spent in the country in the village of Spass-koye–Lutovinovo (district of Mtsensk, Oryol Province) with my elder brother Nikolay (born in 1816 and still alive) and my younger brother Sergey (born in 1821, died in 1837). In 1822 I visited Germany, Switzerland and France with my parents. When I was three I was so seriously ill that I had already been measured up for a grave; in Berne I almost fell into a bear-pit and my father just managed to hang on to me. I was frequently ill; I broke my left arm twice and my right once. My knowledge of Russian literature began with the *Rossiyada*,[1] which a valet of my mother's read to me in secret, repeating each line at first roughly and then exactly. I studied French and German from childhood and English from the age of fourteen.

4. I was educated at first at home and later in Moscow at the private *pension* run by Weidenhammer and at the Armenian Institute under Krause. At home I was educated by a succession of tutors, mainly French, etc.

5. In 1834 I entered the Faculty of Letters at Moscow University and transfer-red to St Petersburg in 1835; I graduated in 1837. I took further examinations in

[102] 1. Epic, patriotic poem by M. Kheraskov (1733–1807), who was known in his day as the 'Russian Homer'.

1838 and was awarded my Master's degree. In the same year I went abroad (and almost drowned during a fire on the steamer *Nicholas I* near Lübeck) and spent three terms at Berlin University. The teachers who had the most influence upon me were – before University, P. N. Pogorelsky (mathematics), I. P. Klyushnikov (history) and D. N. Dubensky (Russian literature); in Petersburg, Graefe and Pletnyov; in Berlin, Werder (Hegelian philosophy), Zumpt and Böck (Greek and Latin literature) and Hans and Ranke (history).

6. During 1843 I served in the Ministry of Home Affairs in the section run by the Minister (Perovsky) under the supervision of V. I. Dahl; but I did not have much to do and only made up the numbers; I retired in 1844 with the rank of Collegiate Secretary.

7. I have never married.

8. I have no legitimate children.

9. My father died on 30 October 1834, and my mother on 16 November 1850.

10. I cannot provide an accurate bibliography of my writings but I can give you certain data. The first things of mine to be published were two unsigned poems called, if I am not mistaken, 'The Oak Tree' and 'Greece'; they appeared in 1842 in Pletnyov's *Contemporary*. And then in 1843 a short poem 'Parasha', signed T.L. At this time I met Belinsky and began to write various things for the *Annals of the Fatherland*, poems, the play *Carelessness*, the story *Kolosov*, and others. I also wrote unsigned critical articles for this same journal, the most extensive of which dealt with Vronchenko's translation of *Faust*. The first of my *Sportsman's Sketches* appeared in the new *Contemporary* in 1847; it also printed the last things I ever wrote in verse. I never wrote poetry again. Almost all my writings appeared in the *Contemporary* up until 1859.

There have been four editions of my collected works: *the first*, in three volumes, in Petersburg in 1856 (published by *Annenkov*); *the second*, very bad, in Moscow, in four volumes, by *Osnovsky* in 1860; *the third*, abroad (published in Karlsruhe), by *Salayev*, in five volumes in 1865; and *the fourth*, also by Salayev, is now coming out in Moscow and will consist of *seven* volumes of which one will be devoted to my plays. Of these the following have been staged: *A Provincial Lady*, *Where it's thin, it tears*, *Lack of Money*, *Lunch with the Marshal of the Nobility*, *Alien Bread* and *The Bachelor*. None of them was very successful, but *Lunch* and *A Provincial Lady* are still in the repertory.

The following have been published in separate editions:

1. 'Parasha', a poem,
2. *The Conversation*,
3. *A Sportsman's Sketches* (two editions),
4. *A Nest of the Landed Gentry*,
5. *Fathers and Sons*,
6. *Smoke* (two editions).

My translation of one of Marko Vovchok's stories has also seen two editions.

In the last – complete – edition of my works the following were omitted: a few long poems and short verses, 'Parasha', *The Conversation*, *The Landlord*, and

Andrey and various critical articles (as the above-mentioned one on Vron-chenko's translation, one on Mme Tur's *The Niece* in the *Contemporary* and another on S. T. Aksakov's *Memoirs of a Sportsman*; there are others), and my translation of the last section of the first part of *Faust*, etc.

I hope that this list is what you want. Nothing important – if anything may be considered important in such a matter – has been omitted.

I beg you to accept the expression of my deepest respect and affection,

Iv. Turgenev

103. To I. P. BORISOV

[Original in Russian]

Karlsruhe, 28 November 1868

Would you believe, dear Ivan Petrovich, that when I received your last letter here I was horrified and even blushed to think how much I was in your debt. It is true that, this time at least, there is some justification. In the first place I did not know your Moscow address, and then I went to Paris for ten days. When I returned I found I had to move to Karlsruhe for the winter, find a flat – so far unsuccessfully – etc., etc. But I am still guilty and lay my head beneath your magnanimous sword! I have moved to Karlsruhe because the Viardots are here for the education of their children, and to have stayed in Baden without them would have been quite awful. So, please write to me here, poste restante for the time being.

I was not intending to go to Moscow in February, but to Petersburg, and as we shall not be far from each other, surely we can meet. Either Mahomet will come to the mountain, or the mountain to Mahomet.

I sent off my latest story to Annenkov and have already received an encourag-ing response. We shall have to see what the public thinks of it. I don't know why the rumour was spread that I was attacking the Slavophiles in the story; there's absolutely nothing like that in it. It is quite simply the story of a young girl who flitted through my life when I was a youth.[1] By the way, about the Slavophiles. You characterized I. S. Aksakov extremely well; I just had to laugh – his pen really does squeak!

I am sincerely pleased about Petya's success; I foresee a brilliant future for him, but not in poetry. His mind is far too lucid and subtle for that. Who knows, but by the time he grows up, we might need political figures! Send him a kiss from me.

It is true that V. P. Botkin is very poorly in Rome, but I wouldn't advise the Fets to make the long journey there: he won't change his will again.[2]

[103] 1. Susanna, the heroine of *The Unhappy Girl*, is based on Emilia Gebel (?–1833), whom Turgenev knew in his teens and who committed suicide after being jilted.

2. The Fets were hoping that Botkin would leave his sister, Fet's wife, a sizeable amount in his will. They were to be disappointed.

The fiasco suffered by Kishinsky over the sale of Uspensky's works has hit my pocket hard.[3] And it just goes to show the turn that public life has taken. Russia is clearly not what it was ten years ago. And we haven't seen such a change this century. The speed with which apparent riches have flown out of the window this year is quite remarkable; I know some fools – real ones – who, thanks to concessions they have been able to obtain, have suddenly acquired millions! And one's conscience forces one to take a mere 400 roubles for each printer's page which has caused so much sweat. There's little profit to be made from literature!

You write nothing about the fifth volume of *War and Peace*; surely it has come out? And what is its author doing?

I have received a long and extremely incoherent letter attacking Kishinsky; it tries to convince me that he is robbing me of thousands, etc. I have sent him a copy, although not the name of the writer. I'm sure it's all lies, but as you are on the spot could you perhaps keep your ears open and possibly find out the truth? You could then let me know.

Karlsruhe is a veritable monastery. The silence on the streets is such that one cannot but feel respectful. I must get down to some work for I have a mass of things to do in the next three months or so. By the way, would you be so kind as to see Salayev[4] and tell him that the portrait has been commissioned from the leading Paris gallery – E. Hédouin – and that the *Memoirs* are nearing their conclusion.[5] Have the first volumes of the new edition appeared yet?

I firmly embrace you. Look after your health.

Yours,
Iv. Turgenev

P.S. I enclose a photograph – awful, as usual.

104. To J. CARO

Jakob Caro (1835–1904), German historian and critic. He had sent Turgenev his article on Lessing's *Nathan der Weise* in which he had attempted to show Lessing's debt to Jonathan Swift.

[Original in German, translated from the Russian]

Karlsruhe, 26 December 1868

Dear Sir,

I have just read your article on Lessing and Swift with the greatest of interest.

3. Turgenev had sold some land on his Spasskoye estate in 1864 to N. V. Uspensky, but had received no payment for it. Uspensky had offered instead the royalties from his writings, which Turgenev later refused; the matter was finally settled at considerable financial loss to Turgenev.

4. Fyodor Ivanovich Salayev (1820–79), Moscow bookseller and publisher. He issued three editions of Turgenev's collected works in 1865, 1869 and 1874.

5. Edmond Hédouin (1820–89), French painter. He provided an etching of Turgenev for the frontispiece of Salayev's 1869 edition of Turgenev's collected works.

Your hypothesis strikes me as not only sensible but also psychologically sound and inherently convincing. Your description of the ideas of Lessing and Swift is quite admirable. I must admit, however, that not being a German I cannot fully appreciate Lessing's creative talents. I deeply respect his intelligence, his personality and his humanity; as a critic he is beyond comparison, and his prose is classical. His plays, though, distress me somewhat. His ideas are always important and well formulated but there is no poetry at all in their expression, and it seems as if he himself were aware of it. Despite the respect I feel towards him I cannot rid myself of the impression that I seem to see the great figure of Lessing himself standing over all his personages, with a gentle smile upon his face. He must surely be well aware that this is all didacticism. But with regard to the *Hamburgische Dramaturgie* and *Laocoön*, his letters and his demolition of Klotz, I know that I am dealing with a giant who has me under his complete command. He is singing here not falsetto but in his proper voice, and there is both life and passion.

The editors of the *Messenger of Europe* have told me that a review of your article will definitely appear in one of the first numbers of next year.

I remain,
Yours very faithfully,
I. Turgenev

105. To M. DUCAMP

Maxim Ducamp (or Du Camp) (1827–94), French novelist, short-story writer and traveller. He and Turgenev first met in the fifties but were not close friends until the second half of the sixties; they were to fall out when Ducamp attacked Flaubert for depicting him as Frédéric in *L'Education Sentimentale*, and Turgenev naturally sided with his great friend Flaubert. They renewed their acquaintance up to a point in 1881, when both were involved in raising subscriptions for a memorial to Flaubert. It was with Turgenev's help that a Russian translation of Ducamp's novel *Forces perdues* appeared, with an introduction by Turgenev. Sixteen of Turgenev's letters to him survive.

[Original in French]

Karlsruhe, 13 January 1869

My dear and good friend,

A thousand thanks for the trouble you are taking over my portrait. I have decided to withdraw my autograph and have written to Hédouin and my editor to this effect. I feel I am decidedly not yet a classic and I think that a portrait is going rather too far. Let us leave it until a 'post mortem' edition, if there should ever be one, and try to ensure that it's as far off as possible! I am pleased that you like the portrait, though.[1]

[105] 1. See note 5 to letter no. 103.

I am happy enough here in Karlsruhe. I have been working here rather more than in Baden-Baden and have had some excellent shooting. I was present at the massacre of some wild boar which had been rounded up into an enclosure (on the Grand Duke's estate). I even shot one myself, which one of the Grand Duke's men then waddled up to, smiling cheerfully, and finished off. He thrust his knife into its heart just as if he were presenting his visiting card, and then wiped the blade on its still heaving body with the smile still on his face. It reminded me of St Bartholomew and it seemed to me as if I were silently and in a cowardly way attending a murder. 'Cowardly' is just the word, for I was placed behind a sort of wooden fence and the unfortunate beasts were made to file past in front of us. But then I told myself that I had to experience this too.

What is Flaubert doing? Have you seen him? How is his novel coming along? Send him my greetings, and also to Mme Husson[2] and her husband and all my friends. The melancholy Viardot is reasonably well and I have passed on to him your handshake.

Pegasus[3] has finally lost the sight of one of his eyes, just like Hannibal, Sertorius, Philip of Macedon and Kutuzov of Russia. Despite his illustrious one-eyed colleagues I have noticed in him a marked degree of Christian humility – of the sort that arises when one can do nothing about things. He's also got a touch of sciatica in his left paw . . . Such are we all!

A thousand greetings,
Iv. Turgenev

106. To P. V. ANNENKOV

[Original in Russian]

Karlsruhe, 24 January 1869

The first number of the *Messenger of Europe* for this year arrived yesterday, dear Pavel Vasilyevich, and today I have been reading Goncharov's novel [*The Precipice*]. I find it difficult to tell you how disappointed I am with it. I shall say nothing about the unbearable, impossible and excessively 'superior' verbosity, nor about Mrs Belovodova, who reminds me of a German pharmacist, nor about her highly repulsive, repetitive and ruminating conversations with Raysky – and the rumination follows eating not grass but hay – but how old, out-of-date, conventional and ⟨commonplace⟩[1] it all is! What an absence of real, living truth! No! After L. N. Tolstoy on the one hand and Reshetnikov on the other (don't be surprised; I think very highly of him), such dank and artificial literature is no longer possible! It should be consigned to a museum. And why this enthusiasm for dealing with such a worn-out type as Raysky? Why so

---

2. Gustave Flaubert, the French novelist; see headnote to letter no. 113. Adèle Husson (1822–?), friend of Ducamp's and Flaubert's.

3. One of Turgenev's favourite dogs.

[106] 1. Original in French.

extensively and affectionately lard him and, again and again, put him in the mouth and spit him out? And what a crowd of old maids with hysterical, nervous complexions! Goncharov's style, which I once admired, now reminds me of the clean-shaven, good-looking but deathly face of a civil servant with his side whiskers delicately smoothed from his ears to the corners of his mouth. But if you take a breath you will come to the home of Tatyana Markovna and the provincial town – these are good, but only of the second rank. Just recall similar things in *War and Peace*. No, I repeat, all this is outdated. I do not know whether the novel will be a success with the public, but I know for certain that it will be praised only by the vulgar – whether intelligent or stupid, it makes no difference. It is written by a civil servant for civil servants and their wives. And what sort of woman could like Belovodova!!! ⟨Well, you can now cut my head off.⟩[1] Look after your health, ⟨you and yours⟩.[1]

Yours sincerely,

Iv. Turgenev

107. To Y. P. POLONSKY

[Original in Russian]

Karlsruhe, 11 March 1869

I thank you, dear friend Yakov Petrovich, for your long and interesting letter. It was really friendly of you. With the exception of yourself no one has said a word to me about my *The Unhappy Girl*, and it will probably suffer the same fate as *Yergunov*. But there's no use grieving about it. I am very well aware that my continual residence abroad is ruining my work as a writer, ruining it to such an extent that it's probably destroying it altogether. But I cannot change anything. As I have always, throughout my literary career, started not from *ideas* but from *characters* (and even Potugin started basically from a well known person), and as such *characters* are appearing less and less frequently, my muse will find nothing from which to paint her pictures. And I shall then hang up my brush and see what others can do.

[Sixteen lines omitted]

My reminiscences of Belinsky will not appear before the April number of the *Messenger of Europe*, but perhaps Annenkov will let you read the manuscript. There's no hurry, though.

The latest number of *Cosmos* has just reached me, the one where Antonovich[1] spends several pages dealing with Korsh and Nekrasov. It's heavy-handed and tasteless. Heavens, what wallowing in the mire! What evil he's sowing!

Let us hope your brother-in-law is not suffering from a mental illness but simply a fever from which he will soon recover.[2]

[107] 1. Maxim Alexeyevich Antonovich (1835–1918), left-wing critic; he wrote mainly for the *Contemporary*.

2. Nikolay Gavrilovich Barshev (?–1873), the husband of Polonsky's sister Alexandra; he was an alcoholic.

108. *To A. I. Herzen*

Farewell until May. I firmly press your hand. Please thank your wife for her kind wishes and send her mine.

Yours,
Iv. Turgenev

108.To A. I. HERZEN

[Original in Russian]

Karlsruhe, 18 March 1869

Dear friend Alexander Ivanovich,

The news about you is being refuted in the Russian papers (and even in Cologne), and they are talking only of the request by *your son* (I don't know if it's true) to return to Russia for a time to settle all your affairs. I've already let it be known in Paris that it's all nonsense. I don't think that on this occasion Shuvalov will put out any feelers;[1] I would be very surprised if they treated you in the same way as Kelsiev.[2] Do not forget that you insulted *the royal family* (the article on Alexandra Fyodorovna – your most *unforgivable* act)[3] and *they will never forgive you* for that. That fool Pogodin[4] is speaking the truth on this occasion, although probably not the whole truth. Any application must come, anyway, from you personally.

We cannot get the *Stock Exchange Gazette* here. If you could send it by letter post, I would return it regularly.

Bakunin has obviously changed his beliefs. When I last saw him in London he still believed in a personal God, and during a conversation we had – in the old romantic way, taking a stroll one moonlit night – he accused you of unbelief. Well? One must open one's eyes to the truth. But it's a question of whether declaring such things has any practical use. Do we have to say *such things* to the workers? There might be a small advantage, I suppose: if strong government does not exist anywhere in the world, then how could it exist under socialism? And then what would remain of socialism?

Some of Lassalle's disciples were here in Karlsruhe. They held meetings in various inns and preached their gospel, but they had no success.[5]

So what can I do? I shall remain an individualist to the very end and I shall not

[108] 1. Count Pyotr Andreyevich Shuvalov (1827–89), Chief of Gendarmes and Head of the Third Section from 1866 to 1873.

2. Vasily Ivanovich Kelsiev (1835–72), writer and revolutionary, who emigrated in 1859 and joined Herzen in London. He later 'repented' his former activities, was 'forgiven' by the Russian authorities and allowed to return home.

3. The wife of Tsar Nicholas I and sister of King Wilhelm III of Prussia. In his 'Most August Travellers' (1856) Herzen had ridiculed the recently widowed tsarina.

4. Mikhail Petrovich Pogodin (1800–75) had told Herzen that if he returned to Russia he would be imprisoned in the notorious Solovetsky monastery and then 'sent somewhere'.

5. Ferdinand Lassalle (1825–64), German socialist. His idea of state socialism envisaged cooperation between workers and government.

be won over by Bakunin's new word *congrégationiste*. I can see in what he wishes to represent by the word, however vaguely, the denial of personal freedom too.

> Look after yourself; I press your hand.
>
> Iv. Turgenev

109. To K. A. L. PIETSCH

Ludwig Pietsch, German painter, illustrator, essayist and critic. He first met Turgenev in Berlin in 1847, but their friendship really belongs to the sixties when he was a frequent visitor to Turgenev and the Viardots in Baden-Baden. It was through Pietsch that Turgenev met many German writers, critics, painters and so on. Pietsch corrected many of the proofs of German translations of Turgenev's works, especially those by Bodenstedt. A hundred and thirty-two of Turgenev's letters to Pietsch have survived.

[Original in German]

Baden-Baden, 3 June 1869

Dear Pietsch,

I wish to place myself on a par with the best of the nineteenth century and ⟨like a beggar⟩[1] crave some publicity for myself. Lend me an ear!

You write to me that you have to do a review of *Fathers and Sons*. Good! But make it one of those which are not only balanced, but vigorous. However, make sure you express in it your incomprehension and surprise that the younger generation in Russia has taken Bazarov for an insulting caricature and a slanderous political pamphlet. And also point out that I have made that young man too heroically idealized (which, actually, he really is) and that the young people in Russia are far too *sensitive*. Because of Bazarov, I have been showered (and still am) with heaps of muck and filth. So much abuse has been poured over my head, so many names have I been called, so often have I been damned to perdition (Vidocq,[2] a Judas who sold his soul for silver, an idiot, an ass, a poisonous toad, *a spittoon* are the *least* I've been called) that I would be gratified if it could be shown that other countries look upon me differently. I make so bold as to request this publicity because it is in full accord with the truth and in no way contradicts your own opinions. I would not otherwise, of course, have worried you. If you agree to comply with my request, please do so quickly, so that I can include a translation of the important passages in your review in my *Memoirs* which are due to be published soon.

Dixi et animam meam salvavi![3]

---

[109] 1. Original in French.

2. Francois Vidocq (1775–1857), French detective dismissed for instigating crimes. Balzac largely modelled his Vaudrin on him.

3. 'I have spoken and saved my soul.'

110. *To I. P. Borisov*

Mme Viardot has been in bed since yesterday; she has a cold but, thank Heaven, it's nothing serious.

Many greetings to all my friends, and keep in good health.

Yours,

I. Turgenev

P.S. And the *Feuilletons?*[4]

110. To I. P. BORISOV

[Original in Russian]

Baden-Baden, 5 September 1869

Dear Ivan Petrovich,

I have just received your letter and also one from Fet. What is meant by his news that he will come here, to Baden, by 20 September? It must be pure fantasy because you say nothing about it and he doesn't mention it again. It goes without saying that we would be delighted to see him here; we would be able to do some shooting. I hope his stomach injury has no serious consequences.

I imagine that you have already returned from Moscow after taking Petya there. The end of the vacation is bitter – I well remember it myself – as are the roots of learning, but its fruits are sweet. So long as you keep in good health!

As for my health I have nothing to complain about. It's improving. I have even been able to go shooting twice, taking great care, naturally; it was reasonably successful.

Your comments about building a new house at Spasskoye are very sensible. I've written to Kishinsky about it.

Would you also do me the favour of discussing with him whether it's worth sending me at the moment the money he received from the sale of my little village at Kholodovo (the last time I got 307 francs for 100 roubles !!!), but I suppose it would be best to send it as it's a rather large sum, 11,500 roubles, and it would be inconvenient to keep it there.

I went to Munich recently, amongst other things, to see the first performance of Wagner's *Das Rheingold*. Munich is an interesting city. As you probably know, the King of Bavaria is Wagner's bosom-friend, even his *odd* friend, and his music is an affair of state in Bavaria. But on account of various highly amusing and complicated intrigues which would have given Aristophanes the subject for a most entertaining socio-political comedy of manners, the opera was not staged, only the dress rehearsal, which I attended. The music and the libretto are equally unbearable, but as you know, there are some Germans for whom Wagner is almost Christ. I found the whole affair most amusing. I'll tell you about it sometime; I might even write something about it.

---

4. Turgenev's title for a series of articles that Pietsch was writing about his visit to Athens and Constantinople. They were printed in the *Vossische Zeitung* in 1869 and as a book in 1870.

I cannot do any work at all. I haven't even finished my damned *Memoirs*. My literary wheels have ground to a halt.

I do not yet know where I'll spend the winter, except that it won't be here. I'll let you know in due course.

Look after your health. I affectionately press your hand.

Yours,

Iv. Turgenev

III. To M. V. AVDEYEV

[Original in Russian]

Baden-Baden, 3 October 1869

I was delighted, dear Avdeyev, to hear from you at last, and I am pleased to learn that you're thinking of bringing out a journal.[1] I have always thought that you had the talent to do something like that and I am impatient to see you ⟨at work⟩.[2] As for whether I can contribute to it, might I explain my position with the sincerity demanded of our old friendship? What you suggest and expect of me goes quite against the grain – to say nothing of the laziness which has overcome me; but I am afraid that I do *not know how* to write the sort of thing you want. The best proof of this is the following fact: *two years ago* I promised to send my Moscow publisher Salayev several extracts from my literary reminiscences which he is publishing as a sort of introduction to a new edition of my works, and I only managed to post the final passage *yesterday*. And it's all so abbreviated, clumsy and poorly developed! But the main thing is how all that nonsense has worn me out, how unwillingly I put pen to paper! I have decided that I shall never do such things again. As I live abroad, far from Russian soil, I am also not up to writing *large-scale* books. A little short story, two at the most, I might be able to manage during the year – but that's all. If I had something finished at the moment, I would have willingly sent it to you, but the only story I have has already been sold to the *Messenger of Europe*. You can see for yourself that I am just not the sort of contributor you envisage. I am sure you will believe me. You may attack me for my laziness and my absenteeism but please do not suspect me of not wanting to help you. If I should finish something this year, I shall of course not forget you.

I wish you all the very best of health and success – and patience. I haven't yet seen a copy of *The Cause* and so I am not at all clear about what exactly it is, but I do know that it has collected together a number of young developing writers whom you must direct along the right road.

[111] 1. Avdeyev had told Turgenev that he was going either to buy the journal *The Cause* or to start up a new one which would be a rival to the likes of the *Russian Herald* and the *Messenger of Europe*; he wanted Turgenev to contribute a series of articles on subjects of his own choosing in the form of letters.

2. Original in French.

112. *To P. V. Annenkov*

I am spending the winter here, perhaps in Weimar, but I shan't leave until December. I affectionately press your hand.

Yours faithfully,
Iv. Turgenev

112. To P. V. ANNENKOV

[Original in Russian]

Baden-Baden, 22 January 1870

I write to you, dear Annenkov, under the influence of some sad news. I heard an hour ago that Herzen has died. I could not hold back the tears.

Whatever might have been the differences in our views, however many arguments we might have had, an old comrade, an old friend has nonetheless passed on. And do you know it is less than a week since I saw him in Paris; we dined together (after a break of seven years) and I had never seen him so cheerful or talkative, even lively. This was last *Friday*; he fell ill in the evening and the following day I saw him in his bed extremely feverish from pneumonia. I went to see his family every day up to my departure on Wednesday, but his doctor would not permit me to see him, and when I left I already knew it was hopeless. The illness worsened terribly quickly. I could not stay any longer in Paris; but I was horrified to think of what would happen to his family. His son had not yet managed to arrive from Florence; his eldest daughter, Natalya, a beautiful, attractive creature, had lost her mind for some six weeks following a series of strange misunderstandings but was gradually improving; the death will probably threaten her reason again. I suppose everyone in Russia will say that Herzen should have died earlier, that he had outlived his usefulness. But what do these words mean? What sense is there in our so-called activities when faced with this silent abyss which draws us down? Is not living, to go on living, the most important thing? I know the 'smell' of death rather well, particularly as I recently and quite unexpectedly had the opportunity to breathe it to the full; a friend invited me (in Paris) to attend not only Tropman's execution but also the reading to him of the death sentence, his *toilette*, etc. There were eight of us. I shall never forget that awful night when ⟨'I have supp'd full of horrors'⟩,[1] and I finally grew to loathe capital punishment in general and the manner in which it is carried out in France in particular. I have already begun a letter to you in which I describe everything in detail and which, if you like, you can later publish in the *St Petersburg Gazette*. I shall say only this: the courage, the contempt for death shown by Tropman was something I just could not imagine. But the whole thing is terrible, terrible.[2]

[112] 1. Original in English. A quotation from *Macbeth*.

2. J. B. Tropman, twenty-one, was publicly guillotined on 19 January 1870 for the brutal murder of an entire family. Turgenev's 'Execution of Tropman', first published in 1870, which spares no detail of the gruesome event, was written to 'supply some arguments to the advocates of the abolition of capital punishment'.

By the way, did you receive my letter about Polonsky? And did you place it in one of the journals? He himself is screeching about it *just like a sea-gull* and assures me in his letters that he is so unhappy and so unsuccessful and that he is convinced his work will never appear. Please prove to him that he's wrong, although I just could not give him any especial *happiness* in my article on him.

Farewell, my friend, and look after your health. I send my best wishes to your wife and press your hands.

Yours,
Iv. Turgenev

P.S. I shall not be going to Weimar before 7 February.

113.To G. FLAUBERT

Turgenev first met Gustave Flaubert (1821–80) at one of the famous dinner parties at Magny's restaurant in Paris in February 1863, and the two remained on very friendly terms ever after. Turgenev liked him more than any other man he ever knew, with the exception of Annenkov, and thought highly of his writings, which he did his best to make better known in both Germany and Russia. In 1877 he translated *La Légende de Saint-Julien l'Hospitalier* and *Hérodias*. Through Flaubert, Turgenev met Zola, Maupassant and Daudet, and on his death organized a subscription for a statue to him in Rouen. His late story, *Song of Triumphant Love*, is dedicated to Flaubert's memory. Ninety-five of Turgenev's letters to Flaubert have survived, and more than 130 of Flaubert's to Turgenev.

[Original in French]

Weimar, 20 February 1870

My dear friend,

The article which M. Julian Schmidt[1] has written on *L'Education Sentimentale* has not yet appeared in the *Preussische Jahrbücher* but as soon as it does I shall send you a copy. If you want me to, I shall ask him to send you his article on *Madame Bovary* which appeared last year. The second number of the (Russian) *Messenger of Europe* which I have just received contains the second and last part of the article of which I've spoken to you. In particular, it is a detailed résumé of the novel. In general he thinks that *women* fill too large a part of Frédéric's life and wonders if it's the same with all Frenchman.

Yes, he has certainly been unjust to you, but now is the time to take courage and throw a real masterpiece at your readers' heads. Perhaps your [*La tentation de Saint-*] *Antoine* will serve the purpose. But do not tarry – I know that's my old refrain. You must not forget that people are measured by the standards they have set for themselves, and you bear the punishment of your own past. You

[113] 1. Julian Schmidt (1818–86), German journalist, critic and literary historian. See headnote to letter no. 132.

have the energy – ⟨'a man must be ferocious,'⟩² says the Spanish proverb – especially an artist. If your book is noticed by only a dozen people of some standing, this will be enough. You must understand that I am telling you this not to console but to encourage you.

I have been here almost a fortnight and my only preoccupation has been to try and get warm. The houses are poorly built here and the iron stoves are no use at all. You will see a small piece of mine in the March number of the *Revue des Deux Mondes*. It's a mere bagatelle, but I'm working on something of more *consequence*, or rather I'm getting ready to work on it.³

I shall go to Paris before returning to Russia, which will be towards the end of April. I shall stay there for about a fortnight and we'll be able to see a lot of each other.

If you should see Mme Sand, please send her every good wish from me.⁴ Greetings to Ducamp and the Hussons.

I embrace you and say: Take courage! You are Flaubert, when all's said and done.

Yours,

I.T.

114. To I. P. BORISOV

[Original in Russian]

Weimar, 27 March 1870

Once again it's a long time since I've written to you, dear Ivan Petrovich. And you've again been unwell, which means I should have thought about you all the more. I *did* think about you, but my accursed laziness prevented me from putting pen to paper. Indeed, I would have hit myself were it not so painful. It's even more stupid that I'm replying to your letter of 7 February and almost six weeks have passed since then – and probably everything has changed! Your letter was melancholy, even gloomy. The picture you painted of contemporary life contained very little consolation, and unfortunately it is very probably close to the truth. But as one cannot do anything about the shape of one's nose (without the help of Venus) and must learn to put up with it, so *even less* can one do anything about one's motherland. But I shall come and see for myself.

And I shall come soon; this time I am not crying wolf! St Nicholas's Day, 9 May, is the definite and unalterable time of my arrival in Spasskoye. I shall stay until the beginning of July and shall of course see you constantly. I have taken your very helpful advice about Kishinsky and the way things are run – I am little disposed towards solemn audits, etc. I like to think that I shall see Fet. I shall try, as a mark of times past, to argue about things with him, but it gets harder with

2. Original in Spanish.
3. *A King Lear of the Steppes*.
4. George Sand (1804–76), the French writer.

every year. I am becoming more and more convinced of the truth of Tyutchev's lines about 'a thought expressed is a lie', or rather such thoughts which their speaker does not willingly accept and which consequently do not help you understand their meaning. But Fet is not like this; he just gets the bit between his teeth.

I have read the sixth volume of *War and Peace*; of course, there are things of the first order, but while passing over the childish philosophy, I find it unpleasant to discover a *system* even in the characters depicted by Tolstoy. Why must all his good women be not only breeding-machines but even fools? And why does he try to convince the reader that if a woman is mature and intelligent then she is always a phrasemonger and a liar? How did he dismiss all the *Decembrist* element in the twenties? And why are all his decent people also nincompoops – with a touch of the holy fool? I am afraid that Slavophilism, into the grip of which he seems to have fallen, has ruined his splendid and poetic talents and removed his freedom of expression, just as it has ruined Kokhanovskaya[1] and others. An artist who has lost all capacity to see *the black* and *the white*, and to look to the left and the right, is on the way to his downfall.

Life proceeds normally here. My health is satisfactory but I am naturally working very little. There were two performances of Gluck's *Orfeo* in which Mme Viardot was as ever quite marvellous. As she has not sung on the stage for a number of years, it was very pleasant for her to be reminded of her past. She is pampered by the public here and they have taken her to their hearts. Weimar is a small town, but some good and interesting people live here.

Although the worst of the winter is over, the weather is awful; but it's warm inside, thanks to the alterations we've made to the stoves.

When you write to Petya, please send him my best wishes. I'm going to bring him a superb rifle and then we can go shooting corncrakes together. Look after your health. I firmly press your hand.

Yours,
Iv. Turgenev

115. To A. F. PISEMSKY

Alexey Feofilaktovich Pisemsky (1821–81), novelist and dramatist. For a number of years he edited the *Reader's Library*. He and Turgenev were friends from the mid-fifties and much admired each other's writings.

While belonging to no particular 'school' – for he always disliked theories and distrusted ideas – Pisemsky showed in his works a love for Russia and things Russian, but he never idealized. His literary fame grew in the 1850s and culminated in his most famous novel, *A Thousand Souls*, in 1858 and the realistic tragedy, *A Hard Lot*, in 1859, which many think is superior to Tolstoy's more celebrated *Powers of Darkness*. In 1863 he published a new novel, *Troubled Seas*,

[114] 1. Pseudonym of the Slavophile writer Nadezhda Stepanovna Sokhanskaya (1823–84).

which contained a satirical attack on the younger, post-Emancipation, generation. This increased the already strong antipathy felt towards him and he grew
increasingly embittered. Family tragedies and a decline in his literary powers led
him to hypochondria and a deepening melancholia. When he died in 1881 he was
a forgotten man. Thirty-five of Turgenev's letters to him have survived.

[Original in Russian]

Weimar, 4 May 1870

Dear Alexey Feofilaktovich,

I do not want to leave your letter unanswered, although I am, as they say, in all
of a rush. I am leaving here in a week and will be in Petersburg in a fortnight. I
shall go from there to Moscow and drop in on you at your home on the
Povarskaya. And then what conversations we shall have! The hatred towards
Russia which you sense in the reviews by German critics of your novel [*A
Thousand Souls*] should not surprise you. No one feels any hatred towards
Sweden or Portugal, but the Germans (especially the Liberals) are rather afraid
of us, as once the Greeks feared Macedonia, even though times have changed
and our present government has different policies from those of Nicholas. The
question of the Baltic States also increases their anxiety a little.

I see from your letter that you are still depressed, but you have no complaints
about your health and that's the main thing. I know my old chum has to work
and it's burdensome. I haven't done any work myself for a long time but I've
started again and I think it's helping me, which is an excellent thing. Even if
you're in need, you don't have to write. I know that you can't work to order, but
at least when the bird approaches you have to say 'cheep, cheep' and not turn
your back on it. As for the civil service, I would suggest that you don't resign
altogether, however unpleasant it is.

My *King Lear of the Steppes* is not a novel but a longish short story. I finished it
about six weeks ago and am taking it with me to Petersburg. It will probably
appear in the June number of the *Russian Herald*, but I shall still read the
manuscript to you in Moscow. You'll perhaps suggest some changes and
corrections.

I think I have already told you once, but never mind, it bears repeating. You
must not forget that *you have won a large sum in life's lottery*; you have a beautiful
wife and wonderful children. Therefore you have no need to feel depressed.

Until we meet. I shall let you know from Petersburg when I hope to arrive.
Meanwhile, I embrace you from afar and send my best wishes to all of you.

Yours sincerely,

Iv. Turgenev

116.To P. V. ANNENKOV

[Original in Russian]

Baden-Baden, 8 August 1870

The sheer size of the paper on which I am about to write to you, dear Pavel Vasilyevich, should convince you of my epistolary intentions. (By the way, why haven't *you* written? It's already a month since I left Petersburg, and not a single line!) I wrote to you last Thursday to the distant rumble of gun-fire; the following day, Friday, a telegram informed me that this was the Germans storming Weissenburg and Moltke's plan being put into effect, which (while the emperor of the French was showing his son between lunch and dinner how a mitrailleuse worked – and with marvellous effect took Saarbrücken, which was defended by a *single* battalion) was to rush the huge army of the Crown Prince of Prussia into Alsace, thus cutting the French army into two. On Saturday, i.e. the day before yesterday, my gardener came to tell me that very heavy firing had been heard since early morning. I went out on to the porch and sure enough dull thumps and rumblings were much in evidence, and the ground was shaking. But they were rather more to the south than on Thursday, and I counted about thirty or forty a minute. I took a carriage and went to Iburg, a castle on the Rhine, resting on top of one of the highest points of the Black Forest. From there the whole valley of Alsace is visible as far as Strasbourg. It was a clear day and the Vosges mountains were clearly sketched on the horizon. But right opposite where I was standing, on the other side of the Rhine, great clouds of black, white, blue-grey and red smoke were rising from behind the dense forests; a whole town was on fire. Further away, towards the Vosges, cannon-fire could still be heard, but now more faintly. It was clear that the French had been defeated and were withdrawing. It was terribly sad to see the shocking signs of war in that quiet, beautiful valley under the pale light of a half-occluded sun. It was impossible not to curse it and its criminally insane perpetrators. I returned to Baden on the following day, i.e. yesterday; from early morning there were telegrams all over the town telling of the latest decisive victory of the Crown Prince over MacMahon, and we learnt in the evening that the French had lost four thousand captured, thirty cannon, six mitrailleuses and two banners – and that MacMahon was wounded! The amazement of the Germans knows no bounds. All roles have been reversed. *They* are attacking, *they* are beating the French in their own country, and more decisively than they did the Austrians! Moltke's plan was put into effect with immense speed and success. The French left flank was annihilated – caught between two fires – and perhaps even today the King of Prussia and the Crown Prince will go down to the battlefield that settled the outcome of the war! The Germans are so amazed that even their patriotic joy is a little confused. They just didn't expect *this*! From the very beginning, as you know, I was wholeheartedly on their side, for I see the complete downfall of Napoleon's empire as the saviour of civilization and as something which would make possible the untrammelled development of free institutions in Europe, although it was unthinkable until *that* disgrace received what he deserved. But I foresaw a long and difficult struggle . . . and suddenly! Everyone's thoughts are now directed towards Paris. What will they say there? A *defeated* Napoleon no longer has any *raison d'être*. But at the present time one may expect even such an improbable event as Paris receiving the news of the defeat of the French armies with equanimity. As you can well imagine I have been reading both the French and the German papers all this time with great care and, with my hand on my heart, I can say that there is no comparison between them. It is impossible to conceive of the chauvinism, the slanders, the complete ignorance about the enemy and finally the naivety of the French papers, to say nothing of journals such as *Figaro* and the most despicable *Liberté* which is utterly worthy of its founder E. de Girardin. But even in the respectable journals such as *Temps* one reads reports of the kind that Prussian junior officers are chasing after their men with iron bars to get them to fight, etc. Their ignorance goes as deep as the *Journal officiel* (a government paper!) reporting in all serious-ness that *the Rhine flows* between France and the Palatinate. One can illustrate the ignorance about the enemy merely in the conviction of the French that Southern Germany will remain neutral despite their clearly expressed wish to unite the Rhine province with the ancient towns of Cologne, Aachen, Trier, etc, probably those parts of Germany dearest to German hearts! The same *Journal officiel* recently affirmed that the object of the war as seen by the French was to restore freedom to the Germans!! And this at a time when the whole of Germany has risen against its ancient enemy! There is no need to say anything about their conviction that they will emerge victorious or about the superiority of their mitrailleuses or their Chassepot rifles. All the French journals are convinced that as soon as the French and the Prussians get together, hey presto, everything will be immediately resolved! I cannot resist quoting one piece of chauvinism: in one of the journals (*Soir*, I think) their correspondent proclaims in describing the mood of the French soliders: 'Ils sont si assurés de vaincre, qu'ils ont comme une peur modeste de leur triomphe inévitable!' (i.e. 'They are so certain of winning that they have as it were a slight fear of their inevitable triumph!') Although you cannot compare this with the truly Shakespearean words of Prince Pierre Buonaparte about the Parisians who accompanied the coffin of Noir, whom he had just *killed*: 'C'est une curiosité malsaine que je blâme' ('I condemn their unhealthy curiosity') – but it does have its interest. And what words these journals put into the mouths of the various highly placed persons they describe, including the Emperor Napoleon! *Gaulois*, for example, reports that when the undefended Saarbrücken had been set on fire on all four sides the Emperor turned to his son and inquired, 'Are you not tired, my child?' This means, ultimately, that they've even lost their sense of shame.

There is also the amusing anecdote of the diplomatic attaché who in the presence of the Empress Eugénie announced that he didn't want victory over Prussia because it would be unpleasant to live on Boulevard Untermunterbirsch-uckroute or to order his carriage to drive along rue Nichtkaputklopsmosfurt.

And he would have to because the French named their streets after their victories! It is possible that on the basis of reports from this same attaché France counted on the neutrality of Southern Germany.

But joking apart, I sincerely love and respect the French people, I recognize their great and noble role in history and do not doubt their future importance; many of my best friends, the people I am closest to, are French and therefore you will not suspect me of a prejudiced or unjust hatred towards their country. But it is now their turn to learn the hard lesson that the Prussians learnt at Jena, the Austrians at Sadova, and – why hide the truth? – we at Sevastopol. But may God grant that they will also learn from it and be able to eat the sweet fruit of a bitter plant. It is high time for them to take a look at themselves, inside their own country, and to see their own ulcers and try to cure them. It is time to put an end to the immorality which has ruled them for almost twenty years. Without serious internal upheavals such self-examination is impossible; it cannot occur without causing deep shame and serious pain. But true patriotism has nothing in common with this arrogant, conceited aloofness which leads only to self-deception, ignorance and irremediable errors. The French need a lesson – because they still have a lot to learn. The Russian soldiers, who died in their thousands in the ruins of Sevastopol, did not perish in vain; may those innumerable sacrifices of the present war be not in vain either, otherwise it will all be equally disgraceful and senseless.

Even though I've finished writing, I still haven't said a tenth of what lies in my heart. Let's leave it to another time. As regards us personally here in Baden, you may rest assured that all is well. The danger of being invaded by unfriendly forces is slight and the necessities of life are now even a little cheaper, despite the reports in the French papers that we are dying from hunger.

If you think it opportune or necessary or of interest to anyone, you can print this letter in the *St Petersburg Gazette*, but sign it simply I.T.

I await some news from you and embrace you. Greetings to you and yours.

Yours sincerely,
Iv. Turgenev

117. To M. A. MILYUTINA

Marya Ageyevna Milyutina (1834–1903), née Abaza, friend and correspondent of Turgenev's since the 1850s, wife of Nikolay Alexeyevich Milyutin.

[Original in Russian]

Baden-Baden, 20 August 1870

I have just received your letter, dear Marya Ageyevna. Yesterday evening, at 10 o'clock, all the bells in Baden suddenly started ringing. News had just arrived of the decisive and probably final defeat of the French at Raisonville. Bazaine's army had failed to get out of Metz after all. One cannot but agree that the incompetence of the French generals and the administration has been twice as great as ours during the Crimean War. The question remains, though, can they make some use, as we did, of this their misfortune, and will this lesson profit them in the future? The French capacity for self-deception and their little love of the truth make that doubtful.

The fact that the whole of Europe expected a French victory just goes to show that we are all incapable of seeing what is going on under our noses. The Prussians, whom I saw on 15 July in Berlin, did not doubt *for one single second* that victory would be theirs – but I ascribed that to national vanity. But it has turned out that they knew what they were talking about.

It is very probable that there will be a revolution in Paris, if there hasn't been one already. Napoleon can hardly survive. But we are living in such unstable times that such an improbable event as the survival of the Empire might just occur.

In any case, though, you should not return to Paris. If I were you I think I would wait for calm weather (you can always tell some two or three days in advance by looking at the barometer) and sail from Le Havre to Ostend and then home via Brussels, Cologne and Berlin – that is, if you have finally decided to spend the winter in Russia. At the moment all the German railways are again working normally. The voyage from le Havre to Ostend only takes a few hours.

It is very quiet here – there are very few sick or wounded. And almost all the doctors (including Heiligenthal) have left – they're wanted in Nancy. Please send my best wishes to all your family and friends; I firmly press your husband's hand. I should be in Russia this winter and shall be in Moscow at the end of January. Will you be there then?

Look after your health,

I remain,
Yours sincerely,
Iv. Turgenev

118. To I. P. BORISOV

[Original in Russian]

Baden–Baden, 24 August 1870

You can now demand, dear Ivan Petrovich, the bottle of wine from Tolstoy, for you have won. The latest attacks by the Prussians have in essence, it would appear, settled the matter . . . The last three battles, on 14, 16 and 18 August, have cost many lives, but the outcome is significant. Nothing now prevents the Crown Prince's army from reaching Paris. MacMahon will now probably withdraw. The final outcome of the war is – at present – impossible to foretell, but it looks as if everything favours the Germans.

I can very well understand why Tolstoy is on the side of the French. He certainly does not like what they say but he hates even more reasonableness, systems, science – in a word, the Germans. The whole of his last novel is constructed on opposition to intelligence, knowledge and consciousness – and suddenly the educated Germans are attacking the ignorant French!! (By the way, is the holy fool who has published some ridiculous prophecies and plans in the *Moscow Gazette* the same *Prince* Urosov with whom Tolstoy is friendly?¹) Without playing the devil's advocate, I can say for my part that I welcome a French defeat, for the Empire of Napoleon, whose existence is not compatible with the spread of freedom in Europe, will be finally defeated too. I expressed such an opinion in some letters to Annenkov, extracts from which were printed in no. 216 (8 August) of the *St Petersburg Gazette*. I quoted there, by the way, some excellent examples of French 'phrasemongering'.

I am delighted that you write of Tolstoy and Fet; it is a pity, though, that the latter still does not wish to part from his Muse. Y. D. Shenshina, whom you describe marvellously, is also one of her children.

I have been out shooting three times already. On the first two I shot terribly, and the third was completely unsuccessful. However, we bagged twenty-three partridges and eight rabbits. My dog was, as always, splendid.

We can hear clearly from here the bombardment of Strasbourg during the night; it's already half destroyed by fire. Even lying in bed with all the windows closed, we can still hear dull rumblings and distant bangs. One cannot help experiencing philosophical, historical and social thoughts of a most unhappy nature. The iron century has still not passed – and we are still barbarians! And will probably remain so for the rest of our days.

The weather has taken a turn for the worse. They say we're in for an early winter.

Send a kiss from me to Petya. I firmly press your hand and remain,

Yours affectionately,

Iv. Turgenev

119. To K. A. L. PIETSCH

[Original in German]

Baden-Baden, 9 September 1870

My dear friend Pietsch,

Life no longer follows its normal course – it surprises us at every turn; one has hardly the time to take a breath before being bewildered yet again! The Emperor taken prisoner, a hundred thousand French taken prisoner – a republic! Perhaps even Paris will be taken in a few days and Ludwig Pietsch borne aloft in triumph through the Arc de l'Etoile, his head crowned with the laurels of victory. And then what?!!

[118] 1. Prince Sergey Semyonovich Urusov (1827–97) had written a series of articles describing various military plans of his own concoction which would guarantee a French victory. He had met Tolstoy during the siege of Sevastopol, and while *War and Peace* was being written had convinced him of the validity of the theory of historical fatalism.

We are living here in the greatest excitement. The first news from the battlefield has arrived, albeit rather delayed. At the beginning of August we were all living here on the qui vive; we were all packed ready to leave for Wildbad, should the Turks cross the Rhine. But we've been calm for a long time now.

All the Viardot family is fit and well. We are helping the wounded, making music, and reading aloud to each other. And thus the hours pass. The downfall of the Empire was a great satisfaction for poor Viardot, and although his heart may be bleeding now, he fully realizes that France has got what she deserved. As for me, as you well know, I am a German at heart, for a French victory would have meant the end of freedom in Europe; but you had no need to set fire to Strasbourg, it was completely uncalled for and inopportune. What will happen now in Paris?

But one may be truly happy to have witnessed that poor fool and his clique falling into the mire. But why is such respect being shown to the fellow? He fully deserved being sent to eat lice in Cayenne.

We will be delighted if you keep your word and come to Baden. Your room is ready and is now waiting for you, empty. An old friend, Müller-Strübing,[1] has just left it.

Sincerest greetings until we meet again,

I. Turgenev

120. To M. Y. SALTYKOV-SHCHEDRIN

Mikhail Yevgrafovich Saltykov (1826–89), satirical writer (under the pseudonym of N. Shchedrin). Born into the landed gentry and educated at the same school as Pushkin, Saltykov entered government service in 1844. He came into contact with the younger, radical, and Westernized generation, and began publishing at a time of severe reaction by the authorities. He was exiled to Vyatka (as Herzen had been some fourteen years before), but stayed in the civil service and rose to the important post of director of the local police. On the death of Nicholas I in 1855 he was transferred back to St Petersburg and resumed his literary career which, in the generally reforming and liberal atmosphere of the time, was greeted with general acclaim. In 1868 he left the civil service to concentrate entirely on writing, and together with Nekrasov he became the editor of the *Annals of the Fatherland*. From this time onward he was one of the leaders of the radical intelligentsia, and he remained such until his death. Although much of his writing is of an ephemeral nature, his *The History of a Town* (1869–70) and his only real novel, *The Golovlyov Family* (1872–6), have ensured him a lasting place in the distinguished list of Russian classics. He

[119] 1. Herman Müller-Strübing (1812–93), German democrat, exiled after 1848. A friend of the Viardots, Herzen and Turgenev.

published a lot on Turgenev's writings, and Turgenev wrote a review of his *The History of a Town* for the London *Academy* in 1871. Twenty-one of Turgenev's letters to him survive.

[Original in Russian]

London, 12 December 1870

Dear Mikhail Yevgrafovich,

I have recently received your *The History of a Town* which was sent to me by Annenkov. I thank you sincerely for remembering me and for the pleasure your book has given me. I read it as soon as I had received it. I shall say nothing of its many other virtues, but it is an invaluable historical document which none of our future writers on social matters will be able to ignore. With its sharply satirical, and sometimes fantastic, style and its rather black humour, reminiscent of the best pages of Swift, your book is one of the most faithful reproductions of one of the most basic facets of the physiognomy of Russia; 'he who has the ears to hear and the eyes to see', as said your law-giver Benevolensky.[1]

Once again, my sincere thanks.

I came here a month or so ago and intend to remain for the time being – but I shall soon come to Petersburg where I shall of course have the pleasure of seeing you.

Please accept the expression of my sincere respect and devotion.

Iv. Turgenev

[120] 1. One of the characters in *The History of a Town*.

IV
1871–1879

Turgenev lived in London from November 1870 until August 1871, except for a five-week visit to Russia in the spring. He renewed his literary contacts with Carlyle, Tennyson, Swinburne, George Eliot and G.H. Lewes; he visited his friends in the country and attended the celebrations of the centenary of the birth of Sir Walter Scott in Edinburgh at the beginning of August; he did a little shooting when he could, and met Robert Browning, whom he found 'vain, not very amusing, boring'.

With the end of the Franco-Prussian War and the restoration of order in Paris after the failure of the Commune, the Viardots decided to return to live in the French capital; Turgenev, of course, had no option but to go with them, however much he professed to dislike the city. Both the properties they owned in Baden-Baden were sold and they moved back into the Viardot's old house in the rue de Douai, where Turgenev occupied the third floor. As all three were now in their fifties they no longer felt the need to keep up any of the pretence of their younger years and Louis Viardot, who had only very rarely shown any resentment at Turgenev's longstanding presence, accepted him fully into the family. Turgenev lived there, or at Bougival, on the Seine, until his death.

With Turgenev settled in Paris, there began his close contacts with the leading French writers of the day, George Sand, Zola, Daudet, Edmond de Goncourt and especially Flaubert, with whom he remained on the most friendly terms until the latter's death in 1880. He did his best to have translations of French literature published in Russia, and arranged to have Zola appointed as Paris correspondent for the journal *Messenger of Europe*. He also continued to champion the cause of writers he considered talented, both in Russia and Europe.

During the seventies Turgenev returned to Russia regularly – for five weeks in 1871, six in 1872, ten in 1874 and eight in 1876, and thereafter annually. Usually these visits, always undertaken reluctantly, were occasioned by family or business concerns. In 1876 he was forced to replace his estate manager Kishinsky for incompetence and for 'having his fingers in the till'; three years later his rich brother Nikolay died, leaving the bulk of his estate, to Turgenev's great chagrin, to his wife's family. The period also sees the decline and collapse of his son-in-law Gaston Bruère's business and the consequent need to support his daughter and her two children; a triumphant reception, much to his surprise, by the young in Moscow in 1879; the award of an honorary Doctorate of Civil Law by the University of Oxford; the friendship with the young and ill-fated Yuliya Vrevskaya; and the beginning of his last infatuation – with the attractive actress Marya Savina. Towards the end of the seventies his health began to show signs of serious deterioration and he grew increasingly more melancholy and resigned.

The decade also sees the publication of the short stories *Knock, knock, knock* (1871), *The End of Chertopkhanov* (1872), *Living Relics, Punin and Baburin* and *There's Knocking* (all 1874), the novella *Torrents of Spring* (1872) – arguably his most characteristic work – and his last novel, *Virgin Soil* (1877), a study of the Russian revolutionaries of the period combined with a romantic love story, which was received with general hostility in Russia but wide acclaim abroad. Between 1877 and 1879 Turgenev also wrote sixty-nine of the eighty-three *Poems in Prose*, a collection of wonderfully evocative (and under-appreciated) short pieces.

121. To L. FRIEDLÄNDER

Ludwig Heinrich Friedländer (1824–1909), German historian, philologist, art historian, archaeologist, literary critic and academic. He first met Turgenev soon after writing a flattering review of the latter's writings in 1868. They met from time to time in the seventies. Seventeen of Turgenev's letters to Friedländer are known.

[Original in German]

London, 6 January 1871

Dear Sir,

I only received your letter of 23 December a few days ago. In all the present confusion even the post is not as punctual as it used to be. I am very sorry that I shall not see you in Berlin but it is highly likely that I shall be able to be in Königsberg for a day, so I shall see you then. My departure from here has been slightly delayed and I shall not be in Berlin before the end of January.

I have written to my publisher in Riga asking him to send you a copy of my *A Nest of the Landed Gentry*, as I gather from what you write that you have not received one. But just in case, I shall bring one with me when I come. *A King Lear of the Steppes* has started to appear in the *Nordische Presse*. *On the Eve* was given that title more because of when it appeared (1860, a year before the Emancipation of the Peasants) rather than because of its actual content; and characters such as Yelena and Insarov are presentiments of what was to come.

And so, heartfelt greetings until we meet again in the near future. All is well with the Viardots, as far as that is possible for the patriotic French.

Yours sincerely,

Iv. Turgenev

122. To PAULINE VIARDOT

[Original in French]

St Petersburg, 13 February 1871

⟨Dearest friend⟩[1] here I am in Petersburg. I only arrived here this morning at eleven o'clock. (I do not know whether you received my letter from Wierzbolovo on the frontier where I spent Thursday night. The man to whom I gave it to post had an untrustworthy look about him and I was stupid enough to give him the money for the stamp. I wrote about my day in Berlin.) I went from hotel to hotel and finally found two fairly awful rooms at great expense, but at least they are warm. My friend Annenkov has already been to see me. He looks a little older but his wife has just presented him with a second son; the christening is next week. After I had washed and changed I went to see Louise[2] but she was not at home. She was at a rehearsal for a concert which will take place tomorrow. But I did see Mme Serova,[3] who struck me as rather eccentric but intelligent; she is much upset over the death of her husband – and very taken with Louise. She spoke of her almost enthusiastically. Unfortunately, according to Mme Serova, Louise is not in very good health; she thinks she has some heart disease. I have arranged to see her tomorrow at noon and will send you all her news in detail. I am now off to the English Club where Annenkov has signed me in. Until this evening.

11 p.m. First of all I must thank you for your kind letter no. 1 which Annenkov passed on to me an hour ago. It was very pleasant to get your news. I hope that more will follow without interruption and that it will always be as good. I thought of you a lot on the evenings of the twenty-third and twenty-fourth. Please tell me if all went well.[4] You say nothing about what you sang at Mrs Keith's. Yes, we must find a teacher for Paul and Marianne as soon as we can. Do not forget to let me know if Gérôme has got the copy of the Velazquez yet.[5]

There was a mass of people at dinner in the club but only a few old friends – and I mean old, as they have all gone amazingly grey! I saw Count Khreptovich,[6] who asked after you. Everyone here believes that the war is more or less over and all that remains is for the peace to be ratified. I spent the evening at Annenkov's with a few initimate friends; I felt rather tired and knew that my bed ⟨would be welcoming⟩.[1]

Everyone here is up in arms at the Germans and very sympathetic towards the French, but they are all a little alarmed by the lack of talent France has shown and

---

[122] 1. Original in German.

2. i.e. Pauline and Louis Viardot's daughter.

3. Valentina Semyonovna Serova (1846–1924), composer and music critic, the mother of the painter V. A. Serov.

4. Pauline Viardot had taken part in two charity concerts in London in aid of the victims of the Franco-Prussian War.

5. Jean Léon Gérôme (1824–1904), painter. It is not known which is the painting in question.

6. Count Mikhail Irineyevich Khreptovich (1809–91), Court Chamberlain and diplomat.

very worried over her future. It would appear that even in high places the Russians desire the success of the modified republic and are pleased to see Thiers at the helm. He was liked during his stay here.

At Königsberg I entered the Kingdom of the Snow. Everything here is white, arch-white, the sky is blue and the snow crunches under one's feet and the wheels of the carriages. It's −15° outside. It's not at all like the London fog – that dear fog, I shall add, as you are there.

I shall write tomorrow and post the letter on Monday. A thousand greetings to Viardot and tell him to look after himself. I kiss Didie, Marianne and Paul and press Mlle Arnholt's hand,[7] and ⟨last not least⟩[8] I tenderly kiss your hands. ⟨With my eternal and unchanging fidelity,

Yours⟩,[1]

I.T.

123. To PAULINE VIARDOT

[Original in French]

St Petersburg, 26 February 1871

Dear and beloved Madame Viardot,

I told you that my reading planned for tomorrow has fallen through. Sadly it wasn't a false rumour. Apparently, though, I am going to read something between Mlle Lovato singing 'It does not tickle my nose' and another young lady of similar talents. It's a proper café chantant, but I am very sympathetic towards its purpose (it's for the French wounded in the war; the announcement doesn't mention it, but everyone knows . . . .). They have placed my name in a prominent position and it shines out next to 'fresh oysters' etc.

I thought of your reception in Brighton and even felt flattered by the coincidence. However, I fear that not many people will turn up, for the public has had its fill of concerts, tableaux vivants, etc. But I'll tell you tomorrow what happens.

Now let us talk of what I've been doing. A sitting for my portrait (the last thank the Lord!), a sitting for some photographs (I am not paying, I assure you!), literary and business matters, visits made and received. My life here is one mad whirl and I shall be happy to leave for the peace of Moscow and the even more peaceful Spasskoye. None of it can be avoided but once it's all over it will be very *agrayable*, as Thérèse[1] would say.

I dined yesterday, Thursday, with three *young* writers; the conversation was lively and animated. And we drank only *one* bottle of wine! I then had to spend the evening at the home of a rather tedious lady whom I think you know, a Mme

7. Louise Arnholt, governess employed by the Viardots.
8. Original in English.

[123] 1. Emma Valadon (1837–1919), famous French opera singer, friend of the Viardots and Turgenev.

M., the one with the fat cheeks. She is worthy of her reputation. Today I dined with Count A. – also a rather tedious man, but full of good intentions with regard to literature. He is about to set up an impressive enterprise to publish a lexicographical encyclopaedia; he is very rich and it needs encouraging – not his wealth, but his enterprise. From there I went to another salon, also politico-literary but of a rather more definite colour and which enabled me to appreciate the different shades of public opinion in my *cara patria*. There is much that I shall be able to tell you of this when we meet face to face.

Saturday evening, 27 February

And so, my dear and good Madame Viardot, the reading has taken place, but it was completely different from what I had anticipated. A small café chantant in effect, with awful music but a huge audience, full of the qualities of youth, a tableau vivant, the apotheosis of Garibaldi, a reading by a lady of her 'Memoirs of a Stay with the Garibaldists', a declaration in a cracked voice by a fat ninny of the 'Deux Grenadiers' by Schumann, which as you will perhaps recall, ends with the Marseillaise, and then an explosion of tempestuous applause and shouts of 'Vive la France!' – in a word, a storm, which lasted ten minutes. A French actor, it is true, read 'Deux Grenadiers', but then a French actress declaimed the 'Pigeons de la République', and that word caused the usual *frisson*.

As for me, I must tell you that never in my life have I received so many – excuse the word – *ovations*. I am telling you this for I know it will give you pleasure, and I thought of you the whole time that I stood there, confused, blushing, an impassive smile on my face, in front of that howling crowd. It felt exactly like a brief but violent rainstorm falling on my bare shoulders. I read an extract from my *Sportsman's Sketches*, 'The Bailiff'. I think I read it rather well; my nerves disappeared in all that din and I was calm – and then the public was so kind!

You will have returned from Liverpool and perhaps I shall receive some news from you tomorrow.

In the meantime, a thousand greetings. I kiss your hands.

Saturday

I continue my letter, dear Madame Viardot.

After dinner I went to a concert at the Russian Society. Beethoven's Third Symphony, rather badly played, and then . . . you will be amazed . . . and at the same time pay due regard to my good faith: they played the overture to *Die Meistersinger* and the entr'acte, which gave me the greatest of pleasure. The entr'acte especially is marvellous – one must admit that it is very powerful music. The audience applauded for a long time and demanded an encore.

That small musician whom you know, Charles Lenz, dragged me off after the concert to the home of one of our best actors, Samoylov,[2] where Rubinstein was

2. Vasily Vasilyevich Samoylov (1812–77), leading St Petersburg actor; he had taken part in various productions of Turgenev's plays.

expected to appear. And he really did! He has conceived an intense hatred for all Germans (!) and refuses to leave Russia. As he must always be organizing something, he has taken it into his head to found a society, an 'Orpheum' or a 'Verein', where the artistic and literary intelligentsia of Petersburg can meet. This idea was debated for a long time and it ended in a decision that we should have a meeting to test the water next Thursday (they chose that day because I'm leaving on Friday), and a list of whom to invite and whom to circulate was drawn up. I am supposed to be in charge of informing literary circles. Naturally, nothing will come of it. As for the rest, it doesn't really concern me as I don't live in Russia. But Rubinstein was pleased with it all – he's a devil of a man, and as obstinate as a mule. I met his wife, a fine-looking woman. It would appear that her son continues to impress.

I think I'll send you my Russian versions of 'Gärtner' and 'Es ist ein schlechtes Wetter'. I chose these two as they are the most difficult. The princess's horse 'Snow White' has become as black as ink, but that's in the nature of things. Get Mme Guryeva to sing it to see how it comes out.[3]

I had a quiet dinner with my old friend Annenkov and afterwards saw a gentleman who wants to rent some of my estates and perhaps buy one of them. He is a fine man whom I have known for a long time – and he is well off.

The whirlpool of life into which I have fallen here in Petersburg and which I hope to escape at the earliest possible moment has not for one instant made me forget either London, my return there, or that which I love most in the world, and now more than ever. I shall be happy only when I have crossed the portals of 30 Devonshire Place!

I have received a letter from Lewes who speaks of one of your Saturdays which he attended and of another which he hopes to in the future. It seems that you have captured his affections.

Until tomorrow, ⟨dearest friend⟩.[4] A thousand greetings to everyone.

Yours,

Iv. Turgenev

124. To Y. P. POLONSKY

[Original in Russian]

London, 6 May 1871

Dear friend Yakov Petrovich,

I received your letter this morning with the enclosed article attacking Saltykov, and I am replying immediately. The reply which you gave to the criticism of your 'Sheaves of Corn' is absolutely logical and incontrovertible, but nonetheless you would have done better not to have published it. You know

3. Turgenev had translated into Russian six poems by Heine, Mörike and Pohl and they were being set to music by Pauline Viardot. 'Die Gärtner' is by Mörike (and also contains 'Snow White') and 'Es ist ein schlechtes Wetter' is by Heine.
4. Original in German.

the famous proverb, 'If you don't touch things, you won't smell of them.' If you reply it means you are justifying yourself which means you are wrong – such is the inevitable syllogism that occurs to the reading public in such cases. But if you feel better for having done so, there's no great harm.

I left Russia much sooner and more quickly than I had planned, in consequence of a number of letters I had received from abroad. I shall stay here until July and then go to Baden; and in October heavens know where – possibly to Russia.

I have heard that Dostoyevsky has 'called me out'. . . Oh, well, let him amuse himself. He came to see me in Baden five years ago, not to pay me back the money he had borrowed from me but to pour abuse on me for *Smoke* which, in his opinion, should have been sent to the stake. I listened in silence to his philippic – and what did I discover? That I had somehow expressed to him some criminal opinions which he hastened to report to Bartenev. (Actually Bartenev wrote to me about it.) This would have been quite simply a slander, if Dostoyevsky weren't mad, which I am positive he is. Perhaps he imagined it all. But, heavens above, what petty unpleasantness!

I am very upset that Princess S. A. Gagarina[1] thinks me arrogant. Please tell her that if I had not taken note of her letter I would not have been arrogant but a boor. The fact is that as soon as I received it I went to the Academy and asked whether I could see her, but her manservant told me she was engaged. Perhaps he mistook my name or perhaps she really was engaged but I intended to try again the following day. However, I was forced to leave by the fear of cholera. Would you please tell her this as soon as you can and add that I beg her to forgive me for not having written to her and that I have the most happy recollection of her.

And so, look after yourself and carry on writing – and don't pay any attention to any of the critics. Please remember me to your wife. I affectionately kiss your hand.

Yours sincerely,
Iv. Turgenev

125. To A. A. FET

[Original in Russian]

Baden-Baden, 28 August 1871

Well, I'm back here again, dear Afanasy Afanasyevich, and have received your letter, i.e. it was waiting for me here. I shall remain in Baden until the end of October, then Paris, and at the end of November Petersburg. I have recently been to Scotland; I attended the celebrations for Sir Walter Scott and even made a speech (very short and learnt by heart beforehand). I am now known in all the

---

[124] 1. Princess Sofya Andreyevna Gagarina (1810–?), née Dashkova. Her husband was vice-president of the Academy of Arts.

papers as ⟨'Mr Torqunoff, a distinguished novelist'⟩.[1] The English have no interest whatsoever in Russia or Russian literature (the Russian government is another matter, especially Russian diplomacy). Then I went to the ⟨Highlands⟩[1] to shoot ⟨grouse⟩[1], a bird half-way between a blackcock and a partridge. It was all very interesting but rather tiring, and because I was so excited I shot badly on the first day. The air in the North of Scotland is quite unique – to breathe it is pure joy. My hosts were extremely pleasant and hospitable.[2]

I am very sorry that Petya[3] is cross at me for my letter and did not feel that perhaps I am right. When he is grown up and if I am still alive and he has become – which I do not doubt – a good man, I shall show him *the first letter he wrote me after the death of his father*, and he will be ashamed and astonished at where the selfishness of youth can lead. Because of his success at the *lycée* he now thinks of himself as a little tsar and, as we all know, it is difficult to make tsars see the truth.

When we see each other, we can talk of recent English *poetry*, about which no one (or almost no one) in Russia knows a thing. I don't much like it, but it's very interesting and there is one huge lyric talent – Swinburne.

It's worrying that 'there is no news of Tolstoy'. One just could not have a higher opinion of him than I do. Let us hope the rumours are exaggerated and that he will recover.[4] If such a talent can be united with a rather more educated and tranquil, i.e. wiser, mind, what can we not expect of him! I am firmly convinced that we shall see the time when we will laugh openly at the stench of all that quasi-philosophical nonsense that he has put into his truly great novel.

And what's this about disliking the name of 'writer'? This is a hobby-horse of yours, but life has taught me to treat the hobby-horses of others with respect. In my opinion 'a writer' is a name, or a definition of one's activities, just like a 'bootmaker' or a 'pastry-cook'. There are, of course, good and bad pastry-cooks – and writers too.

Send my best wishes to Marya Petrovna.[5] I firmly press your hand.

Yours sincerely,

Iv. Turgenev

126. To V. V. STASOV

Vladimir Vasilyevich Stasov (1824–1906), prominent and influential art and music critic. Educated, like Tchaikovsky, at the School of Jurisprudence in St Petersburg, he lived abroad from 1851 to 1854; he was appointed director of the fine arts department of the St Petersburg Public Library in 1872. While his major

[125] 1. Original in English.

2. Mr and Mrs Benson, friends of the Viardots, who lived at Allean House, Pitlochry.

3. P. I. Borisov.

4. Two of Tolstoy's brothers had died from tuberculosis and, fearing he was developing the symptoms, Tolstoy had gone to Samara to take a course of koumiss, fermented mare's milk. The rumours of the seriousness of his illness were indeed false.

5. Marya Petrovna (1828–94), Fet's wife, the sister of V. P. Botkin.

work of literary scholarship on the origins of the Russian *byliny*, or traditional folk epic poems, showed that there was nothing particularly Russian about them, his writings on art did much to further painting and sculpture in Russia and, more particularly, those on music had considerable influence. Besides drafting the libretto of Borodin's *Prince Igor*, he did much to publicize the works of 'the Mighty Handful' of Balakirev, Borodin, Cui, Mussorgsky and Rimsky-Korsakov, who, insisting that they were following the example of Glinka, wished to create a truly *Russian* music.

Stasov and Turgenev first met in St Petersburg in March 1867 at a concert organized by Balakirev at his Free School of Music. Although their artistic interests had much in common, Stasov and Turgenev were to have serious disagreements over their respective views; they nonetheless contrived to remain friends. Twenty of Turgenev's letters survive, and four of Stasov's.

[Original in Russian]

Paris, 10 December 1871

I should have replied to your letter a long time ago, dear Vladimir Vasilyevich, but because of moving house, then an attack of gout, then various literary matters, I am afraid I did not find the time. I have come to Paris for a couple of months and hope to be in Petersburg by the middle of January, if I am alive and well. I am glad that Antokolsky[1] has turned up (I am sending you, by the way, your letter to him). I fear for his marriage more from a physical rather than a moral point of view: people with weak chests are all terribly lustful and wear themselves out – and not on works of art. With your opinion of marriage I am – (in general)[2] – in agreement. I would even go further and apply it to every *permanent* relationship with a woman. You know those unofficial marriages – they sometimes turn out more poisonous than the more accepted form. I know a lot about the problem and have thought deeply about it. If I have failed to deal with it up till now in my literary writings, it is simply because I have always avoided subjects which are too personal; I find them embarrassing. When it has all faded into the past, perhaps I'll think about attempting something – that is if the desire to write has not disappeared. I find the actual labour of writing – and of being satisfied with what I do – grows less easy with every day. I have just finished a long story [*Torrents of Spring*] for the *Messenger of Europe*, which I had to rewrite *three* times; a real labour of Sisyphus. But as the French say, '*qui a bu, boira*' – and nothing else is possible.

I read your article in the *St Petersburg Gazette* about the competition at the Academy and Repin.[3] I was very pleased to hear that this young man is making such rapid and successful progress. He is highly talented and, what is most important, he has the undoubted *temperament* for being a painter. One cannot but

[126] 1. Mark Matveyevich Antokolsky (1843–1902). See headnote to letter no. 212.

2. Original in French.

3. Ilya Yefimovich Repin (1844–1930), one of the most prolific and versatile Russian painters of the nineteenth century, much involved with the *Peredvizhniki*, a society formed with the object of taking paintings of contemporary interest to a wider audience.

rejoice at the decline of the repulsive influence of Bryullov. We shall only have fresh water when that stagnant pool has been removed – when that scab has fallen off.

I haven't been anywhere here yet or seen anyone, so I have nothing to report. The republic is sick, as is the whole nation. What will come of it all God alone knows – and I suspect He doesn't know either.

Send my best wishes to Antokolsky and be assured of my deepest respect.

Yours sincerely,

Iv. Turgenev

127. To Y. P. POLONSKY

[Original in Russian]

Paris, 14 March 1872

Dear friend Yakov Petrovich,

As a meticulous correspondent, I am replying to your letter immediately.

1. Your poem 'The Cliff' has been passed on to Khanykov. He is flourishing.

2. Because of our long-standing custom of being quite open with each other, I can say that I did not like the poem that you sent me, 'Blessed is the *embittered* poet', one bit, even though it bears the stamp of your virtuosity. Somehow it is a clumsy mixture of the ironic and the serious – there is either not enough evil or not enough ecstasy – and it gives the impression of being simultaneously both confused and forced. I have no doubt that Stasyulevich[1] rejected it not because of any political considerations but simply because he did not like it. However, even I do not understand his allusion to the person to whom he thinks *you* were alluding – and if you have worked out whom he means, I shall be even more amazed! I'm not talking about the first half – there it is unquestionably Nekrasov, even though you do not admit it yourself – but who is it in the second half (which is much weaker than the first)? Yourself? No, it just doesn't come off.

3. All the worse for Fet, if he hasn't come to see you. Lev Tolstoy's philosophy has completely confused him and he now sometimes talks such utter nonsense that one is involuntarily reminded of the two insane brothers and their insane sister who had no time for the pleasant poet. The fact that Meshchersky did not understand his article is quite natural.[2]

4. As for the same Prince Meshchersky's *Citizen*, it is without any doubt the most stinking little journal at present appearing in Russia. He sends me copies of it. I foresee its rapid demise – and it won't be a violent death.

5. I have been to see your friends here in Paris and intend to see them again soon. They are very nice and good people.[3]

[127] 1. Mikhail Matveyevich Stasyulevich (1829–1911), editor and publisher. See headnote to letter no. 152.

2. Prince Vladimir Petrovich Meshchersky (1839–1914), right-wing writer and publicist, editor of the *Citizen* from 1872 to 1874.

3. Polonsky had asked Turgenev to see the sisters of his first wife, Y. V. Ustyuzhskaya.

6. I saw Tchaikovsky in Moscow and heard some of his music. We are corresponding, but we have not actually met. He strikes me as a very pleasant man, and he is without doubt very talented or at least more gifted than the likes of the ungifted Cui, Balakirev, etc. who (along with the late Dargomyzhsky)[4] people are trying to suggest are geniuses. I didn't hear the overture [to *Romeo and Juliet*] which you mentioned.

7. You say nothing about your health. What am I supposed to think? Probably, that it's good.

8. I have ceased thinking about my *Torrents of Spring* – as I have, generally speaking, about all my past works which now lie in the archives. I am glad that others have taken to it and praise it. That some hate it is their affair. Let them enjoy other things. *Quod scripsi, scripsi.*[5]

9. I am leaving here on 8 April and so, if nothing awful happens, I shall appear before you during Holy Week and greet you with our traditional triple Easter kiss. And in the meantime, look after your health, work hard and don't get downhearted. Please remember me to your charming wife.

Yours sincerely,

Iv. Turgenev

P.S. Once again, you scoundrel, you have failed to include your address. I spent half an hour rummaging through your old letters to find it.

128. To N. S. TURGENEV

[Original in Russian]

Paris, 16 April 1872

Dear friend and brother,

I have just received your letter, in which you tell me of the cruel and sad loss which you have suffered.[1] I am sure that you will not doubt my deep and sincere sympathy. The woman with whom you passed more than thirty years of your life in such peace and friendship and who could inspire such devotion on your part could not but possess especial qualities and remain dear to me. I can understand that being alone must seem to you so bitter and hard to bear; but what must we do but try to carry on living ourselves, and while we do we must try to find some activity, something to hang on to, even if one's main support has been removed for ever. We are all ephemeral creatures, but ⟨transient moths⟩,[2] as Voltaire says; everyone is condemned to an imminent death; one can

---

4. Alexander Sergeyevich Dargomyzhsky (1813–69), composer and performer, who was largely self-taught; best remembered for his songs, with their unusual harmonies and humour. Up to a point he influenced both Mily Alexeyevich Balakirev (1836–1910) and Tsezar Antonovich Cui (1835–1918), both members of 'the Mighty Handful' (see above, p. 185).

5. What I have written, I have written.

[128] 1. N. S. Turgenev's wife died in March 1872.

2. Original in French.

scarcely look around before everything has perished. ⟨All that one can do is to make the most of one's life.⟩²

Personally, I wish to see you as soon as possible, and to proffer the helping hand of a brother. I shall leave sooner than I had planned and hope to be in Moscow at the beginning of next month. I shall of course stay with you. In the meantime, dear brother, try not to be too despondent and downhearted. Please believe in the immutable friendship of your brother who embraces you from afar with all the tender warmth of his loving heart.

I shall see you soon.

Iv. Turgenev

129. To E. de GONCOURT

Edmond de Goncourt (1822–96), along with his younger brother Jules, with whom he often collaborated, was one of the early representatives of naturalism in literature and a forerunner of Zola. He went to great lengths to present his subject matter with the utmost precision and accuracy. The brothers were also avid collectors of objets d'art and are usually considered the first to have introduced Japanese art into France. The Prix Goncourt, the most highly respected of French literary prizes, was established in 1903 under the terms of Edmond's will. Turgenev first met him in 1863 at one of the famous literary dinners at Magny's restaurant in Paris, although when he first wrote to him nine years later he had obviously forgotten. Although Turgenev had a rather prudish attitude to de Goncourt's scatological humour and frankness about sexual matters, he enjoyed his company. Twenty of Turgenev's letters to him have survived.

[Original in French]

Paris, 14 May 1872

Dear Sir,

I am leaving tomorrow for Russia, but I could not leave without saying how much I regret not having seen you since that charming day we spent at your home. It is all my fault, I know, but that only makes my regret all the more bitter. But I hope to make amends after my return. I have read your book with the greatest of interest; I do not always agree with your opinions but their *maestria* holds me constantly spellbound.

I take the liberty of sending you a volume of my works.

I am writing today to Flaubert. He told me he is about to come to Paris. Please press his hand firmly for me, and be assured of my sincere affection for you.

Yours truly,

Iv. Turgenev

130. To E. DURAND

Emile Durand (1838–1900), French writer and translator. He taught for a number of years at the School of Jurisprudence in St Petersburg and was a regular contributor to the *Journal de St-Pétersbourg*. He translated a number of Turgenev's works into French, notably *Torrents of Spring* and *Virgin Soil*. Eighteen of Turgenev's letters to him have survived.

[Original in French]

Saint-Valéry-sur-Somme, 26 July 1872

Monsieur,

I have never had a more obstinate attack of gout than the one which has had me in its grip for six weeks now. I only managed to walk without crutches for the first time yesterday and it will be impossible for me to get to Paris before the end of next week, but I hope to be there then. I shall let you know on the day before my arrival.

I never had any doubts about the reception you would receive from Hetzel; he is an excellent and sensitive man and I am sure you will easily be able to arrange things with him.

I have found out that M. Franceschi is at present in Valéry. I shall willingly write to him, but I cannot imagine that he really wants to publish *Torrents of Spring* in Belgium in a separate edition.[1]

Could you perhaps find his full address (from the offices of *Nord*) and send it to me?

You have carte blanche to place *Torrents of Spring* in any review or journal, and if the *Revue Universelle* accepts it, so much the better. As for the cuts Hetzel wishes to make I have no advice to give you, as I cannot evaluate critically a work so recently completed. But I agree to anything and shall forget all my susceptibilities as an author. I have the utmost confidence in Hetzel's taste. But it seems to me that any amputation will be difficult as *Nord* has published the thing in its entirety. I repeat, though, that I shall refrain from a decision on it.[2]

The little stories by Count Tolstoy are meant to be read by ordinary people, which is not at all the same thing as saying that they were written for children. I have only read two of them and the second, entitled *The Prisoner of the Caucasus*, is quite charming, and I think that children will like it a lot.[3]

We can talk about all this when we next meet, and until then please accept my very best wishes.

Iv. Turgenev

[130] 1. Franceschi published his translation of *Torrents of Spring* in the Brussels-based journal *Nord*, without Turgenev's permission, in the summer of 1872. It would appear that a separate edition of his version never appeared.

2. It appeared without any cuts.

3. Tolstoy wrote a series of stories for his *ABC Book* (or *Reader*). Two of them, *The Prisoner of the Caucasus* and *God Sees the Truth, but Waits*, were published separately in 1872.

131. To W. R. S. RALSTON

[Original in English]

Paris, 15 October 1872

My dear friend,

You are surely now back in London – and I ought to have written you long ago – but I felt myself very *découragé* – and given up to 'blue devils' – thanks to my gout which still holds me (I have been in bed for ten days a week ago) – and mars and spoils all my projects. I made what the French call 'des efforts surhumains' and went to see Mme G. Sand's château – but could remain there only one day – enough to appreciate the good humour, cordiality and benevolence of this remarkable woman, but not enough to enjoy her society as fully as I wished. She is living in an old French house in a wooded country with her son, her daughter-in-law and two charming grand-children: all is quiet and simple and *naturel* around her. Herself is quite an old woman now – and with the knack she has of hiding her fine brow under a man[e] of curly hair – looks like a Jewess, but the eyes are still very fine and intelligent – and of a grand poetic expression.

I am glad to see that you are deep in your work – but you ought to find some bookseller to publish it – as the ice is broken now. I am still at your absolute disposal for the proof-sheets.[1]

You will soon receive some Russian books I have brought from Russia for you – they will interest you I hope.

Poor Dahl is also dead. But he had done all he had to do on earth – and has left behind a work, which will last – I mean his dictionary. Say something about him in the *Athenaeum* or *Saturday Review* or the *Pall Mall*.[2]

I regret very much your inability to come to Paris this winter – and the necessity of saying you ⟨goodbye⟩[3] – till next year. But *sic fata voluerunt*.[4]

Believe me,

Yours very truly,

J. Tourguéneff

132. To J. SCHMIDT

Heinrich Julian Schmidt (1818–86), German journalist, critic and literary historian, met Turgenev through their mutual friend K. A. L. Pietsch. He wrote extensively and usually very positively on Turgenev's works. Thirty-five of Turgenev's letters to him have been published, although more are known to exist.

[131] 1. Ralston had been working on his *Russian Folk Tales* (London, 1873).

2. Vladimir Ivanovich Dahl (1801–72), of Danish origin, writer of naturalist physiological sketches in the forties, but best remembered for his four-volume *Reasoned Dictionary of the Living Great Russian Language* (1864–8). Ralston wrote a flattering obituary.

3. Original in Russian.

4. Thus have the fates desired.

[Original in German, translated from the Russian]

Paris, 22 January 1873

My dear friend,

Thank you very much for your letter and the cutting from the *Nationalzeitung*. The whole story is now shown in its true light; but I shall not rest until I have discovered the *corpus delecti*, if there really is one.[1]

I am glad you liked the scene where the horse is killed.[2] In the description of the horse's qualities (which is far too long), I did not intend to present a marvellous picture; I simply wanted to list the good points about the Cossack horse. I took what I wrote straight from the mouth of an old Cossack officer, which was being too careful by far. You are quite right about the external wrapping of the story, but I am not always guilty of such things. I think I have fallen upon a good subject this time, or at least a wide-ranging one.[3] I need only to go to Russia, and then . . . I am not involved in writing as much as I used to be, especially as my material is so far away, but I have to force myself.

'Vous me faites venir l'eau à la bouche'[4] as the French say, when you said you wanted to speak of the German soul, and then said nothing. You must tell me, either in person or in a letter.

I cannot deny that I had my knife into Germany when I was writing *Torrents of Spring*, but that was nothing compared with the antipathy I have felt more than once towards Russia or France – do you remember the passage from *Ghosts*? Now that was real hatred. I have never had the slightest enmity towards Sweden, Denmark or Italy, and there is not a man in the whole world who can change my mind about the true love I bear for Germany.

You are quite right in your negative opinion of the last chapter of *Torrents of Spring*. It was weak of me to introduce a moral which I felt I ought to, but it so happened (I ought to have said so earlier) that it cost me nothing.

I do not know what to make of your intention to shout 'Aeneas!' However hard I try I just cannot decipher the meaning of this epithet. What does the joke mean?

Remember me to all our friends. All the very best.

Yours sincerely,
Iv. Turgenev

133. To P. L. LAVROV

Pyotr Lavrovich Lavrov (1823–1900), mathematician, thinker and revolutionary, one of the leaders of the Russian Populists. Exiled in 1866, he emigrated in

[132] 1. There were stories, ostensibly started in certain French papers, that during the Franco-Prussian War Turgenev was reported to have said that he had never known 'a single decent German'. He vigorously denied the statement.
2. In *The End of Chertopkhanov*.
3. *Virgin Soil*.
4. 'You have made my mouth water.'

133. *To P. L. Lavrov*

1870 to Western Europe where he published the revolutionary journal *Forward*; he later joined the First International. Lavrov and Turgenev first met in Paris in 1872, and the latter was to provide much help and material for Lavrov's publications. Seventy-nine of Turgenev's letters survive.

[Original in Russian]

Karlsbad, 13 July 1873

Dear Pyotr Lavrovich,

Please forgive me for not replying immediately to your letter and its enclosed details of your future journal's editorial policies. Taking the waters is such a stupid life that you do nothing all day and still have no time to do anything. I shall begin by saying that I wish to be a subscriber – a serious, paying subscriber – to your journal, and I ask you to send it to my permanent address, 48 rue de Douai, Paris, and also to inform me how, where and how much to pay. I have read your programme twice with the greatest attention. I am in agreement with all the most important points. I have only one objection and one *appréhension*. It seems to me that you have no need to attack the Constitutionalists and Liberals so cruelly or to go so far as to label them our enemies. I think that it would be far easier to pass from their ideal of the form which the State should take to your vision than it would be from the present Absolutism, the more so since you yourself have little faith in violent upheavals and deny that they have any real value. And your announcement that you would summarily remove many Liberals and Parliamentarians will frighten people. As for my *appréhension*, it consists of the following: have you not given your journal too scholarly and philosophical a character, which might harm its circulation and reduce its influence? However, all this will be seen and determined *ipso facto*. I am impatient to see the first number of your *Forward*.

As for all the former Russian female students in Zurich, in the first place my university contacts are too weak for me to be able to provide them with any assistance, and secondly, they should not hide from themselves the fact that they will *not find asylum* in any German university of any standing. It is worth reading the small article in yesterday's *Kölnische Zeitung*, which expresses the opposition not only of the government but also of society to admitting them to university courses. There is not the slightest hope for them there.

I shall leave here in ten days' time, and although I shall be staying in the suburbs of Paris to start with please write to rue de Douai.

I wish you all the best and firmly press your hand.

Yours sincerely,
Iv. Turgenev

134. TO A. A. FET

[Original in Russian]

Bougival, 2 September 1873

Various misfortunes, dear Fet, have clearly befallen your letter. Despatched on 27 July, it reached its destination three days ago; consequently it spent more than three weeks on its journey. I hasten to reply so that I may not be again in your debt. I am delighted that, as far as I can judge, you are in good health and have even had some marvellous shooting. As for me, I am in more or less good health and have also been shooting – but it wasn't marvellous; in fact it was awful. Two days ago, ⟨as an overture to the season⟩,[1] I spent five hours in the company of a poor dog traipsing through the empty countryside and shot one partridge and one quail. I'm finished with it all! In the first place there is *no* game in France and in the second I am getting too old for such diversions. All day yesterday and today my legs have been aching and my right knee is a little swollen. ⟨Enough of it!⟩[2]

The same exclamation might also be applied to literature, which has become ⟨a foreign country⟩[3] to me and rouses but little interest in me in its *latest* manifestations. ⟨I do not read any more; I reread.⟩[1] By the way, I am looking at Virgil again, and with no little pleasure.

And, despite your recommendation, I am not going to read your Strakhov.[4] What I have already read of his lofty phrases will suffice. I feel a strong physical repulsion from everything Slavophile, just as I do from an awful smell or taste, or from Bryullov or G. Doré.[5] It's flabby, unpleasant, rotten and sticks in one's gullet. And it smells of the icon-lamp in church. No, I am an incorrigible Westerner and the slightest mention of the fact that 'Our brother is a Russian, but' etc. grips the pit of my stomach, and my mouth is filled with the bitter taste of bile.

Tyutchev, though, is a different matter. I am deeply sorry about him.[6] He also was a Slavophile, but not in his poetry. And those poems where he was one are decidedly poor. The very core of his being is purely Western, just like Goethe's. Between his 'The light of autumn evenings' and K. Aksakov's 'Lush island, wonderful island' there is absolutely no comparison. The former is like a beautifully shaped lyre while the latter is just a fat little bell, donated by a merchant. Dear, bright, bright as day, Fyodor Ivanovich! Farewell, farewell!

[Six lines omitted]

Why don't you say a word about Lev Tolstoy? He 'hates and despises me', but I continue to take a serious interest in him as the very best of our present writers.

[134] 1. Original in French.

2. Original in Italian.

3. Original in German.

4. Nikolay Nikolayevich Strakhov (1828–96), philosopher, publicist and influential literary critic. In many of his works he showed strong Slavophile influences.

5. Gustave Doré (1832 or 1833–83), French painter and illustrator. Turgenev disliked what he called Doré's 'romantic effects'.

6. Tyutchev had recently died.

135. *To A. A. Fet*

Your recommendation to M. N. Longinov on his departure from Oryol has had its effect; the *Messenger of Europe* has had its second warning.[7] You will no doubt be delighted when this honest, moderate and monarchist journal is closed down for being radical and revolutionary.

Please excuse this somewhat peevish outburst, but anyone can get irritated! Please remember me to your wife. I press your hand.

Yours sincerely,

Iv. Turgenev

P.S. I do not doubt that Kishinsky is feathering his own nest; it is also indisputable that he has never sent any receipts since he has been working for me. But did you really see him drunk? I've never noticed that in him. Could you perhaps – discreetly but accurately – find out what estate he has bought and where it is? As you know, we are rolling in gossip-mongers over here.

135. To A. A. FET

[Original in Russian]

Paris, 12 January 1874

Dear Fet,

I am writing to you on our Russian New Year's Eve. I send you my best wishes and hope to see you sometime during the coming year. I should have replied to your letter of 30 October a long time ago, but I must confess that I have been busy with other things. Mme Viardot's elder daughter, my beloved Didie, is engaged to be married and I have been playing a most active part in this joyous event. Her fiancé, a certain M. Georges Chamerot,[1] is a splendid young man although I shall not say he is worthy of her, for in my eyes no man is; but she is in love with him and he has won the day. I have experienced, and am still experiencing, a variety of feelings – both happy and sad – and I hope you will excuse me for not chatting about much else.

I was always convinced that there was an excellent pedagogue in you and consequently congratulate your fourteen-year-old, although rather immature, niece on coming under your jurisdiction. I have heard from the son of Nikolay Milyutin[2] (our Cavour), who has just arrived here, the best news about Petya Borisov. As far as I can judge, your affairs are progressing reasonably, or at least they are all in order and we must thank Providence for that, although because even Providence cannot return one's youth and everything after it is a hollow sham, I can see little to thank her for.

An almanac (*Pooling our Resources*) has been organized in Petersburg in aid of the victims of the famine in Samara; there is no doubt at all that it will strike

7. Mikhail Nikolayevich Longinov (1823–75), a friend of Turgenev's when both were young men, had been appointed in 1871 director of the government department responsible for the press.

[135] 1. Georges Chamerot (1845–?), publisher and printer; Turgenev liked him a lot.

2. Yury Nikolayevich Milyutin (1856–1912), lawyer, writer and publisher.

everyone as being nothing out of the ordinary. However, all our leading literary figures have agreed to write for it, with the exception of Tolstoy, Pisemsky and you. Why are all our Achilles staying in their tents, especially the first, Tolstoy, who is a real Achilles? Send me news of him – if you can take the trouble to drop me a line.

Karlsbad helped my health and up till now I am fairly all right. I even recently went shooting all day. I bagged, however, only one pheasant, one partridge – and a rabbit.

And so I wish you all the best and send my remembrances to your wife. I affectionately press your hand.

Yours sincerely,
Iv. Turgenev

136. To P. V. ANNENKOV

[Original in Russian]

Paris, 7 February 1874

Dear Pavel Vasilyevich,

First of all I wish to express my joy that nothing unfortunate happened to your family, and I hope your little son will now fully recover and prosper.[1]

The manuscript [*Living Relics*], which you returned to me, has already been sent off to Petersburg. As soon as I read that part of your letter where you expressed your doubts about one short passage I thought immediately that you were referring to ⟨lofty phrases about Emancipation⟩,[2] and the outcome was that the passage was summarily removed. I have never had any regrets about taking your literary advice, and I thank you sincerely and entrust myself to your care for the future.

A funny thing happened to me yesterday, which I must tell you about. There is in America a certain publisher, Henry Holt, who has brought out a number of translations of my works over the past five years. As no copyright agreement exists between America and Europe, it never occurred to Holt to ask my permission, especially as other publishers have printed translations too. You can imagine my amazement when I received a letter from him yesterday where, after many compliments (he even used the word ⟨enthusiasm!⟩[3]), he reports that sales of my books have not gone very well, but as he has managed to make some profit on them he is in the position to send me an honorarium of 1000 francs – and the letter actually contained a money order for this amount! This truly American graciousness really touched me. I must confess that throughout the whole of my literary career I have rarely felt so flattered. People have told me

[136] 1. Annenkov's son Pavel had been very seriously ill with pneumonia.
   2. Original in French.
   3. Original in English.

before that, if I may so express it, I am quite popular in America, but this living proof has made me very happy.

And so I send affectionate greetings and firmly press your hand.

Yours sincerely,

Iv. Turgenev

P.S. The date for the wedding [Didie's] has been fixed for 8 March; so far everything is going well.

137. To P. HEYSE

Paul Heyse (1830–1914), German novelist, poet and playwright, immensely popular in his day but little read today. He received the Nobel Prize for Literature in 1910. He had read the German versions of *A Sportsman's Sketches* in the mid-fifties and wrote two very enthusiastic reviews. He and Turgenev met in Munich in 1861. Eleven of Turgenev's letters to him survive.

[Original in German]

Paris, 2 April 1874

Dear Heyse,

My long, long silence is quite unforgivable, I know, and I shall not even try to excuse myself. But I must explain that it can be divided up into three periods. In the first I failed to read your novel [*Kinder der Welt*]; in the second I did read it and every day intended to write to you, but laziness prevented me; and in the third I was too ashamed to write because I had fallen silent for so long. This will strike you as rather strange, but it's the truth. And now, of course, my letter is too late; your novel's success is just like the old French republic – ⟨'One must be blind not to see it'⟩[1] – and it has already been translated into Russian. My fellow-countrymen are reading it avidly, and I also have passed more than one pleasant hour with your book. But you and I are very alike. Neither of us writes novels but rather extended novellas. I do not have to explain this to you at length; you know it as well as I. I shall press your hand and say: Bravo! Carry on!

But to other matters. Have you received Flaubert's latest book, *La tentation de St Antoine*? I sent it to you because the author is a close friend of mine and the book is very original and striking. And I would like more than anything in the world that the German reading public in particular should render Flaubert his due and thereby encourage him, for the critics here look upon him with disfavour. So could you carry out my wishes? If you like the book, my dear Heyse, please write a review of it. A word from an authority such as you would do a lot of good. Flaubert would be very grateful to you, as I would too. In any case, tell me what you think of the book.

I spent the winter in Paris and am now going to Russia (at the beginning of

[137] 1. Original in French.

May). I shall be in Karlsbad in July and hope to return to Paris via Munich where I shall see you. Your house must surely be finished by now and the bird sitting peacefully in its little nest. Am I right? Please send my best greetings to Frau Heyse.

Yours very sincerely,
I. Turgenev

138. To E. ZOLA

Turgenev first met the French novelist Emile Zola (1840–1902) at the home of Flaubert in 1872 and they remained friends for the rest of Turgenev's life. Zola's popularity in Russia owed much to Turgenev's championing of his cause, and with Turgenev's help Zola became the Paris correspondent of the *Messenger of Europe* from 1875 to 1880; some of his works appeared in Russia before they did in France. Turgenev liked much of Zola's writing, although he had serious reservations about their outspoken realism. Fifty-eight of Turgenev's letters to Zola have survived.

[Original in French]

Spasskoye, 5 June 1874

My dear Zola,

If you have an atlas, find the map of Russia, and starting from Moscow move your finger down towards the Black Sea and you will find, just to the north of Oryol, the town of Mtsensk. Well, my village is ten kilometres from there – and equally unpronounceable, as you will notice! The absolute solitude is peaceful, verdant and sad. If I can do some writing, I shall stay here for a while; if not, I shall flee and after six months in Karlsbad return to Paris, when I shall definitely look you up.

But now, to business!

I became convinced in Petersburg that in view of the present state of international law there is nothing to prevent anyone from translating and publishing your works. This is why I have not been able to place your *Conquête de Plassans*. No translation has yet appeared, but the editor of the journal I mentioned to you[1] does not want to risk commissioning a translation which might not be the first. (When I left Petersburg *La Curée* had just appeared in a bookshop under the title of *Dobycha, broshennaya sobakam* (literally, 'The quarry thrown to the dogs').[2]) But as the editor is very interested in publishing your works in his journal he has suggested that he should pay you (through me) thirty roubles (105 francs) for every printer's page of any manuscript or proof-copy which you send

[138] 1. i.e. M. M. Stasyulevich of the *Messenger of Europe*.

2. *La Curée* had been published with large sections removed by the censor. A longer version was published later in 1874 but was then banned because 'this novel might have a corrupting effect on the inexperienced reader'.

him. As he will have to pay a translator roughly the same amount, I think that is very reasonable of him and that you should accept. Send your reply to the following address: M. I. T., St-Pétersbourg, hôtel Demouth, grande rue des Ecuries. I shall be there in three weeks at the outside and can pass on your answer.

The editor has read your *Conquête* and is in raptures over it.

I am very intrigued by the novel you are writing at the moment; I think it will be excellent. The subject matter is both very ordinary yet very original.

I have just written to Flaubert but I fear my letter will not find him still at Croisset. He was planning to go to Righi in Switzerland to revive his spirits. The Russians haven't been exposed to his *Antoine* and it wasn't even banned![3] But he mustn't be told. Farewell. I wish you health and happiness and cordially press your hand.

Iv. Turgenev

P.S. Political events have taken a strange turn in France.

139. To A. N. OSTROVSKY

Alexander Nikolayevich Ostrovsky (1823–86), dramatist. His plays, both comedies and tragedies and set mainly among the conservative merchant class of Moscow, laid the foundations of Russian realistic drama. His best-known works are *Poverty is no Crime, Easy Money* (based on Shakespeare's *The Taming of the Shrew*), *The Forest* and his masterpiece *The Storm*. His verse fairy-tale *The Snow Maiden* formed the basis for Rimsky-Korsakov's opera.

Ostrovsky and Turgenev first met in the early fifties, when they would read and discuss their works with each other. Although Turgenev preferred his earlier plays to the later ones, he was an enthusiastic admirer of Ostrovsky all his life. It was through Turgenev that the first French version of *The Storm* was published, and also the first article in English on his plays. Eleven of Turgenev's letters to Ostrovsky survive.

[Original in Russian]

Spasskoye, 6 June 1874

Dear Alexander Nikolayevich,

I am writing to you from my home in the country where I arrived yesterday. I must, in the words of Gogol, announce publicly that I am a silly ass . . . What I mean to say is that there is a certain French writer, E. Durand, who is reasonably fluent in Russian. He does various translations and I recommended your plays to him, beginning with *The Storm* as it is probably more accessible and comprehensible to the French. He subsequently translated it – not at all badly. We

---

3. Stasyulevich had refused to publish it because he feared consequences from the censor.

went through it carefully together and corrected all the mistakes, and if we have your permission we shall certainly get it published this winter and even staged in one of the best Paris theatres. On the very day I left Paris Durand, who was in ecstasies over the play, brought round his carefully rewritten manuscript so that I could show it to you and get your opinion of it. I expected that I would definitely find you in Moscow, but when I saw your brother in Petersburg he told me you had left for the country. And that's what I meant when I said I was stupid! So I suggest the following solution: either take my word that the translation is a good one and send me your permission to have it published and, if possible, staged (naturally I shall try to do things in your best interests), or say that you would still prefer to see the manuscript. Write to me in Moscow with your decision. I am staying with Maslov and have left most of my things with him as I'm off to the country myself for a short time. If you have written by the time I return I can then send you the manuscript immediately, and when you have read it through you can send it back to me (if you approve it) in Karlsbad (Bohemia) poste restante – I shall be there for six weeks from 1 July; I'm going to take the waters which help my gout so much. There's no hurry, as we could neither publish nor stage *The Storm* before the winter, and so you will have the time to correct any mistakes which you might find. There are many Russian visitors to Karlsbad and you even might find the opportunity yourself. . . *Dixi et animam salvavi.*[1]

Let me know how things are with you; are you working? And on what specifically? I shall possibly be back in Russia myself towards the end of the year. I do so want to acquaint Europe with your works!

Please send my best wishes to [your brother] Mikhail Nikolayevich.

I firmly press your hand, and remain,

Yours very sincerely,
Iv. Turgenev

P.S. I saw a production of *The Forest* in Petersburg. It was done pretty badly, but the play is a delight! The 'tragic actor' is one of your most successful characters.

140. To P. V. ANNENKOV

[Original in Russian]

Spasskoye, 12 June 1874

Dear friend Annenkov,

I am writing you a few lines from my retreat in the wilds where I arrived ten days ago. I shall be here until Sunday when I am going directly to Karlsbad via Moscow, Petersburg and Berlin. I am staying there for five weeks, so please reply there to this billet-doux, poste restante. If we are all still alive, we shall see each other in Baden at the beginning of August. I know you are there already

[139] 1. I have spoken and saved my soul.

because someone to whom you had written from there has informed me. I hope you are all fit and well under the hospitable roof of Frau Anstett, to whom I send greetings.

I am very pleased with my current visit to Russia, but at the same time I am convinced that if I want to do anything practical, contemporary and important or, in a word, if I want to complete the novel I have been thinking about[1] – and started – I shall have to return to Petersburg for the winter, however awful that may be. I have spoiled myself with my congenial, peaceful and comfortable life abroad. Such pleasant habits have taken root and I do not know whether I can cut myself off from it all. But nonetheless I shall have to try. Perhaps even if I do return nothing will emerge – because my brain has stopped working! – but at least my conscience will not be able to reproach me.

I shall not say anything about all I have seen and heard; I shall leave it all until we meet. But what I will say is that because the Aksakovs are scared (!) at my intention to write an article about their father and their family (just as if I were some sort of pamphleteer!) and Salayev wants something ⟨I haven't published yet⟩[2] in place of the article for his new edition, I have written a short story here in Spasskoye based (as I did with *Living Relics*) on an old manuscript I came across called *There's Knocking*! It's an anecdote from my shooting experiences. It has no especial importance, but I regret that you won't be able to cast an eye over it *before* its publication. From looking over *Punin and Baburin* (I've improved it a little, but it's still poor) I can see how useful your comments are to me. But there's nothing to be done. Let's hope it gets through without too much damage.

I have had a letter from the unhappy Pisemsky. He and his wife are in Göttingen at the moment where his son (now the only one) is studying law. They are planning to go to Switzerland in August and I have advised them to stop over in Baden and see us. I am very sorry for them both. Such a death is harder to bear than others – much more.[3]

Did I tell you about my amazing meeting with Goncharov on a street in Petersburg?! He is now accusing me of stealing all his ideas and passing them on to – whom? French novelists, all of whose works are nothing but *scarcely concealed imitations of* Oblomov *and* The Precipice. And why am I doing this? Simply to prevent his novels being translated (⟨they have been deflowered⟩[2]) and thus retain my reputation as the leading Russian writer in the eyes of the French! Poor Goncharov will end up in an asylum.

And so, farewell. Drop me a line in Karlsbad. I shall write to you as soon as I get there. Greetings to all your family; I affectionately press your hand.

Yours,

Iv. Turgenev

[140] 1. *Virgin Soil*.

2. Original in French.

3. Pisemsky's son, Nikolay, had committed suicide at the age of twenty-two.

141.To S. A. VENGEROV

Semyon Afanasyevich Vengerov (1855–1920), critic, literary historian and bib-liographer, was preparing a chapter on Turgenev for his *Contemporary Figures in Russian Literature* (1874–5) and had asked for information.

[Original in Russian]

Spasskoye, 19 June 1874

Dear Sir,

I have received your letter today. I shall reply frankly to your inquiry.

My father died not in 1836 but on 30 October 1834. I was then sixteen. I even then bore a hatred of serfdom, which, by the way, was the reason why I, who had been brought up amidst torture and beatings, did not defile my hands with a single blow on anyone – although I was still a long way from *A Sportsman's Sketches*. I was simply a boy, hardly more than a child. Furthermore my father was not a rich man. He left 130 distressed serfs who provided us with no income – and we were three brothers. My father's estate was amalgamated with that of my mother, a wilful and power-loving woman, who alone gave us – and sometimes removed from us – the necessities of life; it never ocurred to us, nor to her, that this insignificant estate (I refer to my father's) was not hers. I lived abroad for three years and never received a penny from her, but nevertheless never thought of demanding any inheritance. This inheritance, by the way, because of what was due to my mother as a widow and to my brothers, would have amounted to little more than nothing.

When my mother died in 1850 I immediately freed all the house-serfs and wished to put all the others on quit-rent, and in every way possible I encouraged them to take advantage of complete freedom, with the redemption payments reduced by one fifth. I also took nothing from them for the land they farmed on the main estate – which would have amounted to a sizeable sum. In my place others might have done more – and more quickly – but I promised myself always to tell the truth, whatever that truth might be. It's nothing to boast about, I know, but I suggest that it cannot bring me any disgrace.

As for your second request, it is much more difficult to fulfil. I feel a positive, almost physical, antipathy to all my own poetry. I not only do not possess a single copy of any of my poems but would pay much for their never having existed. 'Andrey' appeared in the *Annals of the Fatherland*, but I cannot recall when: 1845 or 1846. 'Parasha' was published separately in 1843. You might perhaps come across it in Cherkesov's bookshop on the Nevsky, which contains all sorts of rubbish.

I wish you every success in your chosen undertaking. Please accept the expression of my deepest respects.

Your most obedient servant,

Iv. Turgenev

142. To G. FLAUBERT

[Original in French]

Moscow, 30 June 1874

My dear friend,

I received your letter from Righi at the very moment when, painfully supported by two crutches, I was about to climb into my carriage and leave the
country for here. I have not broken both my legs as you might imagine but *the
air in my native land*, so beneficial for the Marseillais, brought on a fresh attack of
gout – this time in *both* feet – which confined me to my bed for a fortnight and
still has not departed. To tell you that this is making me see life through
rose-tinted spectacles – or blue ones (I'm thinking of your dream beneath the
skies of Switzerland) – would be to tell a big lie. Infirmity, long-drawn-out and
cold disgust, painful agitation over senseless memories – this is what, my old
friend, lies in store for a man who has passed fifty. And over and above all that –
resignation, HIDEOUS resignation, the preparation for death. But enough! I
shall try to flee to Karlsbad as soon as I can – not to the Karlsbad where you are
dying from boredom, but to the one in Bohemia where I shall stay for five
weeks. And in the autumn – later! – we shall see. I am not making any plans at the
moment, especially pleasant ones, just in case I tempt Fate.

You do not appear to be a man who is enjoying himself on those sublime
peaks, so sung of by Haller and Rousseau.[1] I must confess that the people who
live most constantly with those peaks – I mean the Swiss – are the most deeply
boring and the least gifted people that I have ever met. 'Whence this paradox?'
the philosopher would ask. But perhaps it is not a paradox at all. What would
Bouvard and Pécuchet say about it?[2]

I am very glad that you have at last found a setting [for your novel] or rather
the setting. But the more I think about it, the more it becomes a subject to be
treated *presto* – in the spirit of Voltaire or Swift. You know that that has always
been my opinion. What you have told me about your planned scenario strikes
me as charming and amusing. If you aren't too expansive, if you aren't too
knowing . . .

But you have your shoulder to the wheel at last.

Zola's *La Conquête de Plassans* has been translated in abridged form in one of
the Russian journals. It will be translated *in extenso* later. He is well liked in
Russia.

What if you were to profit from the Righi glacier to compose something
torrid and burning with passion? Eh? Now there's an idea for you!

But most important, come back refreshed. Unfortunately there are some
people who find that boredom heats their blood and makes it burn. Come back
pale and colourless, like a poem by Lamartine.

[142] 1. Probably a reference to *The Alps* by Albrecht von Haller (1708–77) and to J. J. Rousseau's
Nouvelle Héloïse.
   2. Eponymous heroes of the novel Flaubert was writing at the time.

There is good news of all my friends in Paris and Bougival. That at least is balm for my soul.

And now to politics . . . For seven years you will be governed by an effective but inglorious sword, the sword of the gendarme. And you will see it ending up by governing alone, without an elected parliament.

This reminds me that when I was in the country (where I have an excellent library) I read Robespierre's speech on whether Louis XVI should be brought to trial. I found it quite admirable!

Later, towards the end of his career, Robespierre lost his way and became addicted to sentimentality and to touching, exaggerated and high-flown words. But the fellow had a lot of good in him!

Farewell, my friend, probably till Croisset in September, and let us hope we both stay in good health.

I embrace you.

Your old friend,
Iv. Turgenev

P.S. Are you sure you're in Karlsbad? You twice write Karltbad, but that's not possible.

143. To A. P. FILOSOFOVA

Anna Pavlovna Filosofova, née Dyagileva (1837–1912), liberal and leading figure in the women's movement. She and Turgenev became friends during his visit to Russia in the spring of 1874.

[Original in Russian]

Karlsbad, 18 August 1874

Dear Anna Pavlovna,

You will probably be surprised that I have taken so long to respond to your letter and more particularly to what you enclosed with it. The reason for my silence is illness; gout attacked me two months ago in the country and even here is giving me no peace and delaying my treatment; it will force me to return to Paris before I had planned. Thanks to this illness I have only recently managed to look at the papers I brought with me. My reading has caused me certain doubts which I must lay before you.

The object of sending me the various documents was, as far as I can judge, generally to acquaint me with the cast of mind and the personalities of the 'new people', which I cannot study living abroad. Those which you suggest I should know about show themselves in a very advantageous, almost idealistic light, for otherwise you would not have sent them to me. But with the exception of the *diary*, which impressed me with its honesty, truthfulness and genuine enthusiasm, everything else could provide me with material only from a satirical and humorous point of view. This applies particularly to the 'young man', the Russian 'lion', Mr V. G. Dekhterev.[1] His intoxicated vanity, his remarkable lack of talent (I have read many a poor poem in my time, but Mr D's doggerel surpasses them all) and his dogmatic tone combined with such ignorance can only lead to caricature. And note, I am not at all put off by the *harshness* of his ideas; I am just amazed at the naivety expressed in the statement that 'at twenty all the problems of science and life have been solved'. I beg you to excuse me, dear Anna Pavlovna, for expressing myself so forcefully about the young man for whom you have so much sympathy. But I cannot do otherwise. I think that it's a case of your being deceived by your great kindness of heart. Nothing will ever come of such young men as V. G. D. If you look for *ideas* behind all his high-flown words about his own person, you will see they amount to nothing.

After such an opinion, do I have the right to keep the other papers which you sent with quite different intentions in mind? May I make use of them? My conscience tells me no; it tells me that if you had foreseen the impression they were going to make on me, you would probably not have given them to me; and so I do not have the right to keep them any longer. Consequently please write to me in Paris telling me what I should do and how and where to send them back.

No, dear Anna Pavlovna, these are not *new* people. I know many others among the young who are more worthy of such a title. But in the *diary* I see a beautiful, free soul whom I sincerely wish the greatest happiness, i.e. the realization of all her cherished hopes and dreams of creating good and well-being for her less fortunate brothers.

Please accept the assurance of my deepest respect.

Yours sincerely,
Ivan Turgenev

144. To EMMA LAZARUS

Emma Lazarus (1849–87), American writer and poet. She translated many of Heine's poems into English, and her novel *Alide: An Episode in Goethe's Life* (1874) is very flowery and romantic. Her interest in Russia was inspired by a love for Turgenev's works. Her best poems, which appeared in *Songs of a Semite* (1882) where she glorified the Jewish people, stem from her indignation at the pogroms in Russia. Her sonnet 'The New Colossus' is inscribed on the pedestal of the Statue of Liberty. Three of Turgenev's letters to her are known.

[Original in English]

Bougival, 2 September 1874

Dear Miss Lazarus,

You must excuse my very late answer to the letter which accompanied the gift

[143] 1. Vladimir Gavrilovich Dekhterev (1853–1903), a young medical student, later a psychiatrist, was cruelly satirized by Turgenev as Kislyakov in *Virgin Soil*.

of your book. I was very far off – and ill – in Russia and I came back to France only a few days ago. I have just finished the lecture of *Alide* – and though, generally speaking, I do not think it advisable to take celebrated modern men – especially poets and artists – as a subject for a novel, I am truly glad to say that I have read your book with the liveliest interest. It is very sincere and very poetical at the same time; the life and spirit of Germany have no secret for you – and your characters are drawn with a pencil as delicate as it is strong. I feel very proud of the approbation you give to my works – and of the influence you kindly attribute to them on your own talent; an author who writes as you do is not a 'pupil in art' any more; he is not far from being himself a master. Believe me, my dear Miss Lazarus,

Yours very truly,

J. Tourguéneff

145. To W. D. HOWELLS

William Dean Howells (1837–1920), American novelist, poet and critic, sometime editor of the *Atlantic Monthly*. He wrote a number of articles on Turgenev's works and did much to further his popularity in the USA.

[Original in English]

Paris, 28 October 1874

My dear Sir,

Accept my very best thanks for the gracious gift of your delightful book *Their Wedding Journey*, which I have read with the same pleasure I experienced before in reading the *Chance Acquaintance* and *Venetian Life*. Your literary physiognomy is a most sympathetic one; it is natural, simple and clear – and in the same time – it is full of unobtrusive poetry and fine humour. Then – I feel the peculiar American stamp on it – and that is not one of the least causes of my relishing so much your works.

Hoping to make some day your acquaintance – either in Europe or America (I prefer the latter) – I beg you, my dear Sir, to believe me,

Yours very sincerely,

Iv. Tourguéneff

146. To P. J. HETZEL

[Original in French]

Paris, 5 December 1874

My dear friend,

As I told your son yesterday, I have become a worn-out rag which is good for nothing. However, I have given my *Punin and Baburin*, reworked and rewritten, to be translated, and you will get the manuscript in *three* weeks at the very latest for *Temps*, that is if you don't decide to throw it immediately into the fire.

And that dinner with you that I promised *myself*. I tell you in all truth that I must be in my second childhood. I shall definitely arrive *on Monday* if I don't forget it yet again. If I do, may your curses rain on my head! In the meantime I cordially press your hand, for friendship is not something I ever forget.

Ever yours,

Iv. Turgenev

147. To A. A. FET

[Original in Russian]

Paris, 24 December 1874

Dear Sir,

You will probably be surprised, Afanasy Afanasyevich, to receive a letter from me, and indeed I did not expect to converse with you again. But there was a sentence in your reply [to my last letter] which forces me to take up my pen. You write:

'You say "*I* believe it", and so this "*I*" must be the law for all and in your usual way you hurl insults in the face of even such an irreproachable person as L. T.' (I presume that these initials stand for Lev Tolstoy.)

If by using this phrase you had the intention of simply using a figure of speech, as you did with 'the Fable of Spartacus', then I can only regret that you used that particular phrase; if some piece of gossip lies behind it, I can assure you that I have never said anything to anyone about Tolstoy without having the greatest respect for his talent and his personality; this respect of mine will shortly be shown to the French public with the publication of my foreword to a translation of one of his stories;[1] if, finally, you think that you have seen something similar in my letters, then you should reread them and discover your mistake. I have no doubt at all that you are a just man and am sure that, at least in your own mind, you will withdraw the sentence I have cited.

Furthermore I am not accustomed to throwing either insults or mud at anyone, not because some people are not worth the trouble, but because I am not one to dirty my hands in this way and I leave such pursuits to others.

I cannot help saying that it is futile to bemoan the fact that fate has removed your name from the annals of literature; your fears are without foundation. As Fet you *are* a name, as Shenshin you just have one.

I remain your respectful and most obedient servant,

Iv. Turgenev

[147] 1. Tolstoy's *Two Hussars* was published in French translation in *Temps* in February 1875 with a flattering foreword by Turgenev.

148. To N. V. KHANYKOV

[Original in Russian]

Paris, 12 January 1875

Dear Nikolay Vladimirovich,

Firstly, thank you for your interesting little book; it was a very charming present.[1] Secondly, I accept your invitation for tomorrow with the greatest of pleasure, but might I suggest we dine in a new restaurant which Flaubert has recommended to me and where one can eat *excellently* and at half the price we would pay at the Café Riche or at Véfour's; it's Adolphe et Pellé, 31 boulevard Haussmann, opposite the Opéra.

Be there tomorrow at 6.15 and I'll tell Vyrubov.[2]

I'll see you then. I firmly press your hand.

Yours,
Iv. Turgenev

149. To V. V. STASOV

[Original in Russian]

Paris, 27 January 1875

Dear Vladimir Vasilyevich,

In reply to your letter, I can only say this: I might be mistaken in my opinion of contemporary Russian art and you have the right to accuse me of ignorance or a lack of understanding. But how can you imagine that I say what I do not from my own personal convictions or feelings, but because I am bowing down before foreign authorities? How on earth can I, now an old man who throughout his life has valued nothing more than his independence, bow down before anyone or try to ingratiate myself? If you do nothing else, please allow me enough self-respect to react to any question of ⟨'what will people say?'⟩[1] with complete indifference. In my time I have probably sent as many authoritative notables to the 'pearly gates' as you have in yours – albeit mine were different from yours – and they might have been even more famous than those you have quoted. But that same feeling of inner freedom which I constantly sense in myself 'with every minute of every day' will not permit me to recognize the beautiful in something in which I do not see it. In revenge I could say that you also bow down before authority – even if it is an authority you have erected yourself; but I have made it a rule that when I am arguing with someone I never ascribe to my opponent any opinions or convictions which he has not expressed himself. In a word, I beg you to believe that if I regard Mozart's *Don Giovanni* as a work of genius and Dargomyzhsky's *The Stone Guest*[2] as meaningless rubbish, it is not at

[148] 1. Probably a book on the ownership of land in Iran which Khanykov had edited.
  2. Grigory Nikolayevich Vyrubov (1843–1913), philosopher, naturalist and journalist.
[149] 1. Original in French
  2. Opera based on a short play by A. S. Pushkin dealing with the Don Juan theme.

all because Mozart is an 'authority' and everyone else thinks so too or that Dargomyzhsky is known to nobody outside his own circle, but simply because I like Mozart and dislike Dargomyzhsky. And I dislike *Zigzags* too.[3] That's all there is to it.

In your opinion Kharlamov[4] is decidedly poor because he paints in the French style; but there is nothing at all French about him. The Russian man and the Russian artist stand out in all his works, which are straightforward, sincere and realistic. When you next go to Moscow go and see his recently completed portrait of Sergey Tretyakov's wife, and ask yourself whether we have seen the like before.[5]

The fate of the *St Petersburg Gazette* is as instructive as it is woeful. The same thing will probably happen to the *Messenger of Europe*.[6] The times are as bad as they were in our youth.

As for myself, I am doing nothing, even though my health has improved. There is no desire, so why should I force myself?

I am looking forward to reading Lev Tolstoy's novel in the *Russian Herald*.[7]

I have not thanked you for sending me Shcherbachev's waltzes. They haven't changed my opinion of him, but I am grateful for your kindness.

I wish you all the best and remain,

Yours sincerely,

Iv. Turgenev

150. To J. SCHMIDT

[Original in German, translated from the Russian]

Paris, 13 February 1875

Dear friend,

I am very glad that you liked the photograph. I would have sent you ones of Flaubert and Zola, but that's not so easy. Flaubert has not allowed anyone to photograph him for the past fifteen years, and Zola is never around. He is what the French call *un sanglier* – he stays at home all the time with his wife, never puts his gloves on and doesn't possess a suit; he doesn't want to know anything of life's petty vanities – among which he includes being photographed. However, I don't think it's an absolutely lost cause yet and I shall apply all my powers of persuasion.

I have received no. 4 of the *Wiener Zeitung* and I'll show it to Zola tomorrow;

---

3. Series of pieces for the piano by N. V. Shcherbachev (1853–?).
4. Alexey Alexandrovich Kharlamov (1842–1922), painter and illustrator. He did portraits of Turgenev and both Louis and Pauline Viardot; he illustrated various editions of Turgenev's works, including *A Nest of the Landed Gentry*.
5. Sergey Mikhaylovich Tretyakov (1834–92), art collector.
6. The editor of the *St Petersburg Gazette*, V. F. Korsh, had been dismissed for expressing opposition to the government's changes in secondary education.
7. *Anna Karenina*.

it's about time he came in for some adverse criticism, but the main thing is that you treat him as a major figure.

Do you know Flaubert's *Education Sentimentale* (a terribly bad title)? I hardly expect so. It is probably his most significant book, and the least likeable. It hasn't been at all successful in France – it's too full of bitter truths for the French. It appeared not long before the war and was seen as a prophecy (do you say 'Prophezei' or 'Prophezeihung'?). Would you like me to send you a copy?

I couldn't make out one word in your letter where you speak of Tatyana Borisovna's nephew.[1] 'True . . .' what?

With heartfelt greetings to your charming wife and all our good friends and my best wishes to you.

Yours,
Iv. Turgenev

151. To M. A. MILYUTINA

[Original in Russian]

Paris, 6 March 1875

Well, you have set me a task, dear Marya Ageyevna! I would imagine that no writer has ever received such a request. To describe my personal philosophy of life, briefly, in a letter! It would be easy, and even natural, to reply either negatively or even humorously. It would be equally natural and true to say: heaven knows! I hardly know what my own face looks like! But as I do not wish to create any unpleasantness for your son (although I must admit quite openly that I am amazed at the strange work given to *lycée* pupils), I shall say that I am first and foremost a realist and am interested more than anything else in the living truth of the human physiognomy. I am indifferent to everything supernatural; I do not believe in any absolutes or any systems; most of all I love freedom. As far as I can judge, I have an understanding of poetry. Everything human is dear to me. Slavophile doctrines, like all orthodoxies, are alien to me. However, I think I have said enough; and when it comes down to it, all this is nothing but words. I can add no more about myself.

However, when the time comes, it will be very interesting to read your son's essay.

Thank you for sending me your news. We haven't lacked our share of alarms and worries either, but now everything seems to have settled back into its normal course – *which is the best thing of all*. O, the blessed charm of monotony and the similarity of one day to the next! I find this charm utterly delightful. My gout is leaving me – for the time being – in peace. Everyone here is in good health, including the new arrival, a daughter for my dear Claudie and a granddaughter for Mme Viardot. One could wish for nothing more. And to my great satisfaction, I am doing no work at all.

[150] 1. One of the *Sportsman's Sketches*.

152. *To M. M. Stasyulevich*

I am glad to see that Antokolsky is working on Pushkin, but am not surprised that his bust of your husband is not a success. Such portraits are not in his line.

And talking of portraits, Kharlamov, who is living here now, has painted two marvellous portraits of M. and Mme Viardot. He is now doing one of me.

Please remember me to your family and friends.

Yours very sincerely,

Iv. Turgenev

152. To M. M. STASYULEVICH

Mikhail Matveyevich Stasyulevich (1826–1911), writer, historian and publisher. Professor of History at Moscow and then St Petersburg Universities, he resigned in 1861 in protest at the harsh reaction of the government to student unrest. During the next four years, when he was also a member of the advisory board to the Ministry of Education, he published his three-volume *History of the Middle Ages*. In 1865 he began to publish the *Messenger of Europe*, and the works of many of the leading writers in Russia and Europe appeared in it. Turgenev was a regular contributor from 1867, and through his personal influence many young Russian authors saw their works appearing in Stasyulevich's journal, as did Flaubert, Zola and Maupassant. Three hundred and sixty-one of Turgenev's letters, mainly in connection with the publication of his works, and those of others, survive.

[Original in Russian]

Paris, 13 March 1875

Dear Mikhail Matveyevich,

I am very pleased that you liked the first of Zola's articles[1] and do not doubt that your reaction to the second will be the same. I informed him of your brilliant suggestions and he has willingly agreed to them. You will find him an active contributor with whom both you and your readers will be highly satisfied. I have taken it upon myself to pay him for the first article at the rate you suggested. I enclose his receipt. I trust you approve of my actions. You should know that Zola, although he works from morning till night and lives extremely modestly, can hardly make ends meet. He has been forced to write for various provincial journals, but has now given most of that up in order to work *con amore* for the *Messenger of Europe*. He is not at all greedy for money. As he had *a contract* with Charpentier for *6000* francs (!) a year for two novels, he thought only of one thing: to be in a position to earn a further four. As the correspondent for two or three journals, and the *Messenger of Europe*, he can see his ambitions satisfied.

He agrees to signing his letters either Z-L or Э.З. and leaves the choice to you.

[152] 1. On Turgenev's recommendation Zola was appointed the Paris correspondent of the *Messenger of Europe*.

He doesn't possess a good photograph of himself but has ordered one specifically for you. His address in Paris is 21 rue Saint-Georges (Batignolles). You must add *Batignolles* as there are two rues Saint-Georges in Paris.

As well as being very talented, Zola is a very good man – and *reliable*. He has noted down your terms and will follow them to the last detail.

P. V. Annenkov arrived here yesterday, and will stay for a fortnight.

I affectionately press your hand.

Yours sincerely,

Iv. Turgenev

153. To A. S. SUVORIN

Alexey Sergeyevich Suvorin (1834–1912), journalist, publisher, playwright and theatre critic. In his youth Suvorin was an active liberal, but from the seventies he became increasingly conservative. In 1876 he began to publish *New Time*, which was Russia's first cheap right-wing newspaper. Nine of Turgenev's letters to Suvorin have survived.

[Original in Russian]

Paris, 26 March 1875

You write me such long and interesting letters, dear Alexey Sergeyevich, that I feel guilty at writing briefly; consequently I have been slow to reply.

13 April 1875

I stopped at that juncture – and you have written me yet another letter, and such a nice one too! I bow down my guilty head, and reply.

1. Courrière has been here and brought me his book.[1] He is, as they used to say in the old days, a bit of a fop; he looks like a cross between a commercial traveller and a vet. He's got a round face, broad shoulders, stony eyes and a wheezing voice. You were completely right in your assessment of his book. He has clearly picked up something from living in Russia but it's all rather trite and superficial and written in a poor – non-literary – language. You should write a book on modern Russian literature; it would be better than Courrière's, or even O. Miller's.[2]

2. I am keen to read the first selection of your essays.[3] Your picture of Tolstoy will probably be good. He is remarkably talented, but in *Anna Karenina* he has, as people here would say, ⟨lost his way⟩:[4] the influence of Moscow, the Slavophile gentry, Orthodox old maids, his own seclusion and the absence of

---

[153] 1. Céleste Courrière (1843–?), French literary historian and translator who lived for many years in Russia. His *Histoire de la littérature contemporaine en Russie* was published in 1875.

2. Orest Fyodorovich Miller (1833–89), professor at St Petersburg University, literary historian and publicist. His *Russian Writers after Gogol* appeared in 1875.

3. It contained an article on Tolstoy.

4. Original in French.

real artistic freedom! The second part is simply tedious and *shallow*, that's the real shame! As for details about my biography, everything in Polevoy[5] is correct and it's not worth the trouble collecting any more. (I seem to remember that he has got my father's name wrong – it was Sergey Nikolayevich, and my mother Varvara Petrovna Lutovinova was born on 28 October 1818.) There is indeed a lot of autobiography in *Punin and Baburin*. Your suggestion is a good one; in your place I would go to Moscow and get to know Pisemsky. It's easily done and he's worth a closer look. I have not forgotten my promise to send you information about the writers I have known, but I fear my laziness causes my pen to fall from my fingers. Give us a couple of hours together and I could tell you a tale or two! It is highly probable that after Karlsbad, where I go at the end of May, I shall go to Russia – shall we see each other there?

You seem to be having one scandal after another! I have hardly managed to cool down after Markevich when I am set on the boil by Ovsyannikov![6] Our new financial world is a mystery to me – what delights must lie there! I gather from your articles that you know all you need to about it! Why don't you write something like Proudhon's *Manuel de la bourse* – but amusing, satirical.

It is not exactly cheerful to have passed forty, especially the first ten years. But then under the influence of the cold wind blowing from the grave man learns to rest content. I know an old German lady in St Petersburg who used to say that approaching old age is quite awful, but 'vun must *put up viz it*'. Exactly – *put up viz it*!

I am really grateful for your letters. It is a great pleasure to read them; you can rest assured of that. You can also be sure that I shall reply to them, even if I am sometimes slow in so doing.

N.B. Please don't believe, as almost everyone here does, in the inevitable triumph of Buonopartism in France: *we shall not see the demise* of the republic, even though it's very bourgeois and quiet.

And so I firmly press your hand and remain,

Yours sincerely,
Iv. Turgenev

154. To A. V. TOPOROV

Alexander Vasilyevich Toporov (1831–87), a close friend and factotum of Turgenev's, especially in the seventies and early eighties. At Turgenev's request it was Toporov who organized the removal of his body back to Russia for burial in 1883. One hundred and seventy of Turgenev's letters to him have survived.

[Original in Russian]

5. P. N. Polevoy's *History of Russian Literature* came out in 1874.
6. A reference to two recent court cases. B. M. Markevich, a government official, had been dismissed for taking a large bribe, and S. T. Ovsyannikov, a millionaire merchant, had been exiled to Siberia for the arson of a business rival's mill.

Paris, 1 April 1875

Dear Alexander Vasilyevich,

I feel rather guilty in not replying immediately to your letter. If only I could say that my excuse was that I have been working hard – but no! I am as lazy as ever. And my health is also as ever, i.e. not bad, despite the fact that gout knocks on my door (i.e. my feet) from time to time. In six weeks' time I am leaving for Karlsbad and hope to hold out somehow till then.

The *Citizen* is received regularly by Miss Arnholt and read by me. If the *Cause* is really so empty, may the devil take it! The New Year's present was received and was eaten with gratitude a long time ago. As soon as I discovered it was sent by the Ragozins,[1] I wrote to them. It was very kind and thoughtful of them.

I have written to my estate manager telling him to send you *100* roubles to cover my debt and any future expenses.

I shall now tell you something I wish you to keep an absolute secret. Iogansen has paid me nothing for Mme Viardot's romances. Sparing her modesty, I will tell you he promised her twenty-five roubles for each of them. Please write me a letter in which you say that you have received 125 roubles for the last five and I shall then show it to her (she can read Russian) because she is beginning to doubt my integrity. I shall pay her the money here and you can make out you are keeping the roubles in Russia to help defray some of my expenses. Please do all I have asked, dear Alexander Vasilyevich, and I shall be extremely grateful. But keep it a secret!

We've received a copy of Rubinstein's *Demon* arranged for the piano and have looked it over attentively. We are convinced it's extremely worthy, but tedious and unoriginal. We were even more disappointed (because our expectations were higher) with Tolstoy's novel [*Anna Karenina*]. With all his talent and then to wander off into that high-society bog and mark time there and to treat all that nonsense not humorously but with pathos is, seriously, no trifling matter! Moscow has ruined him; he's not the first, nor will he be the last, but I'm more sorry for him than for all the others.

Dear friend, so you find life tedious; but what can we do about it? Russia is living through tedious times. Being forty is telling on you. We must repeat with I. S. Aksakov:

When will you pass
O Youth, o time of pain!

There is no real work, that's the trouble.

If I manage to shake off my lethargy and finish my novel [*Virgin Soil*], then we shall see each other at the end of the year. But if not, surely you will return to Paris, won't you?

I wish you all the best, and cordially press your hand.

Yours sincerely,
Iv. Turgenev

[154] 1. Yevgeny Ivanovich Ragozin (1843–1906), liberal writer and editor of *The Week*, and his wife.

155.To Y. I. BLARAMBERG

Yelena Ivanovna Blaramberg (1846–1923), writer and translator. She first met Turgenev in St Petersburg in 1871 and they subsequently met frequently, both in Russia and France, where she became a close friend of Pauline Viardot's eldest daughter Louise. Turgenev took a keen interest in her writing and it was through his efforts that her first novel, *Guilty but Blameless*, was published by Stasyulevich in the *Messenger of Europe*. Under the pseudonym of Y. Ardov she published some memoirs in 1904 which provide an interesting picture of Turgenev's life at Bougival. Fourteen of Turgenev's letters to her are known.

[Original in Russian]

Bougival, 25 August 1875

Dear Mademoiselle Blaramberg,
    You have probably received the manuscript which Louise gave me and I shall send you tomorrow those letters of recommendation you asked for, although I am afraid that there are not very many of them. But today, with your permission, I shall give you my opinion of your novel. Naturally it bears the stamp of immaturity and its style is somewhat careless, but there is no doubt that it is the fruit of an observant and well-read mind and a warm, open heart. It also shows a talent which will, I hope, develop with time. But please allow me to point out certain faults which are unavoidable when one is starting out on one's literary career. You return too often to one and the same character trait and so stress it too much. For example, in the very first scene with the mother of your heroine (Nadya) you continuously use the word 'gentle' when referring to her. You also tend to mock your characters, which is something to be avoided. For example, when you are talking, say, about the eyes of one of your female characters you assert that nothing could be more captivating or more ravishing than the way she looks at people, yet you clearly do not think this yourself. What is the point you are making? Irony is a very dangerous weapon, for you are just as likely to injure yourself. Young writers tend to use mockery only because it is easier; tell your story simply and honestly, because this is more your nature as I perceive it. And then there is the fact that in your dialogues you often make your characters say things which they would not say in the given situation but which express what you, the author, think of them; they might well be true, but they are out of place. For example, when the twelve-year-old Nadya first meets her aunt she says to her, 'I like you.' In the mouth of the Nadya you have described these words would be quite impossible, even though she actually does like her. The character Vilda is better conceived than executed: it would have been better if he had said to himself, even when he was alone, between the four walls, that he was a good, honest man. That would have been something new and *true*. I also think that this sort of character is a little hackneyed. Also your dialogues are generally somewhat too long.
    But I nonetheless advise you to continue writing, for you will achieve good

results. From my letter to Louise (and from other sources) you will know that my literary influence is almost nil, if not with my readers then at least with the publishers and critics with whom I have broken off almost all relations. So do not blame me if I cannot do as much for you as I would wish.

I imagine it must have been very hard for you to part from Louise, but we must hope that under different circumstances you will again be able to join the one to whom you are so attached and who herself values your friendship and loves you.[1]

With my sincere good wishes and respects,

Yours truly,
Iv. Turgenev

156. To P. J. HETZEL

[Original in French]

Bougival, 23 September 1875

My dear friend,

J. Verne's story [*Michel Strogoff*] is highly improbable – but that doesn't matter because it's amusing. The improbability lies in the invasion of Siberia by the khan of Bokhara; that's just as if I wanted today to show France being invaded by Holland. It would have been better if he had stressed the danger surrounding the tsar's brother. I also regret that Verne made his heroine a *Livonian*-Russian. The fact is that the Livonians are no more Russian than the Germans. But that is a detail which will pass unnoticed.

I sincerely trust that Mme Hetzel's accident will have no serious consequences. Do you have polished staircases too? France is a terrible place for such things. I shall try to arrange a 'business lunch' for next week and shall let you know in advance.

In the meanwhile I cordially press your hand and remain,

Yours sincerely,
Iv. Turgenev

157. To G. FLAUBERT

[Original in French]

Bougival, 11 October 1875

The sight of your handwriting, my dear old fellow, gave me the greatest pleasure – and the perusal of your letter even more. You are getting back in the swim and are making – I was about to say literary – plans! But at least you're amusing yourself with thinking about what you're going to do. That's a very good thing, and I am sure that you will give us *thirty pages*.

[155] 1. Blaramberg and Louise had been living in Brussels, but the former had to return to Russia in the attempt to get her novel published.

15 October

I had reached that point, my dear friend, when I was interrupted, and to my great surprise I have just found the letter in my blotting pad when I thought I had posted it. You must think me a great imbecile – but I start again.

I was saying that I was very happy at the thought of *thirty* pages, I have just promised my Russian editor a thirty-page story (two printer's sheets) by 26 November – at the latest! – and I haven't the least idea what to write. As my long novel has been postponed until the Greek calends – even later than your *Bouvard et Pécuchet* – my editor is screaming for something else! And so I'm caught. We shall see who gets there first.

Alas, my friend, we are both old; there is no disputing it. Let us at least amuse ourselves like old men. By the way, did you read the story 'The Suicide of a Child' in *La République Française* on 10 or 11 October by X? I was very struck by it. It is clear that the author belongs to your school. If he's young, he has a future. Try and get hold of it and tell me what you think.[1]

Everyone here is well. Only I have had a violent attack of cystitis – at least, I think that's what it's called – an inflammation of the bladder. I had two awful nights and stayed in bed for three days, but it disappeared in the end. These are those small 'mementos', visiting cards left by Mme Death, so that we don't forget her.

We shall be here until 1 November. The weather is quiet, dull and humid – not disagreeable. I shall not be able to live in my new house this year but I go there from time to time to write letters (this one, for example). There's a good fire burning – but it's cold on my back.

There was also a jolly good story by Mme Sand in *Temps* (written in 1829! when she was twenty-five) – you probably read it. Zola has written a marvellous article on the Goncourts for his Russian editor. He's going to translate their novels.

Send me the probable date of your return to Croisset. I imagine that you won't stay much longer at the seaside and will return to Paris in spite of everything. Your friends intend to group themselves around you in such a way as to keep you warm.

In the meantime, please send my best wishes to Mme Commanville.[2]

I embrace you and am your faithful old friend

Iv. Turgenev

158. To M. Y. SALTYKOV-SHCHEDRIN

[Original in Russian]

Bougival, 9 November 1875

I was very pleased to receive your letter, dear Mikhail Yevgrafovich, because I

[157] 1. Flaubert did not much like the story. He thought it was in the style not of himself, but of Zola. The author is unknown.

2. Caroline Commanville, née Hamard (1846–1931), Flaubert's niece.

was beginning to get a little concerned. Your letter is the best present I could have today, my birthday. (I am fifty-seven – as you can see, a good age.) I am also pleased to see that you have found a pleasant corner of Nice to live in, but I am afraid that however nice and amusing Mrs Danilova may be she will suddenly ask you for money! Though that is no great misfortune if you are firm and strong-willed. And you are severe rather than firm! Especially at refusing.

I turn to your latest story in the *Annals of the Fatherland*. I received the October issue yesterday and of course read your *The Family Court* at once. I am completely satisfied with it. All the characters are powerfully and accurately drawn, including the mother, who is very typical – and appears not for the first time with you – and clearly taken from real life. The character who takes to drink out of idleness and is ruined is particularly good. It is so good that I cannot help wondering why Saltykov does not give up his essays and write a big novel on the grand scale, with specific groupings of characters and events and a central theme. But it could be said that up to a point novels and stories are being written by others and what Saltykov does could not be done by anyone else. However that may be, I liked *The Family Court* a lot and am keen to read the sequel – a description of the adventures of the 'Little Jewess'. You complain that you are forced to write and work too much. And I, sinner that I am, instead of sympathizing actually envy you (on the condition, of course, that this work does not ruin your health). I have completely lost the habit of working and writing and hardly ever manage to throw off my lethargy and indifference. And the fact that you are continuously accompanied by Holy Mother Russia should lead to no complaints; she will have to support your activities for a long time yet, even though she shouts at you and batters you in the guise of various 'Prince' Redkins or 'Marquess' Baratynskys. Such circumstances can never remove anyone from his roots. Probably there's no hope of others anyway.

I have not seen your enemy Sollogub since that famous scene. But he's still here and they say he's lost his comedy again and, can you imagine, is still looking for it. Such fools do exist!

Annenkov has at last returned to Baden-Baden and has moved to 4 Sophienstrasse. I am sure your letter to him must have gone astray, for he is a most punctilious man and would have replied. He is fond of you, too.

By the way, I am writing to him tomorrow.

And what do you think of the crash of the Moscow Commercial Bank, etc? Very characteristic! My publisher, Salayev, has lost 55,000 in the affair.

I am staying here for another week and then going to Paris. Please address your letter to 50 rue de Douai.

My greetings to all of yours; I cordially press your hand.

Yours sincerely,
Iv. Turgenev

159. To PRINCESS Y. V. LVOVA

Princess Yelizaveta Vladimirovna Lvova (dates unknown), daughter of V. V. Lvov, the censor who had earlier been dismissed for passing *A Sportsman's Sketches* for publication. She had written to Turgenev for advice.

[Original in Russian]

Paris, 6 January 1876

I can fully appreciate how the busy life which envelops you in Petersburg must at first deafen and confuse you, but one can grow accustomed to anything and you will see that shapes and colours can emerge from all that grey chaos.

Remember Goethe's words:

Delve into the life of humanity;
Whatever you grasp will be of interest.

Organize your life in such a way that you can devote an hour or two every day to yourself, even if you find at first that you do nothing during this time. Good will come of it even so. I would hate it if you stopped half way . . . Force yourself to do some work every day. Read more, but remember what I said when we last met: do not read whatever comes to hand, but choose carefully. If you wish to retain the freshness of your own feelings, do not read novels. Educate your taste and thoughts. The most important thing is to study life and meditate upon it. Do not simply study the general features but its very essence, and try to catch the typical and not the incidental. Get to grips with your subject matter.

At present I am suffering from an attack of gout and am not going out, but I hope to be in Petersburg in April if I am still alive, and we shall be able to see each other. We shall have a lot to talk about!

Please remember me to Sofya Andreyevna Tolstaya.[1]

With my respects,
Yours faithfully,
Iv. Turgenev

160. To M. Y. SALTYKOV-SHCHEDRIN

[Original in Russian]

Paris, 26 February 1876

Well, how are things with you, dear Mikhail Yevgrafovich? How is your health? Can we expect you here soon? Drop me a reply to these questions. Are you still angry with Gambetta?[1] If you are, then you are outdoing all those who voted for

[159] 1. Widow of the writer A. K. Tolstoy.

[160] 1. Léon Gambetta (1838–82), French lawyer and politican. A violent opponent of Napoleon III, he was a member of the government of National Defence in 1870, President of the Chamber of Deputies (1879–81), and prime minister (1881–2) during the Third Republic.

him in such large numbers. Whatever your opinion of him, the future of the Republic and of France is in his hands; and even the *Times* sees him as the embodiment of their fate. The elections made an enormous impression here, and there is no doubt that they marked a turning-point and that the road along which we were going has changed. You will possibly think me an optimist, but it is a long time since I have looked to the future with such confidence; I still have greater hopes for France than I do for Russia, which seems to be sinking daily ever further into a sort of foul-tasting blancmange. The clerical party here is quite simply threatening to kill Gambetta, whom they clearly regard as a thorn in their flesh. And I judge a man by what his enemies say about him.

Thanks to that scoundrel Bazunov[2] I am not getting either the *Annals of the Fatherland* or the *Russian Herald*, and so I haven't yet been able to read your pieces nor the continuation of Tolstoy's novel [*Anna Karenina*].

Our booksellers are a wonderful lot! No one risks as little as they do nor does anyone make money so easily, and yet they go out of business before you can turn round.

Annenkov has been very ill in Baden; his whole head was covered with a red rash; but he is better now and we are corresponding regularly.

My health is reasonable and I am doing a little work.

In the expectation of a reply, I firmly press your hand and remain,

Yours,

Iv. Turgenev

161. To BARONESS Y. P. VREVSKAYA

Baroness Yuliya Petrovna Vrevskaya, née Varpakhovskaya (1841–78), was a close friend of Turgenev's in the seventies. She married a general when she was seventeen but he was killed shortly afterwards in the Caucasus. She served as a nurse in the Russo-Turkish War from 1877 to 1878, during which she died of typhus in Bulgaria. Forty-nine of Turgenev's letters to her have survived, and although they are mostly mild banter and conversational it is clear that Turgenev was physically very attracted to her. There is no evidence that she felt similarly.

[Original in Russian]

Paris, 22 March 1876

And so you have finally moved to Petersburg, dear Yuliya Petrovna, that Petersburg which you always hated. Clearly you cannot avoid your fate. After India, the Liteynaya! For my part I am glad. I am now sure that we shall meet again for, assuming I am alive and well, I shall appear in Petersburg at the beginning of May. I hope you won't be cruel but will wait for me – don't rush

2. Alexander Fyodorovich Bazunov (1825–99), St Petersburg publisher and bookseller.

off to the country or anywhere else! If you have to go to the country then let us travel together – our homes are on the same road, after all.

Thank you for all the news you sent; it breathes of contemporary Russian life. I am glad you have met Meshchersky; he's a splendid fellow.[1] I have sometimes wondered why he doesn't marry Herzen's daughter Natalya of whom he is evidently very fond. They would make an excellent couple. Sound him out about it – but discreetly, mentioning no names.

I see you haven't forsaken your former friends! And Cassagnac is sending you his speeches![2] It would be better to deal with real Cossack brigands, or any other sort, rather than rogues such as he! Please forgive the strong language but, as you know, I am incorrigible. There is only one good thing about it – you are loyal to your friends; but you should be a little careful in your choice. Read Zola's *Son Excellence Rougon*, a remarkable book; one of the characters, Clorinda, is drawn with the pen of a master.

I haven't yet read the continuation of *Anna Karenina* but I can see, with the greatest regret, where the novel is going. However great Tolstoy's talent may be, he cannot get out of the Moscow bog into which he has crawled. Orthodoxy, the nobility, Slavophilism, gossip, the Arbat, Katkov, Antonina Bludova, bad manners, self-importance, the customs of the landowners, the officer class, hatred of everything foreign, sour cabbage soup and a lack of soap – in a word, chaos! And that such a gifted man should perish in that chaos! But it always happens in Russia.

Are they really dying from hunger in Oryol Province? It's bad, very bad; and one can foresee no improvement.

I have lately taken up my novel [*Virgin Soil*], and am working slowly. My health is satisfactory and my gout is, for the time being, at rest. All my friends here are well – that's the main thing.

I press your hands as firmly as I can.

Yours very sincerely,
Iv. Turgenev

162. To V. HUGO

Victor Hugo (1802–85), the influential French poet, dramatist and novelist. While Turgenev remained on amicable terms with him, he detested his plays, regarded his poetry and prose as romanticism in an age of realism, and behaved towards him, at best, somewhat ironically. While he admired the writers Flaubert, Maupassant and Zola (in that order), Hugo came near the bottom of his list. Three of Turgenev's letters to him have survived.

[161] 1. Prince Alexander Alexandrovich Meshchersky (1844–?).
2. Paul Adolphe Granier de Cassagnac (1843–1904), French politician and journalist.

[Original in French]

Paris, 1 April 1876

Dear Sir and Illustrious Master,

Please allow me to make a few observations on M. Vacquerie's article in this morning's *Le Rappel*. They are inspired by the great affection that I have for France and by the desire that nothing should diminish the sympathy towards her that exists in Russia. The premise on which M. Vacquerie bases his argument – the resignation of the Tsar and the regency of his son – is utterly and completely false. I know this for a fact, I assure you. The Tsar is so jealous of his power that he will not renounce one morsel of it until his dying day, and articles such as that by M. Vacquerie (the Tsar is shown daily extracts from the French papers) can only hurt his pride and increase the mistrust he already feels towards his son. The sympathy of the Tsar towards France has never been strong and if he has sometimes shown some, it is simply not to annoy public opinion in his own country. But if the idea should occur to him that his death is desired in France, or at least the end of his reign, he will never forgive you. He is not of a forgiving nature and, like many gentle and outwardly weak-willed people, he forgets nothing. Our unfortunate press, so dependent upon the authorities, would be given instructions what to print – and this in turn would upset the public!

Please excuse me for having written at such length on this matter, and I beg you to accept the expression of my deep respect.

Yours faithfully,
Ivan Turgenev

163. To G. FLAUBERT

[Original in French]

Spasskoye, 6 June 1876

My dear friend,

I have been in my Patmos since this morning and am very down in the dumps. (Have you noticed that this is generally the time when one writes to one's best friends?) It has been 32° in the shade and that, combined with the −9° we had on 21 May, means that the grass in the gardens is scattered with small, dead leaves which remind me a little of dead children, and my old lime trees give such a weak and paltry shade that it is painful to look at them. Add to that the fact that my brother, who should have been waiting for me to discuss some very important – to me – financial matters, left for Karlsbad five days ago; that I think I am about to get another attack of gout (which I did two years ago at the same time and in the same place); that I am almost absolutely convinced that my estate manager is robbing me; and that I shan't be able to get rid of him – and you can see the position I find myself in!

I was very, very upset by the death of Mme Sand. I know that you went to Nohant for the funeral; I wanted to send a telegram of condolence in the name of the Russian reading public but was restrained by a sort of false modesty, by fear of *Figaro*, by the publicity – in a word, by stupidity! The Russian reading public is one of those on whom Mme Sand has had the greatest influence, and it should be said, heaven knows; and I had the right to say it, after all. But there we are!!

Poor, dear Mme Sand! She loved us both, you especially; that's quite natural. What a heart of gold she had! What an absence of any petty emotions, narrow-mindedness, falseness! What a wonderful person and a good woman! And now all of that is – there, in that terrible, insatiable, dumb and beastly pit which does not even know whom it is devouring!

But there's nothing to be done about it and we must just try to keep our chins up.

I am writing to you at Croisset – I assume that you're there. Are you working again? If I can do nothing here, then everything is finished. No one could imagine the silence that reigns here. Not a neighbour for twenty kilometres in any direction. Everything is languishing in immobility! My house is in a sorry state, but not too hot and the furniture is good. An admirable writing-desk and a two-seater cane armchair! There is also a rather dangerous sofa; as soon as you sit on it, you fall asleep. I must try to avoid it. I shall start by finishing your *St Julien*.

There in front of me in the corner of the room hangs an old Byzantine icon, quite blackened and in a silver frame; you can make out only the melancholy, stiff face – it's rather boring really – but I cannot have it removed as my manservant would think me a pagan – and that's no laughing matter here.

Drop me a few lines – more cheerful than these. I embrace you and remain,

Your old friend,

Iv. Turgenev

P.S. Do you know that the Circassian Hassan, who kills ministers like a brace of young partridges, inspires in me a certain respect?[1]
P.P.S. My best wishes to your niece and her husband.

164. To A. S. SUVORIN

[Original in Russian]

Spasskoye, 9 June 1876

Dear Alexey Sergeyevich,

As I was passing through Petersburg, I read in one of your articles: 'George Sand is dead, but I do not wish to speak about it.' You probably meant by this that one should either say a lot about her, or nothing at all. I do not doubt that *New Time* has since filled the gap and like the other journals has at least given the biography of the great writer, but I would still like to write a few words about

[163] 1. An army officer who on 16 June 1876 shot the Turkish Ministers of War and Foreign Affairs.

her for your journal, although at the moment I have neither the time nor the opportunity to say 'a lot' and these few words are not even my own, as you will see. I had the great joy of knowing George Sand personally, but please do not take this phrase in its usual meaning; anyone who saw that rare being at close quarters would truly consider himself fortunate.

I recently received a letter from a French woman[1] who also knew her briefly. This is what she wrote:

'The last words of our dear friend were "leave . . . the greenness . . .", i.e. do not place a stone upon my grave; let the grass grow over it! I find these dying words so touching, so remarkable and so harmonious with her whole life, which had for so long been devoted to the good and the simple. That love of nature and of the truth and her humility before it; that inexhaustible and quiet goodness, natural and never-changing. Oh, what unhappiness her death leaves behind! That dark secret has swallowed up for ever one of the best people who ever lived, and we shall never see that noble face again; that heart of gold will beat no more; everything now lies beneath the ground. Our grief will be sincere and prolonged, but I think that not enough has been said about her goodness. However rare genius is, such *goodness* is even rarer. Yet it is possible to learn something from it (but not from genius) and so we must say something about it, this goodness – glorify it, point it out. This active, living goodness attracted countless friends to her, people of all classes of society, and united them to her and made them utterly loyal to her to the very end. When she was buried, one of the peasants from near Nohant, George Sand's château, went up to her grave, laid a wreath and said, "From the peasants of Nohant; not from the poor, for there are no poor here, thanks to her kindness." But she herself was not a rich woman, and had to work all her life simply to make ends meet.'

I have almost nothing to add to these lines. I can only vouch for their truth. When I first became friends with George Sand some eight years ago, the enthusiasm and amazement which she had once aroused in me quickly disappeared – I had all but worshipped her. But it was impossible to become part of her close circle of friends without worshipping her in a different, perhaps superior, sense. Everyone immediately felt that they were in the presence of an infinitely generous and well-disposed person, in whom everything egotistical had been utterly burnt out by the flame of her poetic enthusiasm, faith and idealism which treated all humanity as equally worthy and valuable, and from which breathed help and concern . . . And over all this there was some unconscious halo, something superior, free and heroic . . . Believe me, George Sand was a saint, and you will, of course, understand what I mean by this.

Please excuse this incoherent and scrappy letter.

Yours respectfully and sincerely,

Iv. Turgenev

[164] 1. Pauline Viardot.

165. To N. S. TURGENEV

[Original in Russian]

Spasskoye, 3 July 1876

Dear brother,

Your letter arrived only yesterday (it took six days – the post is evidently in no great hurry) and I reply immediately. Firstly, I thank you from the bottom of my heart for agreeing to my request, and see in it the continuing friendship of a brother. As for the written promises of loans which you gave me, the one for *50,000* was for my daughter, and the other, for the same sum, I think, was for Mme Viardot; the first I returned to you and you destroyed; the second will *of course count against the 100,000 which you will pay her in the event of my death and your inheriting Spasskoye*; that of course should have gone without saying – I am sorry I forgot to say so. (By the way, when you write to me tell me the figure for Mme Viardot – was it 50,000 or 100,000?) The money intended for my daughter I leave entirely to your discretion; if you can, do something. But she has been told nothing about it, nor will she be. ⟨I think I have done enough for her and her husband already.⟩[1]

I have decided not to sell Spasskoye but shall rent it to my neighbour, A. M. Shchepkin,[2] for twelve years. He owns Katushishchevo and is the son of the famous actor. We shall be signing the contract this very afternoon in Mtsensk. He will take over on 1 January. If I, or my heir, should decide to sell Spasskoye then we have the right to do so, paying 3500 roubles in compensation. But I am not too happy about that. ⟨I shall be forced to carry out a sort of *coup d'état* tomorrow morning and overthrow my Abdul-Asis,[3] Mr Kishinsky, whom I have unmasked as a rogue and caught red-handed with his fingers in the till. His contract runs until 1 April next year and if I honour it he will bleed me to death.⟩[1] I shall replace him with A. M. Shchepkin's son, a young man but very efficient, who will actually live at Spasskoye in his father's name. Which means that I shall have Spasskoye only until the new year. He will also have the rented estates at Tapki and Kadnoye. I don't think that Kishinsky will cause any trouble, but I have decided that come what may I shall rid myself of that gentleman. From all this you will conclude that I do not yet know exactly when I shall leave here. ⟨I seem to be trapped.⟩[1] But the handing over cannot take less than ten days or a fortnight.

I might add that I am well and working hard. I recently saw your family who are also well. But now ⟨for the bad news⟩.[4] Following a terrible storm at Turgenevo the dam was breached and much of the corn was washed away. On Sukhotin's estate at Petrovskoye the miller and a workman were drowned.[5] We

[165] 1. Original in French.

2. Alexander Mikhaylovich Shchepkin (1828–85); he had bought an estate near to Turgenev's in 1870.

3. Sultan of Turkey (1830–76).

4. Original in German.

5. Mikhail Sergeyevich Sukhotin (1850–1914), married to one of Tolstoy's daughters.

had a storm here at Spasskoye – the day before yesterday in the evening. I have never seen anything like it; but luckily there was no flooding.

I still have not lost all hope of seeing you at Bougival. I thank you again with all my heart. I embrace you and remain,

Your affectionate brother,

Iv. Turgenev

P.S. Whatever happens I shall write to you on the day I leave.

166. To PRINCESS Y. A. CHERKASSKAYA

Princess Yekaterina Alexeyevna Cherkasskaya, née Princess Vasilchikova (1825–88), writer of children's stories. She and Turgenev had first met in the forties when she was a young girl; twelve of Turgenev's letters to her have survived.

[Original in Russian]

Paris, 21 November 1876

Dear Princess,

I beg you to excuse me for not replying immediately to your letter with its enclosed translations of 'Croquet at Windsor'.[1] I have had my hands full with the completion, revision and dispatch of my long novel [*Virgin Soil*], which finally arrived in Russia only today. I am very grateful that you should remember me in such troubled times.[2] Mrs Baratynskaya's translation is good and very accurate, but Count Orlov-Davydov's ⟨is quite the contrary⟩.[3] I do not know if you are aware that a translation (from the French, in prose) was sent to the *Daily News* for publication, but the editors ⟨on second thoughts⟩[3] refused it ⟨because it may hurt the feelings of the Queen⟩.[3] No other journal would print it now.[4]

As for your suggestion that I should have written more in the same mode, I should tell you that I wrote it almost unconsciously while on a train between Moscow and Petersburg. I don't at all repent it, but writing poetry is not my line (as the fairly rough verses in 'Croquet' prove). Can you not find a young poet in Moscow?

As you know, I am not a Slavophile, nor shall I ever be one. I do not feel I can sympathize very much with the movement that is sweeping all Russia at present, because it is exclusively religious – even though I recognize its huge and

[166] 1. The British government was supporting Turkey's policies in the Balkans and failed to condemn Turkish atrocities against the Serbian and Bulgarian minorities. Turgenev's bitter forty-line poem 'Croquet at Windsor' depicted Queen Victoria watching a family game of croquet when she suddenly realized that the blood-stained balls were the heads of the victims of the Turkish atrocities.

2. The run-up to the Russo-Turkish War of 1877–8.

3. Original in English.

4. It eventually appeared in English in an anthology of Russian and German poetry published in Baden-Baden in 1882.

elemental force. I myself desire war – but only as a way out of all the anxiety and the gloom; and indeed, seeing here the hatred felt towards Russia by the whole of Europe one cannot but withdraw into oneself and refuse to grant Russia the right of behaving just as she likes. I recognize the unselfishness of I. S. Aksakov[5] but cannot see any reason why I should do the same. The disgraceful events in Bulgaria offended every human feeling in me – yes, I still have some – but if the only thing to be done about them is to go to war, well so be it! Had those slaughtered Bulgarian women and children not been Christians and of our race my indignation at the Turks would have been no less. To leave things *as they are* and to do nothing to secure the future of those unfortunate people would be *shameful*, and, I repeat, it is hardly possible without war. But according to the latest reports, it would appear that such a war will not break out – and we shall again get nothing for our pains.

I have read in the papers about Prince Cherkassky's appointment.[6] If it is true, I wish him every success – and, most importantly, good health. I also trust that your health has not suffered from all the troubles you must have recently had to bear. I cannot complain myself; my gout is at rest – for the moment. I hope to see you at the end of January – I am going to Petersburg and will probably get to Moscow too.

Greetings to all my friends. I firmly press your hand.

Yours very sincerely,

Iv. Turgenev

167. To G. FLAUBERT

[Original in French]

Paris, 19 December 1876

My dear old friend,

I have just returned from a virtuous three-day family visit; but it was not too tedious. Let us deal first with the three stories.

St Julien has been translated and is in the editor's hands. Payment for it will be my usual one, i.e. you will be sent 300 roubles (the rouble varies between 2.85 and 3.30 francs) per printer's page (sixteen pages). But here's the rub. I have had to promise my editor and the public (in a note which I was stupid enough to publish) that I will allow *nothing to appear* with my name *before* my damned novel [*Virgin Soil*]. I have finished it and sent it off to St Petersburg where it is being printed at this very moment. However, that snake of an editor, instead of printing it all at once (which he had formally promised to do), has cut it into two, and it will therefore appear on 1 January and 1 February, and he so confused me

5. Aksakov headed a committee in Moscow set up to send assistance and arms to the Slavs in the Balkans. Turgenev disliked the whole affair because it was organized by the Slavophiles specifically to aid 'our Christian brothers'.

6. Princess Cherkasskaya's husband had just been appointed to a senior diplomatic post in Bulgaria.

that ('soft pear' that I am)[1] I gave my consent to this mutilation, which has pushed the unfortunate *Julien* to 1 March. This means that the other two stories should be published on 1 April. But in any case your *Coeur simple* will *not be published alone*. That would be quite impossible after what you wrote to me. I have given *Coeur simple* to a Russian lady of letters who knows the language very well (she is here in Paris), and if she emerges honourably from the test I shall give her *Hérodiade* as well.[2] Naturally I shall copy it out again if necessary – because my name has to be there! If it isn't, they will say that as I did the first translation, why didn't I do the others as well? They aren't as good, are they? And if we don't do it this way, we shan't be paid so well. But – further embarrassment! I am leaving for Petersburg (this is between ourselves) on 15 February for a month. You will probably not be ready by then, or if you are, I could only take the original without having had the time to do the translation. And then it would be necessary to find someone in Petersburg – which isn't impossible. *Final result*: try to finish *Hérodiade* by the very beginning of February. And then we shall see!

As for the other points in your letter, I shall reply in lapidary style, as I don't want to start another page.

1. An urgent prayer to hasten your return, for I am missing you greatly.

2. On Zola we are in agreement.[3] Our dinner will take place on Friday in the restaurant of the Opéra Comique. Pellé is a swine.[4]

3. Renan.[5] His article is very interesting, coming from him; but what a lack of colour and life! I can *see* nothing; neither Brittany, its saints, his mother, those little girls who were the cause of his first love 'bifurcating', not even Renan himself! And why does he say that *God* gave him a daughter?

4. I haven't read M. Montégut – he disgusts me.[6] There will probably not be a war – which is of incidental interest to you for it would affect the exchange rate of the rouble. The change of minister leaves me cold. Germiny is astounding![7] It makes one believe in a personal, ironic, sneering God!

Mme Commanville has paid me a visit; I was charmed and very flattered. She has a marvellous presence.

And so I embrace you.

Yours,
I.T.

[167] 1. Flaubert's nickname for Turgenev.

2. Possibly Y. I. Blaramberg.

3. Both Flaubert and Turgenev disliked Zola's *L'Assommoir*.

4. Léon Pellé, *maître d'hôtel* at the Café Riche where Turgenev and his French literary friends (Flaubert, Daudet, Zola, E. de Goncourt) often met for prolonged dinners. These meetings were referred to as 'The Dinners of the Failures' (Turgenev qualified as a dramatist).

5. Ernest Renan, French critic, writer and scholar. The reference here is to his *Recollections of Childhood* which had just appeared in the *Revue des Deux Mondes*.

6. Emile Montégut (1826–95), literary critic. Flaubert thought his *The New Novelists* 'gossip' and 'repulsive nonsense'.

7. Count Eugène de Germiny, senior French civil servant, had just been tried for 'insulting public morals', fined and sentenced to prison.

168. To K. A. L. PIETSCH

[Original in German]

Paris, 28 December 1876

A Happy New Year, dear Pietsch. Many thanks for your letter. I fear that it will be a difficult year for Russia. I am definitely going to Petersburg *at the beginning of February* and if you wish or are able we can leave Berlin together.

I have sent off the book you wanted ⟨'by book post'⟩.[1] It was not easy to find. Your enclosed sketch (I mean the photograph) was actually *not* enclosed. So I'm still expecting it.

Here we are all alive and well. Kathi really has sent your charming and friendly article on Paul to Mme Viardot.[2] You are still her faithful old friend!

⟨As for the photographs⟩,[1] would you tell J. Schmidt when you see him ⟨that I do not consider myself released from my promise⟩[1] to send him photographs of Zola and Flaubert? He will get them, come what may.

I have written to Storm, and very politely thanked him for his *Aquis submersus* which he sent me in a very elegant edition. The novella is well written and poetic. But, heavens above, how is it possible, e.g., to have the little boy sing about paradise and the angels *just* before he drowns?! Any little children's song would have had ten times the effect. When the Germans write stories they *always* make two mistakes: a sorry motivation and a quite unforgivable idealization of reality. If you deal with reality simply and *poetically*, the ideal comes of itself. No, the Germans may conquer the whole world but they have forgotten how to tell stories, or perhaps they never learnt how to. If a German author tells me something moving, he cannot refrain from pointing one finger at his own tear-filled eyes and another at me, the reader, giving me a gentle hint not to miss what it is that has so moved him!

The temperature has fallen to −40° in Petersburg, but it's thawing here. How is it in Berlin?

Greetings to all my friends and your family. I press your hand and am,

Yours faithfully,

Iv. Turgenev

169. To K. D. KAVELIN

Konstantin Dmitriyevich Kavelin (1818–85), legal historian, professor of jurisprudence at both Moscow (1844–8) and St Petersburg (1857–61) universities and later at the Military Juridical Academy. A leading liberal Westerner, he originated the *étatist* school of Russian historiography; he strongly advocated the emancipation of the peasants with land, full equality of women before the law, and strong and effective local government.

[168] 1. Original in French.

2. Kathi Eckert (?–1881), wife of the Kapellmeister of the Berlin Opera. Pauline Viardot's son Paul was just beginning his career as a concert violinist.

Kavelin had written to Turgenev praising his recently published novel *Virgin Soil* which had, at first, an extremely hostile reception from the Russian critics, the right-wing resenting the adverse opinions of Russia and the radicals considering his portrayal of the revolutionaries false. Kavelin's daughter, Sofya, also wrote favourably about the novel.

[Original in Russian]

Paris, 29 December 1876

Dear Konstantin Dmitriyevich,

I hope you will believe me when I repeat to you what I have recently written to Stasyulevich, namely, that in the whole of my literary career nothing has given me greater pleasure than your letter. My novel has great importance for me; it is not a question of whether my talent is still as strong or whether it has fallen off, or what success I might have with the reading public – to which I am if not indifferent then at least equanimous, which befits an old man with a grey beard. No, it is a question of whether I have succeeded in the task I set myself, of which the formulation seemed to me accurate but the carrying out (and the whole essence lies there!) capable of arousing in me justifiable doubts – and dangers. These dangers were the more natural because the task was painfully difficult! And then you, such a sensitive and just man – a real friend and a real judge at one and the same time – come along and say, 'The novel is good; everything is excellent and accurate' and even add 'thank you' in terms which could not fail to move me. How could I not be pleased? In thanking you, I am patting myself on the back; and now, whatever the 'literary' fate of *Virgin Soil* might be, I know, I know for certain, that I have not wasted my time and have done good service to my generation, and even perhaps to my country.

And if the young critics are going to take their sticks to me, it does not matter; it will be good exercise for them. Everything will settle down and perhaps they will realize that they were beating themselves.

I concur with your criticisms, however. Please do not think I say *this* out of the fulness of a heart grown tender from your praise. Fomushka and Fimushka are only an interpolation and could be removed without harming the whole. This alone can finally condemn them. I just could not resist the temptation of painting a picture of the old Russia, as a sort of ⟨contrast⟩,[1] or oasis, if you like. As for the depiction of the peasants, the way I did it was to a certain extent deliberate on my part. As my novel could not treat them fully as well (for two reasons: 1) the subject would have been too extensive and I would have lost the thread, and 2) I do not know them well enough *now* to be able to grasp what is unclear and indeterminate in them), I was left only with that hard, sharp side as seen in their contacts with the Nezhdanovs, Markelovs etc. Perhaps I should have drawn the character of Pavel, Solomin's factotum and the future revolutionary risen from the ordinary people, more strongly. But this is a major phenomenon and will become – in time (but not of course from my pen; I am too old and have lived

[169] 1. Original in French.

outside Russia for too long) – the central character of a new novel. For the present I have just prescribed his outline.

That you consider I have succeeded with Solomin is most pleasing to me, for he was the most difficult.

I shall of course read Potekhin's novel, after your recommendation.[2] I thought it would be the same old ethnography and ethnology.

I shall not speak about the disgraceful events outside the Kazan Cathedral, for one cannot know the whole story.[3] But how *stupid*! Thanks to it all I shall probably have to write a letter of explanation to Stasyulevich.

Please remember me to your daughter and tell her that her approval is the pearl in the garland you have placed upon me. I speak slightly allegorically, but it is true. Remember me to Bryullov too.[4]

I firmly, firmly press your hand and say a thousand times thank you.

Yours sincerely,

Iv. Turgenev

170. To BARONESS Y. P. VREVSKAYA

[Original in Russian]

Paris, 7 February 1877

Dear Yuliya Petrovna,

Thank you for your kind letter. I always felt that you were well disposed and sympathetic towards me. I shall not speak to you about *Virgin Soil*, for I have long since settled that problem.

Yesterday's news about the downfall of Midkhat-Pasha might once again alter the state of affairs and increase the chances of Gorchakov – and of war.[1] Nevertheless I have – for the moment – ceased to believe there will be one, and you can hardly count on being of service to the sick and wounded. Although you have no faith in my coming to Petersburg I have not forsaken the idea and feel I shall see you soon. You call me 'secretive', but listen, I shall be so frank with you that you will perhaps regret your epithet.

Since I first met you I have loved you as a friend and at the same time felt a persistent desire to possess you; however, it was not so unbridled (I was of course no longer a young man) as to make me ask for your hand – and furthermore other circumstances prevented it; but on the other hand I knew

2. *The Sick Woman* by the writer and dramatist Alexey Antipovich Potekhin (1829–1908).

3. An anti-government demonstration had taken place on 6 December, led by various elements in the Populist movement and members of the 'Land and Freedom' organization; large numbers of students and ordinary working people participated. A proclamation demanding a constitution and the death of the Tsar was read out.

4. Kavelin's daughter Sofya was married to the painter Bryullov.

[170] 1. Ahmad Midkhat-Pasha, a leading political figure in Turkey, had been dismissed for plotting to overthrow the Sultan. Prince Alexander Mikhaylovich Gorchakov (1798–1883) was State Chancellor at the time.

very well that you would not agree to what the French call *une passade*[2] – there you have the explanation of my behaviour. You wish to assure me that you have never had any 'hidden feelings' for me; alas! I was unfortunately only too well aware of that. You write that your *female* life is over; when my *male* life is past – and there is very little time to wait – I have no doubt that we shall become great friends – because there will be nothing to trouble us. But now I still go hot and a little frightened at the thought: well, what if she pressed me to her heart *not as a brother*? And I want to inquire, like my Marya Nikolayevna in *Torrents of Spring*, 'Sanin, have you learnt to forget?'

Well, now you have my confession. It's frank enough, isn't it?

I was very upset to hear what you said about your accident; I hope it is a false alarm and that you'll live for a long time. I am glad at least that the bruising has left no trace.

I kiss your hands, and remain your

Iv. Turgenev

171. To H. JAMES

Henry James (1843–1916), the American novelist, short-story writer and man of letters. In 1875 James decided to live abroad; he settled in Paris that same year, where he first met Turgenev, and in 1876 moved to England where he spent the rest of his life, becoming a British citizen in 1915. Although Turgenev had no high opinion of James's writings, he enjoyed his company and introduced him to his circle of French friends, notably the Viardots, where he was a frequent visitor on Thursdays ('rigidly musical and therefore, to me, rigidly boring') and on the more relaxed Sundays, where he found Turgenev's antics at playing charades 'both strange and sweet'. Fifteen of Turgenev's letters to James survive.

[Original in French]

Paris, 28 February 1877

My dear M. James,

I have received your letter, which gave me the greatest of pleasure. (Allow me to write to you in French, if you don't mind; it is easier for me.) I expect Ralston told you that I asked him for your address – I wanted to write to you as our relations have been interrupted for a long time. We have missed you a lot here, but we must not complain too much for you are after all happy with your stay in London and are working. Once the personal egotistical life (the only live one) is over (and I think this might apply to you, for it happens to the young as well as to the old), it is only a question of *adapting*; if one can arrange one's life tolerably well, that is all one can ask. However, we shall all be very happy if you wish to return and *adapt* to Paris.

2. A brief love-affair.

I have passed on your good wishes to Princess Urusova and Zhukovsky.[1] The latter has been away for almost three months and has only been back in Paris a few days, as elegant as ever, a little melancholy and sceptical for a young man who is on the threshold of the future – but not crossing it. I should dine with the Turgenevs on Saturday.[2] (It is the anniversary of the Emancipation of the Peasants in Russia and we shall remember the good and venerable N. I. Turgenev for whom the Emancipation had been the ⟨leading thought⟩.[3]) I shall pass on to them all that you told me.

I sent you yesterday the *Fils du Pope*.[4] It is what is called ⟨'a ghastly story'⟩[3] and does not amount to much really. That's what I've been told. When *Temps* has finished publishing my novel (twenty-six episodes have already appeared – there are about fifty in all) I shall send it to you without fail. It has not been very successful in Russia – even the word 'fiasco' has been mentioned. I cannot really agree with the critics, for I think it was not at all bad. But fortune does not favour old men – even in literature. Perhaps it will be viewed with more favour later. I give myself the small consolation of hoping so.

Ralston is an Englishman to his fingertips – a severe and narrow moralist. But with my hand on my heart I cannot see immorality in any of my works.

Nor is *L'Assommoir* an immoral work – but it's devilishly foul. Despite all the talent displayed by Zola, his book won't be successful outside France. If I were a cartoonist on *Punch*, I would amuse myself by drawing Queen Victoria reading *L'Assommoir*.

I have sent your best wishes to Flaubert. He is well and his ⟨'blue devils'⟩[3] have left him. He has just finished a third 'legend' – *L'Hérodiade* – which is very good. His book will appear in May.

Have you read V. Hugo's *Légende des Siècles* – the continuation – which has just appeared? There are wonderful things in it, but there is a lot of verbiage too, and that brass trumpet which assails your ears without stopping for an instant ends up being terribly fatiguing. But no one has *come across* such marvellous verses as he has – he is a real discoverer.

When shall we next see each other? I am leaving in a month for Russia and shall return here in June.

I cordially press your hand and am,

Yours faithfully,

Iv. Turgenev

---

[171] 1. Princess Marya Sergeyevna Urusova, a friend of Turgenev's who lived in Paris for many years. Pavel Vasilyevich Zhukovsky, son of the poet V. A. Zhukovsky.

2. The family of Klara Turgeneva, the widow of N. I. Turgenev.

3. Original in English.

4. The French translation of Turgenev's *The Story of Father Alexis*.

172. To N. S. TURGENEV

[Original in Russian]

Paris, 19 March 1877

Dear brother,

It seems to me that I have written to you rather often recently, and yet in your letter of 1 March you complain of my silence and inquire about my health. It's not bad, although I've recently been suffering from a painful gumboil and neuralgia in my face. But it's nothing serious, and my gout has only been troubling me occasionally.

As for all the critical comments you sent me about my last novel, I learnt nothing new from them. There is no doubt that, as you yourself write, *Virgin Soil* is a failure, and I am beginning to think that it deserves its fate. One must not suppose that all the journals were in some sort of conspiracy against me, but I should recognize that I was wrong to take on a task I was incapable of carrying out and that I failed beneath the burden. It is a fact that one should not write about Russia without living there. It would have been better if I had fallen silent several years ago. But this last lesson will not have been learnt in vain. My literary career has closed for ever and my name will not appear again below any real writing. It will not be exactly easy; the life ahead of me looks rather empty, but one must learn, as they say, to look the devil in the face, or, at least, the truth. Diderot said somewhere that ⟨'before his death a man must several times follow his own funeral procession'⟩,[1] and so I must also walk over my own literary grave. I shall find some other activity and then real old age will have arrived. And those daily petty concerns about keeping body and soul together will absorb all other interests.

But I am still coming to Russia – via Karlsbad, i.e. at the very beginning of May or even at the end of April. I really hope that I shall find you in Moscow and so until then I affectionately embrace you and remain,

Your affectionate brother,

Iv. Turgenev

173. To F. M. DOSTOYEVSKY

[Original in Russian]

Paris, 9 April 1877

Dear Fyodor Mikhaylovich,

My good friend, the well-known writer and expert on the Russian language, Emile Durand, has received a commission from the editor of the *Revue des Deux Mondes* to write a monograph (biographical, literary, critical) on the foremost Russian writers, and he has left for Russia with this objective in mind. You are, of course, in this connection of the first rank and he has asked me to provide him

[172] 1. Original in French.

with a letter of recommendation to you, which I do with the utmost willingness, for personal acquaintance with M. Durand, a man of the highest integrity, education and intelligence, can only give you the greatest pleasure.

I have decided to write this letter to you despite the misunderstandings which have arisen between us and which have led to our breaking off personal contact with each other. You will realize, I am sure, that these misunderstandings have no influence whatsoever on my opinion of your first-class talent and the very highest place which you occupy in our literature.

In the expectation that you will give M. Durand a hearty welcome and sympathize with the reason behind his journey, I beg you to accept the expression of the deep respect with which I have the honour to be,

Your most humble servant,

Iv. Turgenev

174. To Y. P. POLONSKY

[Original in Russian]

Paris, 19 April 1877

My dear friend, Yakov Petrovich,

Your poem, in which there are marvellous lines such as

The damp mists of pathetic night
Look through the window and steal into one's eyes,

caused in me the deepest depression, and because you understood – how? – I repeat to you a few lines from my diary:

'17 March. Midnight. I am sitting again at my desk. Downstairs my poor friend[1] is singing something, but her voice has now completely gone. My soul is filled with a darkness, darker than the night. It is as if the grave is rushing to swallow me up. As the fleeting moment, the day has passed, empty, aimless, colourless. You look up and it's time to roll into bed again. There is no right to live, and no wish to, either. There is no more to do, nothing to expect, nothing even to desire.'

I shall not quote any more: it is too depressing. You forget that I am fifty-nine and she is fifty-six. Not only can she no longer sing, but at the opening of the theatre which you so beautifully describe and in which she once created the role of Fidex in *Le Propète* she was not even sent a ticket. And why? Probably because they have long expected nothing of her . . . And you speak of 'rays of glory' and the 'magic of song'. My friend, we are both two pieces of long-broken china. I, at least, feel like a retired chamberpot.

You can now understand how your lines affected me. (I beg you, however, to destroy this letter.)

In all of this there is only one good thing, although you write nothing about it:

[174] 1. Pauline Viardot.

your wretched illness has passed and you are left only with the old ailments, which are more faithful than friends and never desert one.[2]

The approaching war also is little help in cheering me up. But we shall soon be able to chat about all this in person. We shall see each other in a fortnight as I am soon leaving Paris. Until then, I firmly press your hand and remain,

Yours faithfully,

Iv. Turgenev

175. To W. R. S. RALSTON

[Original in English]

Paris, 19 April 1877

My dear friend,

There is decidedly no French separate book about *nihilism* in Russia – but in the *Revue des Deux Mondes* there has appeared in 1876 or 75 an article intituled 'Le Nihilisme en Russie' by Alf. Rambaud or Leroy-Beaulieu (I am not quite sure of the name of the author) – which I have read and found good and exact enough. I have not been able to put my hand on it. I have given to my bookseller the commission to find it out – but I have not yet received an answer. I imagine, it will be easy for you to find it in the bibliothèque of the British Museum.

The trial[1] of the revolutionists is sad enough – certainly; but you are in a mistake if you imagine that the young girls resemble Mashurina rather than Marianna. Some of them are very handsome and interesting – and (as there still exists in our jurisprudence the barbarous custom of *a bodily* examination of prisoners accused of crimes) they have been found *all* in a state of virginity! There is matter for serious réflexion! I send you in this letter a very touching piece of verses by M-lle Figner, a very pretty blondine of 22 years – in the last stage of phthisis (that explains the last couplet but one) – she did not defend herself nor take an advocate – and was condemned to five years hard labour in Siberia – in the mines. Death will evidently soon release her.[2] I send you likewise a letter (by Zsvilenef)[3] which has been read during the trial – I received it from an unknown person with the remark that it could have been written by Solomine. Russian statesmen ought to think of all that – and come to the conclusion that the only way of stopping the progress of revolutionary propaganda in Russia – is to grant a constitutional reform. But all these considerations will now be swallowed by the turbid waves of war. My conviction is that we stand on the threshold of very dark times . . . There is nobody who can predict what shall come out of all this.

2. Polonsky had just recovered from a mild attack of scarlet fever, but he suffered continually from pains in his legs.

[175] 1. The 'Trial of the Fifty', comprising mainly young idealistic Populists arrested for distributing anti-government and socialist propaganda, took place in Moscow in March 1877.

2. Lidiya Nikolayevna Figner (1853–1920).

3. Nikolay Fyodorovich Tsvilenev (1852–1931), one of the defendants in the 'Trial of the Fifty'.

176. *To N. S. Turgenev*

I leave Paris on 5 May – and come back – if nothing happens – in the middle of July.

Wishing you good health and good spirits, I remain

Yours very truly, Iv. Tourguéneff

176. To N. S. TURGENEV

[Original in Russian]

St Petersburg, 18 June 1877

Dear brother,

Having collapsed beneath a heavy weight in the guise of gout, which I am particularly aware has ruled out the possibility of my seeing you and explaining things in person, I must now commit myself to paper, not even knowing whether you are still in Moscow or have already left for the country. (I conclude it must be the latter because those letters addressed to me at your home which I asked you to send on immediately have not arrived – I repeat my *urgent* request: please forward them.) However that may be, I take up my pen to set out briefly what I wished to discuss with you.

You are probably aware that my affairs have lately taken a rather unpleasant turn. My estate manager, whom I have dismissed, stole from me about 25,000 roubles, but worse than this is the fact that my son-in-law – my daughter's husband – has squandered every penny of her dowry and will probably have to declare himself bankrupt in the very near future. Consquently my daughter and her family are on my hands again and I shall have to see to their needs. I am already paying them an allowance of 4000 francs.

Add to that the fact that I can no longer count on any income from my writings; because the public has cooled towards my labours I thought it better to cease altogether. It must also be remembered that as I live abroad for most of the time the falling exchange rates, to which it is impossible to see an early end, cannot but be reflected in a marked reduction in my income.

It may be concluded from all this that ⟨'those lovely days in Aranjuez have long since passed'⟩.[1]

But you will ask why I am telling you all this. Here is the reason.

You were so good to leave me 100,000 roubles in your will. This was even more generous on your part inasmuch as you will probably not receive a copeck from me should I die first. You also lent me 15,000 roubles, and I cannot hide from you that the 9 per cent I should pay you back soon will be extremely difficult for me at the present time. I wonder, therefore, whether you could add this 15,000 to what you will give me, or more accurately would you leave me only *85,000* in your will, as I have already received 15,000? If you did this you would of course lose the interest I am paying, but it would help me considerably, as the interest I pay you is what I need for my poor daughter's allowance. Please

[176] 1. Original in German; a misquotation from Schiller's *Don Carlos*.

drop me a line with your answer so I shall know whether I shall have to find the 1350 roubles interest this coming year.

I also had an even more impertinent idea. If I had seen you personally I would have asked not only to subtract from your promised *100,000* the 15,000 but to increase it to 20,000, i.e. I would have liked you to give me 5000 now and leave me only 80,000 in your will. That remains, however, only a dream, even if I would have gone down on my knees before you. You know that I am not a money-grubber, nor am I capable even for a second of counting on your death before mine, especially as because of the little difference in our ages, coupled with my poor health, our chances seem about equal; but it would nevertheless have been pleasant to think that such an idea might have occurred to you too. May God grant you live to be a hundred!

Well, enough of that. I've explained everything to you.

I am a little better today and I am trying to hobble about on crutches; but there is no point in thinking about leaving before the end of next week. I repeat my request about *my letters* and *your reply*. I embrace you and have no doubts that you will not be angry with me for my frankness. Please reply in the same spirit.

Yours sincerely,

Iv. Turgenev

177. To A. DAUDET

Alphonse Daudet (1840–97), French novelist of the naturalist school, whose works deal with life in his native Provence and the different social classes in Paris. He and Turgenev became friends in the late sixties, and Turgenev was later to be instrumental in having him appointed as the Paris literary correspondent of the journal *New Time*. This is the only known letter of Turgenev's to Daudet.

[Original in French]

Paris, 24 December 1877

My dear friend,

If I have not spoken to you before of your novel it is because I wanted to do so at length and not simply content myself with one or two banalities. But I shall postpone all that until we meet, which, I hope, will be quite soon; Flaubert will return one of these days and our dinners can recommence. But I wish to say one thing – it is the most remarkable and yet the most uneven novel that you have written; if *Fromont et Risler* is represented by a straight line: ———— , *Le Nabob* must appear like this: ⋀⋀⋀, where the peaks of the zigzags could not have been attained except by a talent of the first rank. I ask your forgiveness for expressing myself so geometrically.

I have had a very prolonged and violent attack of gout and I went out for the first time yesterday – my legs and knees were like those of a ninety-year-old. I fear I have become what the English call 'a confirmed invalid'.

A thousand greetings to Mme Daudet. I cordially press your hand.

Yours,

Iv. Turgenev

178. To P. V. ANNENKOV

[Original in Russian]

Paris, 21 January 1878

So you have deferred your arrival here once again, dear Annenkov! I am beginning to fear that as you defer and defer (what an odd word that is) you will never grant me the favour of your company! And I would have very much liked 1) to see you in person and 2) to introduce you to Miss Lukanina,[1] and, finally, to enrol you into our newly resurrected Society for Assistance to Russian Artists, etc.[2] Let us place our hope in God, and wait!

Yes, Nekrasov is dead. And with him has died the best part of our past and our youth. Do you remember how he was when you and I saw him – in June? And now he has become a legend with the young. But nothing will come of the young until they have freed themselves from this legend, i.e. until some new, powerful and living talent appears. Your characterization of Nekrasov was so *accurate* that I have decided not to burn your letter as you requested, but to return it to you.

You will never find anything more pregnant (as the Germans say) than the words I have underlined. And the fact that Suvorin is lying is not at all beyond the limits he has set himself. What can you expect from such vermin . . . In comparison with him Bulgarin appears almost ideal.[3]

All I did in connection with Pushkin's letter was to pass everything I could. But Stasyulevich has not behaved exactly properly towards me. The passage about the dogs sniffing at the bitches' behinds I deleted in its entirety and he has put most of it back in – as well as Sobolevsky's obscenity.[4] I could not do a different commentary on the letters because I did not know some of the facts . . . but that's all water under the bridge.

And so – the Russians are in Adrianople! Wonders will never cease! But will there now be peace? And what sort of peace? England has her tail between her legs but her malice towards us knows no bounds.

[178] 1. Adelaida Nikolayevna Lukanina, née Rykacheva (1843–1908), doctor and writer. See headnote to letter no. 205.

2. 'The Society for Assistance to Writers and Scholars in Need' had been set up in Paris originally in the sixties, to help impoverished Russians living in France. Turgenev was its Secretary.

3. A. S. Suvorin had published a pseudonymous obituary on Nekrasov where he concentrated not so much on Nekrasov's qualities as a poet but more on what he considered his sharp business practices. Faddey Venediktovich Bulgarin (1789–1859), a member of the extremely reactionary and influential literary 'establishment' during the reign of Nicholas I.

4. Sergey Alexandrovich Sobolevsky (1803–70), a friend of Pushkin's in the twenties.

I am better now; well, almost. My foot still hurts and I cannot walk far. I shall postpone all gastronomic excesses until you get here. All my family are fit and well. But life has definitely lost its lustre. Many people who have been some part of my life have died recently . . . including my uncle of whom I was very fond when I was young.

I shall not say farewell, dear friend, but 'until we meet again'. But come as soon as you can, before my gout dispatches me to my bed again. My greetings to you and yours.

Yours faithfully,
Iv. Turgenev

179. To N. A. SHCHEPKIN

In July 1876 Turgenev was forced to dismiss his estate manager of the previous ten years, N. A. Kishinsky, for incompetence and dishonesty; in his place he appointed Nikolay Alexandrovich Shchepkin (1850–1914), the son of a neighbour of his, A. M. Shchepkin, to whom he had just agreed to rent the estate at Spasskoye. N. A. Shchepkin, a graduate of the Moscow Agricultural School, proved reasonably successful, although it took him a few years to put affairs in reasonable order. A hundred and fifty-two of Turgenev's letters to him survive, most of which contain his instructions.

[Original in Russian]

Paris, 7 February 1878

Dear Nikolay Alexandrovich,

I hasten to reply to your last letter of 19 February with its enclosed accounts.

First of all – Kadnoye. As you are on the spot you can judge better than I, but if you consider that a rent of 4000 roubles is satisfactory, then I will agree. If you need some special certification, then send me a draft here and I shall return it to you. But the main thing is to find someone reliable (not like Volnov), so as to prevent any forfeit in the event of our selling it, which applies to every contract.

As for Volnov, we must of course try to get all we can from that rogue, even if it means going to court.[1] I approve your intention of renting the land at Kholodovo to the peasants; at least they will be more reliable than Volnov.

I would be grateful if you could send me as soon as possible the money from the Kadnoye oats and the first instalment of the rent for Spasskoye, especially as the exchange rate is recovering and will probably recover even more now that the war is over.

Send me a report on Nikita. Is he studying well or not?[2]

[179] 1. Stepan Ivanovich Volnov had rented Turgenev's estates at Kadnoye for 3500 roubles and Kholodovo for 3600 roubles per annum but had not paid for them. Turgenev was forced to sue him for the debt.

2. Nikita Garasichev, a former peasant of Turgenev's for whose education he was paying.

180. *To H. James*

I hope you have fully recovered from your illness. I send my remembrances to your parents and to all of yours. I press your hand.

Yours sincerely,

Iv. Turgenev

P.S. I have received a letter from Mrs Ginter[3] with a copy of your proposal to pay her ten roubles as soon as I inform you that I agree; she says she has already asked me but hasn't received a reply; she also repeats her request about whether I can find her husband a job of steward somewhere on my estates. Would you please tell her that as I have now rented out all my estates I cannot find him a place anywhere, and give her *fifteen* roubles from me, and obtain a receipt.

180. To H. JAMES

[Original in French]

Paris, 30 March 1878

My dear friend,

(You will allow me, won't you, to write in French?) It is a long time since I should have replied to your kind and long letter (which was soon followed by the book you sent me.)[1] But various matters and preoccupations have delayed me, and I make my excuses. (I thank you for your book, which I have promised myself to read with a clear head.)

Your letter was full of kind and cordial words about the peace which has just been concluded between my country and Turkey. They did me good, for they showed once more your sympathy. But I have never for one moment had any illusions; I had a presentiment of the inevitability of war between Russia and England, and everything that was said at the Congress, the diplomatic solutions, left me absolutely incredulous. This war will take place – it has been predestined for a long time now – and the Eastern Question cannot be settled any other way. This war will be long and hard and I hope it will end with the expulsion of the Turks and the liberation of the Slav peoples, the Greeks and all the others. But my country will be ruined for a long time and I shall not see the reforms which have been promised there. You will easily understand that, feeling as I do, the future appears very bleak to me, and you will allow me not to touch on such matters again.

I have stayed in Paris much longer than I intended; my journey to Russia has been postponed until the end of May after the opening of the Salon and the World Exhibition. Will we see you here for it?

I am very happy to learn that you are in good health and getting down to some work. I cannot complain about my health, but as for my work: 'All good things come to an end.'

3. Anna Dmitriyevna Ginter, a neighbour of Turgenev's at Spasskoye.
[180] 1. Probably James's *French Poets and Novelists* (1874), which contained a chapter on Turgenev.

I do not see Princess Urusova and Zhukovsky very often, but I know that they are well.

Our mutual friend, Ralston, was seriously ill when he was here but managed to return to England, and I hope he will make a full recovery in his native surroundings.

I cordially press your hand and remain,

Yours very sincerely,

Iv. Turgenev

181. To L. Y. STECHKINA

Lyubov Yakovlevna Stechkina (1851–1900), writer. Her first story had been published in 1875 and in 1878 she wrote to Turgenev for advice on her writing, which he readily gave. They met soon afterwards and Turgenev followed her literary career with interest. When she later became seriously ill with tuberculosis he helped her financially. Fifty-five of his letters to her survive.

[Original in Russian]

Paris, 7 May 1878

Dear Lyubov Yakovlevna,

I have read your story and this is what I have to say about it: you have an undoubted talent; you are original, lively and even poetic, but *The Crooked Trees* should not be published because – if you will excuse the bluntness of expression – a more ugly or, to be more accurate, a more disfigured work I have yet to come across. Everything you say in your letter about your two heroes is absolutely true and shows that you have a remarkable critical faculty, but that makes what you have produced even more surprising and incomprehensible! You have set yourself a task which is only suitable for a first-class talent, namely the depiction and development of the relationship between your heroine and Mitya; but then, having embarked on it in a truthful and subtle manner, you suddenly introduce into the story for absolutely no reason at all that sick, corrupted and what's more quite unnecessary character, and proceed to deal with him a way that ruins everything – and you bring in the most melodramatic events. In a word, everything is reduced to ashes! How did you not sense yourself, for example, that Yury's nocturnal scribblings would produce a humorous effect – and then your vivacious, marvellous Varya succumbs to this buffoonery!?! And then the quotation from Béranger – what a contrived and freakish pathology! One might well say with Lermontov:

> And if it really did happen to him –
> Then we do not wish to hear about it.

Does it really happen in hospitals that a patient will grab a nurse by the nose and then bite it off? And what does 'to raise the pearl of creation' mean? I am speaking to you like this because I can see in you the most marvellous talent, and it is painful to see that the same person who can describe, for example, the scene where Varenka bathes her hand in the water and the one where Mitya goes into the garden on a winter's night (scenes which are worthy of our best writers) can also get tangled up in such fanciful and tedious arabesques! In my opinion there is only one thing to do: completely remove the second part with this Yury (you can deal with him later in another story), and concentrate on Mitya, Varenka and her husband and present us with a true and accurate account of the development of their story. That would be a lively and interesting tale. But with the following proviso: you have an undoubted gift for psychological analysis, but it often turns into a sort of pernickety nerviness. You wish to catch all the fluctations of a psychological state but you sometimes fall into triviality or just personal whim. It is impossible or at least very difficult to understand you – and sometimes, does it matter? (For example, I must admit that even when I had read the passage twice I still could not understand what was going on in Varenka's heart after her first ride on horseback.) I am sometimes reminded of the words of a young lady I knew in my youth: 'It is very difficult because it's so difficult.' ⟨Now, laugh at that!⟩[1] And then why do all your characters cry so incessantly and even sob their hearts out and then immediately feel an unusual calm? I do not know if you have read a lot of L. Tolstoy, indisputably the leading Russian writer, but I am sure that a study of his methods would be positively harmful for you. You have given ample proof that *you know what you are doing* and so can get rid of all that nonsense, that pirouetting on a pinhead, etc.

But that's enough criticism; I must also praise . . . it is much more pleasant. Your language is admirable despite the occasional Gallicism ('the style *by which* her dress was sewn made one feel' . . . etc.) Your descriptions are excellent – bold, simple, vivid. Every time you deal with nature you are charming, the more so since you describe just a few features, but they are the characteristic ones. You must do the same with your psychological analysis, ⟨for the secret of being tedious is to say everything⟩.[1] In your ability to concentrate on the characteristic I can see your *poetic* gifts. In brief, you could be a very notable writer, for you have everything necessary to become one. But you must take yourself in hand and not destroy your talents. I regret that I do not know how old you are or whether you are married or not.

P.S. I shan't be in Russia before the beginning of July (as I'm going to Karlsbad first), and then not in Petersburg but in the country at my home near Mtsensk, Oryol Province. But as you live near Tula, perhaps we shall see each other. Let me know what I should do with your manuscript. I shall be here for another three weeks.

I firmly press your hand, and remain,

Yours sincerely,
Iv. Turgenev

[181] 1. Original in French.

182. To L. N. TOLSTOY

On 6 April 1878 Tolstoy wrote to Turgenev in very friendly terms stating that all the hostility he once felt towards him had long since disappeared. He begged Turgenev's forgiveness for all that had occurred between them and asked that they should again be friends. Except for one brief letter from Turgenev to Tolstoy in 1875 (very formal, and written in French) concerning the French translations of Tolstoy's *The Raid*, *Three Deaths* and *The Cossacks*, this was the first letter either had written to the other since their quarrel seventeen years before in 1861. In August 1878 Turgenev visited Tolstoy on his estate at Yasnaya Polyana.

[Original in Russian]

Paris, 20 May 1878

Dear Lev Nikolayevich,

I have received your letter, which you sent poste restante, only today. I was delighted and very touched by it. It is with the greatest of pleasure that I say I am quite ready to renew our former friendship and firmly press the hand which you offer me. You are absolutely right when you suggest that I bear you no ill will. If it ever existed, it disappeared long ago. I retain only one memory of you – as a man of whom I was sincerely fond, and as a writer whose first efforts I welcomed before others did and whose every new work aroused in me the most lively interest. I am sincerely happy at the removal of all the misunderstandings which arose between us.

I hope to be in Oryol Province this summer and then we shall be able to see each other. Until then I wish you all the best, and once again most cordially press your hand.

Ivan Turgenev

183. To G. H. LEWES

George Henry Lewes (1817–78), critic and writer on marine biology, physiology, psychology and philosophy. He is probably better remembered for his liaison with George Eliot, with whom he lived from 1854 and whose talent he fostered. He and Turgenev had first met in the forties when both were students in Berlin, but their acquaintance really belongs to the seventies.

[Original in English]

Bougival, 1 November 1878

Dear Mr Lewes,

I have received the two volumes and thank you very much indeed for this gift. My own books will, I hope it, reach your hands before the 9th November and the box with the pills (Capsules de F. Joseph) will leave Paris tomorrow. Try them – and may they be as useful to you as they are to me.

I need not repeat you how happy I have been to meet Mrs Lewes and you at our friend's residence – and with what pleasure I remember those three days; ⟨that of course goes without saying⟩.¹ But be so kind and tell George Eliot how much I admire in her the poet and the woman – and believe me,

Yours very sincerely,
Ivan Tourguéneff

184. To L. N. TOLSTOY

[Original in Russian]

Paris, 27 November 1878

Dear Lev Nikolayevich,

I too did not reply immediately to your letter of 27 October. There have been some rather sad events recently. My old friend N. V. Khanykov died at Rambouillet, near Paris; his funeral had to be organized and his affairs put in order. I have also had a slight cold and my head ached for two days. But that's all over now and I can chat with you.

I am pleased that you are all physically well and hope that the 'spiritual' illness about which you write, has passed. I have suffered from it too. It has sometimes occurred as a mental ferment before I started something, and I suppose this is what happened to you. Although you ask me not to speak of your writings I cannot refrain from saying that I never made fun of them, 'even a little'. Some of your works I have liked a lot, others not at all. Some, like *The Cossacks*, for example, have given me the greatest satisfaction and made me marvel at their author. But why should I make fun of them? I thought that you had got over such 'recurring' thoughts long ago. Why are they known only to men of letters? Why not to painters, musicians and other artists? Probably because in a work of literature there is none of *that* part of the soul which it is not quite proper to show. Agreed, but you are no longer a young writer and you should have got used to that by now.

That I am writing nothing here is unfortunately true. I say 'unfortunately', but that is not true in general, only from my own personal point of view. Boredom is taking over. As I live abroad, I have lost the ability to write (at least, I ascribe my inactivity to living abroad), and as you know these things cannot be forced. Let us wait and see what will happen.

The English translation of *The Cossacks* is dry and ⟨matter of fact⟩,¹ as is Mr Schuyler himself; he was recently here on his way to Birmingham where he has been appointed consul.² I haven't seen the French translation but I fear that it is really not very good – for I know the ways of our Russian ladies who translate

---

[183] 1. Original in French.

[184] 1. Original in English.

2. Eugene Schuyler's English translation of *The Cossacks* was published in London and New York in 1878.

novels.[3] On the one hand I might fear for it, but on the other I am pleased. It is possible that we can still translate it and publish it here.[4]

I see you have been shooting hares; this autumn I have also done a little shooting. I stayed with a friend of mine in England who lives between Oxford and Cambridge and bagged a fair number of pheasants, partridges, etc.[5] But such expeditions – without dogs – are somewhat monotonous. In such circumstances one has to shoot very accurately, and I have always been only an average shot – but I'm used to it. By the way, I visited both the universities. These English educational establishments are the most marvellous and complicated things! And how they hate us!

Tchaikovsky's *Eugène Onegin* has arrived here, transcribed for the piano. Mme Viardot is trying it out in the evenings. It is certainly marvellous music and the lyrical, melodic passages are especially good. But what a libretto! Where Pushkin *tells* us about his characters, here they tell us themselves. For example, where Pushkin says about Lensky that 'He sang of life's faded colour', here we have 'I sing of life's faded colour.' It's like that almost all the way through.

Tchaikovsky has grown in popularity here since the concerts of Russian music at the Trocadéro; he has long commanded interest, if not respect, in Germany. An English professor of music in Cambridge told me, in all seriousness, that Tchaikovsky is the most remarkable contemporary composer. I just stood open-mouthed.

And so, farewell. Please thank the Countess for remembering me. I send my best wishes to everyone, and embrace you.

Yours sincerely,
Iv. Turgenev[6]

185. To P. J. HETZEL

[Original in French]

Paris, 31 December 1878

My dear friend,

Many thanks for sending me *Maroussia* with the preface.[1] All's well that ends well.

This letter will be brought to you by Mme Lukanina whom you already know and who cannot speak too highly of your gracious welcome. I have already mentioned to you that this lady is very talented, and that several of her stories published in the St Petersburg *Messenger of Europe* are quite remarkable. It has occurred to me that I might translate one of them (it's only fifty pages) and

---

3. The French translation was made by Baroness Y. I. Mengden.
4. Turgenev had thought of doing his own translation of *The Cossacks*, which he always thought was Tolstoy's best work.
5. Turgenev had stayed with his friend, W. H. Bullock-Hall, at Newmarket.
6. Tolstoy did not like this letter. He told Fet that Turgenev was nothing but a troublemaker.
[185] 1. Marko Vovchok's story had been adapted and published by Hetzel.

show it to you. I am sure you'll like it, and then you will be able to give her some advice about publishing it. She is worthy of all our support and encouragement.

I wish you all the very best for the New Year and cordially press your hand.

Iv. Turgenev

186. To G. FLAUBERT

[Original in French]

Paris, 21 January 1879

My dear old friend,

You might perhaps be wondering why I am showing no sign of life. Alas, my friend, I am decidedly nothing but an invalid who can no longer 'undertake' anything. It is now a fortnight since I was again caught by my gout, and I have only been able to walk about my room since yesterday – with the help of crutches, of course. I wasn't able to attend the première of *L'Assommoir*, which, castrated as it was, evidently had the success of a good old melodrama. I heard yesterday of the death of my brother; it made me personally very sad, especially when I think about the past. We only saw each other very rarely and we had hardly anything in common – but a brother . . . it sometimes affects you less than a friend but it is still something special. Less strong but more intimate. My brother died a millionaire but he has left everything to his wife's relations. He left me (as he wrote to me) some 250,000 francs in his will (this is about one twentieth of his fortune), but as the people who were with him during the last years of his life are a bunch of rogues it will probably be necessary for me to take myself off to Russia without delay – otherwise my legacy might go up in smoke! And so I shall probably be on my way to Moscow in ten days' time. If I am, when shall we see each other again? I cannot possibly think of coming to Croisset, even though I really would like to see you! Do you really have to stay down there until the end of February? What a sad winter! My life is as solitary as a mole's. To be alone, quite alone – and to do nothing – that gives you a taste – and the after-taste – of your uselessness. But what can be done about it? Patience!

Happily, everyone here is well.

Drop me a line. I trust your work is proceeding normally.

I embrace you.

Yours,
Iv. Turgenev

187. To N. A. SHCHEPKIN

[Original in Russian]

Paris, 29 January 1879

Dear Nikolay Alexandrovich,

As soon as I received your letter I wrote out a certification, had it witnessed at the Consulate and sent it to Mr Stasvulevich, the editor of the *Messenger of Europe* in Petersburg, who will send it on to you at Spasskoye as soon as the Consul's signature has been verified by the Ministry of Foreign Affairs. I have complete trust in all your arrangements and am grateful for all you have done already. There is no question that Mr Malyarevsky[1] has treated me most shamefully; I would also suggest that he is quite capable of purloining the 20,000 roubles about which you wrote. There is one passage in your letter which perplexed me. Which is that populated land near Mtsensk on the Dolgoye estate that wasn't mentioned in the will and that should consequently have come to me? As far as I know, my brother sold Dolgoye.[2] Do you mean *Sychevo*?[3] Or was Sychevo also sold to Mr Malyarevsky along with Turgenevo? I doubt whether my brother would have done that. Mr Malyarevsky would probably have mentioned it when you were discussing Turgenevo. If my brother received 28,000 roubles for it a month before his death, it is impossible to suppose that he gave it all away. He wasn't such a generous person, and whom would he have given it to? I am leaving here in ten days' time and so should be in Moscow in just over a fortnight, and then in Spasskoye. But in the meanwhile please take all the necessary steps. Inform me by telegram as soon as you get the certification. I sent a telegram three days ago concerning my brother's funeral, but I see from your letter that they have decided to bring it forward and bury him before I can get there. I also wrote to you enclosing a letter from Mr Malyarevsky which I asked you to read. If I had known what a crook he is I wouldn't have dreamed of writing to him. If by any chance you haven't yet given it to him, then don't. Even though you say you are going to Moscow, I am writing to you in Spasskoye. It's safer that way. I repeat that if my brother did not sell Sychevo to Mr Malyarevsky while he was alive and it isn't mentioned in the will, then it should legally come to me. In any case it would not be a bad idea to place a temporary restraining order on it so that nothing will be able to be removed and they won't be able to sell the wood, etc. But perhaps that was all sold before, too. Then you must ask Malyarevsky who bought it.

In conclusion may I repeat that I am relying on you and beg you to accept my gratitude in advance.

My greetings to all of yours, and I press your hand. Until I see you in the near future,

Iv. Turgenev

[187] 1. Porfiry Konstantinovich Malyarevsky (?–1896), estate manager for Turgenev's brother Nikolay, and married to one of Nikolay's wife's cousins.

2. Dolgoye, an estate left to Nikolay by his mother. It was not mentioned in Nikolay's will and so legally should have been inherited by Turgenev.

3. Sychevo was in fact left to Malyarevsky by Nikolay Turgenev.

188. To A. V. TOPOROV

Turgenev first met the actress M. G. Savina (see headnote to letter no. 200) on 15 March 1879. Evidently Toporov had told Turgenev to beware of her. The following letter is probably the angriest Turgenev ever wrote.

[Original in Russian]

St Petersburg, 19[?] March 1879

Dear Alexander Vasilyevich,

I am not used to hiding things, especially from you, and therefore I am writing to you in order to say exactly what I mean. I beg you never to speak to me again as you did yesterday in words which if they were not insulting were certainly inappropriate. Never say to me that I am cunning, that *I keep things from you*, just as if you were my rival, or my nanny, and I had to keep things from you! Yesterday you went so far as to express your intention of being present during my conversations with Savina because you fear she might *put me on the spot*(!) and force me to give her money. In the first place Savina is unworthy of such suspicions, and secondly, do you take me for a merchant's stupid little son? And if I intend to give her some money, what right have you to prevent me?! And how could you? Furthermore you have the habit, as by the way do many Russians, of asking me when I am going out somewhere, whom exactly am I going to see? And if I receive a letter – from whom exactly? And who came to see me? And who will be coming? I have grown unaccustomed to such unceremonial questions from Russians, because I have been living abroad where it would never enter anyone's head to ask such things. And at the age of sixty I do not intend to get used to it again. I have always thought of you – and beg you to consider yourself – as my friend, but not as my tutor, or rival, or even saviour. All this is very difficult and tedious at my age – and unseemly. But I've said what I wanted to and I trust that neither of us will ever mention it again.

Farewell.

Yours sincerely,

Iv. Turgenev

189. To PAULINETTE BRUERE (née TURGENEVA)

[Original in French]

Paris, 6 April, 1879

Dear Paulinette,

I returned to Paris only yesterday and must send you all my excuses for not writing to you from Russia, where I was literally overwhelmed by all sorts of things. The question of my brother's will has turned out rather sadly for me; instead of the 100,000 roubles he promised me, he left me scarcely more than a third of that sum, which represents an increase in my income of about 4000 francs. He has left all his huge fortune (more than a million and a half) to his wife's relations. I want nothing more than that you too should profit from this increase, and so from 1 January your allowance will rise from 2400 to 3000 francs. I can also give you a present of 1000 francs. Write to me immediately and tell me up to which date I have paid your allowance. If I am not mistaken, I have already sent you the first half of this year's. As soon as I have your reply, I shall send you what I owe.

I am pleased to learn that things are not going too badly. We must persevere.

My health is not too bad and the attack of gout I had in Russia was not serious.

I still hope to come and see you in the spring. In the meanwhile I embrace you all, starting with you.

Ivan Turgenev

190. To M. NECHELES

Moriz Necheles, German writer and literary critic. His 'Ivan Turgenev, a portrait' had been published in the *Literaturblatt* at the end of March and the beginning of April 1879.

[Original in German]

Paris, 16 April 1879

Dear Sir,

I have received your very flattering letter and read your 'portrait'. I thank you for the honour you have shown me and must say that much of your study is accurate and well written. You yourself know better than I could express it that a writer does not shroud any preconceived ideas in his pictures; everything grows from within him, half unconsciously. Another critic could perhaps have pointed out other aspects of my works with equal justification. If I had to state the true basis of my writings I might say that 'I wrote because it was a real pleasure so to do'. One's own people, human life, the human physiognomy – that is what one takes as one's raw material. The writer makes of them what he can; he cannot do otherwise. This is a very vague theory, but for me it is the only one. In any case I beg you to accept my sincere gratitude for your genuine sympathy. I consider it the greatest happiness of my life that I have managed to bring my native land a little nearer to the European reading public.

With the greatest respect,
Ivan Turgenev

191. To P. V. ANNENKOV

[Original in Russian]

Bougival, 24 June 1879

I returned here the day before yesterday, dear Pavel Vasilyevich, and shall probably not budge before the very end of October. The ceremony at Oxford went off extremely well.¹ There were nine new Doctors in red gowns and mortar-boards (one of them was the Crown Prince of Sweden, a very tall young man with a French-looking – and rather stupid – face). There were swarms of people, especially ladies, in the domed circular hall where such ⟨commemorations⟩² take place. A certain Doctor³ presented us in turn to the Vice-Chancellor, after having extolled us in Latin. The students and the public applauded; the Vice-Chancellor received us, also in Latin, and shook our hands, and we returned to our seats. I shall openly admit that when my turn came my heart was beating wildly. An unaccustomed business for our brother!

I was told that on this particular day the students (⟨undergraduates⟩)² are permitted to do as they like; it is something like a university saturnalia. And as anti-Russian feeling is still strong in England I was told I might expect to be whistled at. But nothing of this nature occurred, and according to the *Times* I was applauded more than the others. The weather was also marvellous that day. And what a wonderful town Oxford is, unique in the whole world, as you probably know. I met a lot of new people and cannot praise too highly the reception I received from the English. The professor there made me a gift of the red gown and mortar-board, and at the behest of the ladies I allowed myself to be photographed in that somewhat foolish get-up. I shall send you one, signed 'J.T., D.C.L'.⁴ It only remains for the Russian journals to tear me to pieces for having agreed to it – but then it will all sink into oblivion, leaving, however, happy memories.

Well, what can one say about the death of the Prince Impérial?⁵ It is true that fate sometimes seems to wish to amuse us with the drama and impact of the events it is causing! Just imagine an author thinking up *such* a denouement! Everyone would be up in arms – what an unnatural antithesis! Born to the sound of cannon, in a palace, laid in a golden cradle, at the centre of the world – and death in an African backwater at the hands of semi-gorilla savages! Anything can happen . . . one can only repeat Gogol's words, 'It's rare, but it happens.'⁶

For the Buonapartists the blow is irreparable. Whether the republic can benefit from this 'grand slam' is another question.

Send me some news. Everyone here sends their greetings; I send mine to you and yours and embrace you.

Iv. Turgenev, D.C.L.

[191] 1. W. R. S. Ralston had first mooted the possibility of the award of an honorary degree by Oxford University to Turgenev in 1874, but nothing came of it. However, in 1879 he enlisted the help of the philologist, Professor F. Max-Müller, whom Turgenev had met a year before on his first visit to Oxford, when he had stayed in 'a large room, but rather cold' with the Master of Balliol College Benjamin Jowett. The ceremony took place on 18 June 1879.
  2. Original in English.
  3. The Public Orator, James Bryce.
  4. Doctor of Civil Law. Turgenev was long bemused by the fact that he thought the initials stood for Doctor of *Common* Law.
  5. Prince Louis Napoleon, son of Napoleon III, was murdered by Zulu tribesmen on 1 June 1879.
  6. Misquotation from N. V. Gogol's short story *The Nose*.

192.To Y. Y. KOLBASIN

[Original in Russian]

Bougival, 17 August 1879

Dear Kolbasin,

I received your letter yesterday with the enclosed story, which is really staggering.[1] I shall try to have it published in one of the Paris journals; it is a pity, though, that none of the French journals which are seen in Russia (e.g. *Temps*) will accept it, for fear of causing themselves trouble – and it might be a good thing if they did. I shall say nothing about the story itself; it's just one of the symptoms of the impossible and unprecedented condition in which Russia now finds herself! But anyway, thank you for sending it.

I have been to Nauheim a few times, but have never stayed there; I hope the waters there will be of some benefit to you.

The Viardot family thank you for your kind wishes and send theirs to you.

Like you I have recently been reading Herzen and got the same impression. We have never had a more intelligent and witty writer (the two don't always go together). And what warmth and sincerity amid all those fireworks! No one has yet replaced him, and I say that even though we are travelling different paths.

As soon as I know *which* journal will publish the story, I shall let you know. Meanwhile I cordially press your hand and remain,

Yours sincerely,
Iv. Turgenev

P.S. I am writing poste restante as I couldn't make out your address.

193.To P. V. ANNENKOV

[Original in Russian]

Bougival, 8 November 1879

Dear friend Pavel Vasilyevich,

I am still writing to you from my beautiful backwater, where I intend to stay until the end of the month.

The Viardots have already returned to Paris, but I have stayed with the children; little James has to stay for another three weeks[1] and Didie must ensure she recovers from childbirth properly. My health is satisfactory and my idleness remarkable. I have written some very short reminiscences of 1848[2] which will be included in the first volume of Salayev's edition of my works. I have also been reading the proofs of some of the other volumes he has already sent me, in which I have discovered a large number of misprints. It would seem that I asked for it as I even made a point about such things in my contract! But such is clearly my fate!

[192] 1. Possibly an account of the treatment of a revolutionary by the Russian authorities.
[193] 1. Jeanne (1874–?), eldest daughter of Claudie Viardot and George Chamerot, had scarlet fever.
2. *The Man in Grey Spectacles.*

I liked Daudet's novel less than you did,[3] probably because in the very nature of the subject matter there are no typical characters, only portraits, somewhat obscured by a thin haze. And surely only the typical is of interest. But he's nonetheless very talented – and hugely successful, which is something you can also say about Zola's *Nana*, which has fast disappeared from the booksellers, despite its obscene subject matter and a mass of unprintable expressions. I have been reading it in the *Voltaire* and have been seized by an unutterable tedium. And that is something my friend Zola did not expect!

By the way, have you read the story in the *Messenger of Europe* called *Stripes*? If I am not mistaken, it is remarkable; we have a new, powerful talent. And just imagine – the author is a woman, a certain poor, sick Lomovskaya, who lives in Moscow![4]

Stechkina's story is appearing in the November number of the *Messenger of Europe*, as I think I told you.[5] I read the proofs here and retained my original impression of it.

Everything you say about the contemporary historical novel in Russia is absolutely true. A sign of the times! I cannot help recalling Goethe's aphorism:

> If you step in the mire, it might be messy,
> But it soon dries out.

I have started reading the last part of Renan's *L'Eglise Chrétienne*. It's interesting but ⟨too ingenious⟩[6] for my profane tastes.

And so I wish you all the best and send my best wishes to all your family. Farewell till Baden!

Iv. Turgenev

P.S. At a recent lunch at Orlov's I met the Tsarevich[7] and his wife. I like him; he has an open, honest face. But what sort of Field-Marshal is Nikolay Nikolayevich?![8] (I also met him.) It passes all understanding!

194. To PAULINETTE BRUERE (née TURGENEVA)

[Original in French]

Bougival, 11 November 1879

My dear Pauline,

I reply immediately to your letter, and I beg you to read my reply as seriously as I have written it.

3. *Les Rois en exil*.
4. Lidiya Filippovna Lomovskaya, née Koroleva (1851–1936), published under the pseudonym of L. N. [elidova].
5. *Varenka Ulmina*.
6. Original in French.
7. The future Alexander III.
8. Grand Duke Nikolay Nikolayevich, third son of Nicholas I, commander-in-chief of the Russian forces in the Russo-Turkish War of 1877–8; he had shown himself fairly incompetent but was still promoted.

You ask me for 19,000 francs at a time when I have only a few hundred at my disposal and when I shall receive nothing from Russia until the second half of December, and then I shall get only five or six thousand at the most. This means I would have to borrow the money. I do not say that I shall not do so, but it is quite obvious that this sum will vanish over the same precipice which swallowed up the 200,000 I gave you before.[1] I promised Gaston (and I shall keep my word) to advance him (or in other words, to give him) the necessary money – *which I shall have to borrow* – which will help him transfer things to another industrialist, who might wish to defer payment. *Once the transaction has been completed* this sum will very probably be lost, but at least you will be rid of everything that would finish by ruining you. At the moment, though, it would only serve to throw oil on the fire. You speak of the possibility of bankruptcy. As I see things, it is quite inevitable. It is unfortunate, but there is basically nothing dishonourable about it. I repeat: it is financially impossible for me to do anything other than what I have already told Gaston:

1. Raise your annual allowance from 1 January by 400 francs – this will make 4800 (I told Gaston 4000).

2. Advance Gaston some of the money which the new manufacturer who will replace him will have to pay and to overcome any delays in payment.

Please be assured that this is all I can humanly do – and act accordingly.

I am also writing to Gaston today at his mother's (64 rue Nicolo, Passy?) and I shall repeat what I have just told you. I shall add two pieces of advice. The first is to ask his mother for the 20,000 francs, the repayment of which I shall take upon myself, instead of lending it to Gaston himself while he transfers the business. Whatever happens I shall pay nothing *until the whole transaction is completed* and there is no question of his still having the factory. It is the least that Mme Bruère can do after the infamous way she and her husband deceived me at the time of your marriage.[2] In this way she will shield her dear Paul[3] from the unpleasantness of his brother's bankruptcy.

My second piece of advice will be to find immediately someone who will take the factory over *without paying anything* but discharging all the debts involved. You will lose everything if he does this, but you will be free of all debt and able to try to start a new life, at first with your 4800 francs and later from any income he can earn from the employment that I shall try to find for him.[4]

With this, I embrace you and the children.

Ivan Turgenev

---

[194] 1. i.e. Gaston Bruère's glass factory.
2. They had kept a quarter of Paulinette's dowry.
3. Younger brother of Gaston.
4. Gaston refused to get rid of the factory or to declare himself bankrupt. Two years later he was quite ruined. (See also letter no. 209).

195.TO Y. P. POLONSKY

[Original in Russian]

Bougival, 22 November 1879

Dear Yakov Petrovich,

I hasten to reply to your letter, in which I see further proof of your undying friendship and concern for me. But you can rest in peace. I have committed no 'great stupidity' in order to spite Mr Zagulyayev[1] (the same Mr Zagulyayev who ceaselessly attacks me in the *Journal de St-Pétersbourg*). In the first place, the piece in *Temps*[2] is in no way a protest, but a simple, unsophisticated and touching story about a man held in prison *about whom there is no hint of any political reproach*. Secondly, in my brief introduction I state simply that while I in no way approve of or share the opinions of Messrs the Nihilists and Revolutionaries, I would suggest that the story serves to show the unsuitability of solitary confinement without trial, ⟨which cannot be justified in the eyes of any healthy legal system⟩.[3] As you probably know, this is something that can be discussed, and there is nothing uncensored in my words. I might add that the interest in the story is purely psychological. That's all. I cannot for one moment imagine that I shall be accused of knowing an exile who is, after all, not exactly a hardened criminal and who was vindicated at his trial (albeit after four years' imprisonment) and sentenced only to administrative exile, from where he escaped to save himself from dying of hunger. And they are going to forbid me to return to Russia for that??!!

I am, if you like, a liberal, but a dynastic liberal who recognizes that no reforms are possible except those which *come from above*, and if such reforms do not take place I repeat to my young friends that they must wait, and wait, and wait; for is not revolution unthinkable in Russia, and against our whole historical tradition? Mr Zagulyayev might think so, but he would probably be the first to welcome such an unprecedented occurrence. I, however, have a much better opinion of our rulers' intelligence and sense of justice.

And so I can say to you without the slightest trepidation that in three or four weeks' time we shall sit down together in Petersburg.

I really did meet the Tsarevich at Orlov's (N.B. – *after* the appearance of the article in *Temps*) and to my great joy found him a sincere, honourable and good man. His wife is also charming.

[195] 1. Mikhail Andreyevich Zagulyayev (1834–1900) published a series of articles on contemporary Russian literature in the French-language *Journal de St-Pétersbourg*; his opinion of Turgenev's writings was generally tepid and he often bemoaned the infrequency of Turgenev's visits to Russia.

2. The story *In Solitary Confinement: Impressions of a Nihilist*, by the political émigré I. Y. Pavlovsky, was published in *Temps* in November 1879. It was prefaced by a short article by Turgenev in the form of a letter of recommendation to the paper's editor, F. Hébrard. Polonsky had told Turgenev that there were rumours in government circles that the authorities were highly displeased with his 'association' with Pavlovsky.

3. Original in French.

And so I affectionately embrace you and wish you all the best.

> Yours,
>
> Iv. Turgenev

P.S. Did you get my letter about *War and Peace*? I also mentioned your own novel.

196. To G. FLAUBERT

[Original in French]

> Paris, 27 December 1879

My dear old friend,

The caviar and the salmon were dispatched *four days* ago to M. Pilon, quai du Havre, Rouen, to be forwarded to you. (I got the address from Commanville.) Would you make the necessary inquiries? I would especially rue the loss of the salmon – it was splendid.

The present cold weather is not only freezing me but stupefying me as well. However, I have started preparing for my departure. 'The wine (and what wine!!) is opened, it must be drunk.'

I shall send you soon a three-volume novel by Count Lev Tolstoy, whom I consider the best contemporary writer. You know who might, in my opinion, rival him?[1]Unfortunately the translation is by a Russian lady and I generally beware these lady translators, especially when they are dealing with writers as powerful as Tolstoy.[2]

Meanwhile, I embrace you.

> Yours,
>
> I.T.

[196] 1. i.e. Flaubert himself.
 2. *War and Peace* had been translated into French by 'une Russe', Princess Irina Ivanovna Paskevich, and published in St Petersburg.

V
1880–1883

The last few years of Turgenev's life were marked by more and more illness, deepening melancholy and resignation, and a decline in his literary output. There were also increasing problems for him in connection with his daughter Paulinette. Her husband had let his business go to ruin, had turned to alcohol, had threatened her life and his own, and had become so difficult to live with that she was forced to leave him. Turgenev, who had never shown much affection towards her, nonetheless felt it his duty to support her and her two young children, and he had to sell his collection of paintings, to which he was very attached, and various other possessions in order to do so. He returned to Russia in 1880 to take part in the celebrations to mark the erection of a monument to Pushkin, during which he made an unremarkable speech (and, much to his annoyance, by far the most notable contribution was by Dostoyevsky), and again in 1881; both these visits were also occasioned by his infatuation with the actress Marya Savina.

He published the stories *Song of Triumphant Love* and *Old Portraits* in 1881 and *Clara Milić* and *The Desperado*, a faithful description of his cousin M. A. Turgenev, in 1882, and wrote his *Poems in Prose* and a few other short pieces.

By the spring of 1882 he was becoming increasingly ill. None of the many doctors he consulted successfully diagnosed his complaint accurately – they preferred a form of angina to the actual cancer of the spine, although one did admit, after Turgenev's death, that he had suspected it. Although he came to regard himself as incurable, Turgenev never really believed his condition was serious. After a painful operation to remove a tumour from his abdomen at the beginning of 1883 his health grew gradually worse, and despite one or two respites from the increasingly unbearable pain, he died on 3 September. His beloved Pauline Viardot and her daughter Claudie were with him to the very end.

197. To L. N. TOLSTOY

[Original in Russian]

Paris, 9 January 1880

Dear Lev Nikolayevich,

Before I received your letter, Chaykovsky[1] came to see me and told me of your plans; I gave him 260 francs (100 roubles). He is a really good man; unfortunately I did not see much of him as he was living most of the time in the country, not far from Paris. I shall be leaving here in just over a week and I know for sure that you and I shall soon see each other, although I do not know yet exactly where. I was very touched by the sympathy you expressed towards me in connection with the article in the *Moscow Gazette*.[2] For my part I almost welcomed its appearance because it led to your kind and friendly words. When I stopped writing for the *Russian Herald*, Katkov told me to be very careful because, he said, I did not know what it was like to have him as an enemy. And now he is trying to show me! Well, let him! My heart and soul are not under his authority.

Princess Paskevich who translated your *War and Peace* finally sent five hundred copies here. I got ten. I sent them to the most influential critics (including Taine, About, etc.).[3] It must be hoped that they can appreciate the force and beauty of your epic. The translation is rather weak but has been done with love and affection. I recently read your truly great work for the fifth or sixth time with renewed pleasure. It is certainly a long way from what the French usually like or what they look for in their books, but it is true to say that in the long run it will hold its own. I trust that if it does not win a brilliant victory it will achieve a lasting, albeit slow, conquest.

You say nothing about your latest work; there are rumours that you are working hard.[4] I can picture you at your desk in that quiet little hut you showed me. But I shall soon be able to get more news – at first hand.

I am pleased at your domestic happiness and ask you to send everyone my affectionate greetings. Yes, Russia is passing through dark and difficult times at present and I am ashamed to live abroad, especially now. The feeling grows stronger and stronger, and for the first time in my life I am setting out for my native land without a thought about when I shall return – and I do not wish to return soon, either.

---

[197] 1. Nikolay Vasilyevich Chaykovsky (1850–1926), leading Populist activist, who was forced into exile after the abortive 'Movement to the People' in 1874 when thousands of young idealistic students had gone out into the country to bring socialism to the peasants.

2. Katkov had reprinted parts of the article by Zagulyayev (see letter no. 195).

3. Hippolyte Taine (1828–93), influential French philosopher, historian and literary critic. Edmond About, writer, and editor of *Le XIX-e siècle* from 1872.

4. At this time Tolstoy was thinking about writing a novel on the Decembrist movement, but he discarded the idea and started on *My Confession*.

I firmly press your hand and thank you for drawing close to me again. I know that I feel the same towards you.

Look after your health; until we meet again.

Yours affectionately,
Iv. Turgenev

198. To A. FRANCE

Anatole France, pen name of Jacques Anatole François Thibault (1844–1924), French novelist, poet, critic and man of letters. He was awarded the Nobel Prize for Literature in 1921. He and Turgenev met in the seventies, but were never close, although Turgenev told him he found much to admire in his 'poetic and noble style'.

[Original in French]

Paris, 15 January 1880

Monsieur,
I take the liberty of sending you *War and Peace* by Count Lev Tolstoy, who is the most popular author in Russia at the present time and quite deserves to be.

His novel is all but a masterpiece and is the most remarkable work in the whole of Russian literature. Knowing the sympathy you have for my country, I hope you might write a few words on it in *Temps*. Every Russian, including the author and the sender of this letter, would be very grateful to you and I dare hope French readers would be too.

Yours sincerely,
Iv. Turgenev

199. To G. FLAUBERT

[Original in French]

Paris, 24 January 1880

My dear old friend,
You can have no conception of the pleasure your letter and what you said about Tolstoy's novel gave me.[1] Your praise has reinforced my own opinion of it. Yes, he is an excellent man, but you have also put your finger on his greatest fault. He has erected for himself a philosophical system, at once mystical, infantile and presumptuous, which has seriously marred both the third volume and the novel he wrote after *War and Peace*.[2] But you will also find there things

[199] 1. Flaubert had written to Turgenev that he thought *War and Peace* first-rate and Tolstoy a marvellous writer and psychologist. But he did not like the last third, where he accused Tolstoy of repeating himself and philosophizing. Turgenev sent Tolstoy a copy of his letter.
2. i.e. *Anna Karenina*.

absolutely of *the first rank*. I do not know what Messrs the Criticis will say (I have also sent *War and Peace* to Daudet and to Zola), but I have made up my own mind about it because *Flaubertus dixit*.[3] Nothing else is important.

I am pleased that your good men are progressing.[4]

I shall leave Paris sometime next week, but I shall remind you of my existence before I go.

In the meanwhile I wish you all the best and affectionately press your hand. Please send my greetings to all of yours.

Iv. Turgenev

200. To M. G. SAVINA

Marya Gavrilovna Savina (1854–1915), real name Podramentsova, thrice-married actress; at the St Petersburg Alexandrinsky Theatre from 1874 until her death. She was twenty-five when Turgenev first met her, when he attended a revival of his play, *A Month in the Country*, in which she played the part of Vera. He was immediately captivated; they often met on his visits to Russia and on hers to France. It is clear that Turgenev dreamed of a relationship with her other than friendship but, true to the themes of his writings, love never brings happiness. Savina was flattered by the attentions of the older, famous man and certainly did not refrain from encouraging his attentions, but her amorous interests lay elsewhere. Seventy-seven of Turgenev's letters to her survive; most of hers to him have presumably been lost or destroyed. For a discussion of their relationship as seen through their correspondence and other sources, see N. Gottlieb and R. Chapman, *Letters to an Actress* (London, 1973).

[Original in Russian]

Moscow, 24 April 1880

Dear Marya Gavrilovna,

Late last night I received both your letters together and was very happy (only not about the fact that you are unwell). I felt that I am sincerely fond of you and, not for the first time since I left St Petersburg, that you have become someone in my life with which I cannot now part.

I have fallen here into a whirl of activity, even more than I did in Petersburg, and won't be able to leave until Tuesday. I shall return here for the Pushkin celebrations on 25 May. But as you will leave St Petersburg on the fifteenth, I fear, as they say in Little Russia, that 'we shall miss each other' As I would not wish that to happen, would you please write to me at Spasskoye, near Mtsensk, Oryol Province, telling me when and on which train exactly you will be setting out from Moscow on the Kursk line. Once I know this, I could wait for you at Mtsensk station and accompany you to Oryol. I would be delighted to ask you

3. Flaubert has spoken.
3. i.e. *Bouvard et Pécuchet*.

to spend a day with me in the country at my home – it's only ten versts from Mtsensk – but this would cause you a lot of trouble as you will not be travelling alone, and then there's the luggage, etc. But do not forget to let me know.

At the very moment on the day of my departure when you were standing in the church and looking at your watch, I, for my part, was gazing at the entrance to the station hoping that perhaps . . . And it turned out that my request to you not to see me off was quite stupid. But you had no right at all to attribute it to the motive which you mentioned; I simply did not wish to say goodbye to you surrounded by a crowd of other people – but there weren't any. It is very difficult for me to forget you – but then I don't want to.

I did not send you the photograph of you wearing the little hat because I recalled that you did not like it.

Do not take the trouble to write me long letters in the midst of all the work that will soon engulf you. I shall be quite content if you send me a postcard with the words: 'I am well', and perhaps you will add: 'Here is my hand; you may kiss it.'

I am doing that now – in my imagination – and more than once; and I hope to do it in reality in Mtsensk. In the meanwhile, look after your health, don't get depressed, and believe in the sincere affection of

Your Iv. Turgenev

201. To E. ZOLA

[Original in French]

Spasskoye, 11 May 1880

My dear Zola,

Thank you for thinking of me. It was like a handshake from a friend. I received the sad news three days ago in a most cruel manner – I was reading an article in the *Voice*.[1] I have no need to tell you of my grief. Flaubert was one of the people I loved most in the whole world. It is not just that a remarkable talent has left us, but also a most wonderful man; he was the centre of all our lives.

I shall be in Paris in three weeks at the latest. I shall see you there, and we can discuss the publication of the novel which he did not manage to complete and which *must* be published. In the meanwhile, I cordially press your hand and am,

Yours sincerely,

Iv. Turgenev

[201] 1. The death of Flaubert was announced in the *Voice* on 2 May.

202. To M. G. SAVINA

[Original in Russian]

Spasskoye, 17 May 1880

Dear Marya Gavrilovna,

It is now half past twelve. I returned here an hour and a half ago and here I am writing to you.[1] I spent the night in Oryol which was both good, because I was thinking of you constantly, and bad, because I could not close my eyes. I hope you slept better than I did in your comfortable compartment. I am accompanying you in my imagination to Kiev. Today, the day you should have come to Spasskoye, is, as if by order, heavenly; not a single cloud in the sky, not a breath of wind, warm . . . If you had been here, you and I and Raisa Alexeyevna[2] would be sitting on the veranda while I talked of nothing in particular. But in my thoughts I would be kissing your feet in an ecstasy of gratitude (⟨the bolt . . .⟩ [3]). At least, this is what I dreamed of, but my dreams remained just dreams. One should drive them away, but it's not easy. I suppose you'll be kind enough to drop me a word when you arrive. I did not manage to speak to you about 'that shadow, which will have an effect on your future . . .'.[4] I can guess what it is but should like to know something more definite. When I was about to return from the station last night and you were at the open window of your compartment, I stood there in silence and then said the word 'desperate'. You thought I meant you, but I was thinking of something quite different. The really *desperate* thought had just occurred to me of seizing you and carrying you off. The third station bell would have sounded, followed by a scream from Raisa Alexeyevna and perhaps one from you too – but it would already have been too late. You would have had to stay with me for the next twenty-four hours – but where and how? It was because of this thought that I said that word. But reason, unfortunately, prevailed, the bell sounded and *ciao!*, as the Italians say.

But just imagine what would have appeared in the papers!! I can just see the report with the headline, 'Scandal at Oryol Station': 'An extraordinary event occurred here yesterday: the writer T. (hardly a young man!), who was seeing off the well known actress S. on her journey to fulfil what would have been a brilliant engagement in Odessa, suddenly, just as the train was leaving, dragged Mrs Savina through the window of her compartment, despite her despairing objections, as if he were possessed of the devil, etc., etc.' What a sensation to rock the whole of Russia! And yet – it hung by a thread! As does everything else in life, I might add in passing.

And so – I shall be here until the twenty-fourth, and then I leave for three days in Moscow from where I shall write to you absolutely without fail. Then two

[202] 1. Turgenev had asked Savina to stay with him at Spasskoye on her way from St Petersburg to Odessa. She refused, but he accompanied her on the train from Mtsensk to Oryol.

2. Raisa Alexeyevna Potekhina (1862–90), an actress friend of Savina's and the daughter of the writer, A. A. Potekhin.

3. Original in French.

4. Possibly a reference to Savina's relations with her future second husband N. N. Vsevolozhsky.

days in Petersburg, then Paris, then Bougival, les Frênes. I do not yet know how long I shall stay here. I confess that I have no great faith in your trip abroad (what *might have been* I have scarcely any need to repeat), but in any case here is my *most reliable* address: M. J. Tourguéneff, bureau de poste restante, rue de Milton, Paris. But you could drop me a note first to 50 rue de Douai, telling me when you plan to arrive, and then write poste restante with your address and so on. But only on the condition that ⟨the bolt is drawn back⟩[3] – otherwise it would be best not to write to me, for you well know from mythology what position Tantalus found himself in. I shall say no more.

I wish you all the best, starting with your health. Please give my regards to your charming companion; I kiss your little hands and feet, everything you permit me to . . . and even that which you do not.

Your
Iv. Turgenev

P.S. I can write ⟨quite openly⟩,[5] can't I? I.e. no one but you will read this? For this reason I am sealing this letter with Pushkin's ring – my talisman.[6] [Address omitted]

203. To M. G. SAVINA

[Original in Russian]

Spasskoye, 19 May 1880

Dear Marya Gavrilovna,

I have never known anything like it. For the third day running the weather here is heavenly. I walk in the park from morning till evening, or sit on the veranda, trying to think – yes, I do think – of various things, but somewhere, deep in my heart, there sounds just one and the same note. I tell myself I am thinking about the Pushkin celebrations when suddenly I realize that my lips are whispering, 'What a night we could have had . . . And what would have happened afterwards? God alone knows!' And then comes the immediate realization that it could never happen and that I shall go into that 'unknown land' without bearing with me any memories of something which I never experienced. For some reason it sometimes occurs to me that we shall never see each other again. I never had any faith, and nor do I now, in your trip abroad, and I shall not come to Petersburg this winter. And there is no need for you to reproach yourself and call me 'your sin'. Alas, I shall never be that! And if we should meet in two or three years' time, I shall be quite an old man and you will probably have finally settled down, and nothing will remain of the past. This will not be very serious for you – all your life is in front of you, mine is in the past; and that hour I spent with you in your compartment, when I almost felt

5. Original in Italian.
6. Turgenev had been given Pushkin's signet ring by the poet Zhukovsky. Pushkin had worn it constantly and called it his 'talisman'.

like a young man of twenty, was the last flicker of the icon lamp. It is even difficult for me to explain to myself what feelings you aroused in me. Am I in love with you? I do not know. Formerly, such things were different. This irresistible need to merge, to possess, and to surrender oneself, when even sensuality is lost in the flickering flame . . . I am probably talking nonsense, but I would have been unspeakably happy if only . . . if only . . . And now, when I know that this can never be, I am not exactly unhappy, I don't feel any particular sadness, but I deeply regret that this delightful night is now lost for ever without touching me with its wing. I regret it for my own sake but – I dare add – also for yours, because I am sure that you would never have forgotten the happiness you would have given me.

I should not have written all this had I not felt that this was a letter of farewell. Not that I wish our correspondence to stop, oh, no! I hope we shall often send news to each other; but the door which was half-opened and behind which something secret and wonderful was hovering, has been slammed for ever. One can really say, ⟨'It's now bolted.'⟩[1] Whatever happens, I shall never be the same – and nor will you.

Well, that's enough. Whatever there *was* (or was not!) has briefly bloomed and died. But it does not prevent my wishing you all the best in the world and imagining that I am kissing your dear hands. You do not have to reply to this letter – but please answer the first.

Your
Iv. Turgenev

P.S. Please have no fears for the future. You will never receive *such* a letter again.

204. To M. M. STASYULEVICH

[Original in Russian]

Spasskoye, 13 June 1880

Dear Mikhail Matveyevich,

When I tell you the following you cannot but be superstitious! About eight years ago, on Friday 13 June, I was at the Vienna Exhibition and hurt my knee getting out of my carriage. I was soon assailed by gout and confined to bed for three weeks. About four years ago, also on 13 June, also on a Friday, I tripped up some stairs and gout struck again, leaving me immobile for a week. And then today, also 13 June, also a Friday, for no particular reason, I've had another attack and am in bed again! I do not yet know when I shall be able to leave, and so our dinner will have to be postponed to some future date. One thing, though, I shall tell you the time of my arrival by telegram – and till then, patience!

[203] 1. Original in French.

I do not know who will report the Pushkin celebrations[1] for you in the *Messenger of Europe*, but I would like you to point out to him the following: both in the speech by I. Aksakov and in all the journals it is said that I am personally quite resigned to Dostoyevsky's speech and even fully approve of it. But that's not true and I have still not cried out, 'You have won, o Galilean!' The speech with all its passion is extremely intelligent, brilliant and cunningly skilful, but it is based on a complete fallacy, though one which flatters Russia's pride no end. Pushkin's Aleko[2] is a purely Byronic figure and not at all typical of the contemporary, rootless Russian; Tatyana's[3] personality is very subtly described, but surely it is not only *Russian* wives who remain faithful to their old husbands? But the main point: 'We shall say the last word to Europe, we shall even give it to her as a present because Pushkin's genius has re-created Shakespeare, Goethe and others.' And that's the point: he *re-created* them, not *created* them, and in exactly the same way we shall not create a new Europe, just as he did not create Shakespeare and the others. And who is this universal man so unrestrainedly applauded by the public? That's not at all what we want; it is better to be an original Russian than this depersonalized universal man. Once again that same old arrogance under the guise of humility. Perhaps that assimilation which the Europeans bring to works of universal genius is even more difficult for them, perhaps they are more original than us. But it's understandable why the public enjoyed such compliments, because the speech is truly remarkable for its beauty and measure. I think that you ought to print something along these lines. Messrs the Slavophiles have not yet swallowed us up.

With which, farewell. I haven't yet sorted everything out here, but I hope to. Perhaps we shall soon see each other. But at the moment, like Socrates, I only know that I know nothing.

I cordially press your hand.

Yours,
Iv. Turgenev

205. To A. N. LUKANINA

Adelaida Nikolayevna Lukanina (1843–1908), née Rykacheva, doctor and wri-

[204] 1. The Society of Lovers of Russian Literature had decided to honour Russia's greatest poet by organizing a three-day festival, during which a monument to him would be unveiled in Moscow. Turgenev was a member of the organizing committee. Many leading literary and academic figures were invited to make speeches. In his own, Turgenev claimed that Pushkin's greatest achievement was the creation of a superb, vital language, essentially Russian in character, but he doubted whether Pushkin was a poet of world class. Naturally enough his speech was not liked. The sensation of the celebration was a speech by Dostoyevsky, which received an ovation without precedent; in it he claimed that the Russian soul, as symbolized by Pushkin, was striving towards the goal of universal man. Turgenev saw the reception of Dostoyevsky's speech as a victory for the nationalist, Slavophile, anti-Western camp, which he always disliked and associated with Moscow and reaction.

2. Hero of Pushkin's narrative poem 'The Gypsies' (1824, published 1827).

3. Heroine of Pushkin's *Evgeny Onegin*.

ter. She first met Turgenev in Paris in 1877 and he did what he could to further her literary career. She published some reminiscences of Turgenev in 1887 and translated his story. *A Fire at Sea* into Russian. Fifty-four of his letters to her survive.

[Original in Russian]

Bougival, 12 August 1880

Dear Adelaida Nikolayevna,

In reply to your letter I can report the following. The convention between France and Russia is so craftily written that anyone has the right, without reference to the author, to translate, abridge, or otherwise mangle any work he likes. Consequently there is no point in suing anybody, and you must succumb to Fate. You could, though, write to the editor of *Réforme* (where is this journal published?), suggesting that you translate your stories yourself, and then you can add the words ⟨'with the authorization of the author'⟩.[1] Although such an 'authorization' is not at all obligatory, at least it provides a sort of moral guarantee, for any journal will prefer a translation by the author.

I shall talk to *Temps* about your *Lyubushka*. It will certainly be published there, but probably not before the winter.

I am very pleased that your story [*Uncle Vanya*] appeared in the *Messenger of Europe*.

Please let me know when you are returning to Paris. I shall be here till November.

With my regards,
Yours sincerely,
Iv. Turgenev

206. To K. A. L. PIETSCH

[Original in German]

Bougival, 11 November 1880

My dear friend,

Many thanks for your letter. Of all my remaining friends only you and a young Russian lady – a great nihilist – sent me birthday greetings. And so again, I thank you.

All the Viardot family has been in Paris since Monday and I remain here all alone. I want to see if solitude can force me to work. Probably not.

I am content with the state of my health. I have even been riding, something I haven't done for twenty years. Didie and her husband (a wonderfully handsome couple) of course rode ahead all the time, and I followed on my sturdy steed. Didie assures me that I looked just like a retired Würtenberg general. Everything is going well with the whole family. Didie's children are delightful. Mme Viardot has composed something – and very good it is too. Paul has played in

---

[205] 1. Original in French. Lukanina had complained to Turgenev that a French version of her story *The Hen-House Keeper* had appeared without her prior knowledge.

Spain – very successfully. Marianne is more charming than ever, but is still not married.

I am very sorry for poor Richter – and his wife.[1] Please remember me to all my old friends, beginning with Kathi. I feel the greatest sympathy for that wonderful creature, although she has perhaps the right to doubt it.[2]

As for the rest, life is as it is. Sweet for the young and for those who can remain young, and sour for the old and those who were born old. As for me, I am quite indifferent for, as you probably know, I shall inevitably die at the beginning of October 1881. There is absolutely *no doubt about it*.

Every greeting to your family, and a cordial handshake for you. Get rid of your rheumatism! What? *Pietschius grandiflorus*, the Apollo of the Spree – with rheumatism!? Look after yourself.

Your friend,
Iv. Turgenev

207. To G. de MAUPASSANT

Guy de Maupassant (1850–93), the French short-story writer and novelist, a 'pupil' of Flaubert and member of the naturalist school. His subject matter is taken mainly from Norman peasant life, the behaviour of the bourgeoisie and fashionable Paris. Turgenev was particularly impressed by the novel *Une Vie* (1883). The two writers probably first met through Flaubert in 1876 at one of the 'dinners of the five', and they became close friends, especially after Flaubert's death in 1880. Turgenev did his best to make Maupassant better known in Russia and arranged for his writings to appear in both the *Messenger of Europe* and *Order*. Six of Turgenev's letters to Maupassant have survived.

[Original in French]

Bougival, 15 November 1880

My dear friend,

I need to talk to you about a rather delicate matter, but I am sure you will understand. You see, after long reflection, I would prefer it if you did not write that article on me. You would do it admirably, with tact and due balance, but I am afraid that people would look upon it – if you would excuse the phrase – as a sort of gesture towards a friend. Seriously, though, I have never had that many readers in France to warrant a special article. But if you still plan to write a series of articles for *Gaulois* on great foreign writers, the idea of which I thoroughly approve and for which I am entirely at your disposal if you need any information, etc., I would ask you to deal with me at the proper level and in my proper turn.

[206] 1. Gustave Richter (1823–84), German painter, was seriously ill.
 2. Kathi Eckert's husband had died earlier that year. Turgenev regretted he had not written to her to express his condolences.

For Russia, for example, start with Pushkin or Gogol, for England with Dickens, for Germany with Goethe – whom Barbey d'Aurevilly[1] has just so stupidly defamed – and then, if you must, go on to *dei minorum gentium*.[2] I am sure that you will take what I say in good part and understand my motives.

Until we meet again, and be assured of the sincere friendship of

Yours very sincerely,

Iv. Turgenev

208. To G. I. USPENSKY

Gleb Ivanovich Uspensky (1843–1902), writer, best remembered for his stories of peasant life which are marked by humour and sympathy and yet are unidealistic. To a marked degree he lived out the contradictions of Russian populism in his own life. He is a striking example of the romance of the Russian intelligentsia with the ordinary Russian peasant. Towards the end of his life he became prey to serious mental delusions, seeing himself on the one hand as Gleb, the personification of everything good, and, on the other, as Ivanovich, the embodiment of everything evil. Only two of Turgenev's letters to him are known.

[Original in Russian]

Paris, 22 January 1881

Dear Gleb Ivanovich,

I hasten to reply to your detailed and friendly letter. I am saddened by the news you sent me of [the journal] *Russian Wealth*. I was genuinely sympathetic towards that new and admirable undertaking and see in its fall a sad 'sign of the times'.

As for my Pushkin speech, I find the reproaches, which you also apply to yourself, unjustified – everything that should have been said about it was said.

I read your latest essays in the *Annals of the Fatherland* with the greatest of pleasure. They are excellent, and 'The Little Boy who did not want to go to School' is a minor *chef d'oeuvre*. It's not just your knowledge of village life, which you always possessed, but your penetration to its very core, your artistic grasp of its characteristic traits and types. In these essays you have almost completely removed all the faults which, if you remember, I pointed out to you during our last meeting in Moscow – all those analytical and (with your talents) superfluous discussions and considerations. When a building is completed, all the scaffolding – without which, as you know, it could not have been built – disappears.

I have been rather seriously ill recently and have not yet fully recovered; my journey to Petersburg has been postponed. I hope to be there, though, within a month.

I received a letter from your wife about six weeks ago, which I have not managed to reply to . . .

[207] 1. Probably a reference to J. Barbey d'Aurevilly's *Goethe et Diderot* (1880).
2. Gods of lower birth.

209.To I. I. MASLOV

[Original in Russian]

Paris, 24 January 1881

My dear friend Ivan Ilyich,

I have recently received from a certain lady in Moscow, one Lidiya Khrebtova,[1] a romance which she has dedicated to me, but as she has not put her address in her letter I am forced to ask you, as an old inhabitant of Moscow, whether you can discover where she lives and pass on to her the enclosed letter.

I have been rather seriously ill and have been in bed for three weeks, I am still not fully recovered. This has meant that my journey to Russia has had to be postponed. But I hope to be there at the end of February – and in Moscow in April.

I embrace you, and remain,

Yours sincerely,

Iv. Turgenev

I have an urgent request. I have in my possession here in Paris an excellent picture by the French landscape-painter T. Rousseau. I never intended to sell it, but circumstances force me so to do.[2] I could get some 25,000 francs for it (it is known to all the artists here, and to Bogolyubov).[3] I seem to remember that both S. M. Tretyakov and Dmitry Botkin[4] have seen it. Tell them of my plans and say that I would let it go for 9500 roubles. If neither of them wishes to buy it, would you please let me know immediately so that I can arrange things here. I hope that you can overcome your laziness on this occasion, and if you cannot write, then please send me a telegram. It is very important.

210.To M. G. SAVINA

[Original in Russian]

Paris, 13/15 March 1881

Dear Marya Gavrilovna,

I received your letter today. At first it cheered me up with the very fact of its appearance, its length, and its tender words, for which I ask your permission to kiss all the little fingers of your right hand; but then it saddened me with some of its contents and the bad news about your health. If you go on not sparing yourself, you are bound to tire yourself out. And quite seriously, I propose that

---

[209] 1. Lidiya Nikolayevna Khrebtova, amateur composer. Turgenev appears to have forgotten that he had given her permission to dedicate to him her 'The Fisherman's Dream' in September 1880.

2. Because of the bankruptcy of his son-in-law Turgenev was forced to sell his collection of paintings in order to support him. Of all his collection he was particularly fond of a landscape by Théodore Rousseau.

3. Alexey Petrovich Bogolyubov (1824–96), academician and painter, mainly of seascapes. He lived for many years in Paris.

4. Dmitry Petrovich Botkin (1820–89), brother of Vasily, who was in charge of the family tea firm. He was a notable art collector.

you grant me the honour and pleasure of resting for a few days – or weeks – at my home this summer.

You will possibly have heard already that Mme Viardot's youngest daughter, my dear Marianne, is getting married (the wedding will be between 3 and 10 April). Two days later I shall leave for Petersburg, where I hope to arrive about the fifteenth, and on St Nicholas Day, 21 May, I shall be back in Spasskoye where I shall stay for the summer. Assuming that your holidays will start in May, I think that nothing better could be suggested – for your health – than a carefree and peaceful visit to the country. At Spasskoye the climate is good, the garden beautiful, the house newly decorated throughout, and the cook excellent; and I shall be able to take you in hand (a very pleasant thought). And as Polonsky and his family will also be staying with me the proprieties will be observed. Also perhaps my dreams of last year will be fulfilled. Think it over and write to me so that I can be happy in advance.

I have read about your triumphs and the ovations you received in the papers and am sincerely glad. When all is said and done, a link has been forged between you and me which nothing can break. By the way, is the author of the play for your benefit performance the same Tchaikovsky[1] whom you once told me about? Do you remember?

One more question: I see that your divorce is proceeding. You are surely only going ahead with it in order to marry Mr Vsevolozhsky? Would you be so kind as to reply to this as well? Or perhaps you just want to be free?

And you have still not sent me your photograph. And how I would bow down at your feet – and kiss them.

I can imagine how Dostoyevsky's funeral must have affected you, and then Levkeyeva's![2] With a nervous system like yours, you must be very careful, and why was there no good friend at hand to stop you driving yourself to exhaustion?

As for myself, I haven't had a very good winter. The gout which had left me in peace for the last three years has been tormenting me no end, and I am still walking as if on pitchforks. I am getting old, but what's to be done about it? Only certain memories have the power to rekindle the old fire in me . . .

Tuesday

I had interrupted the letter there, and then this terrible news from Petersburg arrived – and I was incapable of doing anything.[3] I won't go into the details of it but will say only that with the theatres probably closing for about three months my invitation is very opportune. Please come and stay with me at Spasskoye at the beginning of May for at least a fortnight and then you can set off from here

[210] 1. Modest Ilyich Tchaikovsky (1850–1916), younger brother of the composer. Savina acted in his *The Benefactor* for her benefit performance.

2. Dostoyevsky was buried on 31 January 1881 and Savina's actress friend, Yelizaveta Matveyevna Levkeyeva, on 19 February.

3. Tsar Alexander II was assassinated by revolutionaries on 1 March 1881.

for the Crimea, or Italy, or a spa, or Paris – wherever you want to go. How good that would be, and how your health would improve on our black-earth land! And how splendidly we could pass the time! Tell me of your decision without waiting for my arrival in Petersburg.

In any case I shall see you within the month.

You say at the end of your letter, 'I kiss you affectionately.' How, exactly? As you did on that June night in the railway compartment? If I live for a hundred years, I shall never forget those kisses. I dare think that this is what you mean by 'affectionately'.

Dear Marya Gavrilovna, I love you very much, much more than I should, but it is not my fault. I hope your health has improved, and I ask you not to forget.

Your

Iv. Turgenev

P.S. Please write to me, if only with the words 'I am better.'

211. To N. A. SHCHEPKIN

[Original in Russian]

Paris, 11 April 1881

Dear Nikolay Alexandrovich,

I am leaving here within a week, and as soon as I get to Petersburg I shall let you know. In the meantime would you please send to Yelizaveta Petrovna Kryuger in Moscow 100 roubles in my name. From this year she is one of my pensioners and receives 200 roubles a year.

I shall arrive in Spasskoye by St Nicholas Day, 9 May, together with Polonsky and his family. I trust that all the rooms will be properly furnished by then. I think we shall have to get a proper sprung coach – like a four-seater barouche – and a pair of new horses. And don't forget to buy a nice bath which we can put in one of the small rooms next to the billiard room. As for the rest, the wines, the cook, etc., we can discuss all that when I get to Petersburg. I shall be staying there for three weeks, no longer.

With all my best wishes.

Yours sincerely,

Iv. Turgenev

212. To M. M. ANTOKOLSKY

Mark Matveyevich Antokolsky (1843–1902), sculptor. Turgenev first met him in 1871 in Moscow when he went to his studio to watch him complete his statue of Ivan the Terrible. Perhaps his most successful work is a portrayal of Christ which he completed in Paris. Turgenev tells of the great difficulty he had in persuading the Russian ambassador, Prince Orlov, that Antokolsky, a Jew, could deal with such a subject honestly. He and Turgenev were the leading founder-members of the Society for Assistance to Writers and Scholars in Need in Paris. Twenty-one of Turgenev's letters to him have survived, concerned in the main with Turgenev's postponing sittings for the bust which Antokolsky finally completed in 1880.

[Original in Russian]

Spasskoye, 1 July 1881

Dear Antokolsky,

You have the right to be very angry with me for waiting so long before I replied to your warm and interesting letter. I am sorry and beg you not to take my silence for a lack of friendship towards you or as an indication that I am out of sympathy with what should be the correct treatment of Jews in Russia.

To publish your letter, even with some stylistic corrections, would be quite unthinkable, and would cause you much unpleasantness, if not actual harm. What's more, no journal (not even *Forward*) would print it. The question has lost its immediacy at the present time. But I shall keep the letter as a document that is witness to both the strength of your patriotism and the depth and sincerity of your feelings. I do not lose hope that the time will come when it can be published, but that time is still a long way off, and when it does come there will be freedom and justice not just for the Jews.

Well, I've been here a month now and plan to return to Paris next month, where I shall of course see you and any new work you have been doing. My health is all right. I trust that you are also happy with yours. Please remember me to your wife and accept a cordial handshake.

Yours sincerely,
Iv. Turgenev

213.To G. de MAUPASSANT

[Original in French]

Bougival, 26 September 1881

My dear friend,

I have been back here a fortnight. I went to see you but they told me you were in Africa and that I should write to you in Algiers poste restante, which I am doing. Are you coming back to Paris soon? And what are you doing? Drop me a line and tell me.

Your name is causing quite a stir in Russia and they are translating everything translatable; I've brought back with me a huge article on you (from the *Voice*) which is very well written and sympathetic.[1]

[213] 1. 'A Writer of the Flaubert School. Guy de Maupassant, *La Maison Tellier*', by G. A. Larosh, actually appeared not in the *Voice* but in the *New Newspaper*.

I shall stay here until the end of November. I haven't yet seen any of the others.

Yours,

Iv. Turgenev

214. To Y. P. POLONSKY

[Original in Russian]

Bougival, 1 November 1881

Dear Yakov Petrovich,

I had already picked up my pen to write to you, when your letter arrived. I shall tell you briefly what has happened here during the past two weeks. I have been to England – I just slipped across the sea after a terrible storm – and had some excellent shooting, i.e. I saw a mass of game and shot abysmally! I must clearly give that up too! On the way back our mutual friend Ralston improvised a dinner for me, partly out of sympathy for me and partly (*mainly*, as he himself admitted to me) to present to the English public the main representative of and authority on Russian affairs, Russian literature, etc., etc. In this he succeeded – there were various bigwigs from literature and journalism present; everything was very lively. I made a short speech – naturally stammering and stuttering – and all those gentlemen, of whom hardly one had ever read anything of mine, drank my health. I was very glad when it was all over. Ralston even wants to arrange a banquet (!!?) – but I would rather cut off my nose than agree to such a nonsense. What's the point of a banquet *in my honour* – in England! People in Petersburg would think I had gone in for all sorts of intrigues to warrant such a dinner, had paid for it myself, etc. The devil take them! The game is not worth the candle.

At the moment I am stuck in Bougival. Everyone else has recently left for Paris, and I shall be here for another ten days or so and shall try to do some work. I am very sorry for Zolotaryov[1] and for you. How could he have toyed with the climate in Asia at his age? As for the trick played upon you by Mr Avenarius[2] – a remarkable trick indeed! – you must try and erase it from your memory like a drop of spittle which falls on your clothes.

I was particularly hospitable to Kladishchev,[3] as he had come from you.

I enclose a few lines to Zhozefina Antonovna.[4] Look after your health. I embrace you and remain,

Yours sincerely,

Iv. Turgenev

[214] 1. Ivan Fyodorovich Zolotaryov (1813–81), a friend of Polonsky's, who had just died on a visit to Batumi.

2. Vasily Petrovich Avenarius (1839–1923), writer of children's stories.

3. Lieutenant-General Dmitry Petrovich Kladishchev (1838–1903), senator, later governor of Ryazan Province, an acquaintance of Polonsky's.

4. Zhozefina Antonovna Polonskaya (1844–1920), Polonsky's second wife. See headnote to letter no. 217.

215. To M. G. SAVINA

[Original in Russian]

Paris, 15 December 1881

Dear Marya Gavrilovna,

I have been waiting for your reply to my last letter, but the press reports about your health have begun to alarm me, and now I learn from Toporov that you have been obliged to go away and that you have left your address with him for me to write to you. It made me very sad, although I hope that your illness is not at all dangerous and that you will soon return to the stage. But all the same this is bad news. . . . I shall be in Petersburg at the beginning of *April* and shall of course find you already there. Now, please don't be lazy and write to me from Kiev and tell me how you are and what you are doing. This must have been why you gave Toporov your address. I think there is no need to repeat what you already know, namely that I love you – and how I love you.

As for myself I can tell you that I am as fit as a fiddle and have even begun to do a little work. . . . (By the way, did you expect my *Song* [*of Triumphant Love*] to be so successful? I, at least, did not expect it.) I am awaiting the confinement of my dear Marianne – so far all is going well; she is now in her eighth month. I am cross with my fellow-countrymen who are making such fools of themselves over the unbearable Sarah Bernhardt, who has nothing except a wonderful voice – everything else about her is false, cold and affected – together with the most repulsive Parisian chic. This charlatan, this publicity-seeker has even gone so far as to send a telegram (she herself, mind you!) to all the papers about how the firemen rescued all *her* things from 'that unfortunate theatre in Vienna.[1] Well, really! A thousand people might die – let them! So long as Sarah's things are saved, there is no need to grieve over anything. When I come across this sort of thing the blood of my ancient serf-owning ancestors stirs within me. Honestly, I could flog this poseuse with my own hands. It's only a pity that, because she's so thin, there's nothing to flog! Please forgive me for this somewhat improper stupidity! I am waiting to see how the Petersburg critics deal with this lady.

And so, *be sure* to write to me, and *soon*, otherwise I shall be cross with you and shall not wish to kiss your hands even from afar . . . No, that's nonsense; I shall always want to kiss them, and not only them . . . but . . .

'It's nothing, it's nothing. Keep quiet,' as Gogol says.

But please write.

Your
Iv. Turgenev

[215] 1. There was a disastrous fire in the Vienna Ring-Theatre on 8 December 1881.

216. To P. V. ANNENKOV

[Original in Russian]

Paris, 25 February 1882

I kept putting off writing to you, dear Pavel Vasilyevich, in the hope that I might be in a position to tell you of the successful conclusion to Marianne's confinement. We expected it on the fifth, then the tenth, then the fifteenth – and still nothing, although it could happen at any minute. So I have decided to drop you a line, although there is little good news to report. The long-expected catastrophe between my daughter and her husband has occurred – he has even managed to blue the money which I had intended to guarantee the future of my grandchildren; he has started to drink heavily, threatens to kill now himself, now my daughter – and I daily expect her to arrive here with her children. I shall have to hide her away and start proceedings ⟨for a legal separation⟩.[1] I have already discussed the matter with a lawyer and ⟨a solicitor⟩,[1] and because I must once again reorganize my finances I have had to sell my beloved Rousseau, my horses, carriages, etc. In a word, a minor disaster. Not very cheerful, as you can see.

I read my *Desperado* (not 'A Violent Man') to our circle with some success – the Grand Duke[2] permitted himself to laugh – and by the way, he and I are on friendly terms; he even introduced me to his quasi-wife Kuznetsova with whom he lives here ⟨as man and wife⟩,[1] and her three children. She is like a simple, unattractive, unassuming and modest little housemaid. The critics in Russia have reacted unfavourably to *The Desperado* and the 'illegals' here are insulted. To some extent, it's Bazarov all over again. French ⟨men of letters⟩[1] have liked it. I was even embarrassed by Taine's compliments.

You probably know all about Lavrov[3] and Skobelev.[4] The latter has turned out as brainless as Charles XII, whom he physically resembles. And it looks as if he has the support of the highest circles in Russia, which will only intensify the chaos reigning there. Amen, amen, I say; there has never been anything to rival what is now happening in our dear Fatherland. And what sights we've seen already! If only Skobelev had deserved the gratitude of the French . . . if only! Everyone's cursing him – in the most sincere and friendly manner.

I shall be leaving here in six weeks, and shall of course go via Baden-Baden where I shall still find you in residence. I want to get back to the country as soon as possible. Perhaps I'll get down to some work – or is that a dream too?

We organized an exhibition of works by Russian artists here, but there have been few visitors . . . and it's quite understandable. With the exception of

[216] 1. Original in French.

2. Konstantin Nikolayevich (1827–92), second son of Nicholas I.

3. P. L. Lavrov had had his permission to reside in Paris revoked by the French on the request of the Russian government; he had signed an appeal to the authorities on behalf of the revolutionaries.

4. General Mikhail Dmitriyevich Skobelev (1843–82), while visiting Paris, had made a very belligerent speech attacking Germany.

217. *To Z. A. Polonskaya*

Pokhitonov's tiny landscapes – *mediocritas!*[5]

My health is satisfactory. How is yours? How are your wife and children getting on? Greetings to everyone. I embrace you.

Iv. Turgenev

217. To Z. A. POLONSKAYA

Zhozefina Antonovna Polonskaya, née Ryulman (1844–1920), sculptress, second wife of Y. P. Polonsky. She and Turgenev first met in the late sixties and he became very fond of her. He constantly encouraged her in her art; she modelled the bust which was placed on his grave in 1883. Fifty-four of Turgenev's letters to her have survived.

[Original in Russian]

Paris, 10 March 1882

Dear Zhozefina Antonovna,

I sent you a short note two days ago in which I outlined my present condition. Things have changed little since. The only good thing is the excellent state of health of Marianne and her little baby – this is a great happiness for us. My friend Viardot is still very poorly; one cannot even say that he is out of danger; in any case his recovery will be a slow and prolonged affair. Poor Mme Viardot has hardly left his bedside. As for my daughter, her travails are only just beginning. We had a lot of trouble with lawyers, solicitors, etc., and the case looks as if it will take more than a year to sort out; she has had to hide herself and her children away and might have to flee France for ever. She has lost everything irretrievably. The wheels have started turning and have dragged me along. It is even more difficult for me for, as you know, I have never felt particularly attached to her, and everything I have done for her in the past and shall do for her in the future is only on account of a sense of duty. This unhappy business will in all probability detain me here longer than I had supposed, and there is no hope of my arriving in Petersburg in time for your birthday on 31 March.

As you see, life has become rather grey. Luckily my health is standing up – no gout, even – and only slight palpitations occasionally remind me that I am as mortal as everyone else.

I received a letter today from your husband with the first two acts of his play written out by you. I shall start to read it at once with the greatest attention. Please send the remaining acts without delay and I shall tell you my frank opinion of it.

I am delighted that you liked my photograph and thank you for thanking me. Your husband probably didn't like it much – he hopes to take up his portrait of me again during his coming visit to Spasskoye – this time successfully.

5. Ivan Pavlovich Pokhitonov (1850–1923), painter, who lived for many years in Paris. He painted a portrait of Turgenev in 1882 which was later bought by S. M. Tretyakov.

Naturally I cannot do any work at the moment; I shall leave everything till I get to Spasskoye.

I embrace your husband and the children and with your permission send you a kiss.

Yours,

Iv. Turgenev

218. To PAULINETTE BRUERE, née TURGENEVA

[Original in French]

Paris, 16 March 1882

My dear Paulinette,

The good Mlle Arnholt has just arrived and has put me in the picture. I am very happy to learn that you are safely installed. But let me give you the following advice:

1. Live as quietly as you can, do not show yourself in public too much, speak to few people, do not seek company. Be aware that your husband will make the most detailed investigations to find you, and if he should ever discover your hideout, either from a commercial traveller or through some other source, nothing will save you from his clutches, as you put it. It would be silly to think of writing to him or to M. Pol; I have made out that I do not know where you are. He has already sent me a court summons, and if he should think I am involved he would immediately start proceedings against me.

2. Live as economically as you can. It is quite impossible for me to give you more than *400* francs a month. You will have to manage on that, for you can count on *not a penny more*. Keep an accurate account of everything.

3. Do not forget that you no longer have anything and can demand *absolutely nothing* because you have placed yourself at a disadvantage, and you must think only of ensuring that everyone forgets all about you. You made a mistake in selling the debt you owed to Chamerot to M. Pol – he has already informed me through legal channels that he has taken it over – and Chamerot has told me that he cannot do other than pay him your 1500 francs per annum. The same applies equally to [your daughter] Jeanne's securities. It is your husband who is the administrator of all your income and he can do with it as he pleases. I am in control of all Georges' affairs, but I cannot get any income from them as the company will only pay your husband or the person to whom he transfers his rights. Consequently the income will accumulate but *will not be paid to me* until either your son attains his majority or your husband dies, which is a very long way off because he has never felt better and, now that the die is cast, no longer talks of suicide.

4. He has a perfect right to sell everything of yours, your jewellery, etc., down to the very last trinket. In the eyes of the law you are dead and you cannot, I repeat, claim anything. You must get used to the idea that you now have

277

absolutely nothing and all your rights and possessions have been lost for ever. You can see how carefully you must watch every penny.

Try to keep yourself occupied; look after your children's clothes and your own dresses; educate the children yourself. Do not let anyone in the hotel doubt that your husband is still alive, invent some story or other but only mention it when you really have to. Let people think that your husband has been exiled or has emigrated to America; preferably make something of a mystery of your life. Never reply to any interrogation and try to ensure that they never arise. In heaven's name, do not gossip, do not tell anyone anything. A simple suspicion or a careless word will spread like a drop of oil. It is very easy to send off a telegram, and your husband will land on you like a bomb. You have always been afraid of mere trifles but now you must fear real things, and never forget that you have a sort of sword hanging over your head. Judging from what Mlle Arnholt says, I fear that Soleure is not isolated enough. There were certain words in your letter which made me tremble. 'We have settled in splendidly. *The people are congenial*, we shall go for walks *continuously*, and everything will go *swimmingly*.' Good God! You must not see other people, you must not be seen out of doors all the time, etc. One could truly doubt that you appreciate the position you are in!

'*Keep yourself hidden away, and remain silent*' – that must be your rule.

I shall try to send you some music through Annenkov. Could you tell me two or three pieces you would like?

And so I kiss you and the children and may God grant that all goes well.

Mlle Arnholt has told me that she has left you about 750 francs. That should last you for six weeks starting from 15 March.

I shall try to send you something for a dress and some clothes for the children.

I.T.

219. To G. I. BOGROV

Grigory Isaakovich Bogrov (1825–85), Jewish writer under the pseudonym of Ben-Rabbi. He and Turgenev never met.

[Original in Russian]

Paris, 26 March 1882

Dear Grigory Isaakovich,

I am extremely sorry that I have taken so long to reply to your kind letter and have not thanked you for sending your works. In truth I have had so many unpleasant concerns and worries lately that my head is in a spin. So please forgive me. Of your books I knew only *Memoirs of a Jew*. I remember reading it a couple of years ago in the country with the greatest interest. I am going to start the *Jewish Manuscript* soon. I do not know whether you know, but not only have I never in my whole life had any prejudices against your race, but on the contrary I have always tried to have the greatest sympathy for the Jews, and I have had, and still have, many close friends who are Jews. I would be very happy publicly to express my views on those questions which quite justifiably concern you deeply. But how can I do it without assuming an authority *I do not have as a publicist* and which would of course arouse the wrong sort of response? I have long had the following idea. I was sent from Odessa a very sensible and intelligent little book by Mrs Kalmykova[1] entitled *The Jewish Question in Europe*, and I wished to write a review of it for *Order*; I even started it but then *Order* closed down.[2] So I wondered whether I could place it in one of the Odessa journals. A few days ago I received a positive reply to my inquiries and it will probably appear in a week or two. It could then be reprinted. I shall arrange for you to be sent a copy.[3]

It is superfluous to repeat what I say above about my attitude to the Jews, and I beg you to accept not only my gratitude but also the expression of my deep respect.

Your obedient servant,

Iv. Turgenev

220. To Y. P. POLONSKY

[Original in Russian]

Paris, 3 May 1882

Dear Yakov Petrovich,

As my strange illness is worrying you, then please allow me to give you a short résumé (according to Charcot[1] and others). There are two types of *angina pectoralis*: 1) *essentialis*, which, in good health, arises in the form of attacks of extreme pain in the chest and shoulder, with great difficulty in breathing, etc., and if it does not prove fatal, passes very quickly, leaving no trace and usually recurring after several months, or even years. I do not know if it arises from some condition of the nerves, but it always ends – sooner or later – in death. Fortunately this is *not* the type of angina I am suffering from. But there is another type – *angina pectoralis podagral* (also called *cardialgia nervalis*) – which is a chronic condition. At first there is pain beneath the clavicle and in the shoulder and then there is difficulty walking quickly or climbing stairs and finally in standing up or even simply standing. This is what I have. It lasts for an indeterminate time. I have to lie down simply because it is impossible to stand on my feet. At the moment my shoulder aches, I have a pain in my chest and breathing is difficult, etc., etc. When I'm lying down I have only a slight pain in my shoulder, like

---

[219] 1. Alexandra Mikhaylovna Kalmykova (1849–1926), teacher, and journalist on the Odessa-based *Southern Lands*.

2. A daily political and literary newspaper published by M. M. Stasyulevich from 1881 to 1882.

3. Turgenev never completed the review because of his assessment of the strong anti-Semitic mood in Russia.

[220] 1. Jean Charcot (1825–93), French doctor and neurologist.

toothache. The only cure is to wait. As it does not occur simultaneously with gout, my doctors have told me that it would be a good thing if I had an attack of gout (I haven't had one for a year now) so as to divert the angina! And then, guess what? I actually had an attack – in *three* places at once – in both feet and in my knee! The pain was awful but I thought – so much the better! The attack passed, but the pain in my shoulder remained. Then they burnt the skin on my shoulder in fifty places – I looked like a waffle! – but the pain was still there, and could I stand up? Not on your life!! They want to repeat the treatment but recommend I stay in bed in the meantime and take *bromure de potassium*. Starting from today I shan't be able to get up for at least two months; and as for travelling anywhere, to benefit from the air in Spasskoye and the water, it is quite out of the question. And so, dear friend, let's change the subject. There is neither use nor pleasure in it.

But it is a pity that you and your family do not want to go to Spasskoye.

I am expecting Annenkov here the day after tomorrow. Please send a kiss from me to your children and your wife and tell her that to grieve over much is never any good. I shall write often, but please do not expect a turn for the better. This business is a very, very prolonged affair. I embrace you.

Yours sincerely,
Iv. Turgenev

221. To Z. A. POLONSKAYA

[Original in Russian]

Bougival, 8 June 1882

I was brought here, carried here, the day before yesterday, dear Zhozefina Antonovna, in the hope that the country air would help; but far from there being any noticeable improvement, I am much worse than I was in Paris. The pain in my *left* shoulder prevents my walking or even standing up. This is combined with intercostal neuralgia on the *right* side which prevents me lying down, especially at night. All I can do is to sit – until even that becomes difficult. No one knows what will happen but I imagine that the time has come to give up any idea of going anywhere or even of moving from where I am. However, I shall give myself another *five* days and shall write to you with *definite* news, although I can foresee what I shall say.

I must get used to the idea that *I am finished* even though I might creak along for some time. And all around everything is green, in flower, and the birds are singing, etc. But that's all very well if one is in good health, and I cannot help thinking of Nature's '*indifference*'.

But *you* must be healthy and active; you have more than half your life still ahead of you, you have an excellent husband, charming children. They are your worries – and your joy.

I shall write again in five days' time and in the meantime embrace you all and remain,

Yours very sincerely,
Iv. Turgenev

P.S. Yakov Petrovich once told me I could overcome illness by *will-power alone*. Tell him that I shall take his advice if – by *will-power alone*, without frowning, without waving his arms, or shaking his head – he can remove a fly from his nose, especially if his nose is covered with perspiration and providing the fly with plenty to drink.

222. To M. G. SAVINA

[Original in Russian]

Bougival, 8 August 1882

Dear Marya Gavrilovna,

I have this minute received your letter of 10 July (it took seventeen days!) and am replying immediately. You complain that I haven't written to you for a long time, but I always answer regularly . . . it's the awful distance between us! First of all may I congratulate you not so much on your marriage but rather on having removed yourself from the false position which so troubled you. It was with precisely this in mind that I said that I trusted your wisdom. I sincerely wish (and hope that my wish will be fulfilled) that you never have cause to regret your decision. This could happen if Nikita Nikitich[1] does not keep his word about allowing you to remain on the stage (which he, as your husband, now has the right to do). But he is *trop gentleman* to do that. I thank you too for your detailed replies to my other questions. You are as sweet and charming as ever – and your friend is attached to you *more than ever*.

The condition of this friend remains unsatisfactory. A week ago I was placed on a milk cure (I am permitted to take nothing but milk), and although I seem to be a little better and the pain is not so unbearable, the illness still sticks in me like a nail. There is no point in thinking about going to Russia, even in the autumn. If only I could manage it during the winter! How happy I should be to see you in Petersburg! You too would be glad to see what a self-sufficient man I am!

The Polonskys are living peacefully at Spasskoye and are enjoying the splendid weather there, while we continue to suffer from the cold. I almost had the fire lit today. All the young ones here have left and only we old ones remain. But what can we do about it! Everyone has his turn.

I can't settle down to any work, either. This damned neuralgia has cut right into me. Zhozefina Antonovna [Polonskaya], to whom I wrote that I was finished, wouldn't believe a word I said. But alas! I am beginning to think I am further gone than I had supposed.

[222] 1. Nikita Nikitich Vsevolozhsky (1846–96), Savina's second husband, whom she married in July 1882. The marriage was unhappy and Savina left him eight years later.

But enough of this morbid subject. I am very glad that you say nothing about your health . . . You must have blossomed and be blooming like a rose. Conserve your strength for the coming season, for your new roles – and perhaps I shall be lucky enough to see you in one of them.

Thank you for promising to send me a plaster-cast of your hand, and for the time being I kiss not the plaster but the real hand, and also everythifg else which, in your new condition, you will offer to my caresses. Once again I wish you happiness, joy and all the best.

Your friend,
Iv. Turgenev

P.S. For the moment I am still writing to you as Savina. How do you want me to write in the future?

223. To E. DURAND

[Original in French]

Bougival, 12 August 1882

My dear Monsier Durand,

I am sending you by today's post a small volume called *Stories by V. Garshin*.[1]

M. Eugène Yung[2] has requested me to ask you to translate one of these stories (*Night*, p. 100) for the *Revue politique et littéraire*. Of all the young Russian writers today Garshin is the one whose talents show the most promise. If you think it necessary to show me your translation before submitting it to M. Yung, I am at your complete disposal.

I hope that your health is as good as possible. I cannot say the same about my own. I still cannot walk, and I can't even stand up for more than two or three minutes at a time. I shan't return to Paris before 20 November.

Please send my best wishes to Mme Durand. I have just obtained her *Instruction morale et civique*. That excellent book is as instructive as it is a pleasure to read.[3]

I cordially press your hand.

Yours truly,
Iv. Turgenev

[223] 1. Vsevolod Mikhaylovich Garshin (1855–88); his *The Red Flower* (1883) was dedicated to Turgenev.

2. Eugène Yung was one of the editors of the *Revue politique et littéraire* in the 1870s and 1880s.

3. Durand's wife Alice published her *Instruction morale et civique des jeunes filles* in 1882 under the pseudonym of A. Gréville.

224. To PAULINETTE BRUERE née TURGENEVA

[Original in French]

Bougival, 11 September 1882

Dear Pauline,

I have just received your letter and now reply. I must warn you that this time I am seriously displeased with you and this is why.

It is not because you told me all the gossip, which I had after all asked you for. I learnt nothing new; so let us return it all to the mire whence it came, along with the stupid nonsense from your concierge which you, like a real provincial girl, call the local gossip. I shall not lower myself to refute all those lies.

My chief complaint against you is that you allowed yourself to call Mme Viardot your mistress. In the first place that was very imprudent and could have revealed your true position, and secondly, after the gross ingratitude which you showed to Mme Viardot under the influence of the stupid and ignorant Mrs Innes, you should have held your gossiping tongue and *not dared even to pronounce her name.* You were also ungrateful, stupidly ungrateful, to Mlle Arnholt, who has done nothing but help you and has always had your interests at heart. What right have you to declare that you cannot stand her!? (Another sign of the little provincial madam.) Your *friends* (your underlining) have said she is *insincere.* How the devil would she be insincere towards you and what could she possibly gain from it? Are you some sort of princess or millionairess she could exploit?!!! Come to your senses and be a little less silly in your judgments. One can hardly be insincere to a person to whom one is indifferent or who is a stranger – which is what you are, basically, to her – and she has looked after you only because you are my daughter. Mlle Arnholt was quite right in being disgusted with you for allowing yourself to speak of the presents which I have given the Viardot family and which ruined me, etc. You should have cut your tongue out rather than say such things. In the first place haven't I the right to do what I like with my money? And then, shouldn't you have been the last person to say such things – you, for whom I have done ten times more than was my duty? If anyone has ruined me, it is certainly you and your husband; I have given you a half, if not more, of what I had. It does not take long to add up. Two hundred thousand francs for your dowry (plus what I paid and gave you later), the hundred thousand which passed through my hands on various counts (the debt to Chamerot, the 25,000 etc.), the 70,000 for your children and the 100,000 on which you draw the interest – it comes to near enough half a million. And you dare to complain! And it was not from Mlle Arnholt (whom you can't stand), who has never said a word against you, that I hear such things, but from you yourself. Happily I do not attribute any of this to your heart, which is not at all bad, but to your head which is full of petty and shabby thoughts, suspicious grudges, ridiculous prejudices, stupid gossip and the most unbelievable likes and dislikes – and especially your tongue with which you chatter away in all directions like a magpie – always to your own disadvantage.

You complain of your position, but who has made it what it is if not you yourself? Who was it who rejected the help of a worthy man, M. Lambert,[1] only because he was a friend of Mme George Sand and Mme Viardot, in favour of this brute of a man with whom you are afflicted and for whose sake – having decided that he is so horrible that you must leave him – you still made the most absurd sacrifices, giving him the food from your children's mouths? You went to Switzerland of your own free will, and now you complain you are bored! What do you want me to do? On the money which I am giving you (and to which I cannot add a further penny) you and the children should be able to live quite well. My conscience does not reproach me for anything. Try and ensure that yours leaves you equally tranquil. You speak in your usual hare-brained way of going to Italy, or Germany, or England. Whatever next! To teach, I suppose. All right then, but if you teach French, watch your spelling and do not write 'je veux étudié, être digne d'intérêts, être *allité*', etc.

Well, that's enough. I don't want to worry myself any more about it; but I beg, I demand, that when you reply there will be neither *excuses* nor *explanations*. Make some use of the distasteful things I have had to say to you; think, if it is at all possible, and do not gossip either with your tongue or your pen.

The music will be sent off today and the books will follow shortly. I have no time to reply to Jeanne's note, or Georges', and will content myself for the moment with sending them a kiss – and you too.

Iv. Turgenev

225. To THE PEASANTS AT SPASSKOYE

[Original in Russian]

Paris, 16 September 1882

I have received your letter and thank you all for remembering me and for your good wishes. I am personally very sorry that illness prevented my visiting Spasskoye this year. My health is improving and I hope to come to Spasskoye next summer.

I have heard rumours that you are drinking much less wine lately; I am very pleased to hear it and hope that you can keep it up in the future. Drunkenness amongst peasants leads to their ruin. I regret the other rumour I have heard, that your children are not attending school very often. Remember that in our day and age an illiterate man is no better than a blind man or cripple.

As is my custom of many years, I shall give you a desyatina of forest in a place of Nikolay Alexandrovich's choosing, which he will show you.[1]

I am sure that you will cause no damage to my house or garden, nor to the estate in general. I am relying on you.

[224] 1. Possibly Count Iosif Karlovich Lambert, husband of Countess Y. Y. Lambert, who had previously offered help.

[225] 1. N. A. Shchepkin.

And so, peasants at Spasskoye, I send greetings to you all and wish you every happiness.

Your former landlord,
Ivan Turgenev

226. To M. Y. SALTYKOV-SHCHEDRIN

[Original in Russian]

Bougival, 6 October 1882

Dear Mikhail Yevgrafovich,

I have received your letter and the September number of the *Annals of the Fatherland*. I read *A Contemporary Idyll* immediately and found that your innate *vis comica* has never shown itself with greater brilliance. No! You must press on indefatigably. The censors will probably eat you, but you're very tough; they will chew you but won't swallow you. I also read Mikhaylovsky on Dostoyevsky.[1] He pointed to the basic characteristics of his works extremely well. He might have recalled that something similar occurred in French literature, namely the infamous Marquis de Sade. He even wrote a book entitled *Torments and Tortures*, where with particular pleasure he dwells upon the depraved voluptuousness to be derived from the inflicting of pain and suffering. In one of his novels Dostoyevsky also describes in detail the satisfactions of one such person . . .[2] And just to think that all the most important priests in the Russian Orthodox Church sang requiem masses for our de Sade and even read sermons on this universal man's love of all humanity! We really do live in strange times!

It is bad news that you are unwell (who better to know and appreciate it than myself?), but your complaints that some people hate you, people who pale before your very name, are quite needless. He who inspires hatred also inspires love. Had you been simply the hereditary landowner M. Y. Saltykov, none of that would have happened. But you are Saltykov-Shchedrin, the writer, who will leave his distinctive mark on our literature. That is why you are hated – and loved – depending on the person. And that is 'what your life amounts to', as you put it, and you may be satisfied with it. As for solitude and loneliness, who over the age of fifty is essentially not alone, not a 'hangover' from the older generation? There's nothing to be done about it; it slowly prepares us for death so that we shall not regret parting from life.

Your opinion of our mutual friend P. A. Annenkov is unjust. I know what a high opinion he has of you. He has never been superior or ironic towards anyone – and is hardly likely to start with you! Perhaps you haven't noticed that he is an extremely bashful man, even shy, and you failed to discern this beneath the rather free-and-easy manner he assumes. He is of course a contemporary of

[226] 1. Nikolay Konstantinovich Mikhaylovsky (1842–1904), literary critic, sociologist and one of the leading theorists of Russian populism. His article on Dostoyevsky was entitled 'A Cruel Talent'.
2. *Notes from Underground* (1864).

Belinsky and Gogol but clearly feels he is one of Yazykov[3] and Maslov too – and he never tries to deny it.

I shall stay here another six weeks and then go to Paris. But when I shall get to Russia the gods alone know, if they bother themselves with such trivial matters.

I firmly press your hand and remain,

Yours very sincerely,

Iv. Turgenev

P.S. Is it true that V. Garshin has submitted a story to the *Annals of the Fatherland*? He is an undoubted and original talent.

227. To P. I. VEYNBERG

Pyotr Isayevich Veynberg (1831–1908), poet, translator, critic, and literary historian. He had written to Turgenev asking for his advice on French authors, for he planned to publish a journal containing translations of the best writers outside Russia.

[Original in Russian]

Bougival, 3 November 1882

Dear Veynberg,

In reply to your letter I must say that despite my desire to help you with your plans as much as I can, I am not in a position to promise you any translations. I already owe my publishers a number of original works which I have promised them, so where can I find the time for translations? But anyway, if I did I would prefer to do a few pages of Maupassant or Rabelais, and certainly not Balzac. I could never read more than a dozen pages of his without finding him disagreeable and foreign to my tastes. But, I repeat, I cannot do anything at the moment.

I trust that you will not be angry with me and beg you to accept the expression of my respect and sincerity.

Iv. Turgenev

P.S. To my surprise you failed to include your address – like, by the way, all Russians. I had to write to you through Y. P. Polonsky.

228. To D. V. GRIGOROVICH

Dmitry Vasilyevich Grigorovich (1822–99), novelist, one of the first Russian writers to take his subject matter from peasant life, depicting things from the point of view of the peasants themselves. His best remembered works are *The*

---

3. Mikhail Alexandrovich Yazykov (1811–85), a friend of Turgenev's who worked for many years as a customs and excise officer.

Village (1846) and *Anton Goremyka* (1847). He and Turgenev first met in the 1840s when both were close to Belinsky's circle and the *Contemporary*, and they remained friends thereafter. Twenty of Turgenev's letters to Grigorovich have survived.

[Original in Russian]

Bougival, 12 November 1882

Dear friend Dmitry Vasilyevich,

Yet again you have omitted your address, and yet again I am forced to write to you via Polonsky! Couldn't you even include your business address, the school on Little (or is it Great?) Morskaya Street!

My congratulations on the successful conclusion of all your arrangements for the Exhibition, of which you can feel proud.[1] My congratulations also, and to the public, on the renewal of your literary activities. (I see that *Niva* has announced your forthcoming story, as they have mine – but that is not even started and will hardly be finished in the near future.) The Polonskys, who have heard a reading of your story, shower it with praise. And what do you make of the *comedy* of Petersburg life, with its hero Figaro, by Polovtsov?[2]

Poor I. I. Maslov can do nothing but desire a quick end if he still has the same distressing opinion of his condition; if not, then may he continue to flourish! Assuming, of course, that he is not suffering in any way.[3] I too am leading an existence similar to that of a birch tree or an oyster, thanks to the immobility to which I have been condemned. But, if the truth be told, it's not too bad, and I wish for nothing better.

I recently received from a very charming lady in Moscow[4] that *Confession* by L. Tolstoy which has been banned by the censor. It is remarkable for its sincerity, truth and strength of conviction. But it is based on false premises and leads ultimately to the most melancholy denial of any real living, human life . . . It's also in its way a form of nihilism. And it amazes me how Tolstoy, who denies, amongst other things, Art, surrounds himself with artists – what can they gain from talking to him? But Tolstoy is nevertheless the most remarkable man in Russia today!

[Ten lines omitted]

Please remember me to your wife. I firmly press your hand.

Yours sincerely,

Iv. Turgenev

[228] 1. Grigorovich had organized an exhibition of works by young Russian painters.

2. Anatoly Viktorovich Polovtsov (1849–1905), lawyer, archaeologist and journalist. It is not known to which story Turgenev is referring.

3. Turgenev's old friend was beginning to suffer from various senile mental illnesses.

4. Alexandra Grigoryevna Olsufeva, a neighbour of Tolstoy's.

229. To M. M. STASYULEVICH

[Original in Russian]

Paris, 24 November 1882

Here are the two suggestions I referred to in my letter to you yesterday, dear Mikhail Matveyevich.

1) The story by L. Y. Stechkina has been posted to you today. This poor girl is living here in the most straitened circumstances. She is seriously ill with tuberculosis and her doctors have ordered her to live in the south – but she hasn't a penny. In recommending her story to the *Messenger of Europe*, though, I do so not from feelings of sympathy alone. Nor do I beg any favours from you. Be so kind as to read it and if you think my opinion of it justified and you accept it for publication, then please *send an advance to her immediately*. In this way you will rescue a young girl who fully deserves our sympathy – because of both her talent and her character. In any case, please reply quickly – do this for me.[1]

2) This is my second proposal. You will know of the young novelist Guy de Maupassant. He is undoubtedly the most talented of today's French writers and has written a novel which will be published in serial form in *Gil Blas*, starting on 15 February. I know what the novel contains and it is not at all scabrous, unlike several of his other works. He recently read me several long extracts and I was positively in raptures over it. There has been nothing like it since the appearance of *Madame Bovary*. It is nothing like Zola and the others. I know I have earned the reputation of being too kind as a critic, but either I understand nothing about such matters or Maupassant's book is really remarkable *and absolutely first-class*. He would not be opposed to selling it in manuscript, so that a translation could appear by 15 February next year, i.e. the first part, and the second could appear a month later, i.e. in the March number of the *Messenger of Europe* (assuming the first was published in February). The *Messenger of Europe* has not, I think, done this sort of thing before, but, I repeat, the book is quite out of the ordinary and will make a strong impression. Think it over, and send me your reply as quickly as possible.

This is what I wanted to tell you. The title of the book is *Une Vie*. It is a total picture of a good, honest life, an intimate drama painted by a first-rate artist. It will be no longer than *Madame Bovary*.

I wrote to you yesterday that I agree to re-christen 'After Death' *Clara Milić*.

I cordially press your hand, and remain,

Yours sincerely,
Iv. Turgenev

[229] 1. The story is unknown, as the manuscript was presumably lost in the post.

230. To Y. P. POLONSKY

[Original in Russian]

Paris, 4 December 1882

Dear Yakov Petrovich,

I cannot but regret the alarm you felt in not getting a letter from me, and I recognize in it a sign of your true friendship. But it is not my fault. I reply promptly to every letter from you and Zhozefina Antonovna, and I've even written to Toporov several times with the corrected proofs of the latest edition of my works. And so I must repeat once again my well-known dicta, 'Nothing unexpected has happened' – and 'Bad news travels fast.' It is quite true that I have become worse since moving to Paris, but I have grown accustomed to these ⟨highs and lows⟩[1] and pay no attention to them, because I have finally come to terms with the fact that there is no cure for my illness and that all the medicines are quite useless. I am better, then worse, and then better again – and so on *ad infinitum*. It is not worth talking, writing or even thinking about it; there's no point in grieving over bad weather.

You write that Grigorovich says that he cannot understand my *Poems in Prose*. The expression 'cannot understand' is just a polite way of saying 'do not like'. Grigorovich's opinion will probably be shared by the vast majority of the Russian reading public, and that's as it should be. My *Poems* were written for myself alone and for a small group of people who like that sort of thing. The public will be quite correct in casting them aside. I was horrified when I heard that it was intended to read some of them in public. It would be a fiasco similar to the one which occurred when *A King Lear of the Steppes* was adapted for the Moscow stage. But, thank heavens, the plan was abandoned.

If you see Mrs Abaza, thank her for remembering me.[2]

I have found a new illustrator for your 'The Grasshopper-Musician'.

My dear chap, please don't write again, 'Get better!' It produces an effect on me like, for example, when a deaf man is asked to hear again. A deaf man can live perfectly well and for a long time with his disability, and so can I with mine. But it's still best not to remind him.

My greetings to everyone, and I firmly press your hand.

Iv. Turgenev

231. To I. N. KRAMSKOY

Ivan Nikolayevich Kramskoy .(1837–87), painter. He was a student at the Academy of Arts for six years, but left in 1863 with some fellow students in protest at the subject matter for a competition. He was one of the founders of the *Peredvizhniki* (see p. 185). Kramskoy is a competent draughtsman, but most of

[230] 1. Original in French.
2. Vera Aggeyevna Abaza (1828–1903), an acquaintance of Turgenev's.

his paintings (including the most famous *Christ in the Wilderness*) are rather dry and naturalistic. This is the only letter to him from Turgenev that is known.

[Original in Russian]

Paris, 18 December 1882

Dear Ivan Nikolayevich,

I am writing to you in my capacity of Secretary to the Society of Russian Artists in Paris, and therefore ask you to consider this letter as more or less official and to present it to your Society as such so that I may receive an official reply. But I do not wish to miss this opportunity of expressing my deep respect for you as a man and as a painter.

The discussions held by A. P. Bogolyubov with our Society and the Paris art dealer G. Petit have resulted in the following arrangement. He will lend us *free of charge* his splendid gallery (the best in Paris) for six weeks from 1 November to 15 December 1883 for an exhibition of Russian paintings, on the condition that we undertake to cover all the costs of lighting, security, advertising, presentation, etc., which will amount to about 7000 francs. (The entrance fees are of course at our disposal.) M. Petit would also like the most important of the painters who will be exhibiting, i.e. Bogolyubov, Kharlamov, Leman,[1] Pokhitonov, and, if possible, you and other Russian painters in Paris, each to present him with one of their paintings, naturally not their best ones. The painters here have all agreed, for the following reasons.

Petit is clearly making something of a sacrifice, because until now he has usually been paid between 15,000 and 20,000 francs per month for the hire of his gallery – which is what the water-colourists and others were charged. This shows that from the point of view of *sales* he believes in the future of the Russian school and wishes to ensure it himself. Furthermore the Russians here have already donated some of their paintings to our Society for lotteries etc. In giving them to Petit they will also benefit themselves, as he can use his vast resources for all the advertising etc. Our painters in Russia should also take this into consideration. We have every reason to suppose that for an outlay of 7000 francs we will be able to clear a large amount, enough in any case to be able to pay ourselves for transporting the pictures from Russia. (N.B. They must all be sent to arrive here *no later than 15 October 1883*.) We cannot yet take the responsibility of *returning* them, because that will depend on how many visitors we get (we shall charge two francs for entry) and on how much we finally make.

Might I make the following points? There is no doubt that the French public grew interested in Russia painting *from the time that it became independent*, original and noticeably Russian. (The same thing happened in France with our literature too.) So we probably have nothing to worry about on this score. But it also places upon us the responsibility of being severe and quite unprejudiced in our choice. Those paintings which still express any *tendentiousness* or are trying *to*

[231] 1. Yury Yakovlevich Leman (1834–1901).

make some point (usually a sign of someone young or *immature*) will have to be excluded, as will all genre pictures of the life of the ordinary people which are burdened with ulterior motives. This trumpeting and flaunting of originality, in the main accompanied by a lack of technique – which only serves as a substitute for it – is immediately obvious and dampens all enthusiasm, especially with Europeans who have a developed taste and an innate sense of falsehood from long experience. One may cite as examples Repin's *The Bargees* or Veresh-chagin,[2] whose paintings have been very successful here, while others, also paintings of Russian life, which I've no need to mention, met with fiasco. *Tendentiousness* in art, in poetry, etc. by its very name gives itself away. It is not *an achievement.*

Please excuse me for allowing myself to pass on these thoughts to you; you are a true artist and an example of *complete achievement.* But I thought that the expression of such thoughts would have some significance for our painters.

And so I ask you once again as the Secretary of our Society to tell me the decision of your Society on my proposals and on Petit's conditions, and whether you accept them or will suggest some changes which we will have to consider.

Please accept the expression of my deepest respect.

I remain,
Your obedient servant,
Iv. Turgenev

232. To K. A. L. PIETSCH

[Original in German]

Paris, 25 December 1882

My dear Pietsch,

You are quite right, I made a silly mistake with the stereoscope. Unfortunately it cannot be changed in the original but you could easily do it in the translation. For example, instead of making a stereoscope himself, Aratov can get a photographer to do it (as Clara was an actress she had one done in Moscow in the same pose as in the photograph), or her sister can give Aratov a stereoscope in place of the photograph. You have, as they say, *carte blanche.*[1]

As for the pages from my diary, it's a long story. Over the past four years, as I was not writing anything bigger or longer, I have been jotting down a whole series of 'Short Poems *in Prose*' (as, sadly, I am no poet) on separate sheets of paper. It never occurred to me to publish them. But then my Russian publisher got wind of them and he talked me into giving him about fifty of these 'Senilia' (which is *the title* I gave them) for his journal – naturally with the strong proviso that everything autobiographical or personal was omitted. With the help of

2. Vasily Vasilyevich Vereshchagin (1842–1904) was probably the first Russian nineteenth-century painter to receive wide recognition in Western Europe.
[232] 1. Pietsch had pointed out that in his *Clara Milić* Turgenev had written that the hero Aratov had made a stereoscope of Clara without having a photograph, which is technically impossible.

Mme Viardot more than thirty were translated into French and appeared here in the *Revuè politique et littéraire*. I see that the *Petersburger Zeitung* has done translations from the French. I never thought they had any particular merit and hardly ever mentioned them. These little sketches are intended for a very few people; they will be caviar to the general – especially in Russia. If you like I can send you the French translations, which are at least very accurate. They are actually nothing other than the final pious ejaculations (to put it politely) of an old man.

With me – it's the same old story, but a little worse over the past few days. I am very sorry that you, in the flower of youth, have to taste the bitter apples of old age.

All *mine* here are very well, and that is the main thing. All my best wishes for the New Year.

I press your hand. Look after yourself.

Your

Iv. Turgenev

233. To L. B. BERTENSON

Lev Bernardovich Bertenson (1850–1929), leading physician who treated Tolstoy, Polonsky, Grigorovich and Turgenev amongst many others. He was a prominent figure in Russia's League to Combat Tuberculosis. Twelve of Turgenev's letters to him have survived, all informing him of the progress of his last, fatal illness.

[Original in Russian]

Paris, 18 January 1883

Dear Lev Bernardovich,

Here is a brief description of my operation, which I would be pleased if you passed on to Messrs Stasyulevich, Polonsky and Toporov and also to a journal – *but only in a couple of words* – and mentioning the name of the surgeon. It took place on Sunday morning at eleven o'clock. I was operated on by the young surgeon, a future star, Paul Segond,[1] who was assisted by Brouardel[2] and the son of the famous Nelaton.[3] As it was impossible to give me any chloroform I had just a little ether. They made an incision of some sixteen centimetres in my lower abdomen and from very deep down removed a neuroma the size of a large walnut and resembling a plum. In removing the neuroma they had to cut through two small arteries; they then inserted a rubber pipe into the wound and sewed it up with six stitches; then they bound it tightly with Lister bandages. After all that here I am lying motionless waiting for future blessings. There was

[233] 1. Paul Segond (1851–1912), eminent French surgeon.

2. Paul-Camille-Hippolyte Brouardel (1837 – after 1891), later President of the French Society for Forensic Medicine.

3. His father was the surgeon Auguste Nelaton.

no fever, and indeed my temperature remained normal throughout. They have only changed the bandages once, and tomorrow they will probably remove the pipe. If there are no complications, I shall be able to get up in about ten days' time. The first two days were even more unpleasant because I should have been on my back but my intercostal neuralgia ruled that out. The pain was unbearable and I had to resort to my saviour – morphine.

And so I firmly press your hand and remain,

Yours very sincerely,

Iv. Turgenev

234. To Z. A. POLONSKAYA

[Original in Russian]

Paris, 4 March 1883

Here is my second bulletin, dear Zhozefina Antonovna. There has been no improvement during the past week. The racking pains in my chest and back have not abated; sleep is not possible without injections of morphine and any movement is quite impossible. I spend all day and night either on the sofa or in bed. From time to time I get the most awful convulsions in my chest; I have never experienced such frightful pain. I am then covered with hot poultices. Charcot visited me a day or two ago and announced that I had neuritis – i.e. inflammation of the nerve-ends. I must try and hang on until the spring when I'll be sent to take the waters somewhere if I am in any condition to travel.

I shall send the third bulletin in a week. It's hardly likely to be better than today's.

I embrace you and yours.

Iv. Turgenev

235. To Y. P. and Z. A. POLONSKY

[Original in Russian]

Bougival, 24 May 1883

It is a long time since I wrote to you, my dear friends. My illness does not improve, it just gets worse. Continuous, unbearable pain – despite the most marvellous weather – and no hope whatsoever. My wish to die grows ever stronger, and it only remains for me to ask you too to desire that this wish of your unhappy friend be granted.

I embrace you all.

Yours sincerely,

Iv. Turgenev

236. To L. N. TOLSTOY

[Original in Russian]

Bougival, 11 July 1883

My dear Lev Nikolayevich,

I have not written to you for a long time for I was and still am at death's door. I cannot possibly recover and there's no use thinking about it. I am writing especially to you to say how glad I was to have been a contemporary of yours and to express my final, sincere request. My friend, return to literature! This gift comes to you from where everything else comes. Ah, how happy I would be to think that this request would have some effect on you!! I am finished; even the doctors do not know what to call my illness – *névralgie stomachale goutteuse*. I can't walk, can't eat, can't sleep – nothing! It's tedious even to repeat it all! My friend, great writer of the Russian land, heed my request! Let me know if this note reaches you, and allow me to embrace you tightly, tightly, for one last time, and your wife and all your family. I can write no more. I am tired.

INDEX

Dumas-fils, A., 13, 66, 67
Durand, E., *189*, 198, 233–4, *282*

Eckert, K., 228, 267
Eliot, G., 177, 243, 244
Eugénie (Empress), 148, 170

Feoktistov, Y.M., *37–8*
Fet, A.A., x, 53, 71, *84–6*, 92, 97, *103–4*, 107,
    108, 115, 123, 125, *127–8*, 136, 143, 150, 155,
    162, 166–7, 173, *183–4*, 186, *193–4*, *194–5*,
    206
Feuerbach, L., 9
Filosofova, A.P., x, *203–4*
Flaubert, G., 41, 75, 157, 158, *165–6*, 177, 188,
    196, 198, *202–3*, 207, 208, 209, 210, *215–6*,
    220, 221–2, *226–7*, 232, 237, *246*, *255*,
    259–60, 261, 267, 286
France, A., *259*
Friedländer, L.H., *178*

Gambetta, L., 218–9
Garcia, J., 16, 17, 22, 29, 32
Garcia, M., 16, 22
Garshin, V.M., 282, 286
Gedeonov, S.A., 26
Glinka, M.I., 118, 185
Gogol, N.V., 33, 37, 38–9, 39, 52, 57, 104, 131,
    198, 250, 268, 274
Golovnin, A.V., 100, 109n
Goncharov, I.A., xi, 5, *74–6*, 91, 131, 158–9, 200
Goncourt, E. de, 177, *188–9*, 227n
Gounod, C., 16, 27–8, 32, 37, 116
Granovsky, T.N., *6–9*, *9–11*
Grigorovich, D.V., 57, *286–7*, 289

Hartmann, M., *137–8*, *147*
Hedouin, E., 156, 157
Herwegh, G., 21, 24
Herzen, A.I., x, xi, 86, 91, 93, *99–101*, 105,
    109–10, *115–6*, *119–20*, 138, *160–1*, 164, 174,
    251
Hetzel, P.J., *129–30*, *144*, 149, 189, *205—6*, *215*,
    245–6,
Heyse, P., 109, *196–7*
Holt, H., 195
Howells, W.D., *205*
Hugo, V., 9, 20, 62, *220–1*, 232

Innes, M., 79, 88, 91, 96, 123, 283
Ivanov, A.A., 70
Ivanova, A.Y., 29, 79

James, H., *231–2*, *240–1*

Karatayev, V.V., 52, 74
Kartashevskaya, V.Y., *73–4*, 83, *93–4*
Katkov, M.N., xi, 44, *98–9*, 103, 125, *131–2*,
    134, 137, 258
Kavelin, K.D., 100, *228–9*
Ketcher, N.K., 43
Khanykov, N.V., *112–3*, 186, *207*, 244
Kharlamov, A.A., 208, 210, 290
Kheraskov, M.M., 153
Khmyrov, M.D., *153–5*
Kireyevsky, I.V., 16, 63, 79n
Kireyevsky, P.V., 63, 79n
Kishinsky, N.A., 91, 134, *135*, 136, 150, 156,
    162, 166, 177, 194, 221, 224, 236, 239
Klyushnikov, I.P., 10, 154
Kolbasin, D.Y., 47
Kolbasin, Y.Y., *47–8*, 60n, 62, 102, *251*
Koltsov, A.V., 108, 130–1
Konstantin Nikolayevich (Grand Duke), 275
Korsh, V.F., 144, 159, 208n
Kovalevsky, P.M., 146
Kozlov, I.I., 50
Kramskoy, I.N., *289–90*
Krayevsky, A.A., *26–7*, 45
Krylov, I.A., 3, 130

Lamartine, A., 62, 138, 202
Lambert, Y.Y., x, *54–6*, *76–8*, 83, *87–8*, *94–5*,
    113–4, 119, *121*, *122*
Lavrov, P.L., *191–2*, 275
Lazarus, E., *204–5*
Leontyev, K.N., *44–6*
Lessing, G.E., 59, 156–7
Lewes, G.H., 131, 177, 182, *243–4*
Lomovskaya, L.F., 252
Longinov, M.N., 194
Löwe, S., 8
Lukanina, A.N., 238, 245–6, *265–6*
Lvov, V.V., 33, 218
Lvova, Y.V., *218*

Malyarevsky, P.K., 247
Markovich, M.A. (Marko Vovchok), x, 72, 74,
    83, *86*, 89, *95–6*, 154, 245
Maslov, I.I., 107, *125–6*, 152, 199, *269*, 287
Maupassant, G. de, 165, 210, 220, *267—8*,
    272–3, 286, 288
Maykov, A.N., 58, 102
Maykov, V.N., 58
Maykova, Y.P., 76
Melgunov, N.A., 60

Merck, J.H., 58–9
Mérimée, P., 66, 127, 129, 138n, 145
Mikhaylov, M.L., 109n, 149
Mikhaylovsky, N.K., 285
Milyutina, M.A., *171–2, 209–210*
Minitsky, I.F., 48
Montégut, E., 227
Musin-Pushkin, M.N., 39, 47
Musset, A. de, 16
Mussorgsky, M.P., 185

Napoleon, L., 250
Napoleon III, 148, 169–70, 173, 174, 250n
Necheles, M., *249*
Nekrasov, N.A., 15, 16, 38, 47, *49–51,* 59, 66, 68, 101, 107, 159, 174, 186, 238
Nicholas I (Tsar), 33, 39, 40, 120, 160, 168, 174
Nikitenko, A.V., *5–6,* 75
Nikolay Nikolayevich (Grand Duke), 252

Ogaryov, N.P., 86, 93, 105
Orlov, N.A., 67, 112, 138, 252, 254
Orlova, Y.N., 138
Ostrovsky, A.N., 66, 124, 131, *198–9*

Panayev, I.I., 6, 66n, 88, 109
Panayeva, A.Y., 66, 68
Pascal, B., 20
Pavlovsky, I.Y., 254
Peasants at Spasskoye, *284–5*
Pietsch, K.A.L., ix, 133, 134, *161–2, 173–4,* 190, *228, 266–7, 291–2*
Pisarev, D.I., 107, *139–40*
Pisemsky, A.F., 83, 102, 131, *167–8,* 195, 200, 212
Pletnyov, P.A., 5, 154
Pogorelsky, P.N., 3, 154
Pokhitonov, I.P., 276, 290
Polevoy, P.N., 212
Polonskaya, Z.A., 273, *276–7, 280–1,* 289, *293*
Polonsky, Y.P., x, 59, 83, *142–3, 146–7, 159–60,* 165, *182–3, 186–7, 234–5, 254–5,* 270, 271, *273,* 276, *279–80,* 281, *289,* 292, *293*
Prokhorova-Mavrelli, K.A., 116–7
Pushkin, A.S., 2, 3, 4, 42, 46, 50, 52, 55, 57, 108, 115, 128, 139, 145n, 174, 207n, 238, 245, 263, 264–5, 268

Quincy, T. de, 59

Ragozin, Y.I., 213
Ralston, W.R.S., *130–1, 190,* 232, *235–6,* 241, 250n, 273

Rashet, N.N., 106, 138
Renan, E., 227, 252
Repin, I.Y., 185, 291
Reshetnikov, F.M., 143, 158
Rimsky-Korsakov, N.A., 185
Roland, J.M., 28
Rousseau, T., 269, 275
Rubinstein, A.G., 116, 117, 118, 141, 181–2, 213

Salayev, F.I., 154, 156, 157, 163, 200, 217, 251
Salias de Turnemir, Y.V. (Yevgeniya Tur), 32, 37, 105, 106, 155
Saltykov-Shchedrin, M.Y., x, 69, *174–5,* 182 *216–7, 218–9, 285–6*
Samarin, Y.F., 107, 141
Samoylov, V.V., 181
Sand, G., 13, 16, 57, 62, 166, 177, 190, 216, 221–2, 222–3, 284
Savina, M.G., x, 177, 248, *260–1, 262–3, 263–4, 269–71, 274, 281–2*
Scheffer, A., 70–1
Schmidt, J., 165, *190–1, 208–9,* 228
Schumann, C., 141
Schuyler, E., 140, 244
Scott, W., 177, 183
Scribe, A.E., 18
Serov, A.N., 118, 179n
Serova, V.S., 179
Shakespeare, W., 6, 7, 21, 57, 64–5, 108, 265
Shchepin, A.M., 224, 239
Shchepkin, M.S., 26, 32
Shchepkin, N.A., 224, *239–40, 246–7, 271*
Shcherbachev, N.V., 208
Shcherbina, N.F., 44, 106
Shenshina, Y.D., 29, 173
Shevchenko, T.G., 74, 93, 96
Skobelev, M.D., 275
Sleptsov, V.A., 143
Sluchevsky, K.K., *104–6*
Sollogub, V.A., 35n, 217
Speshnev, N.A., 105
Stankevich, N.V., 6, 7, 9–11, 66, 98
Stasov, V.V., *184–6, 207–8*
Stasyulevich, M.M., 186, 197, *210–1,* 214, 226, 229, 238, *264–5,* 279n, *288,* 292
Stechkina, L.Y., *241–2,* 252, 288
Sterne, L., 20
Storm, T., *132–3,* 228
Strakhov, N.N., 193
Sukhotin, M.S., 224
Suvorin, A.S., *211–2, 222–3,* 238
Swift, J., 156, 157, 175, 202
Swinburne, A., 177, 184